Communications in Computer and Information Science 2727

Series Editors

Rationale

The CCIS series is devoted to the publication of proceedings of computer science conferences. Its aim is to efficiently disseminate original research results in informatics in printed and electronic form. While the focus is on publication of peer-reviewed full papers presenting mature work, inclusion of reviewed short papers reporting on work in progress is welcome, too. Besides globally relevant meetings with internationally representative program committees guaranteeing a strict peer-reviewing and paper selection process, conferences run by societies or of high regional or national relevance are also considered for publication.

Topics

The topical scope of CCIS spans the entire spectrum of informatics ranging from foundational topics in the theory of computing to information and communications science and technology and a broad variety of interdisciplinary application fields.

Information for Volume Editors and Authors

Publication in CCIS is free of charge. No royalties are paid, however, we offer registered conference participants temporary free access to the online version of the conference proceedings on SpringerLink (http://link.springer.com) by means of an http referrer from the conference website and/or a number of complimentary printed copies, as specified in the official acceptance email of the event.

CCIS proceedings can be published in time for distribution at conferences or as post-proceedings, and delivered in the form of printed books and/or electronically as USBs and/or e-content licenses for accessing proceedings at SpringerLink. Furthermore, CCIS proceedings are included in the CCIS electronic book series hosted in the SpringerLink digital library at http://link.springer.com/bookseries/7899. Conferences publishing in CCIS are allowed to use our online conference service (Meteor) for managing the whole proceedings lifecycle (from submission and reviewing to preparing for publication) free of charge.

Publication process

The language of publication is exclusively English. Authors publishing in CCIS have to sign the Springer CCIS copyright transfer form, however, they are free to use their material published in CCIS for substantially changed, more elaborate subsequent publications elsewhere. For the preparation of the camera-ready papers/files, authors have to strictly adhere to the Springer CCIS Authors' Instructions and are strongly encouraged to use the CCIS LaTeX style files or templates.

Abstracting/Indexing

CCIS is abstracted/indexed in DBLP, Google Scholar, EI-Compendex, Mathematical Reviews, SCImago, Scopus. CCIS volumes are also submitted for the inclusion in ISI Proceedings.

How to start

To start the evaluation of your proposal for inclusion in the CCIS series, please send an e-mail to ccis@springer.com

Wentong Cai · Malcolm Low · Gary Tan ·
Gabriele D'Angelo · Duong Ta
Editors

Methods and Applications for Modeling and Simulation of Complex Systems

24th Asia Simulation Conference, AsiaSim 2025
Singapore, Singapore, November 17–19, 2025
Proceedings

Springer

Editors
Wentong Cai
Nanyang Technological University
Singapore, Singapore

Gary Tan
National University of Singapore
Singapore, Singapore

Duong Ta
Singapore Management University
Singapore, Singapore

Malcolm Low
Singapore Institute of Technology
Singapore, Singapore

Gabriele D'Angelo
University of Bologna
Bologna, Italy

ISSN 1865-0929 ISSN 1865-0937 (electronic)
Communications in Computer and Information Science
ISBN 978-981-95-4471-4 ISBN 978-981-95-4472-1 (eBook)
https://doi.org/10.1007/978-981-95-4472-1

This Springer imprint is published by the registered company Springer Nature Singapore Pte Ltd.
The registered company address is: 152 Beach Road, #21-01/04 Gateway East, Singapore 189721, Singapore

Preface

The AsiaSim conference is an annual international conference that started in 1999, and has primarily been organized by the three Asian simulation societies, Chinese Association for System Simulation (CASS), Japanese Society for Simulation Technology (JSST), and Korea Society for Simulation (KSS). In 2011, the Federation of Asia Simulation Societies (ASIASIM) was set up to promote the advancement of modeling and simulation in industry, research and development in Asia and beyond. In 2013, the AsiaSim series finally left the 'Golden Triangle' of China, Japan and Korea and was held in Singapore for the first time. Then in 2017, it was Malaysia's turn to host the conference. We were proud to be the host of the 24th edition of the AsiaSim conference series (the third time it was held in Singapore; the 2nd one was in 2019 before COVID struck). In December 2024, ASIASIM became a full-fledged non-profit international academic organization registered in China. With its tagline "Simulation for Everything", the primary mission of ASIASIM is to promote the advancement and popularization of simulation technology in Asia, foster exchange and collaboration among international organizations, and drive innovation and application of simulation theories, methodologies, generic technologies and frontier technologies. On behalf of the organizing committee of AsiaSim 2025, we were pleased to welcome you to Singapore. AsiaSim 2025 was organized by the Society of Simulation and Gaming of Singapore, the National University of Singapore and Nanyang Technological University. The Society of Simulation and Gaming of Singapore is a non-profit professional organization set up to contribute to the development of Simulation and Gaming in Singapore and the region. It is a focused community for researchers, practitioners and developers who are keen in furthering their professional knowledge through learning and working together and promoting experiential activities for the public.

We received 54 submissions from Austria, China, Greece, Indonesia, Italy, Japan, Malaysia, South Korea, Sweden, the UK, the USA and of course Singapore. After an intensive single-blind review process by a carefully assembled international program committee, where each paper was reviewed by no fewer than 3 reviewers, we finally accepted 19 full papers and 8 short papers. This resulted in a less than 36% acceptance rate for full papers and 50% including short papers.

Based on the peer-review scores, the following four papers were shortlisted for the best paper award. The best paper award committee evaluated the papers and the winner was announced during the conference dinner:

- Jiayi Zhang, Yuanjun Laili, Jiabei Gong, Lin Zhang and Lei Ren, "A Quantitative Learning Method for Simulation Model Evaluation using L-SHADE Optimized Structured Regression".
- Mashiro Shimada, Haruki Omori and Hiroyuki Kamata, "Robust Lunar-Image Matching Under Disturbance: High-Precision Comparison of RANSAC, RL-RANSAC, and MLESAC".

- Yu Qiao, Ping Ma, Ming Yang and Tao Chao, "Aeroassisted Orbital Transfer Optimization Using Sequential Convex Programming".
- Yuteng Zhang, Jiangchuan Hu, Lin Zhang and Pengfei Gu, "Towards Intelligent MBSE: Constructing an MBSE Model Dataset for Generative AI".

The accepted papers are now consolidated in this volume of the Communications in Computer and Information Science series, and are divided into many relevant topics, including Agent-Based Simulation, Simulation Methods and Tools, Visualization, Modeling Methodology, and Simulation Applications in Science and Engineering.

The diversity of topics presented in this conference certainly made for a healthy exchange of research ideas and technical exchanges. We would like to take this opportunity to thank the ASIASIM Federation for allowing us to host AsiaSim 2025 for the third time in Singapore, and we hope that you found the conference enriching and memorable. We also thank the members of the program committee for their valuable effort in the review of the submitted papers. Finally, we would also like to thank our technical co-sponsors and sponsors. Your contributions and support have helped to make AsiaSim 2025 a reality and a success.

September 2025

Wentong Cai
Malcolm Low
Gary Tan
Gabriele D'Angelo

Organization

Conference Chairs

Wentong Cai	Nanyang Technological University, Singapore
Malcolm Low	Singapore Institute of Technology, Singapore

Program Chairs

Gary Tan	National University of Singapore, Singapore
Gabriele D'Angelo	University of Bologna, Italy

Finance Chair

Sun Teck Tan	National University of Singapore, Singapore

Local Arrangement Chair

Chengxin Wang	National University of Singapore, Singapore

Publications Chair

Nguyen Binh Duong Ta	Singapore Management University, Singapore

Sponsorship Chair

Muhammad Shalihin bin Othman	National University of Singapore, Singapore

International Program Committee

Norhaliza Abdul Wahab	Universiti Teknologi Malaysia, Malaysia
Anita Ahmad	Universiti Teknologi Malaysia, Malaysia

Philipp Andelfinger	Nanyang Technological University, Singapore
Salinda Buyamin	Universiti Teknologi Malaysia, Malaysia
Wentong Cai	Nanyang Technological University, Singapore
Chew Wye Chan	D-SIMLAB Technologies, Singapore
Byeong-Yun Chang	Ajou University, China
Yong Cui	Beihang University
Gabriele D'Angelo	University of Bologna, Italy
Stefano Ferretti	University of Bologna, Italy
Boon Ping Gan	D-SIMLAB Technologies Pte Ltd, Singapore
Fred Hardtke	Macquarie University, Australia
Kyoko Hasegawa	Tokai University, Japan
Zhou He	University of Chinese Academy of Sciences, China
Sumin Jeon	Capgemini, Singapore
Nirupam Julka	D-SIMLAB Technologies Pte Ltd, Singapore
Yunbae Kim	Sungkyunkwan University, South Korea
Jaeyoung Kwak	Nanyang Technological University, Singapore
Yuanjun Laili	Beihang University, China
Axel Lehmann	Universität der Bundeswehr München, Germany
Liang Li	Ritsumeikan University, Japan
Malcolm Low	Singapore Institute of Technology, Singapore
Pietro Manzoni	Universidad Politécnica de Valencia, Spain
Zaharuddin Mohamed	Universiti Teknologi Malaysia, Malaysia
Md. Shalihin Othman	D-SIMLAB Technologies Pte Ltd, Singapore
Remya Padinjarapat	Indian Institute of Technology Bombay, India
Alessandro Pellegrini	University of Rome "Tor Vergata", Italy
Tomas Potuzak	University of West Bohemia, Czechia
Xiao Song	Beihang University, China
Yuen Jien Soo	National University of Singapore, Singapore
Serge Stinckwich	United Nations University Institute in Macau, China
Nurul Adilla Mohd Subha	Universiti Teknologi Malaysia, Malaysia
Philip Swadling	Simulation Australasia, Australia
Nguyen Binh Duong Ta	Singapore Management University, Singapore
Gary Tan	National University of Singapore, Singapore
Wen Jun Tan	Nanyang Technological University, Singapore
Sun Teck Tan	National University of Singapore, Singapore
Satoshi Tanaka	Ritsumeikan University, Japan
Bimlesh Wadhwa	National University of Singapore, Singapore
Chengxin Wang	National University of Singapore, Singapore
Jingnong Weng	Beihang University, China
Gregory Zacharewicz	IMT Mines Alès, France

Lin Zhang	Beihang University, China

Best Paper Committee

Axel Lehmann (Chair)	Universität der Bundeswehr München, Germany
Philipp Andelfinger	Nanyang Technological University, Singapore
Zaharuddin Mohamed	Universiti Teknologi Malaysia, Malaysia
Satoshi Tanaka	Ritsumeikan University, Japan

Keynotes

Simulation-Enabled Digital Twins – A Journey from Neutrino Physics at CERN to AI Training for Semiconductor Manufacturing in Singapore

Peter Lendermann

D-SIMLAB Technologies Pte Ltd, Singapore

Digital Twins have become a key element of the ongoing global Industry 4.0 campaign with the objective of speeding up digitalization in production and logistics. The potential of the Digital Twin concept for the enhancement and continuous re-optimization of manufacturing and logistics operations has generally been recognized and accepted in both academia and industry. However, what a Digital Twin entails and what it should be able to do, or rather what it can be used for, especially in the recent light of the rise of Artificial Intelligence techniques, remains controversial to some extent. In this setting, in my Keynote Presentation I will share some my own experiences and challenges faced with creating and making use of Digital Twins, starting from my initial involvement in a neutrino experiment at CERN in Geneva in the early 1990's, all the way to providing a simulation-enabled Digital Twin framework for multiple application use cases including training of AI models, accomplished through our Singapore-headquartered company D-SIMLAB Technologies, to help Semiconductor Manufacturing companies worldwide resolve mind-blowing challenges around capacity planning and WIP flow optimization.

Biography

Peter Lendermann is a Co-Founder and the Chief Business Development Officer of D-SIMLAB Technologies, a Singapore-headquartered company providing simulation-based decision support solutions to Semiconductor Manufacturing companies where he is responsible for business development worldwide. Prior to this he worked at the Singapore Institute of Manufacturing Technology where he led related R&D activities until spinning them off into D-SIMLAB. Peter has been engaged in the field of production logistics, supply chain management and related decision support technologies and solutions since the early 1990's. He holds a PhD in Physics from Humboldt University in Berlin (Germany) and an MBA in International Economics and Management from SDA Bocconi in Milan (Italy).

We Simulate, Therefore We Survive

Fritz Hardtke

Simulation Australasia, Macquarie University, Australia

We are facing a convergence of global challenges that are testing the limits of our systems — environmental degradation, armed conflict, pandemics, economic fragility, and the rapid advance of technologies with far-reaching consequences. These are not distant threats. They are here, now, and unfolding in ways that are complex and often unpredictable. In such times, the role of simulation is not just valuable — it's essential. Simulation enables us to explore scenarios, test decisions before they are made, and understand the interplay of systems under stress. It allows us to prepare rather than react. This keynote will explore how simulation contributes directly to our wellbeing and survival — not in a theoretical sense, but in practical, measurable ways. Drawing on real-world examples across sectors, I will argue that simulation must move from the margins of decision-making to its centre — because our ability to simulate wisely and act on what we learn may be one of the few capabilities that can carry us through what lies ahead.

Biography

Dr. Fritz Hardtke is a seasoned expert in the fields of modelling, simulation, and augmented/virtual reality (AR/VR) technologies. With a career spanning 33 years in defence and aeronautics, he has made significant contributions to the development and implementation of advanced training systems. He is a director at Simulation Australasia.

Throughout his career, Dr. Hardtke has worked with industry leaders such as Rheinmetall, Thales, Boeing, and Raytheon. His expertise extends to diverse domains, including maritime navigation, fast jet operations, submarine systems, ship combat systems, and live electronic warfare. He has been instrumental in defining the fidelity requirements for training systems and overseeing their design and architectural frameworks.

Dr. Hardtke has also delved into the realm of predictive capability modelling for ship combat systems and actively participated in related industry research and development initiatives.

Beyond his industry experience, his academic pursuits have led him to explore the intersection of technology and heritage preservation. As a Research Fellow at Macquarie University, Sydney Australia and a Research Associate at the Frobenius Institute, Frankfurt, Germany, he is at the forefront of innovative approaches to safeguarding cultural heritage. Dr. Hardtke's current research focuses on the recreation of ancient environments using advanced 3D and virtual reality techniques. He leads archaeological expeditions in Egypt, where he applies his technical expertise to bring history to life. By leveraging the power of digital technologies, he aims to provide immersive experiences that bridge the gap between the past and the present.

Organizers

Technical Sponsors

Sponsors

Contents

Best Paper Nominees

A Quantitative Learning Method for Simulation Model Evaluation Using L-SHADE Optimized Structured Regression 3
Jiayi Zhang, Yuanjun Laili, Jiabei Gong, Lin Zhang, and Lei Ren

Robust Lunar-Image Matching Under Disturbance: High-Precision Comparison of RANSAC, RL-RANSAC, and MLESAC 16
Mashiro Shimada, Haruki Omori, and Hiroyuki Kamata

Aeroassisted Orbital Transfer Optimization Using Sequential Convex Programming 28
Yu Qiao, Ping Ma, Ming Yang, and Tao Chao

Towards Intelligent MBSE: Constructing an MBSE Model Dataset for Generative AI 40
Yuteng Zhang, Jiangchuan Hu, Lin Zhang, and Pengfei Gu

Full Papers

Logistics Digital Twin for Sustainability Management 55
Kalyani Alagappan, David Weidong Lin, and Malcolm Yoke Hean Low

Learning to Optimize Capacity Planning in Semiconductor Manufacturing 67
Philipp Andelfinger, Jieyi Bi, Qiuyu Zhu, Jianan Zhou, Bo Zhang, Fei Fei Zhang, Chew Wye Chan, Boon Ping Gan, Wentong Cai, and Jie Zhang

A Credible Evolution Method for Digital Twins Based on LSTM–Decoder-Only Architecture 80
Hongbo Cheng, Lin Zhang, Yiming Qiao, Lei Zhang, Kunyu Wang, and Han Lu

Decentralised Blockchain Management Through Digital Twins 90
Georgios Diamantopoulos, Nikos Tziritas, Rami Bahsoon, and Georgios Theodoropoulos

Implicit Neural Representation for DEM Super-Resolution in Vehicle Motion Simulation 102
Guoqing Hou, Shuaibo Wang, Ni Li, Guanghong Gong, and Bo Tian

A Modeling Method for the Pressing Process of Explosive Molding Powder Based on Particle Size Distribution ... 115
Jin Luo, Yifan Li, Linjing Tang, Xuying Jiao, and Xianzhen Jia

Simulation and Verification of Explosive Powder Compression Molding Based on Thermodynamic Elastoplastic Model ... 124
Jin Luo, Linjing Tang, Xuying Jiao, Yifan Li, and Xianzhen Jia

Research on Speed Control of Permanent Magnet Synchronous Motor Simulation Model Based on FOC ... 134
Yumu Luo, Zhenyu Zhang, Tan Li, Weining Song, Nanjiang Chen, Fangfang Gao, Wenjun Zhang, Congying Wu, Qi Wang, and Min Hu

Modeling and Simulation of Underwater Active Electric Field Detection Based on Compact Electrode Structure ... 148
Yu Pei, Yong Cui, Qinglei Hu, Huafu Cheng, Zirui Wang, Ke Bi, Jianchun Xu, and Huaining Wu

Driving Closer to the Limit: Improved Virtual Racecar Drivers with Data-Driven Control ... 159
Ruslan Shaiakhmetov, Danilo Pianini, Valter Venusti, Gabriele D'Angelo, and Alessandro V. Papadopoulos

B-Spline Based Aerodynamic Table Look-up for Cyber in the Loop Simulation of Air Vehicle Cyber-Physical System ... 171
Bambang Sridadi, Endra Joelianto, and Yul Yunazwin Nazaruddin

Spacecraft Evasive Maneuvering Based on Neural Network Pattern Recognition and an Improved SA-GA Algorithm ... 183
Yisong Wei, Ming Yang, Ping Ma, and Tao Chao

Dynamic Modeling and Motion Control of a Thruster-Assisted Bipedal Robot ... 199
Ze Wei, Jiaying Tan, and Yan Huang

Enhancing Nonlinear Dynamics and Processing Efficiency in Chaotic Stream Cipher via Branching Structures ... 211
Kentaro Yamada, Tatsuki Kamiya, Kouhei Kajima, and Hiroyuki Kamata

Mechanism Simulation of Lithium Polysulfide Conversion Catalyzed by Ti_3C_2 MXene with Different Terminals ... 222
Dezhi Yan, Fangchao Han, Qiang Lu, Ninghan Li, Qianfan Zhang, Yalan Xing, and Weining Song

Short Papers

Analytical 3D Trajectory Solution and Simulation Analysis for Reentry Glide Vehicles Based on the Perturbation Method 237
Yujie Bai, Ju Huo, Zheng Mei, Songyan Wang, and Tao Chao

Evaluating Hospital Disaster Resilience Using Simulation: Integrating Task Duration and Intra-Hospital Patient Transfer 244
Desak Ayu Clara Dewanti, Taro Kanno, Toshiki Nishimura, Kazumi Kajiyama, Michihiro Tsubaki, Sachika Sharikura, Misumi Yamazaki, Haruka Yoshida, Joniarto Parung, and Amelia Santoso

Personalized Federated Learning via Dual Alignment of Semantic Knowledge and Feature Prototypes 252
Bingli Sun, Yuchun Tu, Hongyan Quan, and Xiao Song

A Chain-of-Thought-Based Model Auto-Configuration Method for Customized Production Simulation 259
Na Li, Yuanjun Laili, Lei Ren, and Lin Zhang

Entropy-Based Visualization of Missing Regions in 2.5D Cultural Heritage Point Clouds 266
Qingyu Mao, Liang Li, and Satoshi Tanaka

Modular Physics Simulation Approach for Amazon FC - Case Study 272
Sumant Joshi, Gandhi Chidambaram, Tarciana Almeida, Anish Goyal, and Chin-Yuan Tseng

Knowledge Graph-Enhanced Large Language Model Approach for Device Fault Diagnosis Question Answering 279
Yuchun Tu, Bingli Sun, Zheng Wei, and Xiao Song

On Linking Learning and Game Goal in Serious Games Design 285
Mukarramah Yusuf, Elly Warni, M. Agung Sabillah, and Firmansyah Jaya Kusuma

Author Index 291

Best Paper Nominees

A Quantitative Learning Method for Simulation Model Evaluation Using L-SHADE Optimized Structured Regression

Jiayi Zhang[1], Yuanjun Laili[1(✉)], Jiabei Gong[1], Lin Zhang[1,2], and Lei Ren[1]

[1] Beihang University, Beijing 100191, China
lailiyuanjun@buaa.edu.cn

[2] Hangzhou International Innovation Institute, Beihang University, Hangzhou 311115, China

Abstract. The evaluation of simulation models is a fundamental step in establishing their credibility. Conventional approaches often rely on qualitative expert judgment, a process that is often inefficient and labor-intensive. Additionally, simulation outputs are often limited due to high computational costs or intrinsic model properties. To address these challenges, we propose a Quantitative Learning Method (QLM) that employs a dual-layer architecture. This method is designed to integrate historical assessment scores in small-sample contexts, learning the mapping from raw simulation outputs to evaluation metrics. Validated on two classic simulation models against seven baseline algorithms, QLM demonstrates robust generalization and stable performance, mitigating the overfitting prevalent in machine learning approaches under data constraints. Furthermore, its inherent transparency the mapping between simulation outputs and credibility scores offers considerable interpretability and practical value.

Keywords: Simulation Model Evaluation · Few-shot Learning · Multi-task Regression · Differential Evolution algorithm

1 Introduction

Evaluating simulation models is a critical step in establishing their credibility. The conventional approach relies on qualitative expert assessments [21], a process that is often inefficient and labor-intensive [10,13]. This challenge is compounded by the fact that simulation outputs are frequently limited due to high computational costs or intrinsic model properties, creating a data-constrained context [1]. Such constraints pose a significant hurdle for quantitative alternatives, particularly machine learning approaches [20], which are prone to overfitting in these scenarios [1,6].

W. Cai et al. (Eds.): AsiaSim 2025, CCIS 2727, pp. 3–15, 2026.
https://doi.org/10.1007/978-981-95-4472-1_1

While specialized techniques like Bayesian inference [15] or meta-learning [19] are designed for data constraints, they often depend on strong prior assumptions or the availability of related auxiliary tasks [4]. These limitations motivate the development of a framework that learns evaluation patterns directly from a small set of historical assessment data. Such an approach aims to streamline the labor-intensive evaluation process by capturing knowledge from prior assessments, thereby enabling rapid and repeatable analysis.

To address this challenge, this paper introduces the Quantitative Learning Method (QLM). The method employs a dual-layer architecture to learn the mapping from raw simulation outputs to a final credibility score, thereby encoding the logic from historical assessments. To optimize this mapping, we employ L-SHADE (Success-History based Adaptive Differential Evolution with Linear Population Size Reduction) [17], a state-of-the-art variant of Differential Evolution (DE) [16]. L-SHADE is particularly suited for this task because its mechanisms for self-adapting control parameters based on historical success make it highly effective at navigating complex, non-differentiable fitness landscapes without requiring manual parameter tuning. This focus on a globally robust solution, rather than a locally perfect fit, is critical for developing a reliable quantitative tool for simulation model assessment in data-limited environments.

The remainder of this paper is organized as follows. Section 2 formalizes the model evaluation problem. Section 3 details the proposed QLM framework. Section 4 presents the experimental design and results. Finally, Sect. 5 provides conclusions and outlines future work.

2 Problem Description

The evaluation index system for a simulation model typically exhibits a hierarchical structure, where bottom-level indicators are derived from simulation output data [23]. These base indicators are hierarchically combined [14], typically employing weighted summation, to derive a single, comprehensive credibility score. This evaluative framework is formalized as follows.

We formulate this task as a Multi-task Regression (MTR) problem. For each of the N independent simulation instances, the original output is a multivariate time series $\mathbf{Z}_i \in \mathbb{R}^{M \times T_{orig}}$, representing M state variables recorded over T_{orig} time steps. To create a concise feature representation, we preprocess this time series using a binning and averaging technique [2]. This procedure partitions each of the M state variable sequences into K non-overlapping intervals and computes the mean for each. The resulting $M \times K$ matrix is then flattened into a single feature vector $\mathbf{x}_i \in \mathbb{R}^{M \times K}$.

For each feature vector $\mathbf{x}_i$, the learning targets are its corresponding historical evaluation scores $(\mathbf{y}_i, F_i)$. Here, $\mathbf{y}_i \in \mathbb{R}^D$ represents the vector of D bottom-level evaluation indicators, and F_i is the final aggregated score. These scores originate from an established, often expert-driven, indicator system. The objective is to learn a single, generalizable mapping function $\mathcal{G}$ parameterized by a set of shared weights θ, such that for any given input $\mathbf{x}_i$, the function's output $\mathcal{G}(\mathbf{x}_i; \theta)$

accurately approximates the true scores $(\mathbf{y}_i, F_i)$. The explicit hierarchical dependency within the target scores motivates our choice of a structured regression approach to define this function.

3 The Quantitative Learning Prediction (QLM) Method

The Quantitative Learning Method (QLM) employs a two-stage regression architecture that follows the hierarchical structure of the evaluation process from Sect. 2. To optimize the model's parameters, we use the L-SHADE algorithm [17], an adaptive variant of Differential Evolution. This strategy is robust in exploring complex solution landscapes and is well-suited to mitigate overfitting risks in data-scarce contexts.

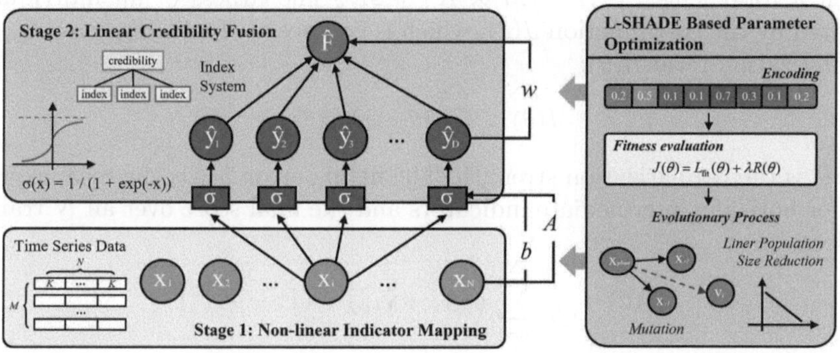

Fig. 1. The two-stage architecture of the QLM. The input feature vector $\mathbf{x}$ is first non-linearly projected to an intermediate indicator space $\hat{\mathbf{y}}$. These indicators are then linearly fused to produce the final credibility score $\hat{F}$.

3.1 Model Architecture

Stage 1: Non-linear Indicator Mapping. This stage maps the input feature vector $\mathbf{x} \in \mathbb{R}^{M \times K}$ to a vector of D intermediate indicators, $\hat{\mathbf{y}} \in \mathbb{R}^D$. The transformation is defined as:

$$\hat{\mathbf{y}} = \sigma(\mathbf{A}\mathbf{x} + \mathbf{b}) \tag{1}$$

where $\mathbf{A} \in \mathbb{R}^{D \times (M \times K)}$ is the weight matrix and $\mathbf{b} \in \mathbb{R}^D$ is the bias vector. The sigmoid activation function $\sigma(\cdot)$ introduces non-linearity and normalizes the indicators to the range $(0, 1)$, aligning them with the scale of typical evaluation scores.

Stage 2: Linear Credibility Fusion. This stage models the final aggregation step as a linear combination of the intermediate indicators, directly corresponding to the weighted summation methods common in hierarchical evaluation frameworks. The final credibility score $\hat{F}$ is computed as:

$$\hat{F} = \mathbf{w}^T \hat{\mathbf{y}} = \mathbf{w}^T \sigma(\mathbf{A}\mathbf{x} + \mathbf{b}) \tag{2}$$

where $\mathbf{w} \in \mathbb{R}^D$ is the fusion weight vector. The complete set of optimizable parameters is denoted by $\theta = \{\mathbf{A}, \mathbf{b}, \mathbf{w}\}$.

3.2 L-SHADE-Based Parameter Optimization

Individual Representation and Fitness Evaluation. In the L-SHADE population, each individual is a real-valued vector representing the complete parameter set θ, with a total length of $D \cdot (M \times K) + 2D$. The fitness of an individual is evaluated by the cost function $J(\theta)$, which is composed of a fitting error L_{fit} and a regularization term $R(\theta)$:

$$J(\theta) = L_{\text{fit}}(\theta) + \lambda R(\theta) \tag{3}$$

where λ is the regularization strength. The fitting error L_{fit} is the mean squared error for both the intermediate indicators and the final score over all N training samples:

$$L_{\text{fit}}(\theta) = \frac{1}{N} \sum_{i=1}^{N} \left(\|\mathbf{y}_i - \hat{\mathbf{y}}_i\|_2^2 + (F_i - \hat{F}_i)^2 \right) \tag{4}$$

The regularization term $R(\theta)$ employs a hybrid L1/L2 penalty to encourage sparsity in the weight matrix $\mathbf{A}$ and prevent large values in the fusion vector $\mathbf{w}$:

$$R(\theta) = \|\mathbf{A}\|_1 + \|\mathbf{w}\|_2^2 = \sum_{u,j} |A_{u,j}| + \sum_i w_i^2 \tag{5}$$

The L-SHADE Evolutionary Process. The optimization is performed using L-SHADE. The algorithm's behavior is defined by the following integrated mechanisms:

- **Parameter Adaptation.** Control parameters F and CR are self-adapted each generation. They are sampled from Cauchy and Normal distributions, respectively, whose means are drawn from a historical memory $(\mathcal{M}_F, \mathcal{M}_{CR})$ of previously successful parameter values. This memory is updated using a weighted Lehmer mean of the current generation's successful parameters.
- **Mutation Strategy.** A *current-to-p-best/1* with archive mutation strategy generates trial solutions. This approach balances exploration and exploitation by using directional information from a top-performing individual $(\mathbf{x}_{pbest})$ and a differential vector derived from two other individuals, one of which $(\mathbf{x}_{r2})$ is drawn from the union of the population $\mathcal{P}$ and an external archive $\mathcal{A}$.

$$\mathbf{u}_i = \mathbf{x}_i + F_i \cdot (\mathbf{x}_{pbest} - \mathbf{x}_i) + F_i \cdot (\mathbf{x}_{r1} - \mathbf{x}_{r2}) \tag{6}$$

- **Crossover and Selection.** Standard binomial crossover is used to create trial vectors based on the mutant vectors. Afterwards, a greedy selection criterion is adopted, and the better solution between the trial vector and the parent enters the next generation.
- **Linear Population Size Reduction (LPSR).** The population size decreases linearly with the cumulative number of function evaluations. This strategy can allocate global computing resources reasonably and avoid redundant calculations.

4 Experiments and Discussion

4.1 Experimental Setup

Datasets. We evaluated our method using two NetLogo agent-based models: Wolf-Sheep Predation and Traffic Flow (Fig. 2). The raw time series outputs ($T_{orig} = 300$ for Wolf-Sheep, $T_{orig} = 100$ for Traffic Flow) were preprocessed via binning into feature sequences of length $K = 50$, as detailed in Sect. 2. To generate diverse behaviors, we used $h = 5$ distinct parameter configurations for the Wolf-Sheep model and $h = 4$ for the Traffic Flow model. For each configuration, we generated independent simulation replicates and partitioned them into mutually exclusive training and testing pools. From these pools, we constructed four datasets of varying sizes for each model: three small-sample datasets using $r \in \{4, 8, 16\}$ replicates per configuration, and one larger "Total" dataset aggregating all available data.

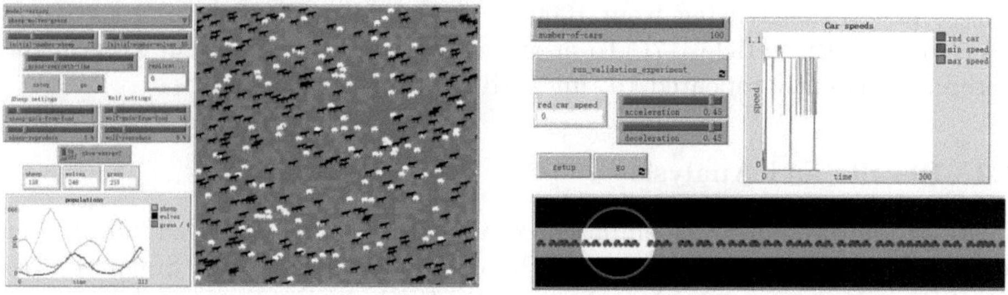

(a) Wolf-Sheep model and its output data.

(b) Traffic Flow model with its output data.

Fig. 2. The simulation models and representative data formats.

Evaluation Index System. Model credibility is quantified using a hierarchical index system, detailed in Table 1. This system translates raw simulation outputs into a vector of D low-level indicators, $\mathbf{y}$, and an aggregated final score, F. The

Wolf-Sheep model employs $D = 6$ indicators to assess its ecological stability, system validity, and pattern fidelity, while the Traffic Flow model uses $D = 3$ indicators to evaluate conformity with traffic theory and internal consistency. The system incorporates both quantitative metrics derived from data and qualitative assessments from experts (denoted by †). As formulated in Sect. 2, our learning objective is to concurrently predict the indicator vector $\mathbf{y}$ and the final score F.

Table 1. Hierarchical structure of the evaluation index system.

Model	Index Category	Component Metric
Wolf-Sheep	Ecological Stability System Validity Pattern Fidelity	Collapse Delay / Population CV Predator-Prey Ratio / Grass Coverage Energy Pyramid†/ Phase Lag†
Traffic Flow	Credibility Metrics	Fundamental Diagram / Dynamic Congestion / Internal Consistency

Baselines and Hyperparameters. We benchmarked our proposed QLM against seven baselines: Multi-task Lasso [18], $L_{2,1}$-Lasso [22], Random Forest [3], and four neural network architectures (DNN, RNN [7], LSTM [12], and GRU [5]). To ensure a fair comparison, all baseline hyperparameters were optimized via 3-fold cross-validated grid search. For QLM, the L-SHADE optimizer was configured with a termination criterion of 5×10^7 fitness evaluations, a population size (N_{pop}) linearly decreasing from 1000 to 4. Others parameter settings can be referred to in the article [17]. To ensure statistical robustness, all experiments were independently repeated 10 times with distinct random seeds.

4.2 Results and Analysis

This section presents the empirical evaluation of the proposed QLM. Performance is primarily measured by the composite Root Mean Squared Error (RMSE) on the test set, with ranks provided for direct comparison. All reported metrics are averaged over 10 independent runs, and statistical significance against QLM is assessed using the Wilcoxon signed-rank test [11].

To diagnose model behavior, we introduce a "Fit Status" metric based on prioritized heuristic rules [8,9]. This status compares training ($\text{RMSE}_{\text{train}}$) and test ($\text{RMSE}_{\text{test}}$) errors against a naive predictor baseline ($\text{RMSE}_{\text{base}}$), which is the error from predicting the mean of the training targets. This metric categorizes performance into four states: Failed to Learn (FL), Severe Overfitting (SVO), Slight Overfitting (SO), and Good Fit (GF). The specific rules are defined as follows:

$$\text{Fit Status} = \begin{cases} \text{FL (Failed to Learn)}, & \text{if } \text{RMSE}_{\text{test}} \geq 0.95 \cdot \text{RMSE}_{\text{base}} \\ \text{SVO (Severe Overfitting)}, & \text{if } \text{RMSE}_{\text{test}}/\text{RMSE}_{\text{train}} > 3.0 \\ \text{SO (Slight Overfitting)}, & \text{if } \text{RMSE}_{\text{test}}/\text{RMSE}_{\text{train}} > 1.8 \\ \text{GF (Good Fit)}, & \text{otherwise} \end{cases}$$

Other edge cases, such as severe underfitting or numerical instability, are also identified during analysis.

Overall Performance Comparison. The primary results presented in Tables 2 and 3 reveal a critical trade-off between raw predictive power and model robustness. When calculating **Ave. Rank**, all other factors (such as SVO, SO, FL) except for GF are increased by 20 ranking positions. In stark contrast to the baselines, QLM demonstrates superior stability across all scenarios. It is the only algorithm to consistently maintain a Good Fit (GF) status, avoiding the Severe Overfitting (SVO) or outright Failures Learning(FL) that plague other methods. This stability is further quantified by its superior overall rank, achieving the top position in both experimental settings and underscoring its reliability. This robustness is the cornerstone of a trustworthy evaluation tool.

While models like Random Forest (RF) often achieve the top rank in Test RMSE, this accuracy comes at the cost of generalization; the Fit Status diagnoses RF with overfitting on multiple datasets (e.g., Wolf-Sheep r = 16, Traffic Flow r = 8, r = 16, Total). Similarly, deep learning models exhibit significant instability, with DNN, LSTM, and GRU failing to learn entirely on the Wolf-Sheep r = 16 dataset.

Table 2. Performance Comparison on the Wolf-Sheep Predation Model. Each cell presents Test RMSE (rank) with Fit Status as a superscript. Best Test RMSE among GF models is in bold. An asterisk (*) indicates statistical significance ($p < 0.05$) compared to QLM. The **Ave. Rank** is based on the average rank across scenarios, penalizing SVO/SO/FL states.

Algorithm	r=4	r=8	r=16	Total	Ave. Rank
QLM (Ours)	0.0836 (3)^{GF}	0.0770 (2)^{GF}	0.0572 (3)^{GF}	0.0755 (8)^{GF}	1
Lasso	0.0672*^{SVO}	0.0417*^{SO}	0.0473*(2)^{GF}	0.0259*(2)^{GF}	7
$L_{2,1}$-Lasso	0.0670*^{SVO}	0.0414*^{SO}	**0.0443***(1)^{GF}	0.0267*(3)^{GF}	7
RF	**0.0490***(1)^{GF}	**0.0156***(1)^{GF}	0.0159*^{SVO}	**0.0210***(1)^{GF}	3
DNN	0.0807 (2)^{GF}	0.1221 (6)^{GF}	0.1011*^{FL}	0.0498 (4)^{GF}	4
RNN	0.1069*(5)^{GF}	0.0949*(4)^{GF}	0.0735*(4)^{GF}	0.0541*(6)^{GF}	2
LSTM	0.0931 (4)^{GF}	0.0909*(3)^{GF}	0.0887*^{FL}	0.0529*(5)^{GF}	4
GRU	0.1121*(6)^{GF}	0.1019*(5)^{GF}	0.0899*^{FL}	0.0618*(7)^{GF}	6

When compared on a level playing field, among models that successfully generalized, QLM delivers consistently strong and competitive performance. It secures a top-tier rank of 2 in the most data-scarce Traffic Flow case (r = 4) and achieves the rank 1 position for the r = 8 dataset. On the Wolf-Sheep model, it consistently places in the upper half of the valid models (e.g., rank 2 for r = 8, rank 3 for r = 4). This outcome validates that QLM not only avoids overfitting but also learns the underlying evaluation patterns effectively. Its ability to provide a reliable and generalizable framework is a paramount quality, establishing it as a dependable alternative to methods that sacrifice robustness for a deceptively low error score.

Table 3. Performance Comparison on the Traffic Flow Model. Each cell presents Test RMSE (rank) with Fit Status as a superscript. Best Test RMSE among GF models is in bold. An asterisk (*) indicates statistical significance ($p < 0.05$) compared to QLM. The **Ave. Rank** is based on the average rank across scenarios, penalizing SVO/SO/FL states.

Algorithm	r=4	r=8	r=16	Total	Ave. Rank
QLM (Ours)	0.0463 (2)^{GF}	**0.1319** (1)^{GF}	0.1265 (4)^{GF}	0.1188 (2)^{GF}	1
Lasso	0.0755^{*SO}	0.1313^{*SVO}	0.1425* (7)^{GF}	0.1196* (4)^{GF}	7
$L_{2,1}$-Lasso	0.0643* (3)^{GF}	0.1322^{*SO}	0.1250* (3)^{GF}	0.1213* (6)^{GF}	5
RF	**0.0441*** (1)^{GF}	0.1285^{SVO}	0.1274^{*SO}	0.1245^{*SO}	8
DNN	0.1185* (7)^{GF}	0.1429^{*SO}	0.1342 (6)^{GF}	0.1202* (5)^{GF}	6
RNN	0.1037* (6)^{GF}	0.1356* (2)^{GF}	0.1312* (5)^{GF}	0.1244* (7)^{GF}	4
LSTM	0.0991* (5)^{GF}	0.1368* (3)^{GF}	**0.1241** (1)^{GF}	0.1194* (3)^{GF}	2
GRU	0.1517* (8)^{GF}	0.1426* (4)^{GF}	**0.1241** (1)^{GF}	**0.1182*** (1)^{GF}	3

Decomposition of Prediction Error. To understand the sources of the composite RMSE, we decompose it into errors from the two model stages: indicator prediction ($RMSE_y$) and score fusion ($RMSE_F$), shown in Table 4. The results reveal that top-performing baselines often exhibit specialized or fragmented strengths. RF, for instance, excels at both sub-tasks on the Wolf-Sheep data, while on the Traffic Flow data, GRU is best at indicator prediction and Lasso at fusion. In contrast, QLM maintains a consistently balanced performance across both stages. This equilibrium, rather than specialized excellence, is the likely source of its robust generalization.

Table 4. Decomposed Test Set RMSE for Both Models on the Total Dataset. Best performance in each column is in bold.

Algorithm	Wolf-Sheep Predation		Traffic Flow	
	$RMSE_y$	$RMSE_F$	$RMSE_y$	$RMSE_F$
QLM (Ours)	0.1038	0.0248	0.1462	0.0827
Lasso	0.0333	0.0153	0.1480	**0.0819**
$L_{2,1}$-Lasso	0.0342	0.0160	0.1505	0.0824
RF	**0.0273**	**0.0115**	0.1532	0.0868
DNN	0.0585	0.0384	0.1470	0.0854
RNN	0.0708	0.0287	0.1516	0.0893
LSTM	0.0685	0.0288	0.1467	0.0836
GRU	0.0831	0.0263	**0.1456**	0.0822

Interpretability and Weight Analysis. The white-box architecture of the QLM framework permits a direct examination of its optimized parameters, offering insights into the learned evaluation logic. Tables 5 and 6 present the learned fusion weights ($\mathbf{w}$), which quantify the contribution of each intermediate indicator to the final credibility score. The learned weights remain relatively stable across the varying dataset sizes. For instance, the consistently negative weight assigned to the "Predator-Prey Ratio" indicator provides actionable feedback, suggesting that this aspect of the simulation may require refinement to improve its credibility.

Table 5. Learned Fusion Weights ($\mathbf{w}$) for the Wolf-Sheep Model.

Indicator	Dataset Size			
	r = 4	r = 8	r = 16	Total
Collapse Delay	0.369	0.478	0.171	0.398
Population CV	0.079	0.032	−0.077	0.184
Predator-Prey Ratio	−0.034	−0.040	−0.260	−0.041
Grass Coverage	0.166	0.178	0.185	0.170
Energy Pyramid	0.218	0.157	0.190	0.080
Phase Lag	0.016	−0.004	0.356	0.042

To analyze the temporal logic learned by the model, we visualize two metrics in Figs. 3 and 4. The heatmap displays the *Indicator-Temporal Importance*, derived from the feature-indicator weight matrix $\mathbf{A}$. The overlaid line plot shows the aggregate influence of all features at a given timestep on the final score $\hat{F}$. This is calculated by first collapsing the model's two stages into an effective weight matrix, $\mathbf{W}_{\text{eff}} = \mathbf{w}^T\mathbf{A}$. The final influence for each timestep t is then the sum of the corresponding effective weights: $\sum_{m=0}^{M-1}(\mathbf{W}_{\text{eff}})_{t,m}$.

Table 6. Learned Fusion Weights (**w**) for the Traffic Flow Model.

Indicator	Dataset Size			
	r = 4	r = 8	r = 16	Total
Fundamental Diagram	0.278	0.264	0.277	0.280
Dynamic Congestion	0.425	0.455	0.479	0.456
Internal Consistency	0.304	0.286	0.243	0.266

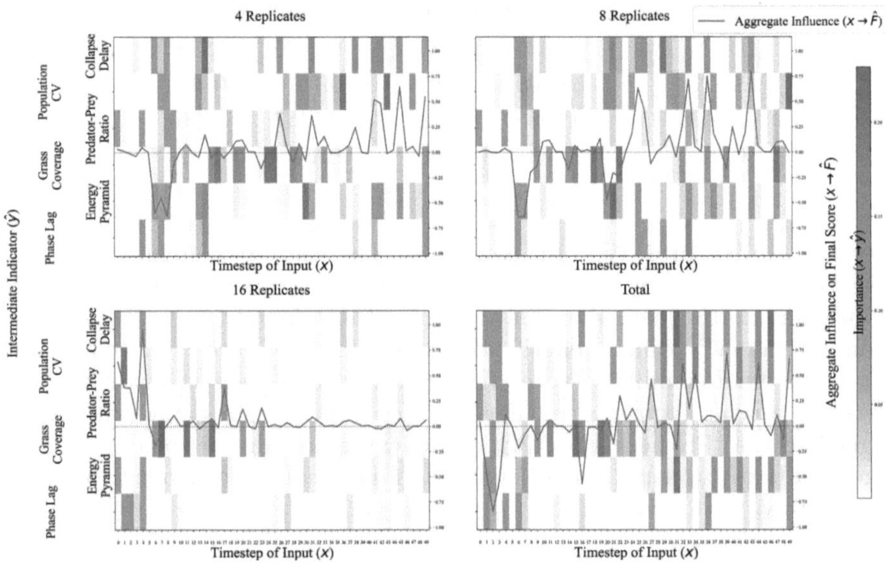

Fig. 3. Temporal analysis of learned weights for the Wolf-Sheep Predation model across different dataset sizes. The heatmap shows the average importance of input data at each timestep for computing intermediate indicators. The overlaid line plot shows the net influence of all features at a given timestep on the final credibility score.

In the Wolf-Sheep model (Fig. 3), the analysis reveals a dual temporal focus. The Net Temporal Influence curve emphasizes the simulation's start and end points, while the heatmap concentrates importance for stability indicators like "Collapse Delay" in the mid-to-late stages. The stability of this logic, even in the few-shot ($r = 4$) case, highlights the model's ability to learn robust patterns from limited data.

The Traffic Flow model analysis (Fig. 4) offers compelling evidence of learned logic. Feature importance peaks mid-simulation, coinciding with traffic state transitions. Crucially, the weights for the "Dynamic Congestion" indicator are highest precisely at these transition points, confirming that QLM successfully captures the intended heuristic of the evaluation metric.

The consistent emergence of these logical, problem-specific heuristics demonstrates that QLM identifies fundamental evaluation patterns, not spurious corre-

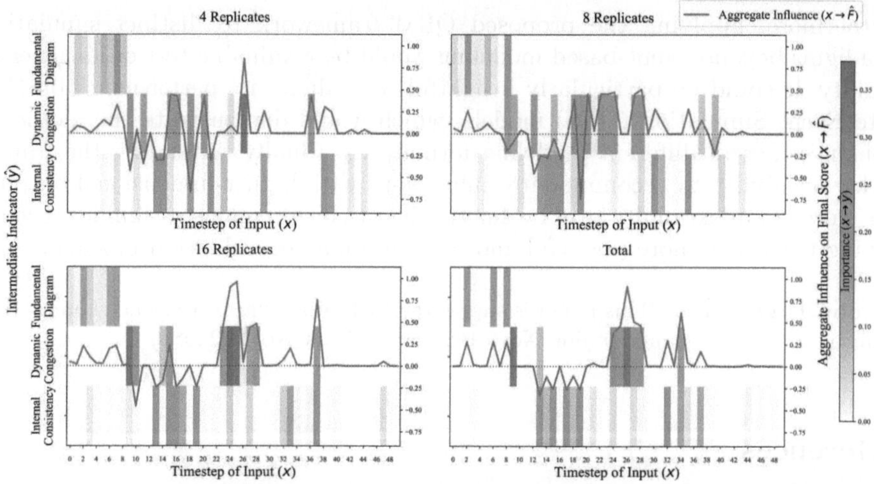

Fig. 4. Temporal analysis of learned weights for the Traffic Flow model. The visualization highlights which timesteps are most critical for assessing indicators like the Fundamental Diagram and Dynamic Congestion, and their overall impact on the final score.

lations. This inherent interpretability, which enables the validation of the learned scoring logic, provides a clear and practical advantage over opaque, black-box alternatives.

5 Conclusion and Future Works

This paper introduced the Quantitative Learning Method (QLM), a framework designed to formalize and automate the evaluation of simulation models, particularly within the constraints of data scarcity. Empirical validation demonstrated that while QLM achieves predictive performance comparable to several baseline algorithms, its primary strength lies in its superior robustness. In few-shot scenarios, QLM successfully mitigates the severe overfitting that afflicted many counterparts, especially deep learning models. Moreover, the framework's inherent interpretability was confirmed through parameter analysis, which showed that the data-driven importance assigned to evaluation indicators aligns with established domain knowledge. These characteristics establish QLM as an effective and reliable tool for enhancing the objectivity, efficiency, and transparency of simulation model evaluation.

Future work will proceed along several promising directions. One key avenue involves enhancing the optimization process, potentially by integrating more advanced search strategies into the L-SHADE algorithm to improve its exploration of the complex parameter space. Concurrently, we plan to refine the current model architecture, exploring alternative non-linear mappings to capture more intricate relationships between simulation data and evaluation scores.

Furthermore, applying the proposed QLM framework to distinct simulation paradigms beyond agent-based modeling would be a valuable test of its generalizability. It could be particularly insightful to evaluate its performance on Discrete Event Simulation (DES) models, which would demonstrate the method's robustness across different modeling formalisms. Finally, extending the framework's scalability to accommodate simulations with higher-dimensional outputs and more complex, multi-level evaluation hierarchies remains a significant goal, moving towards a more powerful and fully automated evaluation pipeline.

Acknowledgements. This paper is supported by Beijing Natural Science Foundation (Grant No. L241018) and Beijing Nova Program (Grant No. 2024085).

References

1. Bean, W.T., Stafford, R., Brashares, J.S.: The effects of small sample size and sample bias on threshold selection and accuracy assessment of species distribution models. Ecography **35**(3), 250–258 (2012)
2. Bella, A., Ferri, C., Hernández-Orallo, J., Ramírez-Quintana, M.J.: Similarity-binning averaging: a generalisation of binning calibration. In: Corchado, E., Yin, H. (eds.) Intelligent Data Engineering and Automated Learning - IDEAL 2009. IDEAL 2009. LNCS, vol. 5788, pp. 341–349. Springer, Berlin, Heidelberg (2009). https://doi.org/10.1007/978-3-642-04394-9_42
3. Breiman, L.: Random forests. Mach. Learn. **45**(1), 5–32 (2001)
4. Carterette, B.: Bayesian inference for information retrieval evaluation. In: Proceedings of the 2015 International Conference on The Theory of Information Retrieval, pp. 31–40. ICTIR '15, Association for Computing Machinery, New York, NY, USA (2015)
5. Cho, K., et al.: Learning phrase representations using RNN encoder-decoder for statistical machine translation. In: Proceedings of the 2014 Conference on Empirical Methods in Natural Language Processing (EMNLP), pp. 1724–1734. Association for Computational Linguistics, Doha, Qatar (2014)
6. Collart, F., Guisan, A.: Small to train, small to test: dealing with low sample size in model evaluation. Eco. Inform. **75**, 102106 (2023)
7. Elman, J.L.: Finding structure in time. Cogn. Sci. **14**(2), 179–211 (1990)
8. Feurer, M., Klein, A., Eggensperger, K., Springenberg, J., Blum, M., Hutter, F.: Efficient and robust automated machine learning. In: Cortes, C., Lawrence, N.D., Lee, D.D., Sugiyama, M., Garnett, R. (eds.) Advances in Neural Information Processing Systems 28 (NIPS 2015), pp. 2962–2970. Curran Associates, Inc. (2015)
9. Goodfellow, I., Bengio, Y., Courville, A.: Deep Learning. MIT Press, Cambridge, MA, USA (2016)
10. Haq, Z.U., Rasheed, R., Rashid, A., Akhter, S.: Criteria for assessing and ensuring the trustworthiness in qualitative research. Int. J. Bus. Reflect. **4**(2) (2023)
11. Hastie, T., Tibshirani, R., Friedman, J.: The Elements of Statistical Learning: Data Mining, Inference, and Prediction, 2nd edn. Springer, New York, NY, USA (2009). https://doi.org/10.1007/978-0-387-84858-7
12. Hochreiter, S., Schmidhuber, J.: Long short-term memory. Neural Comput. **9**(8), 1735–1780 (1997)

13. Law, A.M.: How to build valid and credible simulation models. In: 2022 Winter Simulation Conference (WSC), pp. 1283–1295. IEEE (2022)
14. Meral, A., Eroğlu, E.: Evaluation of flood risk analyses with AHP, kriging, and weighted sum models: example of Çapakçur, Yeşilköy, and Yamaç Microcatchments. Environ. Monit. Assess. **193**(8), 505 (2021)
15. Shiffrin, R.M., Lee, M.D., Kim, W., Wagenmakers, E.J.: A Survey of model evaluation approaches with a tutorial on hierarchical Bayesian methods. Cogn. Sci. **32**(8), 1248–1284 (2008)
16. Storn, R., Price, K.: Differential evolution - a simple and efficient heuristic for global optimization over continuous spaces. J. Glob. Optim. **11**(4), 341–359 (1997)
17. Tanabe, R., Fukunaga, A.: Success-history based adaptive differential evolution. In: 2013 IEEE Congress on Evolutionary Computation, pp. 71–78. IEEE (2013)
18. Tibshirani, R.: Regression shrinkage and selection via the lasso. J. Roy. Stat. Soc.: Ser. B (Methodol.) **58**(1), 267–288 (1996)
19. Vanschoren, J.: Meta-Learning. In: Hutter, F., Kotthoff, L., Vanschoren, J. (eds.) Automated Machine Learning: Methods, Systems, Challenges, pp. 35–61. Springer, Cham (2019). https://doi.org/10.1007/978-3-030-05318-5_2
20. Wang, Y., Yao, Q., Kwok, J.T., Ni, L.M.: Generalizing from a few examples: a survey on few-shot learning. ACM Comput. Surv. **53**(3), 1–35 (2020)
21. Yang, W., Lin, L., Gao, H.: Simulation evaluation of small samples based on grey estimation and improved bootstrap. Grey Syst. Theory Appl. **12**(2), 376–388 (2021)
22. Yuan, M., Lin, Y.: Model selection and estimation in regression with grouped variables. J. R. Stat. Soc. Ser. B (Stat. Methodol.) **68**(1), 49–67 (2006)
23. Zhang, L., Liu, Y., Laili, Y., Zhang, W.: Model maturity towards modeling and simulation: concepts, index system framework and evaluation method. Int. J. Model. Simul. Sci. Comput. **11**(03), 2040001 (2020)

Robust Lunar-Image Matching Under Disturbance: High-Precision Comparison of RANSAC, RL-RANSAC, and MLESAC

Mashiro Shimada[1](✉), Haruki Omori[1], and Hiroyuki Kamata[2]

[1] Graduate School of Science and Technology, Meiji University, Chiyoda, Japan
{ce241013,ce241044}@meiji.ac.jp

[2] School of Science and Technology, Meiji University, Chiyoda, Japan
kamata@meiji.ac.jp

Abstract. This paper proposes a position-estimation method to enable high-precision lunar landing using small unmanned probes in space operating in a low-computational-resource environment. The proposed method extracts feature points from both actual images captured by spacecraft and pre-prepared map images and then estimates the current position through correspondence-point matching. In the lunar environment, outlier removal is crucial, because space-specific disturbances such as radiation can degrade images, thus resulting in false correspondences. Although random sample consensus is commonly used for outlier removal, its inherent randomness can result in unstable estimation accuracy. Hence, this study focuses on reinforcement learning and maximum likelihood estimation sample consensus as correspondence-point-selection strategies. Furthermore, to achieve a more accurate position estimation, local optimization is applied to each method, and its effects on accuracy and stability are evaluated. Additionally, the robustness of the proposed approach against disturbed images under resource-constrained conditions is assessed.

Keywords: Image Matching · MLESAC · Reinforcement-Learning RANSAC

1 Introduction

The Moon is the closest celestial body to the Earth; nonetheless, many of its characteristics are under investigated. To accommodate future exploration and resource utilization, various countries are actively pursuing crewed and uncrewed lunar missions.

In January 2024, Japan's Smart Lander for Investigating the Moon (SLIM) project [1] achieved the world's first high-precision lunar landing, with a landing error of less than 100 m from the designated target. The SLIM project accomplished this by estimating the lander's position and correcting navigation errors through real-time image matching using preloaded lunar-map data. Currently, location matching is performed using ground-based backup processing. However, the ultimate goal is to execute this processing entirely onboard a spacecraft, where computational resources are severely constrained and low power consumption is required.

W. Cai et al. (Eds.): AsiaSim 2025, CCIS 2727, pp. 16–27, 2026.
https://doi.org/10.1007/978-981-95-4472-1_2

A fundamental technology that enables such high-precision landings is the accurate extraction of feature correspondences between images. However, in practical image matching, image degradation resulting from space-exploration-specific disturbances, —such as cosmic radiation and anomalies in camera sensors, —can result in erroneous correspondences (outliers), thereby rendering their removal essential.

This study focuses on outlier-rejection techniques in the context of lunar-image matching and investigates methods for improving the robustness and accuracy of feature correspondence.

The procedure for matching a lunar-map image with a real-time-captured image is as follows: First, feature points are extracted from both images using Accelerated KAZE [2], and candidate correspondences are identified using the k-nearest neighbor (k-NN) algorithm [3]. Next, incorrect correspondences (outliers) are eliminated using random sample consensus (RANSAC) [4–6]. The remaining correspondences after outlier removal are used to estimate the projective transformation matrix, which is subsequently applied to calculate the coordinates in the real-time image. Singular value decomposition is employed for the coordinate estimation.

However, in space environments, radiation and other forms of noise can degrade captured images, thus causing scratches or missing regions. If such damaged areas are mistakenly selected as feature points, then the reliance of RANSAC on random sampling and fixed thresholds can cause incomplete outlier removal, thereby resulting in an unstable estimation accuracy.

Hence, alternative outlier-rejection methods such as reinforcement-learning (RL) -based RANSAC and maximum likelihood estimation sample consensus (MLESAC) [7, 8] were proposed.

RL-RANSAC selects correspondences by assigning higher rewards to more accurate matches. By contrast, MLESAC evaluates all data points by assigning scores based on their likelihood of being inliers, thus identifying a more reliable set of correspondences. Both approaches aim to improve the limitations of random sampling in conventional RANSAC.

Furthermore, local optimization (LO) techniques [9, 10] were introduced to enhance estimation precision by refining the inlier set based on an initially estimated model.

In this study, we comprehensively evaluate four methods—standard RANSAC, RL-RANSAC, LO-RL-RANSAC, and LO-MLESAC—by comparing their number of successful estimations, computation time, and variability in position estimation accuracy. The goal is to assess their robustness and stability when applied to images affected by disturbances, particularly in resource-constrained and low-power environments.

2 RANSAC

As mentioned previously, the correspondence points obtained by the k-NN method include many incorrect matches, which are referred to as outliers. Images can be matched rapidly and accurately by removing these outliers and increasing the proportion of correct matches (known as inliers).

RANSAC is one of the most widely used algorithms for robust model estimation in the presence of outliers. The typical procedure for RANSAC is as follows [11]:

Step1: Randomly sample a subset of correspondence points from the matches detected using the k-NN method.

Step2: Estimate a transformation matrix from the sampled subset and construct a geometric model.

Step3: Apply the model to calculate the estimated coordinates in the map image for all candidate correspondence points.

Step4: Compare the estimated coordinates with the actual feature point coordinates in the map image. Points with distances exceeding a predefined threshold are classified as outliers and thus discarded.

Step5: Repeat steps 1–4 until the termination condition is satisfied. The termination condition based on the number of iterations N is expressed as

$$N = \frac{\log(1-\mathrm{p})}{\log(1-w^s)}. \tag{1}$$

p denotes the desired probability that at least one sampled subset contains only inliers, w is the probability that a randomly selected point is an inlier, and s is the number of points required to estimate the model. In this study, because a projective transformation is used, s is set to 4.

RANSAC generally performs well when the proportion of outliers is less than 50% [12]. However, in the presence of noisy or corrupted images, such as those considered in this study, the outlier rate can be significantly higher. Consequently, the time required to identify valid inliers increases substantially, thus potentially degrading the matching performance.

3 Reinforcement-Learning RANSAC

Reinforcement-learning (RL) is a type of machine learning in which an agent learns to make decisions through interactions with the environment based on the concept of receiving rewards. Unlike supervised learning, which passively learns from data provided, RL aims to "maximize cumulative rewards over time by actively exploring and exploiting the environment."

In conventional RANSAC, samples are randomly selected. When the proportion of inliers is low, the probability of selecting a subset with sufficient inliers is also low, which typically results in inaccurate model estimation. By contrast, RL-RANSAC improves the accuracy, even in such cases, by assigning higher rewards to hypotheses that are more likely to include many inliers, thereby guiding the sampling process toward better subsets over time.

RL algorithms can be broadly categorized into two types: value-based methods, which estimate a value function and select actions based on it; and policy-based methods, which directly learn a policy that maps states to action probabilities. In this study, the value-based approach was implemented using the Monte Carlo method, whereas the policy-based approach adopted the probabilistic upper confidence bound (UCB) policy [5], which is an extension of the UCB algorithm from deterministic action selection to a probabilistic framework.

3.1 Reinforcement Learning with UCB Policy

3.1.1 Update Rating Values

First, we define a method for computing and updating reward values. The reward r assigned to each data point is expressed as follows:

$$r = \begin{cases} \frac{|e-b|}{b} & (|e| < b) \\ 0 & (|e| \geq b) \end{cases}, \tag{2}$$

where e denotes the error between the map image coordinates and the coordinates transformed using the estimated model, and b denotes the error tolerance. This equation yields a high reward when the error e is small and no reward when e is large. In this study, the error tolerance b was set to five [pixels].

The reward value is used to update the evaluation score of each data point as follows:

$$v_i \leftarrow v_i + \alpha \frac{E}{maxE}(r - v_i), \tag{3}$$

where v_i denotes the reward value for each data point; E denotes the total reward across all data points; $maxE$ is the maximum total reward; and α is the tuning parameter, which is set to 0.1 in this study.

3.1.2 Selecting Data

Next, we discuss the methods for selecting correspondence points. These methods can be broadly categorized into probabilistic and deterministic policies.

A representative example of a probabilistic policy is the softmax method, which enables flexible exploration by probabilistically selecting the corresponding points based on their associated rewards.

By contrast, the UCB policy, which is a deterministic policy, selects data points decisively based on both their evaluation values and the number of times they have been selected. A key feature of the UCB policy is its exploratory behavior, which actively favors data points that have been selected less frequently. This increases the likelihood of discovering previously unused, high-quality correspondence points.

In this study, we adopted the UCB policy to enhance the accuracy of correspondence-point selection by balancing the exploration of unselected data and the exploitation of known, high-reward data. This approach is expected to improve the overall accuracy of the final position estimation.

The data-selection method for the UCB policy is expressed as follows:

$$\overline{X_i} \leftarrow \overline{X_i} + C\sqrt{\frac{\ln N}{N_i}}, \tag{4}$$

where $\overline{X_i}$ denotes the average reward of the i-th data point; N is the number of trials; N_i denotes the number of times the i-th data point has been selected; and C is a tuning parameter, which is set to 1 in this study. Additionally, because this study uses the same reward values $\overline{X_i}$, the equation can be rewritten as follows:

$$\overline{X_i} = v_i + \sqrt{\frac{\ln N}{N_i}}. \tag{5}$$

This indicates that the data are selected in the order of increasing values of $\overline{X_i}$; in this study, the top-four points were selected.

3.2 Probabilistic UCB Policy

A probabilistic UCB policy extends the deterministic nature of the normal UCB policy to a probabilistic selection strategy.

In this study, four corresponding points were selected to generate a model based on, the standard procedure for RANSAC-based estimation.

Whereas the normal UCB policy deterministically selects the top four points with the highest evaluation values, the probabilistic UCB policy randomly selects four points from the top eight candidates, thereby introducing sampling diversity and promoting exploration.

4 Maximum Likelihood Estimation Sample Consensus (MLESAC)

MLESAC evaluates model hypotheses based on a probabilistic likelihood function instead of, the binary classification of data points as inliers or outliers, as in RANSAC. Although RANSAC determines the quality of a model by counting the number of inliers, MLESAC uses the sum of log-likelihoods as its evaluation criterion. Consequently, MLESAC tends to yield more stable and accurate model estimates, particularly in scenarios with low inlier ratios or high noise levels in the observed data.

In MLESAC, the likelihood function that represents the probability of a data point being an inlier is modeled as a mixture distribution as follows:

$$P(r) = \gamma \cdot N\left(r;\ 0, \sigma^2\right) + (1-\gamma) \cdot U(r;\ 0, T), \tag{6}$$

$$\mathcal{N}\left(r;\ 0, \sigma^2\right) = \frac{1}{\sqrt{2\pi\sigma^2}} e^{-\frac{r^2}{\sigma^2}},\ U(r;\ 0, T) = \frac{1}{T},$$

where *P(r)* denotes the likelihood, γ is the mixing weight representing the prior probability that a data point is an inlier, r is the residual of a data point with respect to the estimated model, $\mathcal{N}\left(r;\ 0, \sigma^2\right)$ denotes the probability density function of a zero-mean Gaussian distribution with variance, $U(r;\ 0, T)$ denotes the probability density of a uniform distribution over the interval range of 0–T, and T is a threshold parameter defining the support of the outlier distribution. Additionally, the overall score of a model is computed by summing the log-likelihoods of all data points as follows:

$$L = \sum_{i=1}^{N} \log(P(r_i)), \tag{7}$$

where L denotes the total log-likelihood of the candidate model, N is the number of data points, and r_i denotes the residual of the i-th data point. The model hypothesis that maximizes the total log-likelihood L is selected as the best model.

5 Local Optimization (LO)

Local optimization technique [9, 10] is used to refine a hypothetical model obtained by RANSAC or similar methods, to achieve higher accuracy and better overall results.

Even the best model selected by RANSAC may not be optimal, because it is estimated from a limited subset of samples and is thus sensitive to noise. Hence, LO is performed to improve the model by obtaining a larger set of inliers based on the initial estimate and then re-estimating the model using these inliers.

Since the refinement is performed in the vicinity of a promising hypothesis instead of through a global search across the entire data space, the process is referred to as "local" optimization. In this study, we hypothesize that incorporating LO into a learning-based method can enhance the accuracy of feature matching, particularly in addressing the effects of noise unique to the space environment.

6 Experiment

6.1 Experiment Procedure

In this study, four types of captured images generated for simulation and provided by JAXA were used for verification: one actual lunar image and three images with disturbances added to it. The details of the captured images are presented in Table 1, and an example is shown in Fig. 1.

Table 1. Summary of captured images

Pattern No.	Disturbance	Summary	Number of images
1	Nominal	Without disturbance	1000
2	Brightness	Increases or decreases the image brightness	1000
3	Contrast	Increases or decreases the image contrast	1000
4	Radiation noise	Adds sesame-salt noise to the image	1000

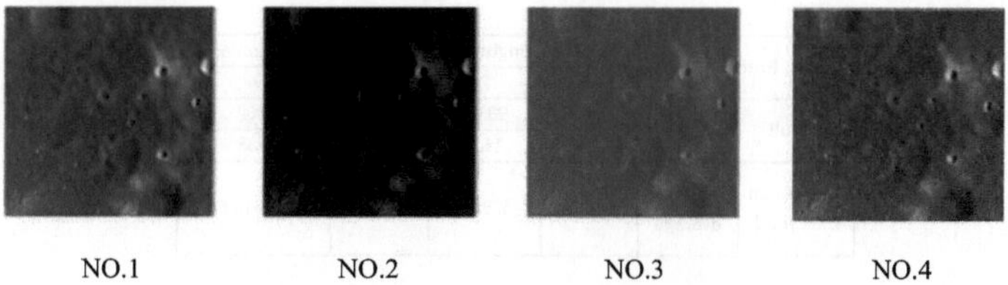

Fig. 1. Examples of captured images

The parameters used in these experiments are listed in Table 2.

Table 2. Parameters used in current experiments

Parameters		Value
AKAZE	Threshold	0.000001
k-NN algorithm	Threshold	Standard RANSAC: 0.93 Other methods: 0.85
RANSAC	Upper limit of number of attempts	5000
	Degree of accuracy [%]	99.99
	Maximum distance [pixel]	5.0
MLESAC	Prior probability of a point being an inlier [%]	70
	Standard deviation of Gaussian error distribution	1.0

Location estimation was performed using lunar-map images and the captured images shown in Table 1. Owing to the inherent randomness of RANSAC and its derivative method, MLESAC, the results varied significantly. Hence, each method was executed 10 times, and the average of the results was used as the evaluation metric.

Five methods were compared: standard RANSAC, RL-RANSAC, LO-RL-RANSAC with rollback, LO-MLESAC with fallback to standard RANSAC, and LO-MLESAC with fallback to RL-RANSAC. In the latter three methods, the application of LO occasionally resulted in estimation failure because of the inability to secure the four correspondences required for projective transformation. Therefore, either a rollback (reverting to the previous hypothesis) or fallback (switching to an alternative method) was employed, depending on the situation.

6.2 Result and Discussion

Tables 3, 4, 5, 6 and 7 present the number of successful estimations and the calculation times for the following five methods: standard RANSAC, RL-RANSAC, LO-RL-RANSAC with rollback, LO-MLESAC with fallback to standard RANSAC, and LO-MLESAC with fallback to RL-RANSAC.

Table 3. Experimental results on standard RANSAC

Pattern		Nominal	Brightness	Contrast	Radiation noise
		1	2	3	4
Result	success	1000	983.8	977.9	762
	failure	0	16.2	22.1	238
Calculation time [ms]	success, average	646.06	629.08	629.5	2861.26

These results are analyzed in detail in the following sections.

Table 4. Experimental results on RL-RANSAC

Pattern		Nominal	Brightness	Contrast	Radiation noise
		1	2	3	4
Result	success	1000	975.4	971	937.7
	failure	0	24.6	29	62.3
Calculation time [ms]	success, average	290.26	280.94	259.34	408.16

Table 5. Experimental results on LO-RL-RANSAC with rollback

Pattern		Nominal	Brightness	Contrast	Radiation noise
		1	2	3	4
Result	success	1000	977.1	973.6	942.5
	failure	0	22.9	26.4	57.5
Calculation time [ms]	success, average	296.44	289.62	266.8	417.05

Table 6. Experimental results on LO-MLESAC with fallback to standard RANSAC

Pattern		Nominal	Brightness	Contrast	Radiation noise
		1	2	3	4
Result	success	1000	984.4	982.9	947.6
	failure	0	15.6	17.1	52.4
Calculation time [ms]	success, average	351.83	340.71	319.91	563.22

Table 7. Experimental results on LO-MLESAC with fallback to RL-RANSAC

Pattern		Nominal	Brightness	Contrast	Radiation noise
		1	2	3	4
Result	success	1000	984.3	983.3	938.6
	failure	0	15.7	16.7	61.4
Calculation time [ms]	success, average	343.43	335.03	305.32	542.26

6.2.1 Estimated Number of Successes

First, a chart comparing the number of successful estimations achieved by the five methods is presented (Fig. 2).

In Pattern No. 1, all five methods performed estimations successfully; therefore, a comparison of the results was omitted. In Pattern Nos. 2 and 4, LO-MLESAC with fallback to standard RANSAC achieved the best performance, whereas in Pattern No. 3, LO-MLESAC with fallback to RL-RANSAC yielded the best results, namely, in terms of the number of successful estimations (i.e., accuracy), MLESAC achieved the best results for all types of disturbances. Because MLESAC determines inliers based on the sum of log-likelihoods, it is considered effective for both brightness and contrast images, where

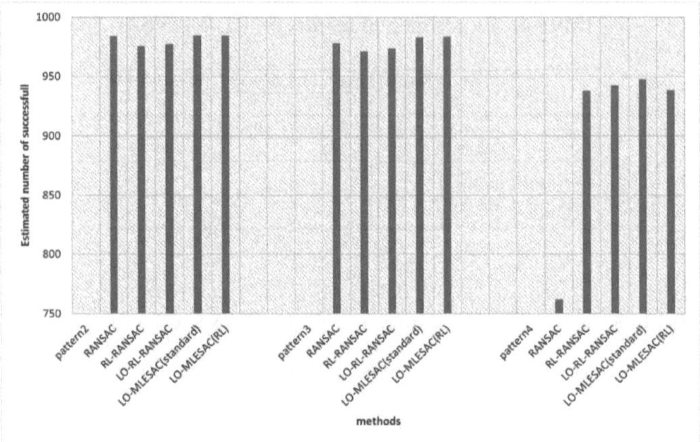

Fig. 2. Estimated number of successes for five methods under three disturbances.

the number of correspondences tends to be small owing to limited luminance variation, and noisy images, where the inlier ratio is reduced.

RANSAC and RL-based methods attempt to efficiently eliminate outliers from the set of correspondences; however, this process may inadvertently remove points that are genuine inliers, thus potentially resulting in failed estimations.

By contrast, because MLESAC evaluates inliers probabilistically using log-likelihoods, it tends to retain borderline points that might otherwise be discarded, thus contributing to improved estimation accuracy.

RL-RANSAC demonstrated high estimation accuracy for noisy images; however, its accuracy degraded for brightness and contrast images. By contrast, MLESAC maintained stable and reliable performances under all disturbance conditions.

For noisy images, the fallback strategy of MLESAC using conventional RANSAC yielded better results than when RL was used. One possible reason is that, although hypothesis generation through RL is generally more accurate, when it is used as a fallback, its effect on model refinement is limited. In such cases, conventional RANSAC can provide a more stable model selection.

6.2.2 Calculation Time

Next, a table comparing the calculation times of the five methods is presented (Fig. 3).

The calculation times were reported only for Pattern No. 1, for which RL-RANSAC achieved the best performance, namely, in terms of calculation time (i.e., speed), RL-RANSAC was superior because the other three methods—LO-MLESAC, LO-RL-RANSAC, and MLESAC—involve more computationally intensive processes. Specifically, LO-MLESAC and LO-RL-RANSAC include LO steps, which require additional processing time beyond simple hypothesis generation and evaluation. Additionally, MLESAC involves more complex likelihood-based computations for inlier classification compared to RANSAC, which in fact requires longer processing times.

Nevertheless, all the proposed methods completed the estimation in approximately half the time required by conventional RANSAC, thus demonstrating their efficiency.

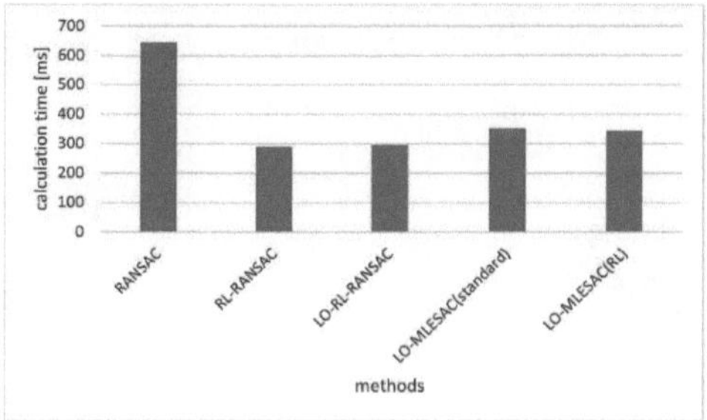

Fig. 3. Calculation times in Pattern 1 for five methods.

Notably, the comparison above is based on images without disturbances. For images with noise, however, all methods completed the estimation in approximately one-sixth of the time, thereby suggesting that the hypothesis convergence accelerated significantly under noisy conditions.

6.2.3 Data Variability

Finally, Fig. 4 shows a comparison of the variability of the five methods under three types of disturbances, and Table 8 summarizes the corresponding standard deviations.

In Pattern No. 1, all five methods performed estimations successfully; therefore, only the results for Pattern Nos. 2 to 4 are presented herein. In Pattern Nos. 2 and 3, LO-MLESAC with fallback to standard RANSAC achieved the highest success rate, followed by LO-MLESAC with fallback to RL-RANSAC, which also performed well. For these two patterns, the MLESAC-based methods outperformed the others methods. By contrast, in Pattern No. 4, LO-RL-RANSAC achieved the highest success rate, followed by LO-MLESAC with RL fallback. These results suggest that RL facilitates the estimation performance.

The variability (i.e., repeatability) of the estimation results is discussed. The standard RANSAC yielded inconsistent accuracies across runs owing to the randomness of the initial sampling process.

In the present evaluation, MLESAC exhibited the most stable estimation accuracy for brightness and contrast images. This stability is likely due to MLESAC's ability to appropriately extract candidate inliers and converge to the correct hypothesis during the subsequent LO stage. As mentioned earlier, MLESAC tends to retain borderline points that may or may not be inliers, thereby contributing to its high repeatability. By contrast, the standard RANSAC and RL-based methods typically classify ambiguous points as outliers, which may result in increased variability in the estimation results.

LO-RL-RANSAC exhibited the best performance for noisy images. This can be attributed to the effective combination of reward-based hypothesis exploration and refinement via LO, which is particularly beneficial under noisy conditions with numerous correspondence points. RL consistently eliminated genuine outliers during each estimation, thereby achieving high success rates. However, the relatively large variability observed in RL-RANSAC without LO may be due to the influence of its initial random exploration stage on the subsequent learning policy.

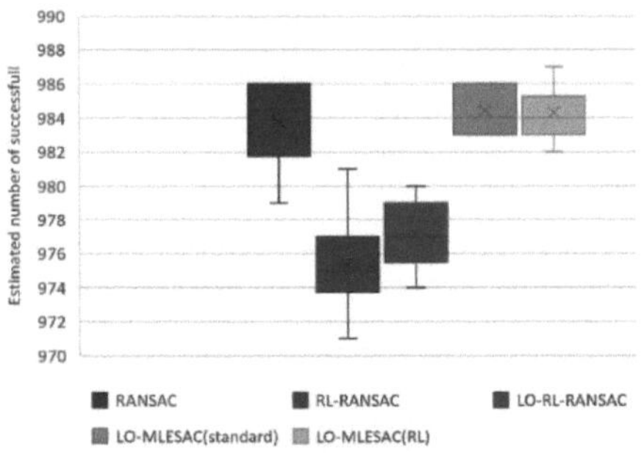

(a)Pattern 1

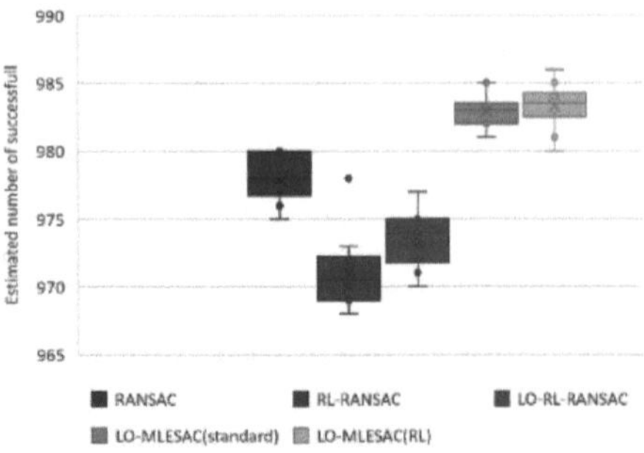

(b)Pattern 2

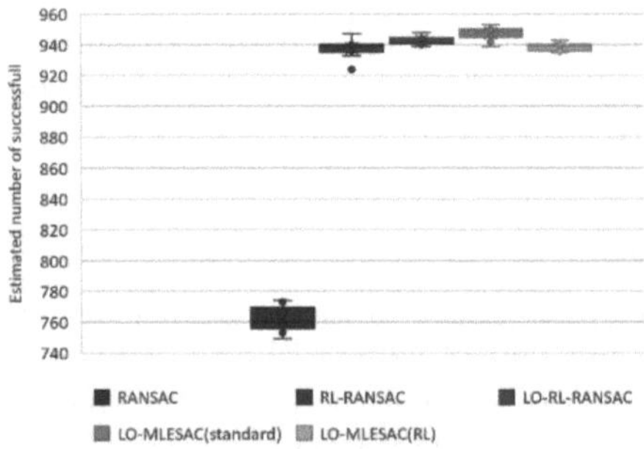

(c)Pattern 3

Fig. 4. Variability of five methods under three types of disturbances.

Table 8. Standard deviations for five methods under three disturbances.

Methods / Pattern No.	RANSAC	RL_RANSAC	LO_RL_RANSAC	LO_MLESAC(standard)	LO_MLESAC(RL)
2	2.27	2.54	1.92	1.20	1.42
3	1.64	2.76	2.01	1.22	1.68
4	7.86	5.69	2.62	4.03	2.29

Nevertheless, MLESAC showed less variability and more stable hypothesis selection than the standard RANSAC. This result is attributable to its likelihood-based inlier scoring, which enables more appropriate outlier rejection.

7 Conclusion

In this study, we aimed to establish an efficient outlier removal method by comparing four approaches: standard RANSAC, RL-RANSAC, LO-RL-RANSAC, and LO-MLESAC.

Our experimental results revealed that the RL-based method excelled in accurately extracting inliers from images with numerous correspondence points. By contrast, MLE-SAC demonstrated robustness across a wide range of image conditions by retaining ambiguous points that might be inliers, thereby offering a balanced performance. However, the estimation accuracy of all these methods was highly sensitive to the threshold settings used in the initial k-NN-based filtering process; thus, their performances may be significantly affected by this parameter.

From the perspective of computational efficiency, all methods required shorter processing times compared with the standard approach. However, the current pipeline involves a two-stage outlier removal process: a coarse filtering step using the k-NN method, followed by a more precise refinement step using RANSAC or MLESAC. This two-stage structure introduces redundancies into the workflow and limits the potential for further acceleration.

Hence, future studies should focus on developing a unified outlier removal framework that does not rely on k-NN-based pre-filtering to, improve both the accuracy and efficiency of the estimation process.

References

1. Yoshikawa, S., et al.: Conceptual Study on the Guidance, Navigation and Control System of the Smart Landing for Investigating Moon (SLIM). Proceedings of the Global Lunar Conference **2010**, 59–62 (2010)
2. Sharma, K.S., Kamal, J.: Image Stitching Using AKAZE Features. J. Indian Soc. Remote Sens. **48**, 1389–1401 (2020)
3. Jorma, L., Erkki, O.: Classification with Learning k-Nearest Neighbors, Proceedings of the International Conference on Neural Networks (ICNN'96) 3, pp. 1480–1483 (1996)
4. Rahul, R., Pollefeys, M., Matas, J.: USAC: A Universal Framework for Random Sample Consensus. IEEE Trans. Software Eng. **35**, 2022–2038 (2013)
5. Shimada, M., Kamata, H.: Highly Accurate Image Matching Using Inlier Extraction of Images via Upper Confidence Bound Policy. Springer Nature, ICGEC **1321**, 65–74 (2025)
6. Omori, H., Shimada, M., Kamata, H.: Improved Correspondence Point Search and Image Matching Accuracy for Disturbanced Images Using TD(0) Method. JSST, Journal of Advanced Simulation in Science and Engineering **12**(1), 191–200 (2025)
7. Torr, P.H.S., Zisserman, A.: MLESAC: A New Robust Estimator with Application to Estimating Image Geometry. Comput. Vis. Image Underst. **78**(1), 138–156 (2000)
8. Zhang, L., Rastgar, H., Wang, D., Vincent, A.: Maximum Likelihood Estimation Sample Consensus with Validation of Individual Correspondences, Springer, Advances in Visual Computing. ISVC 2009. Lecture Notes in Computer Science 5875, pp. 447–456 (2009)
9. Chum, O., Matas, J.: Randomized RANSAC with Sequential Probability Ratio Test. IEEE, Proceeding of the Tenth IEEE International Conference on Computer Vision (ICCV), pp. 1727–1732 (2005)
10. Chum, O., Matas, J., Kittler, J.:Locally Optimized RANSAC, Springer Nature, Pattern Recognition(DAGM2003), pp. 236–243(2003)
11. Fischler, A.M., Bolles, C.R.: Random Sample Consensus: A Paradigm for Model Fitting with Applications to Image Analysis and Automated Cartography. Commun. ACM **24**(6), 381–395 (1981)
12. Lowe, G.D.: Distinctive Image Features from Scale Invariant Keypoints. Int. J. Comput. Vision **60**, 91–110 (2004)

Aeroassisted Orbital Transfer Optimization Using Sequential Convex Programming

Yu Qiao, Ping Ma, Ming Yang, and Tao Chao(✉)

National Key Laboratory of Complex System Control and Intelligent Agent Cooperation, Control and Simulation Center, Harbin Institute of Technology, Harbin 150000, China
chaotao2000@163.com

Abstract. With growing demand for fuel-efficient space missions, aeroassisted orbital transfer (AOT) has become a critical focus in orbital dynamics research. This paper investigates fuel-optimal AOT trajectory optimization under complex constraints using sequential convex programming (SCP). The proposed method introduces auxiliary control variables to decouple state and control dynamics, effectively mitigating high-frequency oscillations caused by linearization. Successive linearization is applied to highly nonlinear dynamics, boundary equality constraints, path inequality constraints, and nonlinear performance indices. Numerical simulations demonstrate that the SCP algorithm outperforms GPOPS in solving fuel-optimal AOT problems, achieving superior solution optimality, path constraint satisfaction, and computational efficiency.

Keywords: Aeroassisted orbital transfer · Trajectory optimization · Sequential convex programming

1 Introduction

With the expansion of human space activities, the complexity of missions such as satellite constellation deployment, on-orbit servicing, and deep space exploration has grown significantly. The inherent energy efficiency limitations of conventional orbital transfer technologies have become increasingly apparent, severely constraining spacecraft operational lifespans and reducing the design flexibility of new space mission architectures. In this context, aeroassisted orbital transfer (AOT) has emerged as a key research focus in orbital dynamics [1]. This innovative method harnesses aerodynamic lift and drag forces, transforming them into orbital energy via controlled spacecraft-atmosphere interactions to dramatically reduce propellant requirements.

The concept of AOT was first proposed by London [2]. Since the1970s, studies have focused on minimum-fuel AOT maneuvers and thermal flux constraint handling [3]. Guidance algorithms have been developed to generate feasible AOT trajectories, but they often lack optimality [4]. Open-loop optimization methods, including indirect [5] and direct methods [6], outperform guidance algorithms in optimality but suffer from low computational efficiency and poor convergence, limiting their use in onboard planning.

W. Cai et al. (Eds.): AsiaSim 2025, CCIS 2727, pp. 28–39, 2026.
https://doi.org/10.1007/978-981-95-4472-1_3

Therefore, developing rapid optimization methods is essential for enabling efficient AOT in complex missions.

In recent years, convex optimization has been widely applied to rapid trajectory planning, including UAV path planning and collision avoidance [7], planetary entry [8], and spacecraft rendezvous and proximity operations [9]. Zhang et al. [10] employed sequential convex programming (SCP) for optimizing the single-pass Mars aerocapture trajectory, improving the optimality of the solution. However, this approach neglects critical path constraints, such as load factor and heating rate, essential for mission feasibility. To address this, Han et al. [11] proposed an SCP-based method using orbital energy as the independent variable to enforce path constraints. However, this method relies on predefined initial and terminal orbital energy values, and fixed entry/exit altitudes constrain flight velocities, limiting optimality. Additionally, Wang et al. [12] introduced bank angle rate as a control variable to decouple control and state dynamics, mitigating high-frequency oscillations. While these advancements enhance SCP's robustness and convergence, SCP-based methods remain unexplored for AOT. In summary, AOT trajectory planning faces challenges such as incomplete constraint handling, limited convergence, computational inefficiency, and sensitivity to initial guesses [13]. Further research on SCP-based AOT trajectory optimization is needed.

Building on prior work, this paper systematically reformulates the AOT problem with complex constraints into a convex-optimization framework. To enhance numerical stability, auxiliary control variables are introduced to decouple state and control dynamics, effectively suppressing high-frequency oscillations induced by linearization. The proposed approach employs successive linearization to convexify the highly nonlinear dynamics, boundary conditions, path constraints, and non-convex performance index. Numerical simulations demonstrate the method's superior effectiveness and computational efficiency in solving fuel-optimal AOT problems.

The paper is organized as follows: Sect. 2 derives the dynamical equations and physical model for AOT, along with the optimal control model. Section 3 presents the sequential convex programming approach for solving the AOT problem. Section 4 validates the method through numerical simulations, demonstrating its effectiveness and convergence. Finally, Sect. 5 concludes the paper.

2 AOT Problem Formulation

Aeroassisted orbital transfer is categorized into coplanar and non-coplanar transfers (Fig. 1), with the latter being the focus of this study. The flight consists of three phases: the Descending Phase (DP), where the vehicle departs its original orbit at point d via a deorbit impulse ΔV_d; the Aeroassisted Maneuvering Phase (AMP), initiating at atmospheric entry (altitude $h \leq 120$ km), where aerodynamic forces enable lateral maneuvers; and the Ascending Phase (AP), where a tangential impulse ΔV_f may be applied at f to compensate for drag-induced velocity loss and establish an ascending transfer orbit. Finally, an insertion impulse ΔV_c at c adjusts the velocity to V_c, transitioning the vehicle into the target orbit.

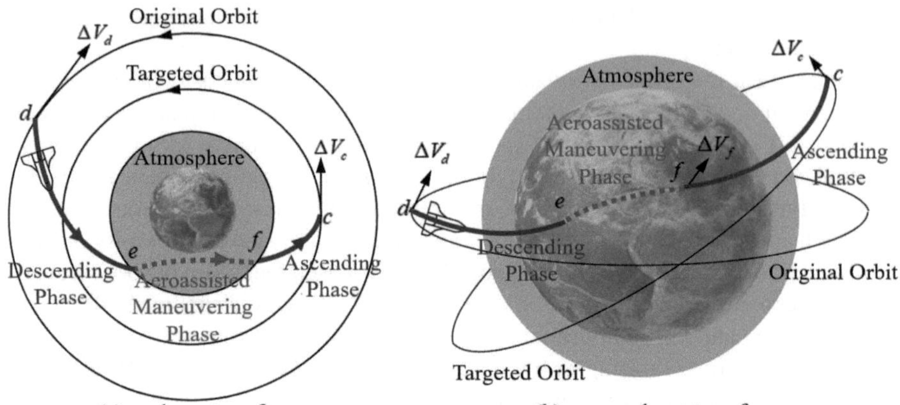

(a) coplanar transfer (b) non-coplanar transfer

Fig. 1. The schematic diagram of aeroassisted orbital transfer

2.1 Equation of Motion and Physical Model

Assuming a stationary atmosphere relative to Earth's surface and modeling Earth as a uniform sphere, the governing equations for unpowered atmospheric flight are formulated in dimensionless form as

$$\begin{aligned}
\dot{r} &= V\sin\gamma \\
\dot{\theta} &= V\cos\gamma\cos\psi \Big/ (r\cos\phi) \\
\dot{\phi} &= V\cos\gamma\sin\psi \Big/ r \\
\dot{V} &= -D - \sin\gamma \Big/ r^2 \\
\dot{\gamma} &= \frac{L\cos\sigma}{V} + \frac{(V^2 - 1/r)\cos\gamma}{Vr} \\
\dot{\psi} &= \frac{L\sin\sigma}{V\cos\gamma} - \frac{V\cos\gamma\cos\psi\tan\phi}{r}
\end{aligned} \tag{1}$$

where r is the radial distance from the Earth's center to the vehicle, normalized by the geocentric distance $R_0 = 6498$ km, which corresponds to the edge of the atmosphere. θ and ϕ are the longitude and latitude, respectively. γ and ψ are the flight-path angle and the heading angle, respectively. V is the dimensionless velocity normalized by $\sqrt{\mu/R_0}$, in which μ is the Earth gravitational parameter. Time is normalized by $\sqrt{R_0^3/\mu}$. The dimensionless lift and drag accelerations, L and D, are normalized by $g = \mu/R_0^2$, which represents the gravitational acceleration at the Earth's surface. They can be calculated as follows:

$$\begin{aligned}
L &= R_0\rho V^2 SC_L \Big/ 2m \\
D &= R_0\rho V^2 SC_D \Big/ 2m
\end{aligned} \tag{2}$$

where m denotes the mass of the vehicle, S represents the dimensional reference area, and $\rho = \rho_0 e^{-h/h_s}$ represents the dimensional atmospheric density. Here, $\rho_0 = 1.225$ kg/m^3 is the sea-level atmospheric density, $h_s = 6.9$ km is the atmospheric density coefficient, and h is the altitude. C_L and C_D represent the lift and drag coefficients, respectively, which are modeled using a standard drag polar [13] as $C_L = C_{L,\alpha}\alpha$ and $C_D = C_{D0} + KC_L^2$, where C_{D0} is the zero-lift drag coefficient, K is the drag polar parameter, and $C_{L,\alpha}$ is the lift slope.

2.2 Optimal Control Model for AOT

During atmospheric flight, the state and control vectors are subject to the following constraints:

$$\mathbf{x}_{\min} \le \mathbf{x} \le \mathbf{x}_{\max} \tag{3}$$

$$\mathbf{u}_{\min} \le \mathbf{u} \le \mathbf{u}_{\max} \tag{4}$$

where $\mathbf{x} = [r; \theta; \phi; V; \gamma; \psi]$ is the state vector, and $\mathbf{u} = [\alpha; \sigma]$ is the control vector. The bounds $\boldsymbol{x}_{\min}, \boldsymbol{x}_{\max}$ and $\boldsymbol{u}_{\min}, \boldsymbol{u}_{\max}$ represent their respective allowable limits.

For a descending transfer orbit with free perigee altitude in the DP, the problem becomes an optimization with free initial and terminal conditions. The dimensionless initial boundary conditions are:

$$r_e = 1, \gamma_e \le 0 \tag{5}$$

$$\theta_e = 0, \phi_e = 0, \psi_e = 0 \tag{6}$$

$$b_1(\mathbf{x}_e) = \left(2 - V_e^2\right) r_d^2 - 2r_d + V_e^2 \cos^2 \gamma_e = 0 \tag{7}$$

where the initial state vector is $\mathbf{x}_e = [r_e; \theta_e; \phi_e; V_e; \gamma_e; \psi_e]$. Equation (5) ensures atmospheric entry, while Eq. (6) constrains all entry points to the equatorial plane for consistent trajectory comparisons. Equation (7) matches the descending transfer orbit's apogee radius to the original orbit. The dimensionless terminal boundary conditions are:

$$r_f = 1, \gamma_f \ge 0 \tag{8}$$

$$b_2(\mathbf{x}_f) = \left(2 - V_f^2\right) r_c^2 - 2r_c + V_f^2 \cos^2 \gamma_f = 0 \tag{9}$$

$$b_3(\mathbf{x}_f) = \cos i_f = \cos \phi_f \cos \psi_f \tag{10}$$

where the terminal state vector is $\mathbf{x}_f = [r_f; \phi_f; V_f; \gamma_f; \psi_f]$. Equation (8) ensures atmospheric exit, while Eq. (9) matches the ascending transfer orbit's apogee radius to the target orbit. Equation (10) aligns the orbital plane change with the target inclination i_f.

During atmospheric flight, path constraints including heating rate $\dot{Q}$, load factor n, and dynamic pressure q must satisfy:

$$p_1(\mathbf{x}) = \dot{Q} = k_Q \sqrt{\rho} \left(V\sqrt{\mu/R_0}\right)^{3.15} \le \dot{Q}_{\max} \tag{11}$$

$$p_2(\mathbf{x}) = n = \sqrt{L^2 + D^2} \le n_{\max} \tag{12}$$

$$p_3(\mathbf{x}) = q = 0.5\rho\left(V\sqrt{\mu/R_0}\right)^2 \le q_{\max} \tag{13}$$

where k_Q is a vehicle-dependent constant, and $\dot{Q}_{\max}$, $n_{\max}$ and $q_{\max}$ are the respective allowable maxima.

The AOT between non-coplanar orbits is formulated as an optimal control problem minimizing fuel consumption, represented by total velocity impulse. Based on orbital energy and angular momentum conservation, the performance index depends solely on initial and terminal states:

$$\begin{aligned} J(\mathbf{x}_e, \mathbf{x}_f) &= \Delta V_d(V_e, \gamma_e) + \Delta V_f\left(V_f, \gamma_f\right) + \Delta V_c\left(V_f, \gamma_f\right) \\ &= \sqrt{\frac{1}{r_d}} - \sqrt{\frac{2(1/r_d - 1)}{1 - (r_d/\cos\gamma_e)^2}} + \sqrt{\frac{2(1 - 1/r_c)}{1 - (\cos\gamma_f/r_c)^2}} - V_f \\ &\quad + \sqrt{\frac{1}{r_c}} - \sqrt{\frac{2(1/r_c - 1)}{1 - (r_c/\cos\gamma_f)^2}} \end{aligned} \tag{14}$$

The AOT trajectory optimization is formulated as an optimal control problem: find the optimal control $\boldsymbol{u}$, that minimizes Eq. (14), subject to the dynamics in Eq. (1), state constraints in Eq. (3), control constraints in Eq. (4), boundary conditions in Eqs. (5) - (10), and path constraints in Eqs. (11) - (13).

3 AOT Using Sequential Convex Programming

3.1 Choice of New Control

Following [12], the introduction of angle of attack rate $\dot{\alpha}$ and bank angle rate $\dot{\sigma}$ as control variables serves to smooth angle profiles by eliminating high-frequency jitter in linearized angle dynamics while decoupling control variables from states, thereby enhancing convex optimization convergence. The augmented dimensionless dynamical system is expressed as:

$$\dot{\mathbf{x}} = f(\mathbf{x}) + \mathbf{B}\mathbf{u} \tag{15}$$

$$\mathbf{x}_{\min} \le \mathbf{x} \le \mathbf{x}_{\max} \tag{16}$$

$$|\mathbf{u}| \le \mathbf{u}_{\max} \tag{17}$$

where the state vector $\mathbf{x} = [r; \theta; \phi; V; \gamma; \psi; \alpha; \sigma] \in \mathbb{R}^8$, and the control input $\mathbf{u} = [\dot{\alpha}; \dot{\sigma}]$ is normalized by $g = \mu/R_0^2$. The control distribution matrix $\mathbf{B} = [\mathbf{0}_{6\times 2}; \mathbf{I}_2]$ and the nonlinear terms $f(\mathbf{x}) \in \mathbb{R}^8$ derived from Eq. (1).

3.2 Convexification

To enable convex optimization, the dynamics must be linearized about both state and control variables. This is achieved through first-order Taylor series approximation of the nonlinear dynamics in Eq. (15) about the reference solution from the previous SCP iteration. The linearized dynamics for the k-th iteration become:

$$\dot{\mathbf{x}} = f(\mathbf{x}^{k-1}) + \mathbf{A}(\mathbf{x}^{k-1})(\mathbf{x} - \mathbf{x}^{k-1}) + \mathbf{B}\mathbf{u} \tag{18}$$

where the Jacobian matrix $\mathbf{A}(\mathbf{x}^{k-1})$ of state vector is

$$\mathbf{A}\left(\mathbf{x}^{k-1}\right) = \left.\frac{\partial f(\mathbf{x})}{\partial \mathbf{x}}\right|_{\mathbf{x}=\mathbf{x}^{k-1}} = \begin{bmatrix} 0 & 0 & 0 & \sin\gamma & V\cos\gamma & 0 & 0 & 0 \\ a_{21} & 0 & a_{23} & a_{24} & a_{25} & a_{26} & 0 & 0 \\ a_{31} & 0 & 0 & a_{34} & a_{35} & a_{36} & 0 & 0 \\ a_{41} & 0 & 0 & a_{44} & a_{45} & 0 & a_{47} & 0 \\ a_{51} & 0 & 0 & a_{54} & a_{55} & 0 & a_{57} & a_{58} \\ a_{61} & 0 & a_{63} & a_{64} & a_{65} & a_{66} & a_{67} & a_{68} \\ 0 & 0 & 0 & 0 & 0 & 0 & 0 & 0 \\ 0 & 0 & 0 & 0 & 0 & 0 & 0 & 0 \end{bmatrix}_{\mathbf{x}=\mathbf{x}^{k-1}} \tag{19}$$

in which

$$a_{21} = -\frac{V\cos\gamma\cos\psi}{r^2\cos\phi},\ a_{23} = \frac{V\cos\gamma\cos\psi\sin\phi}{r\cos^2\phi},\ a_{24} = \frac{\cos\gamma\cos\psi}{r\cos\phi},\ a_{25} = -\frac{V\sin\gamma\cos\psi}{r\cos\phi},$$

$$a_{26} = -\frac{V\cos\gamma\sin\psi}{r\cos\phi},\ a_{31} = -\frac{V\cos\gamma\sin\psi}{r^2},\ a_{34} = \frac{\cos\gamma\sin\psi}{r},\ a_{35} = -\frac{V\sin\gamma\sin\psi}{r},$$

$$a_{36} = \frac{V\cos\gamma\cos\psi}{r},\ a_{41} = -D_r + \frac{2\sin\gamma}{r^3},\ a_{44} = -D_V,\ a_{45} = -\frac{\cos\gamma}{r^2},\ a_{47} = -D_\alpha,$$

$$a_{51} = \frac{\cos\sigma}{V}L_r - \frac{V\cos\gamma}{r^2} + \frac{2\cos\gamma}{r^3 V},\ a_{54} = \frac{\cos\sigma}{V}L_V - \frac{L\cos\sigma}{V^2} + \frac{\cos\gamma}{r} + \frac{\cos\gamma}{r^2V^2},$$

$$a_{55} = \left(\frac{1}{r^2V} - \frac{V}{r}\right)\sin\gamma,\ a_{57} = \frac{L_\alpha\cos\sigma}{V},\ a_{58} = -\frac{L\sin\sigma}{V},\ a_{61} = \frac{\sin\sigma}{V\cos\gamma}L_r + \frac{V\cos\gamma\cos\psi\tan\phi}{r^2},$$

$$a_{63} = -\frac{V\cos\gamma\cos\psi}{r\cos^2\phi},\ a_{64} = \frac{\sin\sigma}{V\cos\gamma}L_V - \frac{L\sin\sigma}{V^2\cos\gamma} - \frac{\cos\gamma\cos\psi\tan\phi}{r},$$

$$a_{65} = \frac{L\sin\sigma\sin\gamma}{V\cos^2\gamma} + \frac{V\sin\gamma\cos\psi\tan\phi}{r},\ a_{66} = \frac{V\cos\gamma\sin\psi\tan\phi}{r},\ a_{67} = \frac{L_\alpha\sin\sigma}{V\cos\gamma},\ a_{68} = \frac{L\cos\sigma}{V\cos\gamma},$$

$$D_r = \frac{\partial D}{\partial r} = -\frac{R_0^2\rho V^2 SC_D}{2mh_s} = -\frac{R_0}{h_s}D,\ D_V = \frac{\partial D}{\partial V} = \frac{R_0\rho VSC_D}{m},\ L_r = -\frac{R_0}{h_s}L,\ L_V = \frac{R_0\rho VA_{ref}C_L}{m},$$

$$D_\alpha = \frac{R_0\rho V^2 SKC_{L,\alpha}^2\alpha}{m}, L_\alpha = \frac{R_0\rho V^2 SC_{L,\alpha}}{2m}$$

To ensure convergence of the linearized problem, a trust region constraint is introduced as follows:

$$|\mathbf{x} - \mathbf{x}^k| \leq \boldsymbol{\delta} \tag{20}$$

where $\boldsymbol{\delta} \in \mathbb{R}^8$ defines the trust region boundary, with its components scaled proportionally to the corresponding state variables in $\boldsymbol{x}$.

The strongly nonconvex boundary conditions specified in Eqs. (7), (9) and (10) are similarly linearized about the reference solution from the preceding iteration, yielding the following approximate boundary conditions:

$$b_i(\mathbf{x}) \approx b_i(\mathbf{x}^{k-1}) + b_i'(\mathbf{x}^{k-1})(\mathbf{x} - \mathbf{x}^{k-1}) = 0, \text{ where } i = \begin{cases} 1, \text{ if } \mathbf{x} = \mathbf{x_e} \\ 2, 3, \text{ if } \mathbf{x} = \mathbf{x}_f \end{cases} \tag{21}$$

where the first-order derivatives are

$$b_1'(\mathbf{x}^{k-1}) = \left[\frac{\partial b_1}{\partial V_e}, \frac{\partial b_1}{\partial \gamma_e}\right] = \left[2(\cos^2\gamma_e^{k-1} - r_d^2)V_e^{k-1}, -2(V_e^{k-1})^2 \cos\gamma_e^{k-1} \sin\gamma_e^{k-1}\right]$$

$$b_2'(\mathbf{x}^{k-1}) = \left[\frac{\partial b_2}{\partial V_f}, \frac{\partial b_2}{\partial \gamma_f}\right] = \left[2(\cos^2\gamma_f^{k-1} - r_c^2)V_f^{k-1}, -2(V_f^{k-1})^2 \cos\gamma_f^{k-1} \sin\gamma_f^{k-1}\right]$$

$$b_3'(\mathbf{x}^{k-1}) = \left[\frac{\partial b_3}{\partial \phi_f}, \frac{\partial b_3}{\partial \psi_f}\right] = \left[-\sin\phi_f^{k-1}\cos\psi_f^{k-1}, -\cos\phi_f^{k-1}\sin\psi_f^{k-1}\right]$$

The strongly nonconvex path constraints specified in Eqs. (11) - (13) are similarly linearized about the reference solution from the preceding iteration, yielding the following approximate conditions:

$$p_i(\mathbf{x}) \approx p_i(\mathbf{x}^{k-1}) + p_i'(\mathbf{x}^{k-1})(\mathbf{x} - \mathbf{x}^{k-1}) \le p_{i,\max},\ i = 1, 2, 3 \tag{22}$$

where the first-order derivatives are

$$p_1'(\mathbf{x}^{k-1}) = \left[\frac{\partial p_1}{\partial r}, \frac{\partial p_1}{\partial V}\right] = \left[-0.5R_0k_Q\left(V\sqrt{\mu/R_0}\right)^{3.15}\sqrt{\rho}\Big/h_s, 3.15k_Q\left(V\sqrt{\mu/R_0}\right)^{2.15}\sqrt{\rho}\right]_{\mathbf{x}^{k-1}}$$

$$p_2'(\mathbf{x}^{k-1}) = \left[\frac{\partial p_2}{\partial r}, \frac{\partial p_2}{\partial V}\right] = \left[-0.5\left(V\sqrt{\mu/R_0}\right)^2 R_0\rho\Big/h_s, \rho V\sqrt{\mu/R_0}\right]_{\mathbf{x}^{k-1}}$$

$$p_3'(\mathbf{x}^{k-1}) = \left[\frac{\partial p_3}{\partial r}, \frac{\partial p_3}{\partial V}\right] = \left[-0.5R_0^2S\sqrt{C_L^2 + C_D^2}\rho\left(V\sqrt{\mu/R_0}\right)^2\Big/mh_s, R_0S\sqrt{C_L^2 + C_D^2}\rho V\sqrt{\mu/R_0}\Big/m\right]_{\mathbf{x}^{k-1}}$$

Given the nonlinear characteristics of the performance index, it is reformulated to conform to second-order cone programming (SOCP) requirements through convex approximation:

$$J = J(\mathbf{x}_e^{k-1}, \mathbf{x}_f^{k-1}) + J'(\mathbf{x}_e^{k-1})(\mathbf{x}_e - \mathbf{x}_e^{k-1}) + J'(\mathbf{x}_f^{k-1})(\mathbf{x}_f - \mathbf{x}_f^{k-1}) \tag{23}$$

in which

$$J'(\mathbf{x}_e^{k-1}) = \left.\frac{\partial J}{\partial \gamma_e}\right|_{\mathbf{x}^{k-1}} = \frac{r_d^2 \sin\gamma_e^{k-1}\sqrt{2(1 - 1/r_d)}}{\left(r_d^2/\cos^2\gamma_e^{k-1} - 1\right)^{1.5} \cdot \cos^3\gamma_e^{k-1}}$$

$$J'(\mathbf{x}_f^{k-1}) = \left[\frac{\partial J}{\partial \gamma_f}, \frac{\partial J}{\partial V_f}\right]_{\mathbf{x}^{k-1}} = \left[-\frac{\cos\gamma_f^{k-1}\sin\gamma_f^{k-1}\sqrt{2(1 - 1/r_c)}}{\left(1 - \cos^2\gamma_f^{k-1}/r_c^2\right)^{1.5} r_c^2} + \frac{r_c^2 \sin\gamma_f^{k-1}\sqrt{2(1 - 1/r_c)}}{\left(r_c^2/\cos^2\gamma_f^{k-1} - 1\right)^{1.5} \cdot \cos^3\gamma_f^{k-1}}, -1\right]$$

3.3 Discretization

As a convex optimal control formulation, problem must undergo discretization before numerical solution. This study transforms the continuous-time problem into a finite-dimensional optimization framework using the trapezoidal discretization scheme [12]. Specifically, the time domain $[t_e, t_f]$ is discretized into N-1 intervals with N nodes. The step size is $\Delta t = (t_f - t_e) \big/ (N-1)$, and the nodes are represented as $\{t_1, t_2, ..., t_{N-1}, t_N\}$ with $t_1 = t_e, t_N = t_f$, and $t_{i+1} = t_i + \Delta t, i = 1, 2, ..., N-1$. The dynamics in Eq. (18) and the path constraints in Eq. (22) admit the following approximations:

$$\begin{aligned} \hat{\mathbf{h}}_i = \mathbf{x}_{i+1} - \mathbf{x}_i - \frac{\Delta t}{2}\Big[\Big(f_i^{k-1} + \mathbf{A}_i^{k-1}\mathbf{x}_i - \mathbf{A}_i^{k-1}\mathbf{x}_i^{k-1} + \mathbf{B}\mathbf{u}_i\Big) \\ + \Big(f_{i+1}^{k-1} + \mathbf{A}_{i+1}^{k-1}\mathbf{x}_{i+1} - \mathbf{A}_{i+1}^{k-1}\mathbf{x}_{i+1}^{k-1} + \mathbf{B}\mathbf{u}_{i+1}\Big) = 0,\ i = 1, 2, \ldots, N-1 \end{aligned} \tag{24}$$

$$\hat{\mathbf{g}}_i = \begin{bmatrix} p_1(\mathbf{x}_i^{k-1}) + p_1'(\mathbf{x}_i^{k-1})(\mathbf{x}_i - \mathbf{x}_i^{k-1}) - \dot{Q}_{\max} \\ p_2(\mathbf{x}_i^{k-1}) + p_2'(\mathbf{x}_i^{k-1})(\mathbf{x}_i - \mathbf{x}_i^{k-1}) - q_{\max} \\ p_3(\mathbf{x}_i^{k-1}) + p_3'(\mathbf{x}_i^{k-1})(\mathbf{x}_i - \mathbf{x}_i^{k-1}) - n_{\max} \end{bmatrix} \le 0,\ i = 1, 2, \ldots, N \tag{25}$$

where $\mathbf{x}_i^k = \mathbf{x}^k(t_i)$, $\mathbf{A}_i^k = \mathbf{A}^k(x_i^k)$, $f_i^k = f(\mathbf{x}_i^k)$.

3.4 Sequential Convex Programming

Following above processing, the optimal control problem is transformed into a SOCP problem: find the optimal control $\boldsymbol{u}$, that minimizes Eq. (23), subject to the dynamics in Eq. (24), state constraints in Eq. (16), control constraints in Eq. (17), boundary conditions in Eqs. (5), (6), (8) and (21), and path constraints in Eq. (25).

The procedure for determining the optimal trajectory of aeroassisted orbit transfer via sequential convex programming is summarized as follows:

Step1: Initial Trajectory Generation. Set $k = 0$, and initialize the state vector as $\mathbf{x}_i^0, i = 1, 2, ..., N$. As outlined in [11], convergence is found to be insensitive to specific values of $\mathbf{x}_i^0$ during the solving process. Based on aeroassisted trajectory characteristics, the initial radial distance profile is defined as $r^0 = [r^{01}, r^{02}, r^{03}]$, where r^{01} is a straight line from 1 to $r_m = (1 + r_e) \big/ 2$ with $\lfloor N/10 \rfloor$ components ($r_e = R_e/R_0$, R_e is Earth radius), and r^{02} is a straight line from r_m to r_m with $N + 1 - 2\lfloor N/10 \rfloor$ components, and r^{03} is a straight line from r_m to 1 with $\lfloor N/10 \rfloor$ components (where the symbol $\lfloor\ \rfloor$ denotes rounding to the nearest integer). Additionally, the longitude profile is chosen to be a straight line from $\theta_e^0 = 0$ to $\theta_e^0 + 90°$, and the latitude profile is chosen to be a straight line from $\phi_e^0 = 0$ to $\phi_e^0 + i_f$. The flight-path angle profile is chosen to be a straight line from $\gamma_e^0 \le 0°$ to $\gamma_f^0 \ge 0°$, and accordingly, the velocity profile is chosen to be a straight line from V_e^0 (Eq. 7) to V_f^0 (Eq. 9). The heading angle, the angle of attack and the bank angle profiles are chosen as constant values ψ^0, α^0 and σ^0, respectively. Note that the initial control profile $\mathbf{u}^0$ is set to zero.

Step2: $k = k + 1$, and parameterize SOCP problem using $\mathbf{x}^{k-1}$ and solve for the solution pair $\{\mathbf{x}^k, \mathbf{u}^k\}$.

Step3: Check the following convergence condition:

$$\sup_{0\le i\le N}\left|\mathbf{x}_i^k-\mathbf{x}_i^{k-1}\right|\le\boldsymbol{\varepsilon},\ k>1 \tag{26}$$

where $\boldsymbol{\varepsilon}\in\mathbb{R}^8$ is a prescribed tolerance for convergence. If the preceding condition is satisfied, proceed to Step 4; otherwise, proceed to Step 2.

Step4: The solution of the SOCP problem is found to be $\mathbf{x}^*=\mathbf{x}^k$ and $\mathbf{u}^*=\mathbf{u}^k$.

4 Numerical Demonstration

The AOT mission profile and key simulation parameters are presented in Table 1. Furthermore, the flight time is fixed at $t_f=1650$ s, the boundary of the trust region is $\delta=[20000/R_0;\ 40\pi/180;\ 40\pi/180;\ 1000/\sqrt{\mu/R_0};\ 40\pi/180;\ 40\pi/180;\ 40\pi/180;\ 40\pi/180]$, and the tolerance is $\varepsilon=[500/R_0;\ 1\pi/180;\ 1\pi/180;\ 25/\sqrt{\mu/R_0};\ 1\pi/180;\ 1\pi/180;\ 1\pi/180;\ 1\pi/180]$. For all cases in the simulations, the discretization process employs $N=200$ nodes.

Table 1. AOT mission profile and associated physical parameters

Parameter	Value	Parameter	Value
R_d	42164 km	C_{D0}	0.032
R_c	6678 km	K	1.4
i_f	16°	k_Q	9.437×10^{-8} KW/m^2
m	4944 kg	$\dot{Q}_{\max}$	3000 KW/m^2
S	16.48 m^2	$n_{\max}$	5 g
$C_{L,\alpha}$	0.5699	$q_{\max}$	18 KN/m^2

The SOCP problem is solved using MOSEK [14], a commercial solver implementing a primal-dual interior-point method. For performance comparison, we select GPOPS-II [15], a commercial optimal control package that employs an adaptive Legendre-Gauss-Radau orthogonal collocation method to transcribe optimal control problem into a sparse nonlinear programming problem, which is then solved using IPOPT.

Figure 2 demonstrates close agreement between the state solutions obtained from both algorithms. However, Fig. 3 reveals significant differences in control characteristics: while the SCP algorithm generates smooth control profiles, GPOPS produces unrealistic high-frequency oscillations in angle of attack, bank angle, and their rates. More critically, Fig. 4 shows that GPOPS violates the heating rate constraint at 300 s, rendering its solution infeasible for practical implementation. This constraint violation also accounts for the minor discrepancies observed in the altitude-velocity profiles of the state solutions.

Table 2 presents a comparative analysis of algorithm performance, showing that both SCP and GPOPS achieve nearly identical optimal velocity increments (1551.6 m/s), with

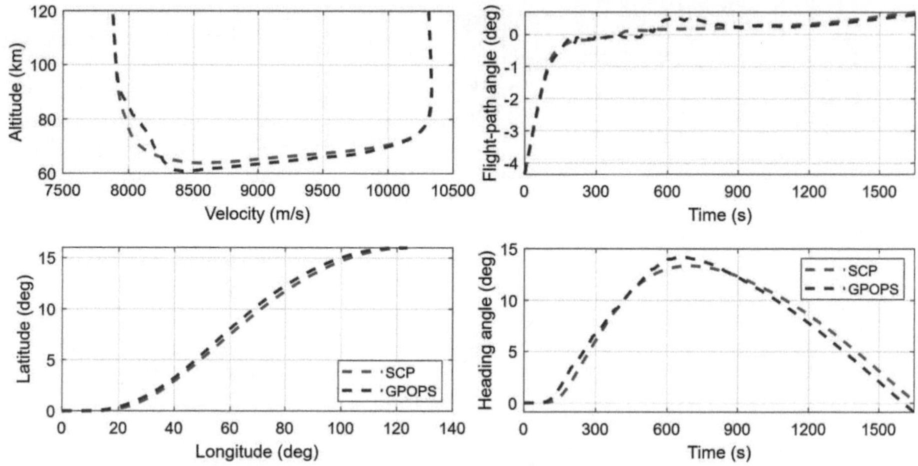

Fig. 2. Comparison of the state vector solution

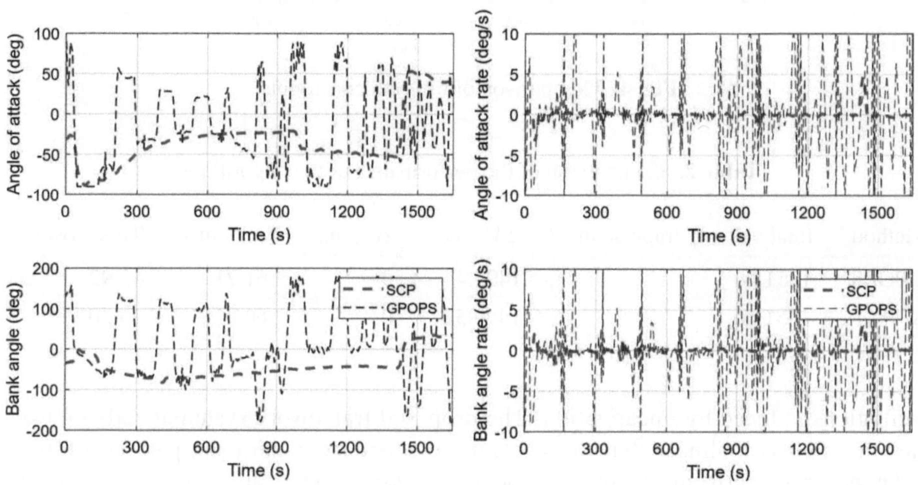

Fig. 3. Comparison of the control vector solution

matching partial velocity components, thereby validating the SCP solution's optimality. Notably, the SCP algorithm demonstrates superior computational efficiency, converging in 5.20 s compared to GPOPS's 43.92 s - an order-of-magnitude improvement in solution speed while maintaining equivalent solution quality.

5 Conclusion

This paper uses a sequential convex programming approach to solve the fuel-optimal control problem in aeroassisted orbit transfer. By introducing auxiliary control variables to decouple state and control dynamics, the method effectively suppresses high-frequency

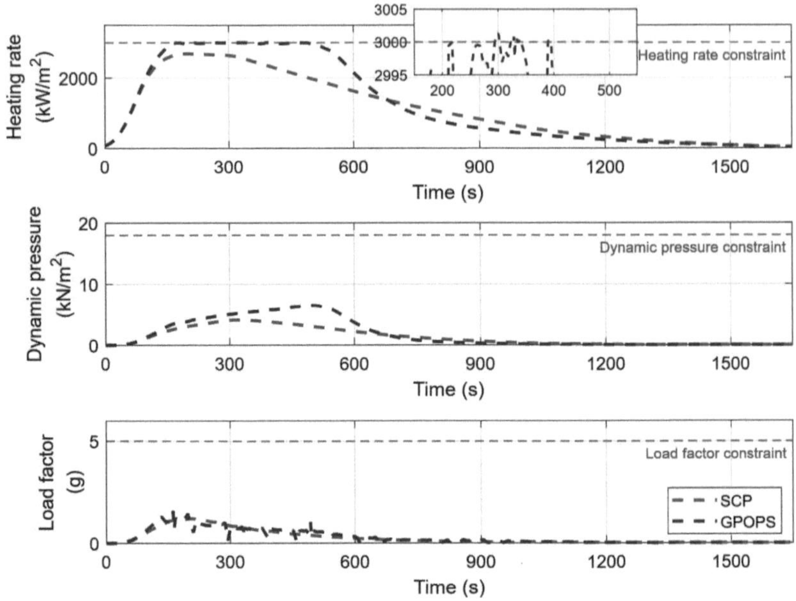

Fig. 4. Comparison of the path constraints

Table 2. Comparison of the performance of two algorithms

Method	total velocity impulse m/s	ΔV_d m/s	ΔV_f m/s	ΔV_c m/s	Time cost s
GPOPS	1551.66	1490.44	0	61.21	43.92
SCP	1551.56	1490.52	0	60.95	5.20

oscillations induced by linearization. The proposed framework systematically convexifies the highly nonlinear dynamics, complex boundary conditions, path constraints, and non-convex performance index through successive linearization, approximating the original solution via a series of second-order cone programming problems. Comparative results with GPOPS demonstrate the algorithm's superior performance in fuel optimization, constraint satisfaction, and computational efficiency, establishing it as an effective solution for aeroassisted orbit transfer problems.

Acknowledgments. This study was funded by the National Natural Science Foundation(NNSF) of China under Grant 62273119.

References

1. Falcone, G., Williams, J.W., Putnam, Z.R.: Assessment of aerocapture for orbit insertion of small satellites at Mars. J. Spacecr. Rocket. **56**(6), 1689–1703 (2019)

2. London, H.S.: Change of satellite orbit plane by aerodynamic maneuvering. J. Aerosp. Sci. **29**(3), 323–332 (1962)
3. Fuhr, R., Rao, A.V.: Minimum-fuel low-earth-orbit aeroglide and aerothrust aeroassisted orbital transfer subject to heating constraints. J. Spacecr. Rocket. **55**(3), 723–748 (2018)
4. Lu, P., Cerimele, C.J., Tigges, M.A., et al.: Optimal aerocapture guidance. J. Guid. Control. Dyn. **38**(4), 553–565 (2015)
5. Zeng, X., Gong, S., Li, J.: Fast solar sail rendezvous mission to near Earth asteroids. Acta Astronaut. **105**(1), 40–56 (2014)
6. Han, H., Qiao, D.: Optimization for the aeroassisted orbital plane change with the synergetic maneuver using the hp-adaptive pseudospectral method. J. Aerosp. Eng. **30**(6), 04017076 (2017)
7. Wang, Z., McDonald, S.T.: Convex relaxation for optimal rendezvous of unmanned aerial and ground vehicles. Aerosp. Sci. Technol. **99**, 105756 (2020)
8. Liu, Z., Cui, N., Du, L., et al.: Sequential convex programming for reentry trajectory optimization utilizing modified hp-adaptive mesh refinement and variable quadratic penalty. Aerospace **11**(9), 785 (2024)
9. Zhang, Z., Zhao, D., Li, X., et al.: Convex optimization for rendezvous and proximity operation via birkhoff pseudospectral method. Aerospace **9**(9), 505 (2022)
10. Zhang, S.J., Agikmese, B., Swei, S.S.M., et al.: Convex programming approach to real-time trajectory optimization for Mars aerocapture. In: 2015 IEEE Aerospace Conference, pp. 1–7. IEEE (2015)
11. Han, H., Qiao, D., Chen, H., et al.: Rapid planning for aerocapture trajectory via convex optimization. Aerosp. Sci. Technol. **84**, 763–775 (2019)
12. Wang, Z., Grant, M.J.: Constrained trajectory optimization for planetary entry via sequential convex programming. J. Guid. Control. Dyn. **40**(10), 2603–2615 (2017)
13. Zhang, G., Wen, C., Han, H., et al.: Aerocapture trajectory planning using hierarchical differential dynamic programming. J. Spacecr. Rocket. **59**(5), 1647–1659 (2022)
14. ApS, M.: Mosek optimization toolbox for matlab. User's Guide Ref. Manual Vers. **4**(1), 116 (2019)
15. Patterson, M.A.: GPOPS-II: a MATLAB software for solving multiple-phase optimal control problems using hp-adaptive Gaussian quadrature collocation methods and sparse nonlinear programming. ACM Trans. Math. Softw. **41**(1), 1–41 (2014)

Towards Intelligent MBSE: Constructing an MBSE Model Dataset for Generative AI

Yuteng Zhang[1,2,3], Jiangchuan Hu[1,2,3], Lin Zhang[1,2,3](✉), and Pengfei Gu[1,2,3]

[1] Hangzhou International Innovation Institute, Beihang University, 166 Shuanghongqiao Street, Pingyao Town, Yuhang District, Hangzhou, China
[2] School of Automation Science and Electrical Engineering, Beihang University, Xueyuan Road No. 37, Haidian, Beijing, China
[3] State Key Laboratory of Intelligent Manufacturing Systems Technology, Yongding Road No. 51, Haidian, Beijing, China
zhanglin@buaa.edu.cn

Abstract. As the complexity of complex product system design continues to increase, Model-Based Systems Engineering (MBSE) has demonstrated significant advantages in the process of system modeling and simulation. In recent years, Generative AI (GenAI) has introduced an innovative modeling paradigm to MBSE. However, the scarcity of high-quality, structured simulation model datasets remains a significant bottleneck, hindering further advancements of large models in this field. This paper constructs a system simulation model dataset aimed at industrial complex system modeling and simulation. The dataset, based on X language, encompasses multi-level modeling information such as system requirements, use cases, architecture, and physical behaviors, boasting excellent structural consistency and executability. We have designed a comprehensive data generation process, including domain task setting, LLM-driven model generation, syntax verification, structural normalization, and manual review. Experimental results indicate that the dataset demonstrates high performance in terms of syntactic accuracy and structural completeness, and can be successfully applied to fine-tuning tasks for large language models. This dataset provides high-quality training material for intelligent system modeling tasks and offers a reliable baseline support for subsequent research.

Keywords: Model-Based Systems Engineering · Generative AI · modeling and simulation

1 Introduction

With the increasing complexity of modern engineered systems—such as aircraft, spacecraft, and intelligent vehicles—there is a growing demand for advanced system design methodologies. In response to these challenges, Model-Based Systems

W. Cai et al. (Eds.): AsiaSim 2025, CCIS 2727, pp. 40–52, 2026.
https://doi.org/10.1007/978-981-95-4472-1_4

Engineering (MBSE) [5] has emerged as a key paradigm for managing the design, analysis, and verification of complex systems. By using formal, digital models as the central artifacts throughout the system lifecycle, MBSE improves consistency across domains, enhances traceability of requirements, and enables early validation through simulation. While SysML remains the most widely adopted language in current MBSE practices, it exhibits notable limitations in supporting the simulation of physical system behaviors [2,7]. As a result, system-level design workflows are typically split into two separate stages: conceptual modeling using SysML [6], followed by physical behavior simulation using domain-specific co-simulation tools or semi-physical platforms. In our previous research, we proposed an integrated modeling and simulation language based on Discrete Event System Specification (DEVS) [15] extension development—X language [16,17]. While X language addresses the integration of modeling and simulation within a unified formalism, the process of constructing high-quality system models still heavily relies on expert knowledge and manual effort. This underscores the need for further advancements toward automation and intelligent assistance in MBSE.

The rapid progress of Generative Artificial Intelligence (GenAI) has opened up new possibilities for intelligent modeling and simulation [1,3]. Recent advances in GenAI have demonstrated strong potential in understanding system design patterns, generating domain-specific models, and assisting in the creation of simulation code. By shifting the modeling process from manual efforts to AI-assisted generation, it becomes possible to streamline development workflows, improve the accuracy of models, and enable more flexible and scalable approaches to complex system design. Despite the promising capabilities of GenAI in code and model generation, its performance is largely constrained by the availability of high-quality, domain-specific datasets [11]. Most existing code datasets focus on general-purpose programming languages and lack the structural, semantic, and physical constraints of system simulation modeling. Compared to general-purpose code, simulation models used in complex engineered systems have clear modular structures, use specialized syntax, and include executable logic that reflects real-world physical behavior. However, a notable gap remains in publicly available datasets that capture these unique characteristics.

To address this challenge, we construct a new dataset specifically designed for AI-driven modeling and simulation of complex systems in MBSE. Each instance in the dataset represents a complete system model with well-defined structure, consistent syntax, and executable semantics, making it suitable for training and evaluating generative modeling approaches in MBSE. The structure of this paper is organized as follows: Sect. 2 introduces the modeling language employed in this paper and the relevant research on the application of GenAI in the field of modeling and simulation. Section 3 presents the structure of the dataset, along with a detailed construction process. Section 4 evaluates the quality of the dataset and utilizes the dataset for fine-tuning open-source models.

2 Related Works

In the related work section, we will give a brief introduction to X language and some related works of GenAI for simulation models in MBSE.

2.1 Basic Concepts of X Language

X language is a modeling and simulation language based on XDEVS [14]. The structure of the X language is illustrated in Fig. 1. Compared to SysML and SysML 2.0, X language provides a more comprehensive description of a product's system architecture and physical characteristics. This capability is particularly significant during the system integration phase, as SysML typically lacks the ability to describe physical models, necessitating integration with other physical simulation languages to achieve accurate simulation and verification of overall system behavior.

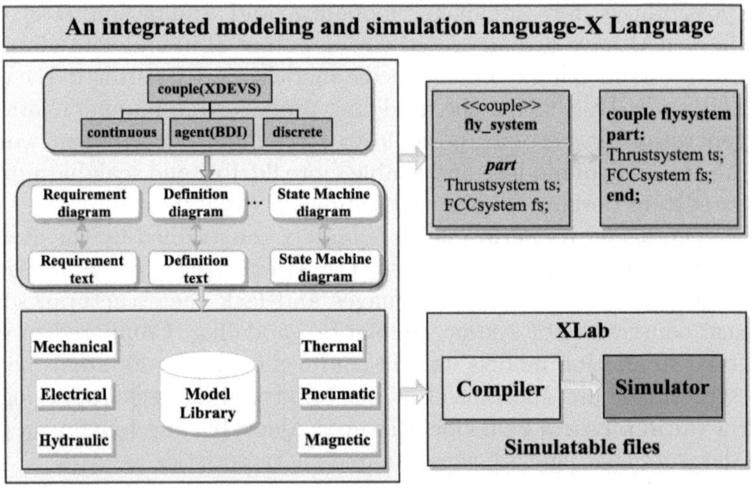

Fig. 1. The composition and architecture of X language

X language specifies a range of classes, such as discrete, continuous, and agent classes, and facilitates both graphical and textual forms of representation. X language is capable of modeling continuous, discrete, and hybrid systems and allows for the compilation and simulation of these models through X language development tools, XLab. X language supports dual-form descriptions, both graphical and textual, which endows it with greater flexibility and adaptability. Specifically, graphical modeling can be accomplished through various diagrammatic forms such as requirement diagrams, use case diagrams, definition diagrams, connection diagrams, equation diagrams, activity diagrams, and state machine diagrams. These graphical models can be automatically converted into corresponding textual models, which are then transformed into simulation files by X language interpreter and executed by X language simulation engine to validate system performance. This dual-form description not only enhances the potential applications of the X language but also lays the foundation for intelligent modeling, providing possibilities for automatic model generation and simulation processes in the future.

2.2 GenAI for Model Generation and Simulation

Recent years have seen growing interest in applying AI, especially Large Language Models (LLMs), to automate various tasks in model-based systems engineering. However, the development and evaluation of such models rely heavily on the availability of high-quality datasets. Most existing datasets focus on general-purpose programming languages or textual system descriptions, while datasets specifically tailored for executable system simulation models remain scarce.

Code-focused datasets such as CodeSearchNet [10] and HumanEval [4] have enabled significant advances in general-purpose code generation. However, they are not designed to capture the hierarchical, domain-specific, and semantically executable nature of system simulation models. Some studies have explored using structured representations, such as SysML or engineering specifications, for model generation; however, these sources often lack formal, executable semantics and are frequently detached from simulation workflows. A few recent works have attempted to use LLMs to generate simulation models [9,13] from textual prompts. However, the aforementioned methods for generating simulation models remain at the experimental stage and are not capable of producing high-quality datasets suitable for training LLMs.

In contrast to these existing efforts, our work provides a structured dataset of system simulation models that integrates both model structure and executable behavior. This dataset is designed to support research in GenAI-driven modeling and offers a realistic foundation for training, evaluating, and benchmarking generative approaches in MBSE.

3 Dataset Construction

This section provides a detailed overview of the complete process we followed to construct the system simulation model dataset. We will cover each phase, starting from initial data generation through to data cleaning, preprocessing, and validation. Our goal is to present a clear and systematic methodological framework for achieving a high-quality system simulation dataset.

3.1 Overall Technical Implementation Framework

The overall process for generating a system simulation model dataset is illustrated in Fig. 2. The initial step involves preparation before generation. In this phase, we catalog several prevalent domains within the general industrial sector, accompanied by the identification of typical products associated with each specific domain. Furthermore, we have extended our efforts in the aerospace industry by delineating a more comprehensive list of commonly encountered products in aerospace industry. This enhancement is aimed at augmenting the value of the dataset, specifically within the realm of aerospace industry products. Subsequently, leveraging the aforementioned product names and descriptions, we utilized LLMs to generate more detailed and natural language descriptions. In the second step, we crafted appropriate prompts tailored to each generation process. By defining these prompts, we guide the language model in creating detailed representations that align with the specific requirements and complexities of each tier within the simulation framework. Finally, we perform data cleansing and structure the data according to the established sample framework. After completing the aforementioned steps, we employ language models followed by manual review to examine the generated dataset, ensuring a high degree of accuracy.

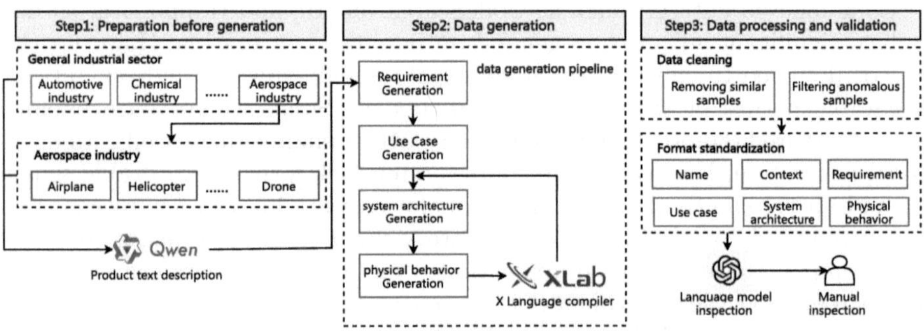

Fig. 2. The overall technical implementation framework is divided into three parts: Preparation before generation, data generation, data processing and validation.

3.2 Dataset Architecture

The structure of the samples in the dataset is as follows. The dataset built in this work uses a multi-tiered architecture, incorporating the requirements, functions, and architecture of the system simulation model into a single sample. This implicitly includes the relationships between different levels of simulation models in the dataset. These implicit relationships can be used for subsequent fine-tuning of LLMs.

```
{
  "name": "name of the model",
  "context": "more detailed and natural language descriptions",
  "childElement": [
    {
      "text": "requirementModels",
      "type": "requirement",
      "childElement": [
        {
          "text": "name of the requirement model",
          "type": "requirementDiagram",
          "code": "code of the requirement diagram"
        }
      ]
    },
    {
      "text": "usecaseModels",
      "type": "requirement",
      "childElement": "Similar to the childElement structure in usecaseModels."
    },
    {
      "text": "architectureModels",
      "type": "architecture",
      "childElement": [
        {
          "text": "name of the couple class model",
          "type": "couple",
          "code": "code of the couple class model"
        },
        {
          "text": "name of the atomic class model",
          "type": "discrete or continuous",
          "code": "code of the atomic class model"
        }
      ]
    }
  ]
}
```

The structure mentioned above is just a simple example; the actual samples are much more complex. For instance, in a typical sample, the "childElement" of "architectureModels" usually contains multiple atomic models. Similarly, the "childElement" of "requirementModels" and "usecaseModels" may also contain multiple elements. The detailed content of the samples can be found at the GitHub repository: https://github.com/ZhangMazi9/TowardsIntelligentMBSE.

The dataset proposed in this paper covers the following domains: automotive and transportation, aerospace and defense, energy and power, electronics and semiconductors, chemical and process industries, medical equipment, marine and offshore engineering, construction and heavy engineering, consumer goods industry. This diversity enables language models fine-tuned on this dataset to exhibit enhanced generalization capabilities across tasks spanning various domains. Furthermore, to augment the dataset's applicability within the aviation sector, we have specifically increased the quantity of aviation-related samples. During the training process, these aviation samples are utilized alongside those from other domains. This approach not only facilitates the model's efficient learning of characteristics inherent to aviation system simulation models but also effectively mitigates the risk of catastrophic forgetting.

3.3 Data Generation

To create the multi-tiered system model architecture described in Sect. 3.2, this paper has developed a data generation pipeline. For each product sample, the detailed process of data generation is described as follows:

Requirement Generation: First, based on the product text description, an LLM is used to generate the top-level requirements for the product. Subsequently, more detailed requirements are generated based on these top-level requirements. During this process, the relationships between requirements, such as "include," "refine," and "derive," need to be established.

Use Case Generation: Based on the requirements generated above, the functionalities and use cases of the model are further refined and developed. The corresponding use case diagram text is then generated according to standards.

System Architecture and Physical Behavior Generation: Based on the generated requirements and use cases mentioned above, a system simulation model is constructed. Initially, an LLM is used to build X language couple class models, which describe the composition of the model and the interactions between subsystems. Subsequently, using the interaction relationships of the subsystems as constraints, generating X language atomic models, which describe the behavior of the subsystems and their interactions with the external environment.

Model Syntax Checking: We employ X language compiler to conduct a syntax checking of the generated system simulation model, subsequently relaying the outcomes of this analysis to the LLM. This process enables the LLM to regenerate the system simulation model, rectifying any previously encountered errors. The types of compiler errors are delineated in Table 1.

Table 1. Types and meanings of compiler errors

Error	Definition
Structural Integrity Error	"Each state block must have an independent end marker 'end;"' "All end markers must exist independently"
Missing End Marker in State Definition	"The state definition section ends with an independent 'end;"' "The state definition section must have an independent end marker 'end;"'
Missing Initial State	"The first state must be 'initial state"' "The first state of each system must be 'initial state"'
(10 items total, others omitted)	

3.4 Comparison with Traditional Datasets

A comparison between traditional system design methods and the X-SEM [8] based on X language is shown in Fig. 3. Traditional system design methods often involve two separate tools, making it difficult for simulation results to be directly fed back to the requirement and functional levels. In contrast, the X language supports the integrated description of requirements, functions, architecture, and physical behavior, enabling simulation feedback to have a broader impact across different design stages.

For datasets, traditional ones that aim to cover multiple stages of MBSE typically include models written in various languages such as SysML, Modelica, and Simulink. These models, described in different languages, need to be executed on different platforms or tools, which not only increases the workload for users but also reduces the consistency among models across different stages. In contrast, the dataset proposed in this paper uses the X language to describe requirements, functions, architectures, and physical models uniformly. When using this dataset, there is no need to deal with integration or transformation between different languages or tools. This inherent semantic consistency provides LLMs with ideal end-to-end modeling paradigm learning samples.

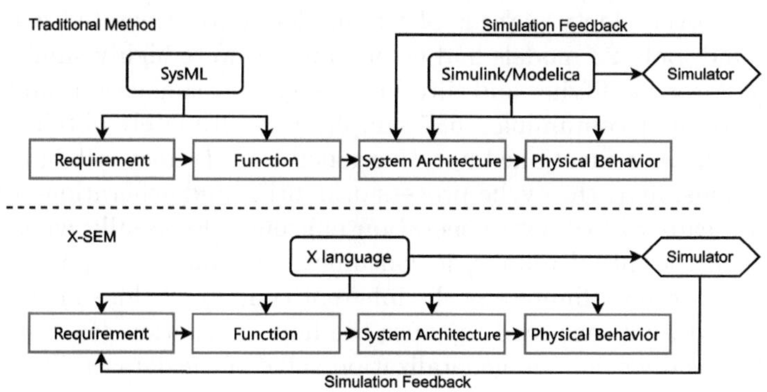

Fig. 3. The comparison between traditional system design methods and the X-SEM

4 Experiment

In this section, we will assess the quality of the generated dataset. Additionally, we will employ this dataset to fine-tune the LLM, thereby demonstrating its efficacy in aiding the development of system simulation models.

4.1 Dataset Quality Assessment

During the dataset generation, the API of the open-source LLM, Qwen2.5-max [12], was utilized. The workflow for this generation process was constructed using the open-source framework Dify. In the raw generated model collection, a significant portion of the samples exhibited issues such as syntax errors, incomplete structural components, and inconsistent naming conventions. Common problems included missing or malformed state and equation modules, undefined variables, and unclosed control structures. These issues rendered many models unparseable or unexecutable within the simulation environment.

In the "Model Syntax Checking" step of Sect. 3.3, we employed X language compiler to check the syntax of the generated models and provide feedback. Thus, the process of generating the dataset will proceed as follows: Initially, we utilize LLM to generate the dataset, then compile it using the X language compiler, using the compilation results as feedback to attempt model correction. For models that cannot be corrected with the X language compiler, we opt to regenerate them with LLM. This process is repeated until the number of uncorrectable models is ultimately reduced to a minimal quantity. Concurrently, we filtered out structurally incomplete and highly repetitive data to ensure that the released dataset comprises only models that are syntactically valid, structurally complete, and ready for simulation. The assessment results of the original dataset are presented in Table 2. A total of 1626 samples were generated in this study. In the first round of generation, a total of 910 models contained syntax errors, and 9 models were highly similar to previously generated ones. After five rounds of generation, over ninety percent of the models were generated correctly. By the final round, only 23 models had errors, and 16 were highly similar to existing models. After modifying and filtering the system simulation model code, a high-quality dataset containing 1,587 samples was ultimately obtained.

However, the aforementioned iterative generation strategy still has two significant limitations: first, the cyclic process of multi-round generation-verification-regeneration leads to low data generation efficiency. Especially when the error rate is high in the initial rounds, it consumes substantial computing resources and time costs; second, limited by the inherent consistency bias in the output of LLMs, repeated iterations tend to cause the homogenization of generated models, reducing the diversity and generalization value of the dataset. To address the generation efficiency issue, an error type mapping library can be constructed to establish the mapping relationship between error types and correction strategies, reducing untargeted regeneration attempts. For the homogenization issue, the "dynamic prompt diversification" strategy is implemented: before each round of generation, the Prompt is reconstructed by randomly replacing domain term expressions, adjusting the description perspective of model structures, introducing different scenario constraints, etc., to break the output inertia of LLMs. These methods will be explored and attempted in future research.

Table 2. Dataset quality assessment results

iteration count	Total number	Syntax Error	repetitive data
1	1626	910	9
2	1626	563	14
...	...	...	...
ultimately	1626	23	16
filtered	1587	0	0

4.2 Dataset Fine-Tuning

To examine the efficacy of the dataset in LLM fine-tuning, this section will employ the dataset for fine-tuning a local LLM and evaluate the performance of the model after fine-tuning.

The experimental hardware configuration comprises an NVIDIA A100 GPU with 80 GB of VRAM, paired with an i9-13900K processor and 256 GB of RAM. In terms of the software environment, the system operates on Ubuntu 20.04 LTS and is equipped with PyTorch version 2.4 for deep learning, alongside CUDA 12.4 and cuDNN 9.1 to accelerate graphical processing. This paper utilizes the open-source framework Llama Factory [18] for model fine-tuning, renowned for its flexible modular design and optimized resource management, enabling effective support for high-quality model training. As shown in Fig. 4, the LLM fine-tuning process is as follows: First, X language model dataset constructed in this study is divided into training set, validation set, and test set at a ratio of 8:1:1, and the data is formatted according to the input requirements of LLama Factory. Second, the base LLM is loaded in the framework, and fine-tuning parameters (including learning rate of 5e-5, batch size of 1, training epochs of 3) are configured. Finally, through the Low-Rank Adaptation lightweight fine-tuning module of the framework, the dataset is input into the LLM for parameter update, enabling the model to learn X language modeling knowledge.

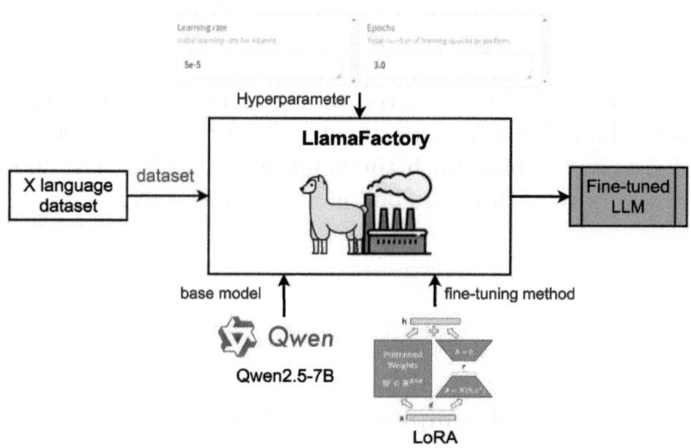

Fig. 4. The LLM fine-tuning process based on Llama Factory

The Qwen2.5-7B model serves as the base model. Initially, we employ the unfinetuned Qwen2.5-7B to assist in constructing X language models. As shown in Fig. 5, the unfinetuned Qwen2.5-7B fails to accurately understand our intent. Subsequently, we reorganize the information related to logical and physical simulation models from the dataset—specifically the content in "architectureModels"—into the format required by the fine-tuning dataset. This processed data is then used to fine-tune the Qwen2.5-7B model. We then use the fine-tuned Qwen2.5-7B model to assist in constructing X language models. As shown in Fig. 5, the fine-tuned model is able to understand our intent and generate simulation models that not only generally conform to the X language specification but also possess meaningful physical semantics.

This experiment demonstrates that the dataset constructed in this study can be used to fine-tune open-source LLMs for tasks related to simulation automation. This section describes only one possible usage of the dataset. For different task scenarios, the dataset can provide a variety of information. For example, when aiming to obtain a requirement-oriented LLM, we can fine-tune it using the "requirementModels" section of the dataset. Furthermore, for tasks involving the full lifecycle of MBSE, the samples in our dataset contain information from different stages of product design. By constructing a fine-tuning dataset with appropriate methods, the LLM can more effectively learn the relationships among various stages of product development.

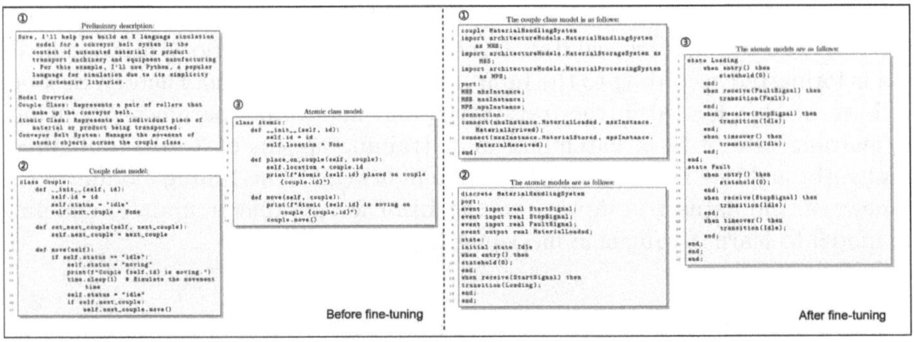

Fig. 5. On the left is the output generated by the unfinetuned Qwen2.5 model, which does not conform to the X language specification. On the right is the output from the fine-tuned Qwen2.5 model, where both the generated coupled class model and atomic class model largely comply with the X language specification.

5 Conclusion

This paper targets the tasks of complex product system modeling and simulation, constructing an MBSE model dataset that is structurally standardized, semantically complete, and capable of simulation. The dataset is uniformly modeled using the X language, encompassing system requirements, functional use cases, architecture, and atomic-level physical behavior models, forming multi-layered, traceable modeling samples. We designed a systematic data generation process that integrates the capabilities of generative large models with syntax verification mechanisms, automatically constructing and cleansing a substantial amount of high-quality model data. Through evaluation methods such as syntax checks and structural integrity analysis, the quality and usability of the dataset are validated. Furthermore, we employed this dataset for fine-tuning of open-source language models, preliminarily verifying its effectiveness in enhancing model modeling capabilities. In the future, we plan to expand the scale and domain coverage of this dataset and further explore its potential in intelligent modeling tasks by integrating methods such as self-supervised pretraining.

Acknowledgments. This work was supported by Beijing Natural Science Foundation - Fengtai Innovation Joint Fund (Grant No. L241018). The authors would like to express their gratitude for the financial support provided by the funds.

Disclosure of Interests. The authors declare that they have no known competing financial interests or personal relationships that could have appeared to influence the work reported in this paper.

References

1. Achiam, J., et al.: Gpt-4 technical report. arXiv preprint arXiv:2303.08774 (2023)
2. Amissah, M., Toba, A.L., Handley, H.A., Seck, M.: Towards a framework for executable systems modeling: an executable systems modeling language (esysml). In: Proceedings of the Model-Driven Approaches for Simulation Engineering Symposium, pp. 1–12 (2018)
3. Bai, J., et al.: Qwen technical report. arXiv preprint arXiv:2309.16609 (2023)
4. Chen, M., et al.: Evaluating large language models trained on code. arXiv preprint arXiv:2107.03374 (2021)
5. Friedenthal, S., Griego, R., Sampson, M.: Incose model based systems engineering (mbse) initiative. In: INCOSE 2007 Symposium, vol. 11. sn (2007)
6. Friedenthal, S., Moore, A., Steiner, R.: Omg systems modeling language (omg sysml) tutorial. In: INCOSE International Symposium, vol. 9, pp. 65–67. Citeseer (2006)
7. Fu, C., Liu, J., Yu, H., Xu, W.: A visual transformation method of sysml model to modelica model. In: Journal of Physics: Conference Series, vol. 1684, p. 012058. IOP Publishing (2020)
8. Gu, P., et al.: X-sem: a modeling and simulation-based system engineering methodology. J. Manuf. Syst. **74**, 198–221 (2024)
9. Hummel, P., Grimstad, J., Xia, Y., Morozov, A.: Generation of matlab simscape models using large language models for training reliability evaluation methods. In: ASME International Mechanical Engineering Congress and Exposition, vol. 88698, p. V011T14A010. American Society of Mechanical Engineers (2024)
10. Husain, H., Wu, H.H., Gazit, T., Allamanis, M., Brockschmidt, M.: Codesearchnet challenge: evaluating the state of semantic code search. arXiv preprint arXiv:1909.09436 (2019)

11. Manduchi, L., et al.: On the challenges and opportunities in generative ai. arXiv preprint arXiv:2403.00025 (2024)
12. Team, Q.: Qwen2.5 technical report. arXiv preprint arXiv:2412.15115 (2024)
13. Xiang, J., Ye, T., Liu, P., Zhang, Y., Wang, W.: Modigen: a large language model-based workflow for multi-task modelica code generation. arXiv preprint arXiv:2503.18460 (2025)
14. Xie, K., Zhang, L., Laili, Y., Wang, X.: Xdevs: a hybrid system modeling framework. Int. J. Model. Simul. Sci. Comput. **13**(02), 2243001 (2022)
15. Zeigler, B.P., Praehofer, H., Kim, T.G.: Theory of Modeling and Simulation. Academic Press, San Diego (2000)
16. Zhang, L., et al.: X language: an integrated intelligent modeling and simulation language for complex products. In: 2021 Annual Modeling and Simulation Conference (ANNSIM), pp. 1–11. IEEE (2021). https://doi.org/10.23919/ANNSIM52504.2021.9552057
17. Zhang, L., et al.: An integrated intelligent modeling and simulation language for model-based systems engineering. J. Ind. Inf. Integr. **28**, 100347 (2022)
18. Zheng, Y., Zhang, R., Zhang, J., Ye, Y., Luo, Z.: Llamafactory: unified efficient fine-tuning of 100+ language models. arXiv preprint arXiv:2403.13372 (2024)

Full Papers

Logistics Digital Twin for Sustainability Management

Kalyani Alagappan(✉), David Weidong Lin, and Malcolm Yoke Hean Low

Singapore Institute of Technology, Singapore, Singapore
alagappankalyani@gmail.com, {david.lin, malcolm.low}@singaporetech.edu.sg

Abstract. With increasing regulatory pressure and the introduction of carbon taxes, reducing carbon emissions has become a strategic priority for healthcare supply chains. These networks are critical for ensuring timely delivery of essential medical supplies but are also significant contributors to greenhouse gas emissions, particularly in warehousing operations and transportation. This study applies a digital twin approach, developed using FlexSim, to evaluate carbon reduction strategies in warehouse operations while considering their implications for downstream transportation. Two operational improvements were explored: (1) rearranging storage locations based on SKU velocity classification using ABC analysis, and (2) implementing batch picking to consolidate order fulfillment and reduce travel distances. A digital twin of a healthcare warehouse was created to simulate baseline and optimized scenarios, enabling quantification of carbon emissions for each strategy. Results show that both strategies reduce emissions, and batch picking achieved the largest reduction, primarily by minimizing forklift travel and improving efficiency. These findings highlight the potential of digital twin technology as a decision-support tool for achieving compliance with emerging carbon regulations and supporting sustainable logistics operations in the healthcare sector.

Keyword: Digital Twin · Sustainability · Carbon emissions · Supply chain · Warehouse · Healthcare

1 Introduction

The healthcare supply chain is critical for ensuring the timely delivery of medical supplies, pharmaceuticals, and life-saving equipment. However, its operations are a significant source of carbon emissions, primarily from warehousing and transportation activities. Warehousing contributes substantially due to energy-intensive storage systems and frequent material handling tasks such as order picking and replenishment. With increasing regulatory pressures such as carbon taxes and heightened focus on sustainability, healthcare organizations face growing demands to reduce emissions while maintaining service quality [3].

Digital twin technology is a key enabler of sustainable logistics, allowing warehousing operations to test alternative strategies and assess their impact on efficiency and environmental performance [8].

W. Cai et al. (Eds.): AsiaSim 2025, CCIS 2727, pp. 55–66, 2026.
https://doi.org/10.1007/978-981-95-4472-1_5

This study uses a simulation-based digital twin developed in FlexSim to evaluate two emission-reduction strategies: (1) SKU velocity-based storage assignment, leveraging ABC classification to reduce travel to frequently picked items, and (2) batch picking, which consolidates orders to minimize forklift travel. By comparing these approaches against the current baseline, this research quantifies potential emission reductions and highlights the value of digital twins as decision-support tools for sustainable healthcare logistics.

2 Literature Review

The healthcare supply chain is a vital enabler of patient care but is also a significant contributor to carbon emissions, primarily from warehousing and transportation activities. Warehousing accounts for a substantial share of these emissions due to energy-intensive storage systems and frequent material handling tasks such as order picking and replenishment. With the growing implementation of carbon taxes and increased focus on sustainability, healthcare organizations are under pressure to reduce their carbon footprint while ensuring service quality [6].

Digital twin technology has emerged as a promising approach for evaluating operational strategies and supporting sustainable logistics. A digital twin is a virtual representation of a physical system that enables real-time monitoring, scenario testing, and performance optimization [3]. In warehousing, digital twins have been used to analyze storage layouts, workforce allocation, and picking strategies, demonstrating measurable improvements in efficiency and energy consumption [5]. Similarly, simulation-based approaches for route optimization have yielded notable reductions in delivery distances and transportation emissions by optimizing vehicle routes and delivery schedules [14].

However, most existing studies treat these areas in isolation. While previous research has explored route optimization and general digital twin applications, there is a gap in the literature regarding the integrated application of specific operational strategies—such as SKU velocity-based storage (ABC analysis) and batch picking—and their direct, quantitative impact on carbon emissions within a healthcare-specific context. This gap is particularly important because healthcare warehouses have unique operational constraints, including temperature-sensitive products, critical delivery time windows, and highly variable demand patterns.

This study addresses these gaps by using a digital twin to evaluate the combined effects of storage optimization and batch picking strategies on carbon emissions in a healthcare warehouse, while also acknowledging the parallel deployment of route optimization tools for outbound delivery.

3 Methodology

This study employed a simulation-based digital twin approach to evaluate carbon emission reduction strategies in a healthcare warehouse. Digital twins can be developed at different maturity levels—ranging from static models to simulation models, to data-integrated and real-time twins. The present research adopts a simulation-level digital twin, where warehouse processes are virtually replicated for scenario testing and performance analysis. A discrete-event simulation software widely applied in logistics and supply chain studies, FlexSim, was used for modeling, visualizing, and analyzing complex warehouse operations. FlexSim's 3D simulation capabilities [5] enabled realistic modeling of material flows, equipment interactions, and operator movements, facilitating accurate scenario testing without disrupting live operations. It was used to replicate core warehouse operations, including receiving, storage, order picking, and dispatch. The model was calibrated and validated using six months of historical operational data from inbound, order picking and packing, and outbound processes to ensure its accuracy in representing real-world performance. Two strategies were evaluated: (1) SKU velocity-based storage assignment using ABC classification to optimize item placement, and (2) batch picking to consolidate order fulfillment and minimize forklift travel. Carbon emissions were estimated based on forklift travel distances and energy consumption, applying appropriate emission factors. Three scenarios—baseline, SKU velocity-based storage, and batch picking—were simulated under identical demand conditions, and key performance indicators such as travel distance, order cycle time, and estimated emissions were compared to quantify the effectiveness of each strategy.

3.1 Warehouse Baseline

The healthcare warehouse studied functions as a central distribution hub for consumables, pharmaceuticals, and equipment. A Warehouse Management System (WMS) provided real-time data on inbound, storage, picking, and outbound flows, while historical WMS transactions and equipment logs formed the baseline dataset. Key data included SKU master records (categories, storage needs, demand frequencies), order profiles (daily volumes, line items, time windows), equipment logs (forklift travel and energy use), and process cycle times (put-away, picking, staging, dispatch). These inputs ensured the simulation model accurately reflected real operations and enabled robust scenario comparisons.

3.2 Strategy Design

Two operational strategies were formulated to reduce warehouse-related carbon emissions:

1) SKU Velocity-Based Storage Assignment

A velocity-based storage assignment method was implemented using ABC classification [2], which groups items based on their demand frequency. ABC classification was used to rank SKUs based on their cumulative demand frequency, following the Pareto principle where a small number of fast-moving items account for the majority of order volume. Items were categorized as A (high-frequency), B (medium-frequency), and C (low-frequency), enabling optimized storage placement to minimize travel distance. Items were ranked according to their total order quantity Q_i:

$$Q_i = \sum_{t=1}^{n_t} D_{i,t} \tag{1}$$

where $D_{i,t}$ is the demand of item i in period t, and n_t is the total number of periods considered.

Items were sorted in descending order of Q_i and cumulative percentages of demand were calculated:

$$P_i = \frac{Q_i}{\sum_{k=1}^{n_p} Q_k} \times 100\% \tag{2}$$

P_i is the cumulative percentage demand and n_p is the number of products. Items with $\leq P_i 80\%$ were classified as A-class, those within 80–95% as B-class, and the remaining as C-class. A-class SKUs were positioned closest to primary picking zones to reduce travel distances, while B- and C-class items were progressively located farther away.

2) Batch Picking

The batch picking strategy [1] consolidated multiple orders into a single picking trip when orders shared common SKUs or were released within a predefined time window Δt. A grouping algorithm minimized repeated travel paths by generating a combined pick list:

$$L = \bigcup_{k=1}^{m} O_k \tag{3}$$

where O_k represents individual order lines and m is the number of orders batched together. Here, L represents the combined pick list generated by grouping m individual orders (n_o) into a single batch. The combined batch pick list L was treated as a single picking tour. The picking route was optimized to minimize total travel distance:

$$d_{batch} = \min \sum_{(i,j) \in P(L)} d_{ij} \tag{4}$$

where d_{ij} is the travel distance between locations i and j, and $P(L)$ is the set of all paths in the route for products in batch L. d_{batch} represents the minimum total travel distance for a single batch-picking route.

3.3 Emission Estimation Framework

The primary emission source considered was forklift travel within the warehouse. The total carbon emissions for each scenario was calculated using:

$$E = d \times \alpha_F \tag{5}$$

where:

- E = total carbon emissions ($kgCO_2$)
- d = total forklift travel distance (km)
- α_F = emission factor of forklifts ($kgCO_2/km$)

For electric forklifts, emissions were based on energy consumption:

$$E_{electric} = \frac{\beta_F \times t \times \alpha_g}{\eta} \tag{6}$$

where:

- β_F = forklift rated power (kW)
- t = operational time (h)
- α_g = regional grid emission factor ($kgCO_2/kWh$)
- η = charging efficiency

The carbon emissions from lighting and HVAC were excluded, as these were constant across scenarios and did not influence comparative results. In this study, we assumed a fleet of electric forklifts, which aligns with the current warehouse setup and sustainability goals. Emission factors were sourced from national and international guidelines:

- Electricity Grid Factor: Singapore's average grid factor (0.408 $kgCO_2/kWh$).
- Diesel Fuel Factor: IPCC default emission factor (2.68 $kgCO_2$/litre).

These factors were applied consistently across all scenarios to ensure fair comparison. The simulation output provided the total forklift travel distance (km) and operating time (hours) for each scenario. These values were fed into the emission calculation formulas. For example:

$$E_i = \sum_{k=1}^{n_f} (d_k \times \alpha_F) \tag{7}$$

where:

- n_f = number of forklifts
- d_k = travel distance by forklift k
- α_F = emission factor for the relevant forklift type

The change in carbon emissions between baseline and each strategy i was then expressed as a percentage reduction:

$$\Delta E_i = \frac{E_{baseline} - E_i}{E_{baseline}} \times 100\% \tag{8}$$

where:

- ΔE_i = percentage change in carbon emissions for scenario i compared to baseline (%)
- $E_{baseline}$ = total carbon emissions for the baseline scenario ($kgCO_2$)

Granularity: Emissions are directly tied to actual forklift activity, making results sensitive to changes in travel distance. Scalability: The same approach can be adapted for different types of material handling equipment and energy sources in future studies.

4 Digital Twin Model Development

To assess the impact of the proposed strategies on carbon emissions, a simulation-level digital twin of the healthcare warehouse was developed. While digital twins can range from static models to fully integrated, real-time systems, this study focuses on the simulation level, where processes are virtually replicated for scenario testing. Using data from the Warehouse Management System (WMS) and operational logs, the model captured layout, workflows, equipment, and demand patterns. Simulating both baseline and optimized practices allowed robust comparison of travel distance, cycle time, and emissions without disrupting live operations [5].

4.1 Modelling Environment

A digital twin of the healthcare warehouse was built in FlexSim 2025, a discrete-event simulation tool widely used in logistics. The model replicated static features such as layout, racks, and staging areas, along with dynamic elements including equipment movement, order arrivals, and operator workflows. Simulation logic was parameterized using observed data on forklift speed, picking time, and staging cycles [7].

4.2 Warehouse Layout and Process Presentation

The baseline layout comprised conventional pallet racking arranged in parallel aisles, with dedicated areas for receiving, put-away, picking, packing, and outbound dispatch. All inbound goods were staged, verified, and placed into racking using forklifts. Picking was performed using a single order picking strategy, where each order was picked and transported individually to the packing area before release.

For simulation purposes:

- Physical assets such as racks, aisles, and staging areas were modeled with their actual dimensions.
- Material handling flows replicated real-world travel paths, queuing at aisles, and staging bottlenecks.
- Order profiles were modeled based on six months of historical data, representing demand variability and product mix.
- Labor resources were parameterized by staffing levels and shift patterns from actual operations.

4.3 Scenario Configuration

Three scenarios were designed to evaluate carbon emission reduction strategies:

1. Baseline (Current Practice): Existing warehouse layout and single order picking.
2. Strategy 1 – Velocity-Based Storage Assignment: SKUs re-slotted based on ABC classification. A-class SKUs (top 80% of demand) were placed in high-access zones near primary picking aisles, reducing forklift travel distance for frequently picked items.

3. Strategy 2 – Batch Picking with Velocity-Based Storage: Orders released within defined time windows ($\Delta t = 30 minutes$) and sharing common SKUs were consolidated into batch pick lists. Forklift operators retrieved multiple orders in a single trip, following optimized nearest-neighbour routing.

4.4 Model Calibration and Validation

Calibration involved adjusting travel speed distributions, picking times, and staging delays until simulation outputs matched observed performance. Key parameters were cross validated against historical logs from the WMS.

Validation was conducted using three key performance indicators (KPIs): orders processed per day, average travel distance per day, and average order cycle time. Table 1 compares actual versus simulated KPIs for the baseline configuration, demonstrating a difference of less than ± 9%, which is within accepted thresholds for discrete-event simulation studies (Fig. 1).

Table 1. Model Validation Results

KPI	% Difference
Orders processed per hour	−9%
Avg. Pick time per order	−5.5%
Avg. Forklift travel distance per hour	+ 4.0%
Packing Time per Order	−3.3%

Fig. 1. Simulation Model of Warehouse

4.5 Strategy Implementation Logic

To evaluate opportunities for emission reduction in warehouse operations, two operational strategies were implemented. The first strategy focused on optimizing SKU placement based on historical picking frequency, while the second employed batch picking to consolidate order fulfillment and minimize redundant travel paths.

1) Velocity-Based Storage (Strategy 1):

- SKUs were ranked by historical picking frequency.
- Slotting optimization assigned A-class SKUs to high-access areas nearer to the packing zone, B-class SKUs to mid-tier zones, and C-class SKUs to low-access zones.
- The new slotting plan reduced average forklift travel distance per pick by reducing travel to high-frequency SKU locations.

2) Batch Picking (Strategy 2):

- Orders were grouped based on time window releases and SKU overlap.
- A nearest-neighbour heuristic determined optimized pick paths, ensuring that travel loops were minimized when collecting multiple SKUs.
- The batch picking logic slightly increased order release time (waiting for batch window closure) but significantly reduced travel per fulfilled order.

5 Route Optimization

5.1 Background

Transportation is a major source of healthcare supply chain emissions, driven by frequent, dispersed deliveries to hospitals and clinics. Route optimization can cut travel distance, fuel use, and carbon output while sustaining service levels.

5.2 Route Optimization Tool

A route optimization tool is currently being implemented and tested within the outbound delivery network. The tool uses delivery location data, time windows, and vehicle capacity constraints to generate optimized delivery routes. Algorithms based on variants of the Vehicle Routing Problem (VRP) and Time Window Constraints are applied to minimize total distance traveled while satisfying delivery service commitments.

5.3 Expected Benefits

Preliminary tests indicate that optimized routing could reduce total delivery distance by 8–15%, translating into proportional reductions in fuel consumption and associated carbon emissions. Although the tool is still in its testing phase and not fully deployed, its integration with warehouse operations (e.g., aligning order batching with delivery scheduling) has strong potential for end-to-end emission reductions.

5.4 Implementation

Once fully deployed, route optimization can complement the warehouse strategies. Together, these initiatives support a holistic approach to emission reduction, addressing both internal material handling and external transportation activities.

6 Results and Discussions

6.1 Overview of Experimental Outcomes

The digital twin simulations provided quantitative insights into how each strategy affected travel distance, order cycle time, and resulting carbon emissions. Ten replications were performed for each scenario to account for stochastic variation in order arrivals and equipment utilization. The mean results are presented in Table 2, with standard deviations kept within 9% of the mean values, ensuring robustness of the simulation outcomes.

Table 2. Emission Reduction Results

Strategy	Travel Distance	% Emission Reduction
Rearranging Fast/Slow Movers	↓ 10–30%	↓ 10 ± 2%
Batch Picking + Optimized Routes	↓ 15–30%	↓ 15 ± 2%
Combined	↓ up to 40%	↓ 20 ± 2%

The results indicate that rearranging storage based on SKU velocity reduced travel distance and energy use while slightly improving processing time. Batch picking, when combined with optimized storage, further reduced travel distance and energy consumption but introduced a slight increase in processing time due to batching delays. The combined application of both strategies achieved the highest overall reduction in travel distance and energy use, confirming their effectiveness in reducing operational carbon emissions.

6.2 Effects of Velocity Based Storage

Implementing velocity-based storage resulted in a reduction in forklift travel distance compared to the baseline scenario. This was primarily achieved by relocating high-frequency (A-class) SKUs closer to the primary picking and packing zones, thereby reducing the average travel distance per pick task.

The improvement in travel efficiency translated into a reduction in carbon emissions. Since forklift emissions are directly proportional to travel distance (as shown in the emission calculation framework), this result aligns with expectations. Additionally, average cycle time improved slightly, demonstrating that better SKU placement reduced order fulfillment time without requiring additional labor resources or new equipment.

These findings are consistent with previous literature, which reported 10–15% travel savings and corresponding emissions reduction through slotting optimization in warehouse settings. For healthcare supply chains, where item criticality and demand frequency vary significantly, such a strategy offers a low-risk approach to sustainability improvements without impacting service levels.

6.3 Effects of Batch Picking

Batch picking [1], combined with the velocity-based storage optimization, delivered the most significant sustainability benefits. Forklift travel distance reduced, and this was achieved by consolidating multiple orders into single picking runs, which minimized redundant aisle travel.

Carbon emissions were also reduced. However, the strategy introduced a slight increase in average cycle time, primarily because orders were released in batches, resulting in short waiting times before picking commenced.

This trade-off highlights a common operational tension between sustainability and service level: while batch picking significantly reduces energy use and emissions, it may not be suitable for facilities with strict real-time order fulfilment requirements (e.g., emergency medical supplies). Instead, it is better suited for bulk or scheduled deliveries, where minor delays are acceptable. Table 3 shows the impact by the strategies.

Table 3. Impacts by both strategies

Area	Impact
Travel Efficiency	Reduced significantly, especially for high-frequency items.
Picking Time	Decreases because picking is faster.
Forklift/Operator Fatigue	Less forklift/battery/diesel usage per order.
Energy Consumption	Reduction due to shorter forklift routes and lower energy used.
Carbon Emissions	Higher throughput with same resources.

6.4 Implications for Sustainability Goals

Both strategies demonstrate that warehouse-level operational changes can yield measurable carbon reductions:

- Velocity-Based Storage is relatively easy to implement, requiring only re-slotting of SKUs, and can deliver 5–15% emission reductions without workflow changes.
- Batch Picking requires operational adjustments and may slightly delay order release but offers significantly greater reductions (10–20% or more) when applied effectively.

These results highlight the value of digital twins as decision-support tools for sustainability, enabling dynamic testing of operational strategies before implementation and reducing the risks of trial-and-error changes.

6.5 Limitations

Although this study shows the potential of digital twin simulation for reducing warehouse carbon emissions, some limitations remain. Only forklift and material handling emissions were modeled, excluding fixed sources like lighting, HVAC, and IT systems; this may change absolute values but not relative reductions. Workforce productivity and equipment availability were assumed to be constant, which may differ during peak periods. Demand was also modeled as fixed, without seasonal or emergency fluctuations that could influence batching efficiency and emission outcomes.

6.6 Future Research Directions

Building on these findings, future research could expand the scope to dynamic demand scenarios, multi-facility networks, and the integration of renewable energy into warehouse operations. In addition, AI-driven strategies could be explored, where machine learning models dynamically decide between single-order and batch picking based on real-time order patterns, further enhancing both efficiency and sustainability outcomes. [10].

7 Conclusions

This study demonstrated the use of digital twin technology to evaluate carbon reduction strategies within a healthcare warehouse. By replicating actual operations in FlexSim and integrating historical WMS and equipment data, the digital twin provided a risk-free environment for testing operational changes without disrupting live activities.

Two strategies were investigated: (1) SKU velocity-based storage assignment, which re-slots fast-moving SKUs closer to picking points, and (2) batch picking combined with velocity-based storage, which consolidates multiple orders to minimize redundant travel. The results showed that:

- Velocity-based storage reduced forklift travel distance and warehouse-related emissions by 5–15%, while slightly improving average cycle time.
- Batch picking combined with velocity-based storage achieved a 10–20% reduction in emissions, the highest among the scenarios, but resulted in a small increase in average order cycle time due to batching delays.

These findings highlight that sustainable warehousing practices can be achieved through relatively low-cost operational changes when supported by digital twin analysis. Velocity-based storage offers quick and easy sustainability gains with minimal operational disruption, while batch picking is suited for bulk or scheduled deliveries where minor delays are acceptable.

Future work should extend beyond a single facility to multi-echelon healthcare networks, account for dynamic demand and order priorities, and examine renewable energy use in material handling. By combining digital twins with data-driven emission models, healthcare supply chains can advance sustainability goals while preserving operational efficiency.

References

1. Aboelfotoh, A., Singh, M., Suer, G.: Order batching optimization for warehouses with cluster-picking. Proc. Manufact. **39**, 1464–1473 (2019) [Online]. https://doi.org/10.1016/j.promfg.2020.01.302

2. Dhoka, D., Choudary, Y. L.: ABC classification for inventory optimization. IOSR J. Bus. Manage. (IOSR-JBM) **15**(1), 38–41, Nov.–Dec. (2013) [Online]. https://doi.org/10.9790/487X-1513841
3. Frazzon, E. M., Freitag, M., Ivanov, D.: Intelligent methods and systems for decision-making support: toward digital supply chain twins. Int. J. Inf. Manage. **57**, 102281 (2021) [Online]. https://doi.org/10.1016/j.ijinfomgt.2020.102281
4. Greenhut, R. F., Dufour, R., Kendall A. M.: Life-cycle assessment in agricultural systems. Butte, MT, USA: National Center for Appropriate Technology (2013) [Online]. https://attra.ncat.org/wp-content/uploads/2022/12/life_cycle_assessment.pdf
5. Guo, D., Mantravadi, S.: The role of digital twins in lean supply chain management: Review and research directions. Int. J. Prod. Res. (2024) [Online]. https://doi.org/10.1080/00207543.2024.2372655
6. Hezam, I. M., Ali, A. M., Sallam, K., Hameed, I. A.: Digital twin and fuzzy framework for supply chain sustainability risk assessment and management in supplier selection. Sci. Rep. **14**, 4891 (2024) [Online]. https://doi.org/10.1038/s41598-024-67226-z
7. Javaid, M., Haleem, A., Suman, R.: Digital twin applications toward industry 4.0: A review. Cogn. Robot. **3**, 100116 (2023) [Online]. https://doi.org/10.1016/j.cogrob.2023.100116
8. Kliment, M., Pekarcikova, M., Trebuna P.: Design and development of digital twins: A case study in supply chain. Sustain. **13**(16), 8963 (2021) [Online]. https://doi.org/10.3390/su13168963
9. Mahat, D., Niranjan, K., Naidu, C. S.: AI-driven optimization of supply chain and logistics in mechanical engineering, in Proc. 2023 10th IEEE Uttar Pradesh Section Int. Conf. Electrical, Electronics and Computer Engineering (UPCON), Prayagraj, India, pp. 1–6 (2023). https://doi.org/10.1109/UPCON.2023.10434905
10. Min, H.: Artificial intelligence in supply chain management: Theory and applications. Int. J. Logistics Res. Appl. **13**(1), 13–39 (2010). https://doi.org/10.1080/13675560902736537
11. Perez, H.D., Wassick, J.M., Grossmann, I.E.: A digital twin framework for online optimization of supply chain business processes. Comput. Chem. Eng. **166**, 107972 (2022). https://doi.org/10.1016/j.compchemeng.2022.107972
12. Srai, J. S., Settanni, E., Tsolakis, N., Aulakh, P. K.: Supply Chain Digital Twins: Opportunities and Challenges Beyond the Hype, in Proceedings of the 23rd Cambridge International Manufacturing Symposium, Cambridge, UK, Sep. (2019). https://doi.org/10.17863/CAM.45897
13. Nordgren, W. B.: Flexsim simulation environment, in Proceedings of the 2002 Winter Simulation Conference, 250–252 (2002). https://doi.org/10.1109/WSC.2002.1172892
14. Xin, L., Xu, P., Gu, M.: Logistics distribution route optimization based on genetic algorithm. Comput. Intell. Neurosci. **2022**, 1–12 (2022). https://doi.org/10.1155/2022/8468438

Learning to Optimize Capacity Planning in Semiconductor Manufacturing

Philipp Andelfinger[1], Jieyi Bi[1(✉)], Qiuyu Zhu[1], Jianan Zhou[1], Bo Zhang[1], Fei Fei Zhang[2], Chew Wye Chan[2], Boon Ping Gan[2], Wentong Cai[1], and Jie Zhang[1]

[1] College of Computing and Data Science, Nanyang Technological University, Singapore, Singapore
jieyi001@e.ntu.edu.sg
[2] D-SIMLAB Technologies Pte Ltd., Singapore, Singapore

Abstract. In manufacturing, capacity planning is the process of allocating production resources in accordance with variable demand. The current industry practice in semiconductor manufacturing typically applies heuristic rules to prioritize actions, such as future change lists that account for incoming machine and recipe dedications. However, while offering interpretability, heuristics cannot easily account for the complex interactions along the process flow that can gradually lead to the formation of bottlenecks. Here, we present a neural network-based model for capacity planning on the level of individual machines, trained using deep reinforcement learning. By representing the policy using a heterogeneous graph neural network, the model directly captures the diverse relationships among machines and processing steps, allowing for proactive decision-making. We describe several measures taken to achieve sufficient scalability to tackle the vast space of possible machine-level actions. Our evaluation results cover Intel's small-scale MiniFab model and preliminary experiments using the popular SMT2020 testbed. In the largest tested scenario, our trained policy increases throughput and decreases cycle time by about 1.8% each.

Keywords: Deep Reinforcement Learning · Semiconductor Manufacturing · Optimization · Graph Neural Network

1 Introduction

Semiconductor manufacturing is highly complex, involving hundreds of machines and re-entrant operations [17]. As a result, capacity planning plays a critical role in allocating resources to meet product demand and maintain target performance metrics [8]. Typical decisions in capacity planning include changes to machines and their recipe dedication, improving machine uptimes, and improving machine throughputs [24], which are captured in so-called future change lists. In current

P. Andelfinger, J. Bi and Q. Zhu—Equally contributed.

W. Cai et al. (Eds.): AsiaSim 2025, CCIS 2727, pp. 67–79, 2026.
https://doi.org/10.1007/978-981-95-4472-1_6

industry practice, static and dynamic capacity planning tools rely heavily on expert knowledge to identify potential capacity problems and create appropriate future change lists [24]. These decisions are driven by combinations of expert knowledge and heuristics. While heuristics rules may consider certain observable statistics of the fab operations, they cannot fully capture the dynamic relations among machines and operations. Moreover, small variations in machine uptime and product mix can cause negligible or enormous impacts on factory performance at different periods and are difficult to consider as part of a heuristic [24]. Hence, heuristic-driven capacity planning is likely to leave significant opportunities for process improvements untapped.

In the present work, we explore the use of deep reinforcement learning (DRL) to train a capacity planning policy that considers the dynamically evolving fab situation and proposes suitable actions in order to improve key performance indicators such as throughput and cycle time. In contrast to classical optimization approaches (e.g., [8]), the evolving fab state is represented by discrete-event simulations, which allows for detailed consideration of the time-varying machine and operation features, but also introduces higher complexity and significant computational demands. A heterogeneous graph neural network (HGNN) captures the interactions of nodes and the associated operations, extending the scope of the decision-making beyond the local machine level. We present our formulation of the Markov decision process underlying the reinforcement learning task and describe in detail our overall training framework. An industry-grade simulation software suite forms the environment and is exercised in a parallelized setting to quickly gather a diverse set of fab state trajectories and the consequences of capacity planning decisions. Our experiments are targeted towards understanding the scalability of our framework. To this end, we evaluate its performance both for the small-scale MiniFab testbed [26] and the larger SMT2020 [10], showing substantial improvements in performance indicators in both cases.

2 Related Work

Traditionally, capacity planning approaches from the literature take the form of mathematical models that are solved heuristically to tackle the problem scales of real-world fabs [16]. In contrast, data-driven approaches using observations from simulations or real-world fabs can more closely represent and exploit the complex relationships among fab states, actions, and performance indicators [15,30].

To exploit learned relationships for planning under unpredictable situations such as unplanned downtimes, digital twin architectures that allow for rapid decision-making employ learned models, often based on reinforcement learning (RL). A comprehensive survey covering works on capacity planning using RL until 2021 is provided by Kulmer et al. [12].

Waschneck et al. employed cooperative Deep Q-Learning (DQN) agents for scheduling in a semiconductor fab comprised of four machine groups [31]. Agents representing machine groups were trained one by one to carry out local scheduling decisions, while observing actions of other agents.

Lee et al. applied a DQN to schedule lots in a manufacturing line covering 60 machines and ten wafer types [14]. Here, the reward measures the adherence of the chosen actions with a pre-determined production plan that prescribes the quantities to be produced, generated by solving a linear program.

Capacity planning for a cement factory was studied by Danket et al. [5]. As in our work, they rely on deep RL via Proximal Policy Optimization (PPO). However, in place of our HGNN, deep feed-forward networks represent the actor and critic. Taking a mixture-of-experts approach, four agents are trained on different demand patterns. During inference, a gating agent aims to select the best-suited expert for observed emerging demand patterns.

Kuo et al. presented a DQN-based digital twin framework for semiconductor manufacturing, focused on handling demand uncertainty [13]. In contrast to other works, the learned policy does not propose actions directly, but selects from a pool of traditional mathematical models.

Tassel et al. trained a DRL-based dispatching policy using a feed-forward network with double-headed self-attention [29]. At each step, the policy assigns scores to define an order on the waiting lots, which are represented by a combination of lot-level features and features describing applicable machine families.

Recently, HGNNs have been employed in DRL using PPO with great success to solve flexible job-shop scheduling problems [19,25,28]. By capturing interactions across machines and operations, richer policies can be learned. However, to our knowledge, HGNNs have not previously been applied to simulation testbeds for semiconductor manufacturing.

Unlike prior works, we focus on actions on the planning rather than operation level. Our experiments include capacity planning for the SMT2020 testbed, which covers more than 1,300 machines and over 4,000 operations.

3 Preliminaries

3.1 Problem Definition and MDP Formulation

Capacity planning (CP) aims to dynamically allocate production resources to accelerate the manufacturing process. In semiconductor manufacturing, a CP instance consists of a product set $\mathcal{P}$ (different models of lots of wafers), a machine set $\mathcal{M}$ and an operation set $\mathcal{O}$. In particular, the operation types include lithography, diffusion, dry etching, wet etching, implantation, etc. Each product $p \in \mathcal{P}$ consists of n_p operation steps $\{O_{p,j}\}_{j=1}^{n_p} \subseteq \mathcal{O}$ required to be processed subject to precedence constraints, i.e., $O_{p,1} \rightarrow O_{p,2} \rightarrow \cdots \rightarrow O_{p,n_p}$. Each operation $O_{p,j}$ can only be processed by any of the compatible machines $\{m_1, m_2, \ldots, m_k\} = M_{p,j} \subseteq \mathcal{M}$, where m_k represents a single machine. We consider three types of decision variables in this paper: (1) *dedication*, assigning machines to operations $d^+(m_k, O_{p,j}) : \mathcal{M} \rightarrow \mathcal{O}$ or removing the assignment $d^-(m_k, O_{p,j}) : \mathcal{M} \rightarrow \mathcal{O}$; (2) *uptime* $u(m_k)$, increasing a machine's percentage of uptime by 3% (but not exceeding 100%); and (3) *efficiency* $r(m_k)$, reducing a machine's per-lot processing time to 90% of its original value. These decision types follow those in [24], while the specific parameter values are defined in this work. The objective of a CP solution is to maximize the total production output $N = \sum p$ and minimize the average cycle time $T = \frac{1}{N}\sum_{p=1}^{N} T_p$, subject to a limited number of changes to the decision variables.

We formulate the long-horizon capacity planning as an MDP $(\mathcal{S}, \mathcal{A}, \mathcal{T}, \mathcal{R}, \gamma < 1)$. At each step t, the **state** s_t describes the factory status, and the **action** a_t consists of σ changes to decision variables. In the MINIFAB setting, $a_t = \{u(m_i)\}_{i=1}^{\sigma_u} \cup \{r(m_i)\}_{i=1}^{\sigma_r}$ with $\sigma_u = \sigma_r = 1$. In contrast, the SMT2020 setting uses the full action set: $a_t = \{u(m_i)\}_{i=1}^{\sigma_u} \cup \{r(m_i)\}_{i=1}^{\sigma_r} \cup \{d^-(m_i, O_{p,j})\}_{(i,p,j)\in\mathcal{I}_{d^-}} \cup \{d^+(m_i, O_{p,j})\}_{(i,p,j)\in\mathcal{I}_{d^+}}$, with $|\mathcal{I}_{d^-}| = \sigma_{d^-}$, $|\mathcal{I}_{d^+}| = \sigma_{d^+}$ and $\sigma_u = \sigma_r = \sigma_{d^-} = \sigma_{d^+} = 5$. The action space in SMT2020 is substantially larger, as $u(m_i)$ and $r(m_i)$ are defined over $|\mathcal{M}|$ machines, while d^+ and d^- span $|\mathcal{M}| \times |\mathcal{O}|$ combinations, introducing significant complexity. The **state transition** function $\mathcal{T}$ is deterministic and updates s_t to s_{t+1} based on the simulation behavior. At each decision step t, we evaluate the simulation both with and without applying the selected actions. This allows us to better distinguish the effects of actions from the simulations' stochasticity by defining the **reward** as $r_t = \mathrm{KPI}_1 - \mathrm{KPI}_0$, where KPI_1 and KPI_0 denote the performance metric with and without applying the selected actions. In this work, we adopt the fab-level daily going rate as the reward KPI, which is defined as $DGR = \sum_{i=1}^{I} \frac{r_i}{L_i} \sum_{l=1}^{L_i} DGR_{i,l}$, where $DGR_{i,l}$ is the daily output of operation l for product i, L_i is the number of operations of product i, and r_i is the WIP ratio of product i.

3.2 Simulation Environment

We consider two common semiconductor manufacturing models, SMT2020 and MINIFAB, whose key properties are summarized in Table 1.

Table 1. Statistics of the SMT2020 and MINIFAB testbeds.

Model	$\lvert\mathcal{P}\rvert$	$\lvert\mathcal{M}\rvert$	$\lvert\mathcal{O}\rvert$	$\lvert\mathcal{O}_p\rvert$
SMT2020	10	1,314	4,014	242 to 583
MINIFAB	3	5	18	6

Intel's MINIFAB [26] models a small fab with five machines (two for diffusion, two for ion implantation, one for lithography) and three products with six operations each, incorporating typical wafer fab attributes such as batch processing, reentrant operations, and operation-dependent setups [7,9,20]; while detailed enough for controlled studies, it is far smaller than real-world fabs. In contrast, the SMT2020 testbed [10] represents 1,314 machines and up to 583 processing steps per product, with two datasets, "high-volume, low-mix" (HV/LM) and "low-volume, high-mix" (LV/HM), commonly used to evaluate dispatching and scheduling approaches [11,18,29]. We use the more diverse LV/HM dataset, increasing wafer arrivals by 25% to accentuate bottlenecks and test scalability. Both models are simulated in D-SIMCON [4], a discrete-event engine with

Python interface for optimization and machine learning [3,22,27], which captures process flows, dedication, wafer starts, downtimes [23]. D-SIMCON supports state copying during policy rollouts [2], which allows us to periodically realign a no-action baseline trajectory for variance reduction.

4 Methodology

To address the capacity planning MDP formulated in Sect. 3.1, we train a policy π_θ parameterized by an encoder-decoder network. A heterogeneous graph encodes machine-operation and operation-operation interactions; the encoder generates node embeddings, which the attention-based decoder uses to compute action probabilities. The policy is trained via n-step PPO.

4.1 Heterogeneous Graph Construction

To model the complex interactions between machines and operations in a production pipeline, we construct a heterogeneous graph $\mathcal{H}$ with two types of nodes: $\mathcal{M} = \{\mathcal{M}_1, \mathcal{M}_2, \dots\}$ and operation nodes $\mathcal{O} = \{\mathcal{O}_{11}, \mathcal{O}_{12}, \dots\}$. Different types of edges capture key relationships in the production process: operation-operation edges reflect logical dependencies between sequential operations, while operation-machine edges denote assignment relations. Each node and edge in the graph is associated with a feature vector extracted from manufacturing logs and configuration metadata:

- **Machine node features:** $m_k \in \mathbb{R}^{d_1}$ encode machine attributes, including min/max batch sizes, waiting lot number, completed lots and wafers, average cycle time, queue time, and processing time, as well as utilization-related metrics such as productive time, down time, idle time, setup time, interval time, dispatch queue length, and end-of-period work-in-progress (WIP) lots and wafers.
- **Operation node features:** $o_{ij} \in \mathbb{R}^{d_2}$ capture operation-specific properties, including completed wafers, completed lots, completed wafer layers, completed main-process wafers (excluding optional steps), average WIP lots, average out-of-process wafers, average cycle time, average remaining due time, average queue time, average processing time, average remaining processing time, average operation-specific remaining due time, average fab cycle time, daily going rate, and dynamic cycle time.
- **Operation-Machine edge features:** $\varepsilon_{ij,k} \in \mathbb{R}^{d_3}$ represent contextual assignment data (i.e., processing time, setup cost).
- **Operation-Operation edge features:** $\varepsilon_{ij,i(j+1)} \in \mathbb{R}^{d_4}$ include dependency-specific information (i.e., process flow).

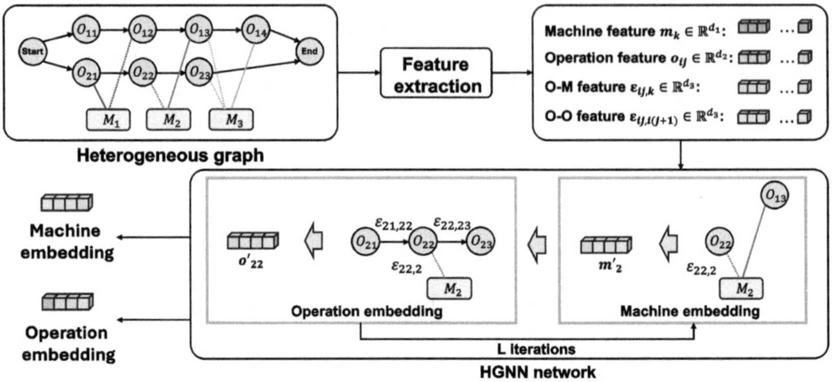

Fig. 1. Overview of feature extraction and HGNN network.

4.2 Model Architecture

Our model learns meaningful embeddings for both machine and operation nodes using an edge-aware heterogeneous graph neural network (HGNN), following [25]. As illustrated in Fig. 1, the architecture consists of two main components.

- **Machine Embedding (Edge-aware Attention)**: Each machine node aggregates information from its associated operation nodes using an attention mechanism that accounts for both node features and edge attributes. This allows the network to capture the varying importance of different operations assigned to the same machine.
- **Operation Embedding (MLP Aggregation)**: Each operation node updates its embedding by integrating information from its immediate neighbors in the process flow (i.e., preceding and succeeding operations) as well as the embedding of the assigned machine. This is implemented using a multi-layer perceptron (MLP) to flexibly combine diverse sources of information.

These two components are applied iteratively over L message-passing layers to capture complex, higher-order dependencies between operations and machines. At each layer, node representations are updated based on their local neighborhoods. The final node embeddings are computed by averaging the representations across all layers: $m_i^{\text{final}} = \frac{1}{L}\sum_{\ell=1}^{L} m_i^{(\ell)}$, and $o_{ij}^{\text{final}} = \frac{1}{L}\sum_{\ell=1}^{L} o_{ij}^{(\ell)}$, where $m_i^{(\ell)}$ and $o_{ij}^{(\ell)}$ denote the embeddings of machine node $\mathcal{M}_i$ and operation node $\mathcal{O}_{ij}$ at the ℓ-th layer, respectively.

Attention-Based Decoder. Final machine and operation embeddings are passed to a lightweight decoder to compute action probabilities. For machine-level uptime and efficiency, separate MLPs with sigmoid activations are applied to machine embeddings, yielding independent one-dimensional probabilities for each machine: $\pi_i^u = \text{Sigmoid}\left(\text{MLP}_u\left(e_i^{\text{final}}\right)\right)$ and $\pi_i^r = \text{Sigmoid}\left(\text{MLP}_r\left(e_i^{\text{final}}\right)\right)$.

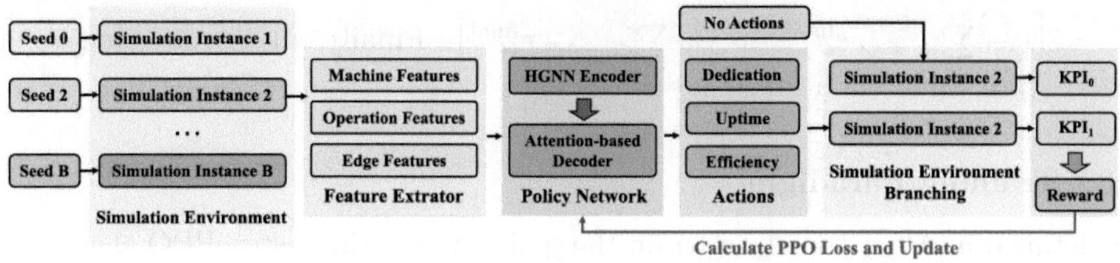

Fig. 2. Overview of the training framework.

Algorithm 1. n-step Training with PPO

Require: Initial **policy network** parameters θ; initial **critic network** parameters ϕ; clipping threshold ϵ; learning rate η_θ, η_ϕ

for epoch $= 1$ to E **do**
  for $b = 1$ to B **in parallel do**
    Generate environment instance $\mathcal{D}_b$ with unique random seed
    Set initial state $s_{b,0}$
  $t \leftarrow 0$
  while $t < T_{\text{train}}$ **do**
    for $b = 1$ to B **in parallel do**
      Collect experiences $\{(s_{b,t'}, a_{b,t'}, r_{b,t'})\}_{t'=t}^{t+n}$ by running policy π_θ for n time steps, where $a_{b,t'} \sim \pi_\theta(a_{b,t'}|s_{b,t'})$
    $t \leftarrow t + n$, $\pi_{\text{old}} \leftarrow \pi_\theta$, $v_{\text{old}} \leftarrow v_\phi$
    for $k = 1$ to K **do**
      $\hat{R}_t \leftarrow v_\phi(s_t)$
      for $t' \in \{t-1, \ldots, t-n\}$ **do**
        $\hat{R}_{t'} \leftarrow r_{t'} + \gamma \hat{R}_{t'+1}$
      Normalize $\hat{R}_{t'}$ by Z-score
      $\hat{A}_{t'} \leftarrow \hat{R}_{t'} - v_\phi(s_{t'})$
      Compute PPO loss $\mathcal{L}_\theta^{\text{PPO}}$ and Critic loss $\mathcal{L}_\phi^{\text{Critic}}$ as in [21]
      $\theta \leftarrow \theta + \eta_\theta \nabla \mathcal{L}_\theta^{\text{PPO}}$
      $\phi \leftarrow \phi - \eta_\phi \nabla \mathcal{L}_\phi^{\text{Critic}}$

For operation-machine dedication actions, we use an attention mechanism to model pairwise interactions between machine and operation embeddings. These interactions are then passed through a scaled tanh and sigmoid to produce normalized probabilities: $\pi_{ij}^{d^+} = \text{Sigmoid}\left(-C \cdot \text{Tanh}\left(\frac{e_i^{\text{final}} \cdot r_{ij}^{\text{final}}}{\sqrt{d}}\right)\right)$, where C is a scaling factor that encourages exploration; following [1], we set $C = 10$. The probability of removing a dedication is defined as the complement of the probability of adding one, i.e., $\pi_{ij}^{d^-} = 1 - \pi_{ij}^{d^+}$.

Critic Network. The critic network, parameterized by ϕ, shares the HGNN encoder with the policy network. To estimate the value of the overall factory state, it aggregates both machine and operation embeddings via separate mean pooling, which are concatenated to form the graph state embedding $h_t \in \mathbb{R}^{2d}$:

$h_t = \left[\frac{1}{|\mathcal{M}|}\sum_{m_i \in \mathcal{M}} e_i^{\text{final}} \;||\; \frac{1}{|\mathcal{O}|}\sum_{O_{p,j} \in \mathcal{O}} r_{ij}^{\text{final}}\right]$. Finally, h_t is projected to a scalar state value via a linear layer.

4.3 Training Paradigm

As detailed in Algorithm 1, we train the policy π_θ via the n-step PPO algorithm in an online setting, where our agent interacts with the simulation environment during training. As shown in Fig. 2, multiple simulation instances are executed in parallel to enable batch training. During training, the parameters of the policy network θ and critic network ϕ are updated accordingly.

5 Experiments

We evaluate our method on two common simulation-based testbeds (cf. Sect. 3.2): Intel's small-scale MINIFAB and SMT2020.

We train using Adam with learning rates $\eta_\theta = 3 \times 10^{-4}$ (policy) and $\eta_\phi = 10^{-4}$ (critic). PPO is configured with $n = 5$, $K = 20$, clipping parameter $\epsilon = 0.2$, and discount factor $\gamma = 0.99$. We use a batch size of $B = 16$. In MINIFAB, actions are taken daily over $T_{\text{train}} = 5$ simulation days; in SMT2020, actions are taken weekly over $T_{\text{train}} = 25$ weeks. We set the HGNN's layer count to $L = 1$ for MINIFAB, to $L = 2$ for SMT2020, and the hidden dimension to $d = 64$. As baselines, our results include three strategies: taking no actions, taking random actions, and a heuristic that samples target machines and dedications based on their work-in-progress levels.

5.1 Results on MINIFAB

We first assess the HGNN's sensitivity to its hyperparameters by varying the hidden dimension $d \in 32, 64, 128, 256$ and the layer count $L \in 1, 2$. Each strategy is tested across 16 simulation instances using the same sequence of random seeds to ensure fairness. We evaluate three fab performance indicators: completed lots, average cycle time and daily going rate. As shown in Table 2, the best results are obtained with $d = 64$ and $L = 1$, showing that larger dimensions or deeper networks may lead to overfitting or increased optimization difficulty.

We evaluate the effectiveness of our HGNN in the MINIFAB environment by comparing it against our baselines. As shown in Table 4, our method consistently outperforms all baselines: it achieves a 1.59% increase in completed lots and a 2.70% reduction in cycle time compared to the heuristic and random decisions. Against the no-action baseline, the improvements are more pronounced, with 13.85% higher throughput and 14.96% lower cycle time.

5.2 Results on SMT2020

We now turn to our SMT2020 scenario, which involves a substantially larger state space and spans a duration of 25 weeks per episode. Figure 3 shows the

Table 2. Impact of HGNN hyper-parameters on performance in MINIFAB.

Hyperparameter	Completed Lots ↑	Cycle Time ↓	Daily Going Rate ↑
$d = 32$	55.06	1.10	265.73
$d = 64$	**55.50**	**1.08**	**266.56**
$d = 128$	54.69	1.09	265.26
$d = 256$	54.69	1.10	266.26
$L = 1$	**55.50**	**1.08**	**266.56**
$L = 2$	55.06	1.11	266.09

Table 3. Comparison of fab performance metrics across strategies.

Strategy	Completed Lots ↑	Cycle Time ↓	Daily Going Rate ↑
GNN	**55.50**	**1.08**	**266.56**
Heuristic	54.63	1.11	265.42
Random	54.63	1.11	265.00
No Action	48.75	1.27	251.09

Table 4. Improvement of GNN over the baseline strategies in MINIFAB.

GNN vs.	Completed Lots	Cycle Time	Daily Going Rate
Heuristic	1.59% (+0.87)	2.70% (–0.03 days)	0.43% (+1.14)
Random	1.59% (+0.87)	2.70% (–0.03 days)	0.59% (+1.56)
No Action	13.85% (+6.75)	14.96% (–0.19 days)	6.16% (+15.47)

fab-level KPIs over the course of the training. The main observation is a substantial improvement in the KPIs over the first 30 to 40 epochs, with a subsequent decline towards the initial values. We also recorded the concrete efficiency actions taken with respect to machines of different families. Figure 4 shows that the policy increasingly targets lithography and diffusion before returning to the initial frequencies. Most of the frequencies for other families such as dry etching slightly decreased, but with less clear trends over the course of the training. At epoch 40, we evaluated against the baseline strategies. Table 6 shows that, in line with the training curves, our policy outperforms the other strategies substantially, with increases of 1.87% and 1.74% in throughput and daily going rate, and a reduction in 1.8% in average cycle time compared to the heuristic.

To investigate potential causes for the observed decline after the initial improvement in the KPIs, we designed a restricted SMT2020 scenario. By limiting each epoch to 5 weeks and employing a constant seed for all simulator instances, we expect significantly lower variance in the rewards. Furthermore, to constrain the action space, we omit dedication actions, allowing only for changes to the machines' efficiencies and uptimes. In addition to our reward formulation using the difference in KPIs with and without actions, we include a variant

Table 5. Performance comparison across different methods in SMT2020.

Strategy	Completed Lots ↑	Cycle Time ↓	Daily Going Rate ↑
GNN	**6019.75**	**59.100**	**749.79**
Heuristic	5909.44	60.181	736.99
Random	5904.13	60.211	736.65
No Action	5872.94	60.507	732.58

Table 6. Improvement of GNN over the baseline strategies in SMT2020.

GNN vs.	Completed Lots	Cycle Time	Daily Going Rate
Heuristic	1.87% (+110.3)	1.80% (–1.08 days)	1.74% (+12.80)
Random	1.96% (+115.6)	1.85% (–1.11 days)	1.78% (+13.14)
No Action	2.50% (+146.8)	2.33% (–1.41 days)	2.35% (+17.21)

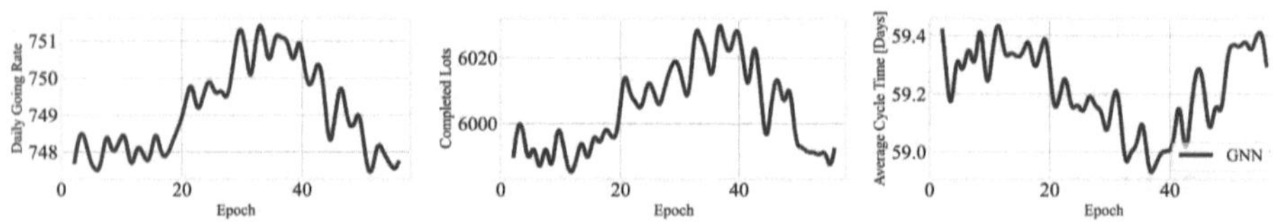

Fig. 3. Fab-level KPIs during training in SMT2020.

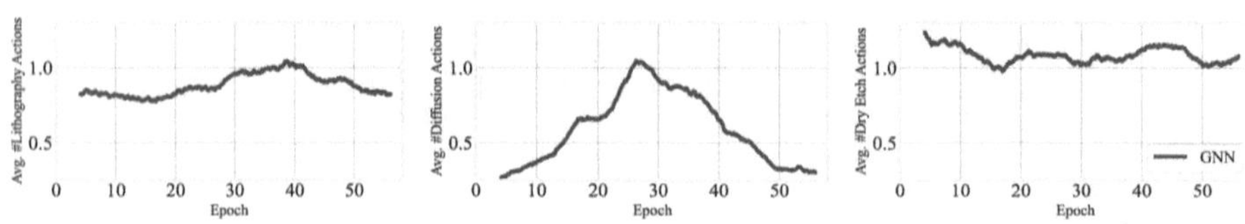

Fig. 4. Frequency of efficiency actions on different machine families in SMT2020.

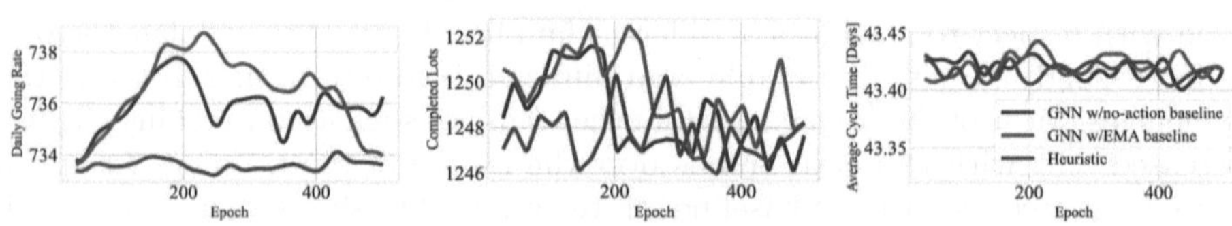

Fig. 5. Fab-level KPIs in the five-week SMT2020 scenario.

using the difference between the current KPI and an exponential moving average (EMA) of the weekly KPIs from previous epochs. The results shown in Fig. 5 suggest that the observed decline is not dependent on these factors. As in the 25-week training, the learned actions trend towards their initial frequencies as the KPIs begin to decrease. We are currently investigating appropriate regularization measures [6] in order to achieve reliable convergence to high-quality policies in long-term training runs.

6 Conclusion and Future Work

We presented a GNN-based deep reinforcement learning framework for optimizing capacity planning decisions in semiconductor manufacturing. Experiments using the small-scale MiniFab testbed allowed us to select suitable hyperparameters and showed the general ability to learn effective capacity planning decisions. We subsequently applied our approach to the larger-scale SMT2020 testbed, which includes many of the characteristics of real-world wafer fabs and approaches their scale, increasing throughput by about 1.8%, which is a significant improvement in the semiconductor manufacturing context.

Our future work will explore three main avenues. Firstly, we will explore improvements to the training stability to support gradual improvement of the policy during long-term training. Secondly, to support real-world decision-making, the costs incurred by different actions must be taken into account and unprofitable actions avoided. Finally, experiments on industry-scale simulation models will evaluate the scalability of our framework beyond common testbeds. To support targeted proactive decisions in more dynamic settings, information about future wafer starts will be incorporated in the fab state representation.

Acknowledgments. This research is supported in part by the National Research Foundation, Singapore under its AI Singapore Programme (AISG Award No: AISG3-RP-2022-031) and in part by the National Research Foundation, Singapore under its AI Singapore Programme (AISG Award No: AISG2-100E-2024-130).

References

1. Bi, J., et al.: Learning to handle complex constraints for vehicle routing problems. Adv. Neural Inf. Process. Syst. **37**, 93479–93509 (2024)
2. Bosse, T., et al.: A standard framework for ai-driven optimizations in various complex domains, pp. 1966–1977 (2024)
3. Chan, C.W., Gan, B.P., Cai, W.: Combining time series data and snapshot data for situation aware dispatching in semiconductor manufacturing. In: 2023 Winter Simulation Conference (WSC), pp. 2310–2312 (2023)
4. D-SIMLAB: Forecaster and Scenario Manager (2023). http://www.d-simlab.com/category/d-simcon/products-d-simcon/forecaster-and-scenario-manager. Accessed 15th April
5. Danket, T., Tanachutiwat, S., Rungreunganun, V.: A mixture-of-experts approach to production capacity planning for diverse demand patterns via deep reinforcement learning. Engineering Access **10**(2), 154–165 (2024)
6. Dohare, S., Lan, Q., Mahmood, A.R.: Overcoming policy collapse in deep reinforcement learning. In: Sixteenth European Workshop on Reinforcement Learning (2023)

7. Drießel, R., Mönch, L.: An integrated scheduling and material-handling approach for complex job shops: a computational study. Int. J. Prod. Res. **50**(20), 5966–5985 (2012)
8. Gopalakrishnan, M., Skoogh, A.: Machine criticality based maintenance prioritization: identifying productivity improvement potential. Int. J. Product. Perform. Manag. **67**(4), 654–672 (2018)
9. Hassoun, M., Kopp, D., Mönch, L., Kalir, A.: A new high-volume/low-mix simulation testbed for semiconductor manufacturing. In: 2019 Winter Simulation Conference (WSC), pp. 2419–2428. IEEE (2019)
10. Kopp, D., Hassoun, M., Kalir, A., Mönch, L.: Smt 2020–a semiconductor manufacturing testbed. IEEE Trans. Semicond. Manuf. **33**(4), 522–531 (2020)
11. Kovács, B., Tassel, P., Ali, R., El-Kholany, M., Gebser, M., Seidel, G.: A customizable simulator for artificial intelligence research to schedule semiconductor fabs. In: 33rd Annual SEMI Advanced Semiconductor Manufacturing Conference (ASMC), pp. 1–6. IEEE (2022)
12. Kulmer, F., Wolf, M., Ramsauer, C.: Medium-term capacity management through reinforcement learning-literature review and concept for an industrial pilot-application. Procedia CIRP **107**, 1065–1070 (2022)
13. Kuo, H.A., Hong, T.Y., Chien, C.F.: A deep reinforcement learning based digital twin framework for resilient production planning under demand uncertainty and an empirical study in semiconductor wafer fabrication. Comput. Ind. Eng. 111389 (2025)
14. Lee, Y.H., Lee, S.: Deep reinforcement learning based scheduling within production plan in semiconductor fabrication. Expert Syst. Appl. **191**, 116222 (2022)
15. Meidan, Y., Lerner, B., Rabinowitz, G., Hassoun, M.: Cycle-time key factor identification and prediction in semiconductor manufacturing using machine learning and data mining. IEEE Trans. Semicond. Manuf. **24**(2), 237–248 (2011)
16. Missbauer, H., Uzsoy, R.: Production Planning with Capacitated Resources and Congestion, Springer Books, vol. None. Springer, Cham (June 2020). https://doi.org/10.1007/978-1-0716-0354-3
17. Mönch, L., Fowler, J.W., Dauzère-Pérès, S., Mason, S.J., Rose, O.: A survey of problems, solution techniques, and future challenges in scheduling semiconductor manufacturing operations. J. Sched. **14**(6), 583–599 (2011)
18. Mönch, L., Zimmermann, J.: Simulation-based assessment of machine criticality measures for a shifting bottleneck scheduling approach in complex manufacturing systems. Comput. Ind. **58**(7), 644–655 (2007)
19. Peng, Y., Lyu, Y., Zhang, J., Chu, Y.: Heterogeneous graph neural-network-based scheduling optimization for multi-product and variable-batch production in flexible job shops. Appl. Sci. **15**(10), 5648 (2025)
20. Pfund, M.E., Balasubramanian, H., Fowler, J.W., Mason, S.J., Rose, O.: A multi-criteria approach for scheduling semiconductor wafer fabrication facilities. J. Sched. **11**(1), 29–47 (2008)
21. Schulman, J., Wolski, F., Dhariwal, P., Radford, A., Klimov, O.: Proximal policy optimization algorithms. arXiv preprint arXiv:1707.06347 (2017)
22. Schulz, B., Jacobi, C., Gisbrecht, A., Evangelos, A., Chan, C.W., Gan, B.P.: Graph representation and embedding for semiconductor manufacturing fab states. In: Proceedings of the 2022 Winter Simulation Conference, pp. 3382–3393 (2022)
23. Seidel, G., et al.: Harmonizing operations management of key stakeholders in wafer fab using discrete event simulation. In: 2017 Winter Simulation Conference (WSC), pp. 3670–3678 (2017)

24. Seidel, G., et al.: An integration of static and dynamic capacity planning for a ramping fab. In: 2019 Winter Simulation Conference (WSC), pp. 2304–2311 (2019)
25. Song, W., Chen, X., Li, Q., Cao, Z.: Flexible job-shop scheduling via graph neural network and deep reinforcement learning. IEEE Trans. Ind. Inf. **19**(2), 1600–1610 (2022)
26. Spier, J., Kempf, K.: Simulation of emergent behavior in manufacturing systems. In: Proceedings of SEMI Advanced Semiconductor Manufacturing Conference and Workshop, pp. 90–94. IEEE (1995)
27. Stöckermann, P., et al.: Scalability of reinforcement learning methods for dispatching in semiconductor frontend fabs: a comparison of open-source models with real industry datasets. Int. J. Adv. Manuf. Technol. (2025)
28. Tang, H., Dong, J.: Solving flexible job-shop scheduling problem with heterogeneous graph neural network based on relation and deep reinforcement learning. Machines **12**(8), 584 (2024)
29. Tassel, P., Kovács, B., Gebser, M., Schekotihin, K., Stöckermann, P., Seidel, G.: Semiconductor fab scheduling with self-supervised and reinforcement learning. In: 2023 Winter Simulation Conference (WSC), pp. 1924–1935. IEEE (2023)
30. Wang, J., Zhang, J., Wang, X.: A data driven cycle time prediction with feature selection in a semiconductor wafer fabrication system. IEEE Trans. Semicond. Manuf. **31**(1), 173–182 (2018)
31. Waschneck, B., et al.: Optimization of global production scheduling with deep reinforcement learning. Procedia Cirp **72**, 1264–1269 (2018)

A Credible Evolution Method for Digital Twins Based on LSTM–Decoder-Only Architecture

Hongbo Cheng[1,2,3], Lin Zhang[1,2,3](✉), Yiming Qiao[2], Lei Zhang[1], Kunyu Wang[1], and Han Lu[1]

[1] Hangzhou International Innovation Institute, Beihang University, 166 Shuanghongqiao Street, Pingyao Town, Yuhang District, Hangzhou 311115, Zhejiang, China
{chenghongbo,zhanglin,wangky2020,luhan}@buaa.edu.cn
[2] School of Automation and Electrical Engineering, Beihang University, Xueyuan Road, Beijing 100191, China
qiaoyo@buaa.edu.cn
[3] The State Key Laboratory of Intelligent Manufacturing Systems Technology, Beijing 100854, China

Abstract. To address the challenges of accuracy, adaptability, and trustworthiness in digital twin modeling for complex dynamic systems, this paper proposes an evolutionary digital twin approach based on a hybrid architecture that integrates LSTM with a Transformer Decoder-Only framework. This method combines the strengths of LSTM in extracting local sequential features with the capability of the Decoder-Only Transformer to model global temporal dependencies. In addition, a dynamic self-adaptive evolution mechanism, driven by a sliding-window credibility metric, is introduced to enable online calibration and continuous optimization of the digital twin model. Experimental results on a publicly available quadrotor UAV dataset demonstrate that the proposed approach offers significant improvements over mainstream methods in terms of prediction accuracy, robustness, and responsiveness to system changes, thereby validating the effectiveness of the credibility-driven evolution strategy.

Keywords: Digital twin · Dynamic evolution · Credibility assessment

1 Introduction

Digital Twin (DT) has been extensively adopted in manufacturing, healthcare, and smart cities as a critical bridge between the physical and cyber domains [1]. A digital replica of a physical asset enables real-time state monitoring, prediction, and decision optimization. Nevertheless, field data are high-dimensional and strongly time-dependent, and are continuously perturbed by internal and external dynamics. Consequently, the twin model must be persistently calibrated and evolved to retain accuracy [2]. A novel DT model that provides

W. Cai et al. (Eds.): AsiaSim 2025, CCIS 2727, pp. 80–89, 2026.
https://doi.org/10.1007/978-981-95-4472-1_7

high-resolution temporal modeling, adaptive evolution, and measurable trustworthiness is urgently required by both academia and industry.

Conventional DT approaches are challenged by rising system complexity and dynamics. First, classical temporal learning techniques—e.g., ARIMA and shallow RNNs—are limited in capturing long-range dependencies, nonlinear kinetics, and multi-scale variations [3]. Second, during operation, drifted sensors, anomalous data, and system evolution continuously shift the twin state away from the physical counterpart, thereby degrading decision safety [4]. Therefore, robust temporal modeling and quantifiable credibility mechanisms are required to enable dynamic, adaptive evolution of the twin.

Long short-term memory (LSTM) is widely adopted for temporal data, because its gating mechanism effectively captures long-range dependencies [5]. Transformer architectures and their variants, empowered by self-attention, excel at global relationship extraction and have been introduced into sequential tasks. Recently, decoder-only Transformers have demonstrated strong generative performance while remaining lightweight and output-focused. Nevertheless, a systematic model that fuses LSTM's sequential feature extraction with the global modeling capacity of decoder-only Transformers, while simultaneously supporting credibility-driven adaptive evolution, has not yet been reported.

To address the aforementioned challenges, a credibility-driven evolutionary digital twin method based on LSTM-augmented Transformer Decoder-Only (LTDO) is proposed. The principal contributions are summarized as follows:

(1) A hybrid LTDO structure is devised. Local short-to-mid-term patterns are extracted by the LSTM module, while global temporal relationships are captured by the decoder-only Transformer.
(2) A credibility metric is formulated from the model outputs to dynamically quantify the deviation between the twin and the physical entity in real time.
(3) An adaptive evolution mechanism is introduced. Model recalibration and optimization are triggered whenever credibility variation exceeds a predefined threshold, thereby enhancing accuracy and robustness under complex environments.

2 Related Works

2.1 Temporal Feature Extraction

Effective extraction of temporal features is essential for accurate state perception and prediction in digital twins. To address the multi-scale and multi-modal characteristics of industrial time series, recent efforts have concentrated on multi-scale modeling and representation learning. A hierarchical recurrent structure is adopted in reference [6]. Slow-varying trends and fast dynamics are modeled separately, yielding enhanced resolution and interpretability. Feature redundancy, however, leads to excessive computation and model complexity. A multi-scale feature selection and compression method is introduced in reference [7]. Dynamic weighting across scales is performed, enabling effective integration under complex operating conditions. Despite these advances, balancing representational power with computational efficiency remains a critical challenge.

2.2 Transformer and Self-attention in Temporal Modeling

Transformer-based self-attention has been widely adopted for industrial temporal analytics owing to its global dependency modeling capacity. In reference [8], a lightweight Transformer is tailored for industrial scenarios. Parameter sharing and sparse attention significantly reduce inference latency and resource overhead. Edge deployment is enabled in reference [9] by pruning and quantizing the Transformer, yielding viable solutions for resource-limited devices. Although global modeling capabilities have been advanced, the effective integration of local temporal features with global dependencies remains unresolved.

2.3 Credibility Modeling and Adaptive Evolution

Credibility assessment and adaptive evolution have been identified as critical enablers for sustained operation of industrial digital twins. A credibility metric combining sliding-window residual detection with Bayesian confidence analysis is proposed in reference [10]. Real-time performance monitoring and anomaly alerting are thereby achieved. Reference [11] presents a closed-loop adaptive digital twin. Incremental samples are automatically collected and incorporated when new conditions arise, and parameters are fine-tuned online to enable autonomous model evolution. Efficient and low-cost credibility-driven evolution mechanisms that support cross-cycle and cross-process autonomous upgrades remain an open research direction.

3 Proposed Method

3.1 Overall Framework

A credibility-driven evolutionary digital-twin method is proposed that integrates local temporal patterns with global dynamic correlations. Short-to-mid-term dependencies are captured by LSTM modules, whereas global spatial temporal features are extracted by decoder-only Transformer. The outputs are continuously evaluated through a credibility metric computed within sliding windows. Guided by this metric, fine-tuning and structural adaptation are triggered online, enhancing robustness and adaptability under evolving conditions. The entire pipeline—feature extraction, global modeling, credibility assessment, and dynamic evolution—is closed-looped, as illustrated in Fig. 1.

3.2 LTDO Model

The LSTM module excels at capturing short-term variations and non-stationary disturbances. Gated dynamics are exploited to reweight historical inputs, suppress noise, and retain salient features. However, long-range dependencies that span extended intervals cannot be fully addressed by local modeling, leading to predictive bias. Consequently, intermediate features produced by the LSTM module are forwarded to a decoder-only Transformer. Multi-head self-attention is then applied in parallel to extract distant, high-order spatio-temporal couplings across the sequence.

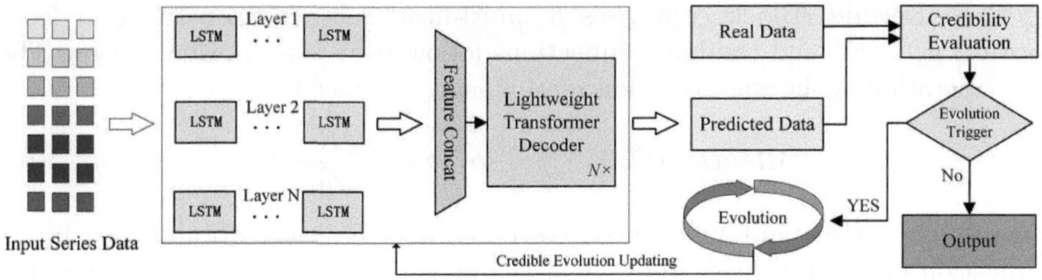

Fig. 1. Dynamic evolution architecture of digital twin based on LTDO.

3.2.1 Local Dynamic Feature Extraction

The LSTM module is tasked with preliminary temporal-dependency modeling. Given the historical observation sequence $x_{1:t}$, it yields the contextual hidden-state sequence $h_{1:t}$. To further strengthen temporal modeling, the LSTM is extended to multi-scale processing. Multiple LSTM instances are deployed, each fed with data aggregated at a distinct temporal scale. The resulting hidden-state sequences are fused, yielding an enriched multi-scale representation, expressed as:

$$h^s = h_1^s, h_2^s, h_3^s, \cdots, h_{T_s}^s \tag{1}$$

And concatenate them to form the final temporal feature representation, expressed as:

$$H_t = FUSE(h_t^1, h_t^2, h_t^3, \cdots, h_t^s) \tag{2}$$

The LSTM stage is tasked with compressing mid-to-short-term dependencies, thereby reducing computational load and training cost for the subsequent Transformer module.

3.2.2 Global Dynamic Correlation Modeling

The aggregated sequence H_t encapsulates scale-specific dynamics while jointly reflecting the global state. To explicitly capture long-range and cross-variable dependencies among subsystems, a decoder-only Transformer is employed. Multi-head self-attention is leveraged to model complex spatio-temporal interactions across both temporal and system dimensions.

The aggregated sequence H_t is first arranged as a temporal input to the decoder-only Transformer:

$$\mathcal{H} = H_1, H_2, H_3, \cdots, H_t \tag{3}$$

$$Z = Transformer(\mathcal{H}; \theta) \tag{4}$$

where θ denotes the Transformer parameters and Z represents the fused global feature.

The decoder-only stack is composed of identical decoder blocks. For each position j, the output z_j is calculated as follow:

$$Z_j = DecoderBlock(H_j, Z_{<j}) \tag{5}$$

Each Decode rBlock comprises a multi-head self-attention layer, a feed-forward network, and residual connections followed by layer normalization. The core operation is the self-attention mechanism, expressed as:

$$Attention(Q, K, V) = softmax(\frac{QK^\top}{\sqrt{d_k}})V \tag{6}$$

where Query, Key, and Value matrices $Q, K, V \in R^{td_k}$ are obtained by linear projection of the input; d_k represents the attention dimension (the dimension of Key/Query); t represents the sequence length. The multi-head self-attention mechanism enhances the model's ability to focus on different feature relationships through multi-head calculations.

After obtaining the global embedding Z, the prediction result of the twin model is output through the decoder block:

$$\hat{y}_t = f_{out}(Z) \tag{7}$$

where f_{out} denotes a stack of fully-connected layers.

3.3 Credibility Evolution

To achieve sustained perception of digital-twin output quality, a sliding-window normalized mean square error (NMSE) is introduced as the core credibility metric. Specifically, at time t, the system collects the twin prediction $\hat{y}_t$ and the corresponding physical observation y_t. Within a historical window of length L, the normalized average of the prediction error relative to the observation variance is computed to evaluate the recent agreement between the twin output and the physical reality. The metric is formulated as follow:

$$NMSE_t = \frac{1}{L} \sum_{k=t-L+1}^{t} \frac{(\hat{y}_k - y_k)^x}{Var[y_{t-L+1:t}] + \varepsilon} \tag{8}$$

where $Var[y_{t-L+1:t}]$ denotes the variance of the physical observations within the window; ε is a regularization term to avoid an excessively small denominator. This metric reflects both the relative error and automatically adapts to data volatility under varying environments. Furthermore, to uniformly quantify twin credibility, the credibility score $C(t)$ is defined as follows:

$$C(t) = 1 - NMSE_t \tag{9}$$

During evolution, the twin system is governed by $C(t)$. The evolution threshold α is set. If $C(t) \geqslant \alpha$, the twin is deemed healthy and remains unchanged. When $C(t) < \alpha$, it indicates a significant deviation between the prediction of the twin model and the actual observation, which triggers evolution and fine-tuning of the model parameter. This workflow can be expressed as follow:

$$\theta \longleftarrow \theta - \eta \cdot \nabla_\theta \mathcal{L}(\hat{y}_{t-L+1:t}, y_{t-L+1:t}) \tag{10}$$

where $\mathcal{L}$ is the MSE loss and η is an adaptively adjusted fine-tuning learning rate.

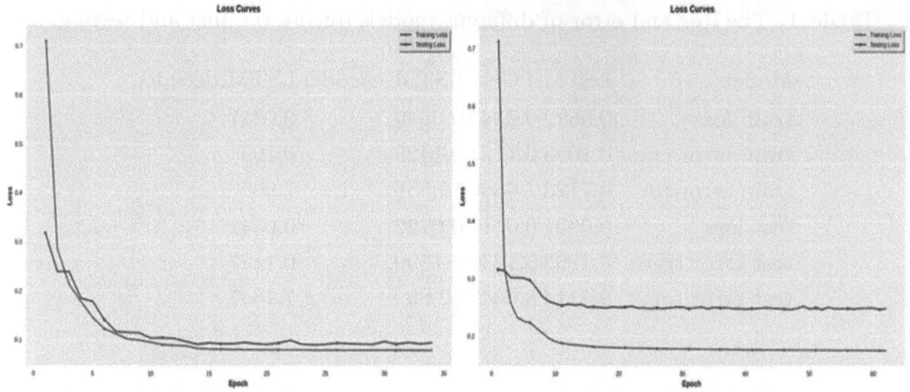

(a) Window size = 40 (b) Window size = 190

Fig. 2. Training and Testing Loss Curves of the LTDO Model under Different Window Sizes.

4 Case Study

4.1 Description of the Experiment

The experimental dataset used in this study is the publicly available Wavelab "Pelican Dataset" of quadrotor UAV flight data. The data was collected by an AscTec Pelican quadrotor during indoor flight [12]. The original dataset was divided into pre-training (875k time steps), testing (286k time steps), and online evolution (210k time steps) subsets in a ratio of 3:1:1, with the window length set to different numbers of time steps. During the experiments, we implemented the models in PyTorch on an Intel Core i7-10750H CPU and an NVIDIA GeForce RTX 2060 GPU. The Adam optimizer was used with a batch size of 128.

4.2 Experiment Result

4.2.1 Performance of the Proposed Model Under Different Window Sizes

In the experiments, to evaluate the impact of different window sizes on the model, we selected two cases with window sizes of 60 and 190 to test the performance of the LTDO model. Figure 2 shows the time series prediction results of the six degrees of freedom states of the UAV under different window lengths. It can be observed that, compared to longer windows, shorter windows are better able to track the changes in the true signal, and this effect is especially notable in the first three degrees of freedom. As the window size decreases, the predicted curves fit the real curves more closely, with the trends and amplitudes of fluctuations becoming more consistent. The model's response to complex dynamic changes and sudden signals becomes more accurate with smaller window sizes.

Table 1. The loss and error of different models during training and testing.

Model	LSTM	TCN	LSTM_encoder	LSTM_decoder
train loss	0.0582	0.0349	0.0649	0.0387
train error trans	0.1096	0.112	0.1425	0.109
train error rot	9.1123	7.0366	10.558	7.006
test loss	0.0691	0.061	0.0722	0.0541
test error trans	0.1293	0.1236	0.1399	0.1127
test error rot	9.2114	8.0048	12.89	7.7647

4.2.2 Comparison with Other Models

To validate the effectiveness of the proposed model, we systematically compared the proposed LSTM_decoder model with mainstream sequence modeling methods, including standard LSTM, TCN, and LSTM_encoder. Detailed results are shown in Table 1. The comparison is conducted from two perspectives: (1) Comparison of loss curves during training and testing (Fig. 3), to evaluate the convergence speed and generalization ability of different models; (2) Statistical analysis of the distribution of training and testing losses after convergence, for a further assessment of the stability and performance of each model during the convergence phase.

Figure 3(a) shows the loss reduction process of different models on the training set, while (b) illustrates the loss trends on the test set. All models exhibit a rapid decline in loss at the early stages of training, followed by gradual convergence. Comparisons reveal that the LSTM_decoder achieves the best performance in both training and testing losses, featuring fast convergence, the lowest final loss values, and simultaneously demonstrating a very narrow confidence interval (indicating higher stability and robustness). The testing loss and its fluctuations for the LSTM_encoder are noticeably higher than those of the decoder structure, reflecting weaker generalization ability. The TCN's loss decreases at a slightly slower rate compared to the LSTM_decoder but overall outperforms the standard LSTM. Although the standard LSTM performs well on the training set, its loss and fluctuations on the test set are relatively large, indicating a limited ability to model the long-term dependencies of complex UAV dynamic time series systems.

For the testing loss distribution, the LSTM_decoder again achieves the best results: it not only has the lowest mean, but also the narrowest fluctuation range, indicating superior generalization ability and robustness to real-world application data compared to the other methods. The TCN and LSTM follow, with concentrated distributions, but both are higher than the LSTM_decoder. The LSTM_encoder has the worst performance in terms of testing loss and variability, suggesting that it has difficulty effectively capturing the true distribution characteristics of dynamic time series systems.

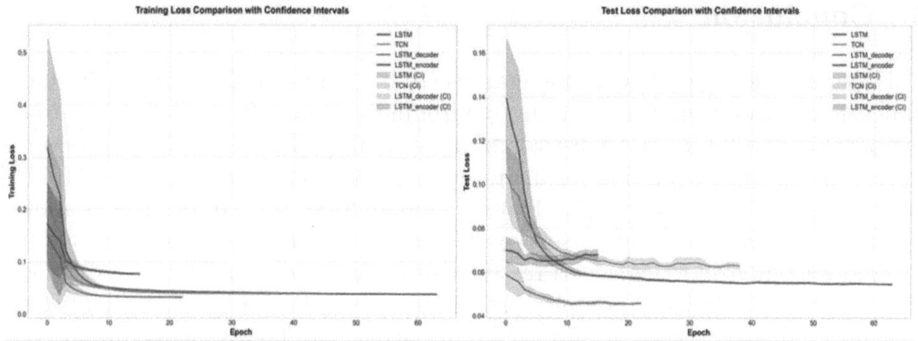

(a) Training Loss Curves (a) Testing Loss Curves

Fig. 3. The training and testing curves of different models.

4.3 Performance with and Without Evolution

To investigate the impact of the presence or absence of the "evolution" mechanism on the pose prediction accuracy and dynamic response capabilities of the digital twin model for UAVs, we conducted sequence prediction for the UAV's six degrees of freedom (Pitch, Roll, Yaw, x, y, z) under two conditions: without the evolution mechanism and with the evolution mechanism introduced. In Fig. 4, it can be observed that the model's prediction ability is significantly improved after introducing the evolution mechanism. The predicted curves for all degrees of freedom (red lines) fit the true curves (blue lines) much more closely—not only do the overall trends match, but the response to dynamic changes and sharp turns is more accurate and timely.

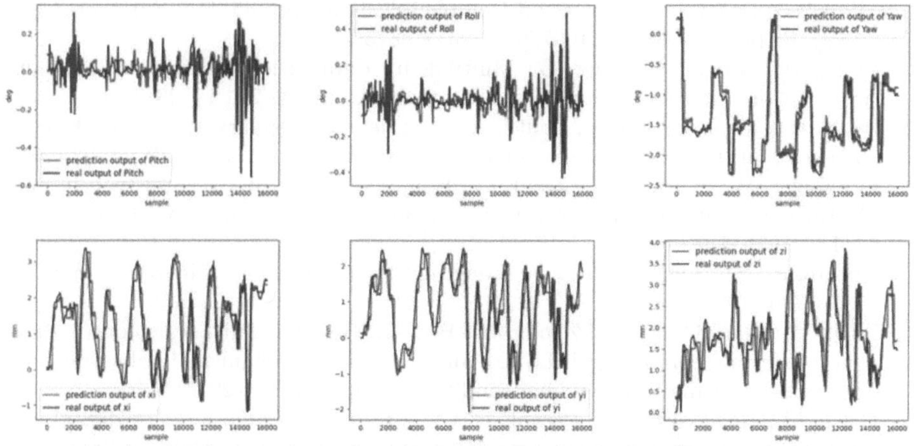

Fig. 4. UAV pose prediction with evolution.

5 Conclusion

This paper addresses key challenges faced by digital twin systems in high-dimensional and complex dynamic environments, namely modeling accuracy, temporal dependency, and trustworthy adaptability. To this end, we propose a reliable evolutionary method for digital twins, based on the integration of LSTM networks with a Decoder-Only Transformer architecture. While the proposed approach demonstrates promising performance in terms of modeling capability and system robustness, certain limitations remain: (1) The overall model architecture is relatively complex, resulting in higher computational resource consumption compared to traditional approaches. (2) The trustworthiness metrics and evolution-triggering strategies utilized in this study are primarily based on statistical indicators such as mean squared error; the responsive capacity of trustworthy evolution under complex fault patterns or non-Gaussian distributions requires further enhancement. (3) Experimental validation has thus far been primarily focused on UAV trajectory data, so the generalizability and cross-domain applicability of the model need to be further verified and extended across a broader range of practical scenarios and engineering objects.

Acknowledgment. This work is supported by the National Natural Science Foundation of China [Grant No. 62373026] and the Fundamental Research Funds for the Central Universities.

References

1. Grieves, M., Vickers, J.: Digital twin: mitigating unpredictable, undesirable emergent behavior in complex systems. In: Kahlen, F.-J., Flumerfelt, S., Alves, A. (eds.) Transdisciplinary Perspectives on Complex Systems, pp. 85–113. Springer, Cham (2017). https://doi.org/10.1007/978-3-319-38756-7_4
2. Wang, H., Song, X., Zhang, C.: Multifidelity data fusion mechanism for digital twins via the internet of things. IEEE Internet Comput. **29**, 16–23 (2025)
3. Längkvist, M., Karlsson, L., Loutfi, A.: A review of unsupervised feature learning and deep learning for time-series modeling. Pattern Recogn. Lett. **42**, 11–24 (2014)
4. Kritzinger, W., Karner, M., Traar, G., Henjes, J., Sihn, W.: Digital twin in manufacturing: a categorical literature review and classification. IFAC-PapersOnline **51**(11), 1016–1022 (2018)
5. Hochreiter, S., Schmidhuber, J.: Long short-term memory. Neural Comput. **9**, 1735–1780 (1997)
6. Zhao, D., Tian, C., Fu, Z., Zhong, Y., Hou, J., He, W.: Multi scale convolutional neural network combining BiLSTM and attention mechanism for bearing fault diagnosis under multiple working conditions. Sci. Rep. **15** (2025)
7. Dietz, M., Reichvilser, T., Pernul, G.: A data-driven framework for digital twin creation in industrial environments. IEEE Access **12**, 93294–93304 (2024)
8. Guo, H., et al.: Lightweight compressed temporal and compressed spatial attention with augmentation fusion in remaining useful life prediction. In: IECON 2023- 49th Annual Conference of the IEEE Industrial Electronics Society, pp. 1–6 (2023)

9. Wen, J., Kang, J., Niyato, D.T., Zhang, Y., Mao, S.: Sustainable diffusion-based incentive mechanism for generative AI-driven digital twins in industrial cyber-physical systems. IEEE Trans. Industr. Cyber-Phys. Syst. **3**, 139–149 (2024)
10. Maculotti, G., et al.: A shared metrological framework for trustworthy virtual experiments and digital twins. Metrology (2024)
11. Wang, K., Zhang, L., Jia, Z., Cheng, H., Han, L., Cui, J.: A framework and method for equipment digital twin dynamic evolution based on IExATCN. J. Intell. Manuf. **35**, 1571–1583 (2023)
12. Mohajerin, N., Mozifian, M., Waslander, S.L.: Deep learning a quadrotor dynamic model for multi-step prediction. In: 2018 IEEE International Conference on Robotics and Automation (ICRA), pp. 2454–2459 (2018)

Decentralised Blockchain Management Through Digital Twins

Georgios Diamantopoulos[1,2], Nikos Tziritas[3], Rami Bahsoon[2], and Georgios Theodoropoulos[1,4(✉)]

[1] Southern University of Science and Technology, Shenzhen, China
georgios@sustech.edu.cn
[2] University of Birmingham, Birmingham, UK
[3] University of Thessaly, Lamia, Greece
[4] Research Institute of Trustworthy Autonomous Systems, Shenzhen, China

Abstract. The necessity of blockchain systems to remain decentralised limits current solutions to blockchain governance and dynamic management, forcing a trade-off between control and decentralisation. In light of the above, this work proposes a dynamic and decentralised blockchain management mechanism based on digital twins. To ensure decentralisation, the proposed mechanism utilises multiple digital twins that the system's stakeholders control. To facilitate decentralised decision-making, the twins are organised in a secondary blockchain system that orchestrates agreement on, and propagation of decisions to the managed blockchain. This enables the management of blockchain systems without centralised control. A preliminary evaluation of the performance and impact of the overheads introduced by the proposed mechanism is conducted through simulation. The results demonstrate the proposed mechanism's ability to reach consensus on decisions quickly and reconfigure the primary blockchain with minimal overhead.

Keywords: Blockchain · Digital Twins · Blockchain Management · Blockchain Governance

1 Introduction

As blockchain matures, increasingly sophisticated applications are proposed to leverage its decentralisation, transparency, and security properties. With the advent of permissioned blockchain, the technology has found novel use cases beyond finance, providing the infrastructure for storing traceable and immutable records serving applications in IoT, supply chain management, e-governance, and more [1]. However, as the technology matures and blockchain applications evolve and scale, managing blockchain systems becomes challenging.

Blockchains are complex and dynamic systems that experience varying over their lifetime. Consequently, blockchain systems that are unable to adapt to such conditions dynamically are likely to experience periods of inefficiency.

W. Cai et al. (Eds.): AsiaSim 2025, CCIS 2727, pp. 90–101, 2026.
https://doi.org/10.1007/978-981-95-4472-1_8

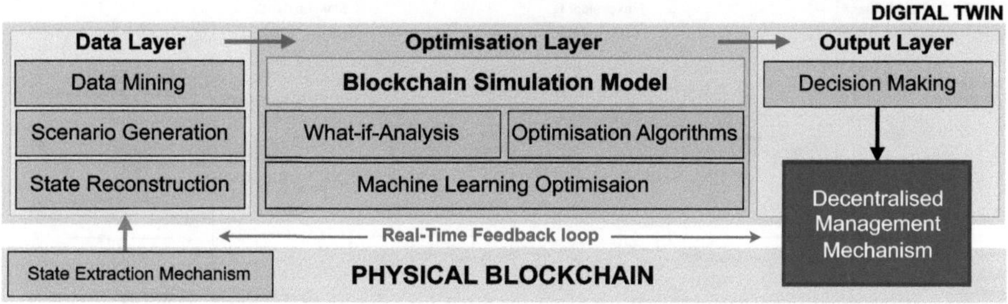

Fig. 1. Proposed digital twin architecture as conceptualised in [6]

This strongly motivates dynamic blockchain management and optimisation. However, blockchain systems rely on their decentralisation property to provide their core features (immutability, transparency and security) necessary for trust. This introduces a novel constraint to managing blockchain systems, maintaining decentralisation, which is not satisfied by traditional approaches [15].

Digital Twins [3] are identified as a promising technology for the problem of dynamic blockchain management and governance. In previous work, a dynamic digital twin architecture for managing blockchains was proposed, and a preliminary evaluation of its ability to manage blockchains was conducted [6,7]. A high-level architecture for blockchain digital twins is presented in Fig. 1. The system relies on a feedback loop between the blockchain and its Digital Twin. In [8] the physical-to-virtual direction of the loop was considered, namely extracting and synchronising the state of blockchain networks to update the model within the Digital Twin.

This paper focuses on closing the feedback loop, proposing a mechanism to implement the virtual-to-physical direction, updating the blockchain system based on the output of the Digital Twin. A core challenge of the above is ensuring that the mechanism does not introduce any centralisation into the blockchain system, as that could result in catastrophic damage. To this end, a mechanism utilising multiple digital twins controlled by the system's stakeholders is proposed. To facilitate agreement, the twins are organised in a secondary blockchain network, which orchestrates decentralised agreement on management decisions and their propagation to the managed blockchain system. The former is enabled by the consensus process and the latter through the resulting blockchain structure. Leveraging the power of digital twins organised in a blockchain network allows for granular control while maintaining decentralisation.

The paper structure follows: Sect. 2 presents the challenges and proposed solution to decentralised blockchain management. Section 3 presents the experimental setup and the evaluation results. Section 4 presents the relevant literature while Sect. 5 concludes this paper.

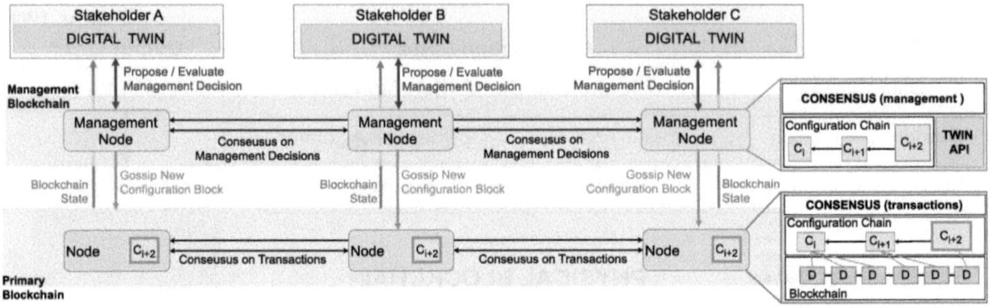

Fig. 2. A generic blockchain system managed by the proposed mechanism

2 A 'Blockchain-Based' Approach for Decentralised Blockchain Management

Any system designed to manage blockchains must ensure that the decentralisation of the managed system is not violated. In the context of digital twin-based blockchain management, this manifests as the problem of who controls the digital twin. Blockchain systems provide a decentralised, trusted platform to enable cooperation between a set of stakeholders. Thus, the stakeholders of the blockchain system must collectively steer the management process. This necessitates multiple digital twins to represent the system holders. However, the introduction of multiple twins gives rise to two core challenges: **i)** How can agreement on a global decision be reached while simultaneously tolerating possible Byzantine behaviour (a core assumption of blockchains)? **ii)** How can the agreed-upon decisions be applied to the primary blockchain in a decentralised manner while ensuring the resulting blockchain structure can remain verifiable?

A notable observation, that forms the basis of this work, is that blockchain systems are designed to address this set of problems. Blockchain enables decentralised Byzantine fault tolerance consensus while providing a traceable, immutable, and verifiable ledger that tracks the system's evolution. Inspired by the above, this work proposes a 'blockchain-based' approach to blockchain management that utilises a secondary blockchain system. Through this, the stakeholder-controlled digital twins can agree upon and propagate management decisions to the primary blockchain system. Specifically, the proposed architecture targets consortium blockchain systems [9]; permissioned blockchains instantiated by mutually untrusting entities to facilitate their cooperation.

2.1 Agreement

To ensure decentralised management, multiple twins representing the stakeholders of the primary blockchain must participate in the process, which creates an agreement problem. The proposed solution addresses this by organising digital twins in a secondary blockchain network called the 'management blockchain', which comprises 'management nodes'. Within this system, the management

Algorithm 1: Management Node Logic

Data: management node n, configuration block interval CBI, current cycle r

begin
- calculate proposer for r
- **if** *n is proposer* **then**
  - create and propose configuration block CB_r for cycle r
  - **if** *consensus reached* **then**
    - gossip signed CB_r
  - **else**
    - begin cycle $r + 1$
- **else**
  - wait for proposal (CB_r) or cycle timeout
  - **if** *CB_r is a valid under r* **then**
    - validate configuration included in CB_r and cast appropriate vote
  - **else**
    - begin cycle $r + 1$

nodes reach consensus on management decisions for the primary blockchain through the blockchain's consensus process. Drawing a parallel to traditional blockchain systems, the digital twins act as the application layer, while the management nodes provide them access to the blockchain network, enabling participation in the consensus process. Figure 2 depicts a generic blockchain system managed by the proposed mechanism.

To arrive at global decisions, a proposer digital twin computes and proposes a decision to the management blockchain through its local management node. This initiates a consensus round with the remaining twins acting as validators. Specifically, the proposer management node packs the decision of its digital twin in a configuration block before proposing it to the system. When acting as validators, management nodes use their respective digital twin to validate the proposed configuration blocks. Since blockchain consensus protocols are agnostic to the content of the blocks, any off-the-shelf protocol can be used. The use of Byzantine Fault Tolerant (BFT) protocols ensures that Byzantine behaviour from the twins can be tolerated.

The above process is governed by the configuration block interval (CBI) hyperparameter, which defines the minimum interval between two subsequent configuration blocks. This provides a mechanism to control rapid fluctuations between configurations, specifically designed to limit fluctuations under unstable conditions in the primary blockchain.

To fairly select proposers, a deterministic Tendermint-style proposer selection algorithm is used [2]. Given the hash of the latest configuration block (denoted as h_l), the next proposer can be computed as $p_{next} = h_l \mod |MN|$ where $|MN|$ is the number of management nodes. To handle offline or non-quorum proposers, the process is organised into proposal cycles (propose + vote). The

Algorithm 2: Node reconfiguration

Data: node index i, local management chain MC_i, height of active configuration block H^i_{cc}, gossiped configuration block CB_{new}, proposed data block B

begin
  while *active consensus round* **do**
    if *received valid* CB_{new} **then**
      gossip CB_{new} to peers
      if CB_{new} *is future* **then**
        request missing blocks
      else
        append CB_{new} to MC_i
    if *configuration of* $B \neq H^i_{cc}$ **then**
      B is invalid
  after consensus round ends (success or fail)
  wait for any missing blocks
  if *new configuration blocks in* MC_i **then**
    update to configuration in latest block
    $H^i_{cc} \leftarrow MC_i[last]$.height
  start next round according to H^i_{cc}

agreement process triggered by the CBI allows up to $|M_N|$ cycles. The proposer selection is modified to $p_{next} = (h_l + FC) \pmod{|M_N|}$, where FC is the number of failed cycles since the CBI. This guarantees that if a quorum exists, a live quorum member will get to propose a configuration block. Algorithm 1 presents the agreement process in a structured manner.

Configuration Block Structure: The configuration blocks of the management blockchain contain system configurations. Specifically, a configuration block at height i (CB_i) contains the following:

$$CB_i = \{H_i, H_{i-1}, P, C^{prim}, proof, height\}$$

where H_i, H_{i-1} are the current and previous configuration block hashes, P is the block proposer, C is the proposed configuration, and $proof$ a proof that consensus was reached. The definition of a configuration C is specific to the application and therefore outside the scope. In general, the configuration of a blockchain system refers to configurable parameters or settings that define its operation. Examples include consensus mechanisms and their parameters (e.g., block interval, validator set), peer discovery, node roles, smart contract upgrade policies, and network topology, among other aspects.

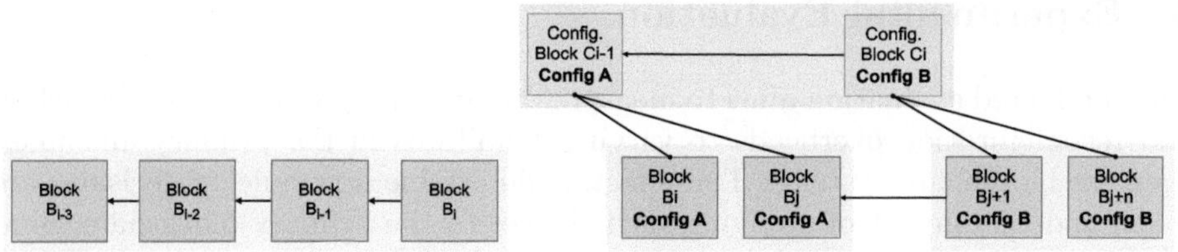

(a) Traditional Blockchain Structure (b) Managed Blockchain structure

Fig. 3. Differences between a traditional blockchain structure and the proposed digital twin-managed blockchain structure.

2.2 Reconfiguration

Once agreement is reached, the scope shifts to the primary blockchain, where the agreed-upon configuration must be verified by the primary nodes and applied. To allow this, the primary blockchain nodes participate in the management blockchain as observer nodes; nodes that do not participate in the consensus process but are aware of the management nodes and keep an up-to-date copy of the blockchain structure (see Fig. 2). Giving primary nodes the ability to see and verify configuration blocks enables the configuration of the primary blockchain to be controlled by the management blockchain structure. Specifically, the latest configuration block controls the active configuration of the primary blockchain. To avoid new configuration blocks from disrupting ongoing consensus in the primary blockchain, reconfiguration is only allowed between consensus rounds. Algorithm 2 showcases the reconfiguration logic.

2.3 Verifiability

A fundamental blockchain property and an enabler of blockchain's trust model is verifiability. Blockchain systems achieve verifiability by maintaining a decentralised, immutable, and back-linked list of blocks that contain cryptographic signatures and proofs. This enables nodes to individually verify the system's state by rebuilding it block by block, checking that each block includes valid signatures and a correct reference to the latest block.

In a reconfigurable blockchain system, the configuration details must be known to allow for validation (active validator list, consensus protocol, block size, etc.). The management blockchain offers a natural solution to the problem of block verification, as all past system configurations are stored in an equally immutable and verifiable blockchain structure. Linking transaction blocks to configuration blocks ensures the configuration details remain immutably linked to the block, allowing future verification. Figure 3 showcases the differences between a traditional blockchain structure and the proposed structure. Furthermore, the links between transaction blocks and the management blockchain structure enable nodes to validate whether newly proposed transaction blocks adhere to the latest configuration.

3 Experimental Evaluation

The conducted evaluation aims to measure the sensitivity of management delays and reconfiguration overheads to varying conditions in the primary and management blockchain systems. These factors determine how quickly decisions are taken and the impact of applying such choices to the primary blockchain. Simulation was used to provide the experimental platform for the above evaluation. The proposed mechanism was implemented by modifying the SymbChainSim blockchain simulation [4,5]. Specifically, an API was implemented to allow the simulated management blockchain to interface with the simulated primary blockchain. The API allowed the primary blockchain to request the simulation of a consensus round in the management blockchain and receive the resulting configuration block along with its associated delay. A gossip event containing the new configuration block is then injected into the primary blockchain simulation at the appropriate time to simulate the propagation of the configuration block along the primary blockchain nodes.

Experimental Set-Up: The experimental setup consists of a primary blockchain system comprising 32 nodes connected to 16 random peers over network links, forming a peer-to-peer (P2P) network. The bandwidths of the links are dictated by a normal distribution with $\mu = 10MB/s$ and $\sigma = 0.5MB/s$ (sampled per message), and the latency is dictated by their geographical distance (calculated based on [11] and randomly assigned geographical locations). The management blockchain configuration consists of 16 nodes randomly drawn from the 32 primary blockchain nodes at the start of the simulation. The consensus protocol utilised by both blockchain networks is PBFT. The maximum allowed block size for transaction blocks is $1MB$, and the block interval is set to $0.1s$. The configuration block size is $0.25MB$. The CBI was drawn from a normal distribution ($\mu = 30s, \sigma = 5s$) over 1 hour-long simulations. To eliminate noise, the produced configuration blocks always contained the same configuration. In the following experiments, only the parameter under examination varies. This baseline configuration serves as a constant reference for the observation of relative fluctuations in response to changes in system conditions.

3.1 Evaluation of the Management Delays

The management delay measures the interval between the CBI and the resulting management decisions being reflected in the primary blockchain. In the proposed mechanism, this delay can be broken down into three phases: agreement, propagation, and update. Agreement delay refers to the time required for the management nodes to reach a consensus on a decision. Propagation delay refers to the time needed for the produced configuration block to arrive at the primary blockchain system nodes. Finally, update delay refers to the time between a primary node receiving a new configuration block and the time required to update its local configuration to reflect the contents of that configuration block. The propagation and update phases need only take place on $2f + 1$ nodes for

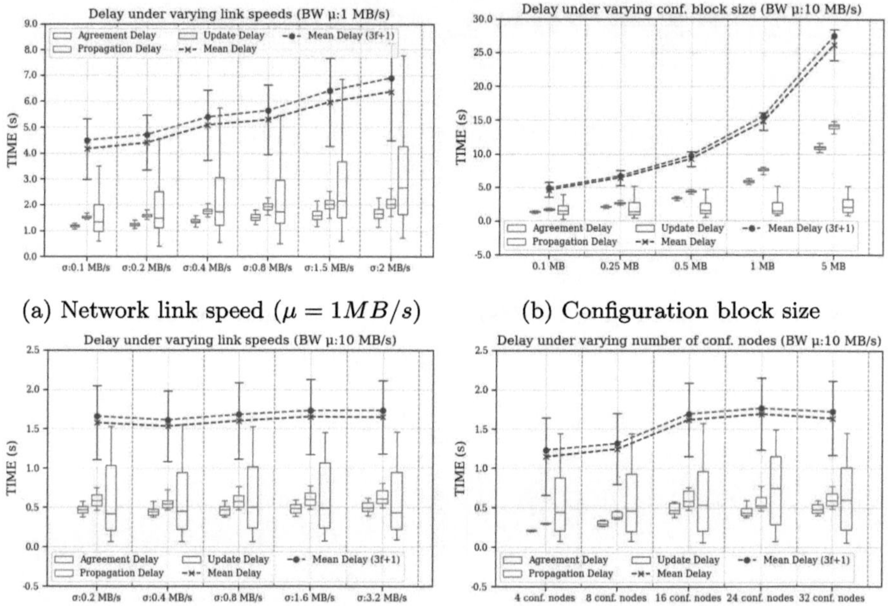

(a) Network link speed ($\mu = 1MB/s$) (b) Configuration block size

(c) Network link speed ($\mu = 10MB/s$) (d) Number of configuration nodes

Fig. 4. Evaluation of management delays

the system to start functioning under the new configuration. Consequently, the following results present the delays as observed on the fastest $2f + 1$ nodes for each configuration block.

Figures 4a and 4c show that the impact of varying link bandwidth is pronounced when the mean link bandwidth is low, with the effects concentrated on update delays. This phenomenon is attributed to the fact that high variation in link performance leads to uneven dissemination of information, that is, some nodes receive information faster than others. This effect can compound and result in a 'split' network where nodes with faster links update their configuration earlier than others. The effect was not observed in the case of higher mean bandwidth (Fig. 4c), which diminishes the impact of variations.

Finally, Figs. 4b and 4d evaluate the effect of parameters related to the management blockchain. The results show that the size of the configuration block has a pronounced effect on the agreement and propagation delay, but has little impact on the update delay. This is expected as larger blocks increase the size of the network messages that are necessary to facilitate agreement and, of course, propagate the block to the primary blockchain. The number of configuration nodes, on the other hand, has little effect on the reconfiguration delay. This is a positive observation as systems with numerous stakeholders can adopt this approach without worry about increased decision overheads.

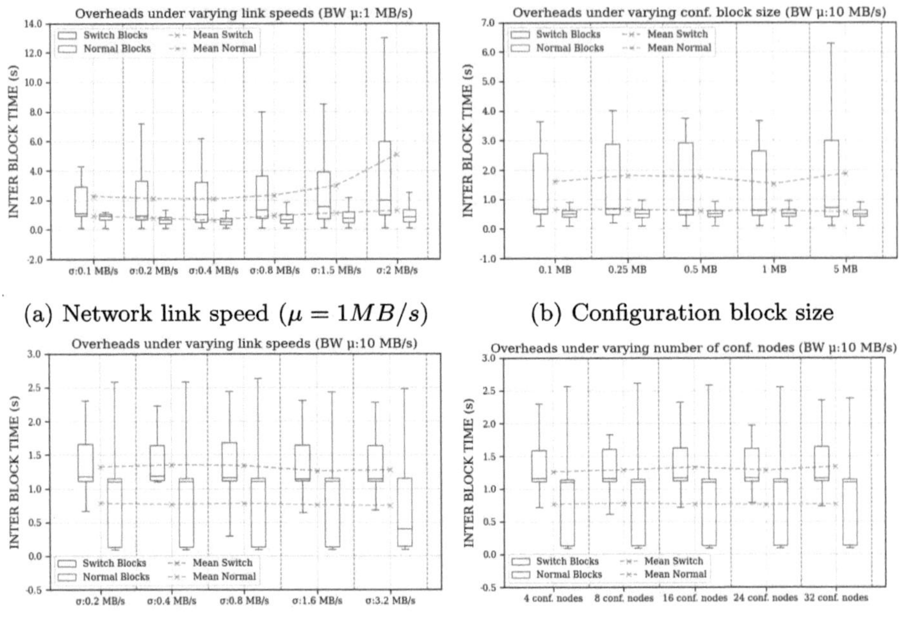

(a) Network link speed ($\mu = 1MB/s$) (b) Configuration block size

(c) Network link speed ($\mu = 10MB/s$) (d) Number of configuration nodes

Fig. 5. Evaluation of the impact on the primary blockchain (overhead)

3.2 Evaluation of the Reconfiguration Overheads

Besides the management delay, another critical factor to consider is the impact of the dynamic management process on the primary blockchain system. Due to the nature of reconfiguration, overheads are contained in the interval between two sequential transaction blocks produced under different configurations. Intuitively, this is the case because blocks produced before that were created under the old configuration, and later blocks will be made under the new configuration. Thus, measuring the overhead of reconfiguration can be effectively captured by comparing the inter-block times between sequential blocks under the same configuration (normal blocks) to those of sequential blocks under different configurations (switch blocks). The observed differences in duration constitute the reconfiguration overhead.

The reconfiguration overheads appear to be less sensitive to the same system parameters as compared to the management delays (Figs. 5a, 5c, 5b, 5d). This observation suggests that the effects of reconfigurations have minimal impact on the operation of the primary blockchain system. It is worth noting that the above overheads are in the context of the CBI, meaning they are only incurred once each time the management blockchain produces a new configuration block. Another interesting phenomenon is that, in most observations, the median switch block delay is close to the median delay of normal blocks (denoted by the bar inside the box component of the box plots). This demonstrates that most reconfiguration operations added minimal overheads, with the observed difference in the mean being attributed to outliers. This behaviour can be exploited to allow timing reconfiguration operations to minimise overhead.

4 Related Work

The problems of dynamic blockchain management and governance have been gaining traction in the blockchain literature. As dynamic systems, blockchains stand to benefit significantly from dynamic optimisation as it directly leads to improved performance and quality of service. Furthermore, as blockchain establishes itself as a mainstream technology, combined with its integration in critical applications, the need for novel governance mechanisms suitable for blockchain systems has become increasingly vital.

Dynamic Blockchain Optimisation: One of the most influential works in dynamic blockchain optimisation/management is [14], which proposes a reinforcement learning-based approach for dynamic adaptation of a blockchain system's consensus protocol, block size and block interval to improve performance under varying system conditions. However, despite the impressive results exhibited by the above mechanisms, the challenge of integrating these dynamic decisions into the blockchain system in a decentralised manner was not addressed. Furthermore, previous work [6,8], conducted by the authors, has also showcased the performance benefits of a digital twin-managed blockchain, including improved transaction latency, transaction throughput, and block times. However, these experiments were also performed under a centralised management model. In conclusion, the challenge of decentralised blockchain management remains an open problem in the blockchain literature and constitutes the main challenge addressed by this work.

Decentralised Blockchain Governance: Updating blockchain systems in a way that maintains decentralisation is also a core challenge in the blockchain governance literature. Current approaches to blockchain governance can be categorised into two major categories: on-chain and off-chain (these approaches are explained in detail in [16]). On-chain approaches rely on hard-coded rules within the blockchain network, typically in the form of smart contracts. Although decentralised, on-chain solutions offer limited control. On the other hand, off-chain solutions rely on external platforms, through which the community system stakeholders can propose and discuss changes. Although off-chain approaches can control most aspects of a blockchain system, the decentralisation of off-chain solutions is often poor and hard to verify. Furthermore, agreed-upon changes are slow to reflect in the blockchain system. To this end, the proposed mechanism can offer both the flexibility of off-chain approaches, with the decentralisation guarantees of on-chain solutions, while additionally enabling automated decision-making powered by the digital twin.

Multiple Blockchain Structures: Ideas utilising multiple blockchain data structures have been explored in the blockchain literature; however, existing approaches focus on either increasing security by storing sensitive data into a separate blockchain [13] or enhancing the system's performance by balancing transaction processing across multiple chains [17]. Furthermore, the proposed mechanism fundamentally differs from layer-two protocols [12] and side-chains [10]. Specifically, layer-two protocols explore ways to utilise external mechanisms to improve blockchain systems while relying on the consensus protocol of the primary blockchain system itself. In contrast, the proposed mechanism is a fully featured blockchain network with a separate consensus protocol. On the other hand, side-chains focus on methods for securely sharing value (such as tokens or coins) between existing blockchain networks that serve different underlying applications. To the best of our knowledge, the proposed solution is the first to suggest a secondary blockchain layer utilised for dynamic blockchain management.

5 Conclusion

This work presents a 'blockchain-based' decentralised blockchain management mechanism based on digital twins, completing the feedback loop of blockchain digital twins. The basis of this work is that a blockchain-based approach to blockchain management can inherently satisfy all requirements for decentralised blockchain management. The proposed mechanism thus revolves around a secondary management blockchain network whose participants are the digital twins controlled by the system stakeholders. The management blockchain implements a consensus process to reach agreement on new system configurations driven by the decisions of the digital twins. To reflect these decisions in the primary blockchain, the nodes of the primary blockchain participate as observer nodes in the management blockchain, keeping an up-to-date version of its blockchain structure. Thus, the active configuration in the primary blockchain can be dictated by the latest block in the management blockchain. An experimental evaluation of a simulated blockchain system assessed the sensitivity of reconfiguration delay and overheads to various system conditions. The results of the experimental evaluation showed that the management blockchain can produce configuration blocks quickly, while the overhead of switching configuration observed in the primary blockchain remains minimal.

Acknowledgments. This research was supported by: Research Institute of Trustworthy Autonomous Systems, Southern University of Science and Technology, Shenzhen 518055, China; Program for Guangdong Introducing Innovative and Entrepreneurial Teams under Grant 2017ZT07X386; SUSTech-University of Birmingham Collaborative PhD Programme.

References

1. Amiri, M.J., Agrawal, D., El Abbadi, A.: Permissioned blockchains: properties, techniques and applications. In: Proceedings of the 2021 International Conference on Management of Data, pp. 2813–2820 (2021)
2. Buchman, E.: Tendermint: byzantine fault tolerance in the age of blockchains. Ph.D. thesis, University of Guelph (2016)
3. Buscher, V.: Digital twin towards a meaningful framework. Arup, Foresight, Research and Innovation (2019)
4. Diamantopoulos, G., Bahsoon, R., Tziritas, N., Theodoropoulos, G.: SymBChainSim: a novel simulation tool for dynamic and adaptive blockchain management and its trilemma tradeoff. In: Proceedings of the 2023 ACM SIGSIM Conference on Principles of Advanced Discrete Simulation, pp. 118–127 (2023)
5. Diamantopoulos, G., Bahsoon, R., Tziritas, N., Theodoropoulos, G.: SymBChainSim: a novel simulation system for info-symbiotic blockchain management. ACM Trans. Model. Comput. Simul. **35**(2), 1–25 (2025)
6. Diamantopoulos, G., Tziritas, N., Bahsoon, R., Theodoropoulos, G.: Digital twins for dynamic management of blockchain systems. In: 2022 Winter Simulation Conference (WSC), pp. 2876–2887. IEEE (2022)
7. Diamantopoulos, G., Tziritas, N., Bahsoon, R., Theodoropoulos, G.: Dynamic data-driven digital twins for blockchain systems. In: International Conference on Dynamic Data Driven Applications Systems, pp. 283–292. Springer (2022)
8. Diamantopoulos, G., Tziritas, N., Bahsoon, R., Zhang, N., Theodoropoulos, G.: Dynamic digital twins of blockchain systems: state extraction and mirroring. arXiv preprint arXiv:2412.05527 (2024)
9. Dib, O., Brousmiche, K.L., Durand, A., Thea, E., Hamida, E.B.: Consortium blockchains: overview, applications and challenges. Int. J. Adv. Telecommun **11**(1), 51–64 (2018)
10. Garoffolo, A., Viglione, R.: Sidechains: decoupled consensus between chains. arXiv preprint arXiv:1812.05441 (2018)
11. Goonatilake, R., Bachnak, R.A.: Modeling latency in a network distribution. Netw. Commun. Technol. **1**(2), 1 (2012)
12. Gudgeon, L., Moreno-Sanchez, P., Roos, S., McCorry, P., Gervais, A.: SoK: layer-two blockchain protocols. In: Bonneau, J., Heninger, N. (eds.) FC 2020. LNCS, vol. 12059, pp. 201–226. Springer, Cham (2020). https://doi.org/10.1007/978-3-030-51280-4_12
13. Kan, L., Wei, Y., Muhammad, A.H., Siyuan, W., Gao, L.C., Kai, H.: A multiple blockchains architecture on inter-blockchain communication. In: 2018 IEEE International Conference on Software Quality, Reliability and Security Companion (QRS-C), pp. 139–145. IEEE (2018)
14. Liu, M., et al.: Performance optimization for blockchain-enabled industrial internet of things (IIoT) systems: a deep reinforcement learning approach. IEEE Trans. Industr. Inform. **15**(6), 3559–3570 (2019)
15. Lumineau, F., Wang, W., Schilke, O.: Blockchain governance–a new way of organizing collaborations? Organ. Sci. **32**(2), 500–521 (2021)
16. Reijers, W., et al.: Now the code runs itself: on-chain and off-chain governance of blockchain technologies. Topoi **40**(4), 821–831 (2021)
17. Sohan, M.S.H., Mahmud, M., Sikder, M.B., Hossain, F.S., Hasan, M.R.: Increasing throughput and reducing storage bloating problem using IPFs and dual-blockchain method. In: 2021 2nd International Conference on Robotics, Electrical and Signal Processing Techniques (ICREST), pp. 732–736. IEEE (2021)

Implicit Neural Representation for DEM Super-Resolution in Vehicle Motion Simulation

Guoqing Hou, Shuaibo Wang, Ni Li(✉), Guanghong Gong, and Bo Tian

School of Automation Science and Electrical Engineering, Beihang University, Beijing 100191, China
lini@buaa.edu.cn

Abstract. High-resolution digital elevation models (DEMs) are essential for accurate vehicle motion simulation, yet are costly to obtain and store. We propose a DEM super-resolution method based on a coordinate-based multilayer perceptron (MLP), which represents elevation as a continuous function over spatial coordinates. A hypernetwork predicts the parameters of the MLP from low-resolution inputs, enabling direct querying of elevation and slope values at arbitrary locations via automatic differentiation. To enhance terrain detail reconstruction, we incorporate periodic activation functions and terrain-aware loss functions, including slope and frequency-domain components. Experimental results show that the proposed method outperforms bicubic interpolation in both elevation and slope prediction, while reducing memory usage to just 14.9% of explicit DEM storage. Furthermore, it enables efficient end-to-end generation of a parameterized MLP. We further demonstrate its integration into a vehicle simulation system, where the continuous and differentiable terrain model significantly improves simulation realism. The proposed method is compact, accurate, and easily deployable in real-time terrain-aware applications.

Keywords: DEM Super-resolution · Implicit Neural Representation · Vehicle Motion Simulation

1 Introduction

Digital Elevation Models (DEMs) are widely used to represent terrain surfaces in a raster-based format and serve as essential input for various geospatial applications such as vehicle motion simulation. The resolution of DEMs directly impacts the accuracy of such tasks. However, high-resolution (HR) DEMs are often difficult to obtain due to sensor limitations and acquisition costs. To address this, many DEM super-resolution (SR) methods have been developed. DEMs have a similar data structure with images, where each cell in the DEM raster can be viewed as a pixel. Therefore, many image SR methods can be directly applied to DEMs. Recently, inspired by the success of deep learning-based image SR techniques [1, 2], a number of DEM SR methods have been proposed [3–6] with improved performance.

W. Cai et al. (Eds.): AsiaSim 2025, CCIS 2727, pp. 102–114, 2026.
https://doi.org/10.1007/978-981-95-4472-1_9

In vehicle motion simulation, elevation and slope values at arbitrary positions are frequently required for accurate dynamic modeling. Raster-based DEM requires interpolation and finite-difference approximations to estimate such parameters, which introduces errors and computational overhead. However, most existing DEM SR methods generate discrete 2D raster arrays, facing two limitations in vehicle motion simulation: (1) high memory cost due to resolution scaling; (2) lack of support for continuous slope and elevation queries without interpolation. Inspired by implicit neural representations (INR), we propose a DEM SR framework that models HR DEM as a continuous function of spatial coordinates using a coordinate-based MLP. This compact representation supports direct querying of elevation and slope via automatic differentiation. A hypernetwork with an encoder–decoder architecture generates the MLP parameters from low-resolution (LR) DEM inputs in an end-to-end manner.

The proposed method achieves higher accuracy than bicubic interpolation in both elevation and slope prediction, while reducing memory usage than storing full-resolution DEM. Furthermore, the proposed method enables efficient end-to-end generation of a parameterized MLP which enables continuous and differentiable queries of DEM and is validated in the vehicle motion simulation system, where it enhances simulation accuracy.

The main contributions of this paper are as follows:

1. We propose an end-to-end DEM SR method combining a hypernetwork and a coordinate-based MLP, which enables continuous DEM representation and direct querying of elevation and slope at arbitrary positions.
2. We improve the coordinate-based MLP expressiveness by modifying its activation function and introducing terrain-aware loss functions.
3. We conduct extensive experiments to validate the proposed method, demonstrating its effectiveness in vehicle motion simulation.

2 Related Work

2.1 INR

Recent advances in INR have enabled the modeling of spatially continuous signals by using parameterized coordinate-based MLPs [7–9]. Unlike traditional discrete signal representations, INR represents signals as continuous functions offering several advantages, such as resolution independence, memory compactness, and differentiability. This method has proven effective in 3D shape modeling, scene representation, and 2D image fitting [10]. In image SR, the Local Implicit Image Function (LIIF) [11] enables arbitrary-scale SR by mapping spatial coordinates to pixel values using latent codes. Building on this idea, many subsequent methods have enhanced image SR performance [12–14].

The proposed method builds on this idea, using coordinate-based MLPs to represent DEMs, and introduces a hypernetwork [15, 16] to generate MLP parameters conditioned on LR DEM, providing a more efficient solution compared to traditional INR-based DEM SR methods.

2.2 DEM SR

Due to the structural similarity between DEMs and images, many DEM SR methods have adopted image SR methods, achieving better performance than traditional interpolation methods such as bicubic interpolation [17–19]. However, DEMs differ from RGB images in having unbounded elevation values and more complex topographic structures. Several recent methods have explicitly addressed these differences. For example, TfaSR [4] leverages terrain feature extraction through deformable convolutions, and TTSR [6] employs a Transformer-based architecture for terrain feature extraction. Despite their success, these methods still generate discrete raster outputs, requiring significant memory to store HR DEMs. They also have limited flexibility when querying terrain derivatives like slope at arbitrary locations. EBCF [5], inspired by LIIF, proposes a more efficient and scalable solution by learning latent codes from LR DEMs. However, it requires precomputing separate latent codes for each LR DEM, and lacks direct support for slope computation.

In contrast, the proposed method uses a lightweight coordinate-based MLP to represent the HR DEM, enabling efficient elevation queries and direct computation of slope.

3 INR Based DEM SR

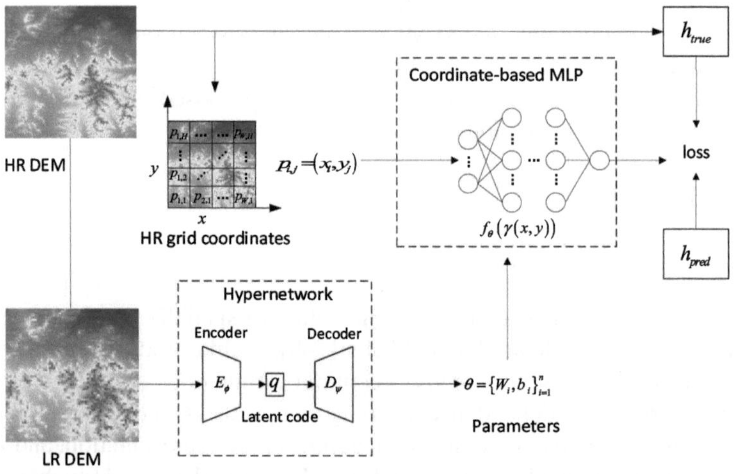

Fig. 1. Overview of the proposed INR-based DEM SR method.

We propose an INR-based model for DEM SR. An overview of the proposed framework is shown in Fig. 1. The framework consists of two main components: the hypernetwork and the coordinate-based MLP. The hypernetwork takes LR DEM as input and generates the parameters for the coordinate-based MLP, which represents the HR DEM as a continuous elevation function. The HR grid coordinates of the DEM are extracted from the HR DEM. These coordinates are used as inputs to the coordinate-based MLP.

3.1 Model Formulation

In most existing DEM SR methods, querying the elevation at any location requires accessing the entire HR DEM. In contrast, our proposed INR-based method treats the DEM as a continuous function $f : \mathbb{R}^2 \rightarrow \mathbb{R}$, which maps 2D spatial coordinates to corresponding elevation values. Specifically, this function can be expressed as:

$$f_\theta(x, y) = h \tag{1}$$

where h is elevation value corresponding to the 2D spatial coordinate (x, y), f_θ is a parameterized coordinate-based MLP.

Our objective is to learn an end-to-end mapping from a LR DEM to the parameters of a coordinate-based MLP. As shown in Fig. 1, the proposed method is based on a hypernetwork with an encoder–decoder architecture. Where the coordinate-based MLP serves as the target network of the hypernetwork. The hypernetwork can be formally expressed as:

$$q = E_\phi(I) \tag{2}$$

$$\theta = D_\psi(q) \tag{3}$$

where $I \in \mathbb{R}^{h \times w}$ is the input LR DEM, E_ϕ is the encoder with learnable parameters ϕ, $q \in \mathbb{R}^m$ is the latent code, D_ψ is the decoder with learnable parameters ψ, $\theta = \{W_i, b_i\}_{i=1}^n$ are the parameters of the MLP, W_i, b_i are the weight matrix and bias vector of the i-th layer, respectively, and n is the total number of layers in the MLP.

The encoder takes a LR DEM as input and generates a latent code. This latent code is then passed to the decoder, which generate the parameters of the coordinate-based MLP. The hypernetwork shares parameters, enabling it to generate corresponding MLP parameters for each input LR DEM. Detailed architecture of the coordinate-based MLP and hypernetwork is provided in Sects. 3.2 and 3.3.

3.2 Coordinate-Based MLP

By leveraging automatic differentiation, the first-order derivatives of the coordinate-based MLP output with respect to the input coordinates can be efficiently computed. Slope corresponds to the first-order derivative of elevation. Unlike conventional MLPs, Sitzmann et al. [7] demonstrated that periodic functions such as sine allow for more accurate signal representation and precise modeling of derivatives. We adopt this principle and construct the MLP using sine activations in layers. To further enhance frequency support and gradient stability, we replace the sine activation function in the first layer with the hyperbolic periodic activation sin(sinh(2x)) proposed in H-SIREN [20]. The architecture of the final coordinate-based MLP is illustrated in Fig. 2.

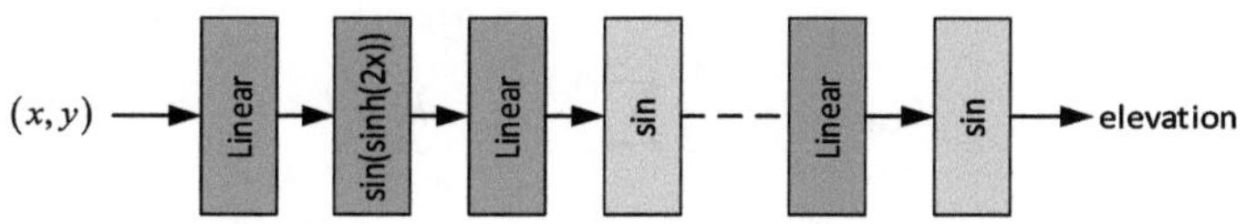

Fig. 2. Architecture of the coordinate-based MLP.

3.3 Hypernetwork

As mentioned above, the hypernetwork, consisting of an encoder and a decoder, is used to generate the parameters of the coordinate-based MLP. The encoder is used to extract the latent code from the input LR DEM, serving as a feature extraction module. To enhance the modeling of spatial dependencies, we adopt a Transformer-based encoder built upon the SwinIR [2], which has demonstrated strong performance in image SR tasks. The detailed structure is shown in Fig. 3.

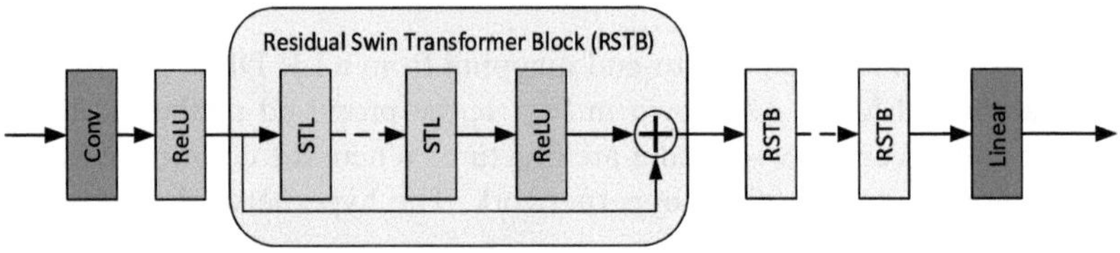

Fig. 3. Transformer-based encoder, STL refers to the Swin Transformer Layer [2].

In the encoder, a final linear layer projects the spatial feature map to a scalar representation, ensuring that the dimensionality of the latent code matches the channel dimension of the output feature map. The decoder takes this fixed-dimensional latent code as input and comprises multiple lightweight MLPs. Each MLP corresponds to one layer in the coordinate-based MLP and generates its associated weight and bias parameters, as illustrated in Fig. 4.

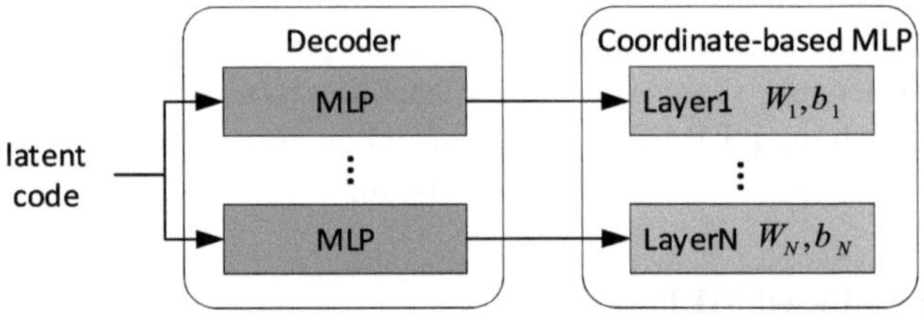

Fig. 4. Structure of the decoder. W_i, b_i are the parameter of the i-th layer.

3.4 Loss Function

As shown in the Fig. 1, the coordinate-based MLP predicts elevation values at the HR coordinate grid positions, which are then reshaped and compared with ground truth to compute the loss. Loss function consists of three components: content loss L_{content} to improve global elevation accuracy, slope loss L_{slope} to preserve local topographic gradients, and frequency-domain loss $L_{\text{frequency}}$ to enhance high-frequency detail reconstruction. The content loss and terrain slope loss, both formulated as mean squared error (MSE), are defined as follows:

$$L_{\text{content}} = \frac{1}{N}\sum\nolimits_{i}^{N}\left(h_i - \widehat{h}_i\right)^2 \tag{4}$$

$$L_{\text{slope}} = \frac{1}{N} \sum\nolimits_{i}^{N} \left(s_i - \hat{s}_i\right)^2 \tag{5}$$

where N is number of DEM cells, h_i and $\widehat{h_i}$ denotes the predicted and true elevation values respectively, s_i and $\hat{s}_i$ denote the slope values of SR DEM and the ground-truth HR DEM respectively. The terrain slope $s_{i,j}$ of cell (i, j) can be computed using finite difference approximation as follows:

$$dx_{i,j} = \frac{\left[h_{i-1,j+1} + 2h_{i,j+1} + h_{i+1,j+1} - h_{i-1,j-1} - 2h_{i,j-1} - h_{i+1,j-1}\right]}{(8r)} \tag{6}$$

$$dy_{i,j} = \frac{\left[h_{i+1,j-1} + 2h_{i+1,j} + h_{i+1,j+1} - h_{i-1,j-1} - 2h_{i-1,j} - h_{i-1,j+1}\right]}{(8r)} \tag{7}$$

$$s_{i,j} = \arctan\sqrt{dx^2 + dy^2} \tag{8}$$

where $h_{i,j}$ denotes the elevation of cell (i, j), r denotes the spatial resolution of the DEM, $dx_{i,j}$ and $dy_{i,j}$ represent the slope components along the longitudinal and latitudinal directions at cell (i, j).

The frequency loss is defined as the MSE between the magnitudes of the Fast Fourier Transform (FFT) of the two DEMs:

$$L_{\text{frequency}} = \frac{1}{N} \left\| \text{FFT}(D) - \text{FFT}(\widehat{D}) \right\|^2 \tag{9}$$

where D and $\widehat{D}$ denote SR DEM and the ground-truth HR DEM, respectively.

The total loss is defined as follow:

$$L = L_{\text{content}} + \alpha L_{\text{slope}} + \beta L_{\text{frequency}} \tag{10}$$

where α and β are the weights of L_{slope} and $L_{\text{frequency}}$ respectively.

4 Experiments and Results

4.1 Experimental Setup

We conduct experiments on the TfaSR30 [4], which is collected from ten diverse regions covering plateau, mountainous, and basin areas. It contains a wide range of terrain features such as ridges, rivers, saddles, cliffs, and mountains. The dataset provides DEMs at a 30-m resolution, consisting of 25088 non-overlapping tiles for training and 6272 for testing, with each tile having a fixed size of 64 × 64. LR DEMs are generated by downsampling HR DEMs using the nearest-neighbor method.

Experiments are implemented on the PyTorch platform with a SR scale factor of 4. Both elevation values and the 2D spatial coordinates are normalized to the range (−1, 1) using min-max normalization. We use the ADAM optimizer with an initial learning rate of 0.0001. The model is trained for 500 epochs, and the learning rate is halved every 100 epochs. The weights of loss function are set as $\alpha = 0.5$ and $\beta = 0.2$.

The latent code dimension in the hypernetwork is set to 256. The encoder follows the same parameter configuration as proposed in the original SwinIR implementation. The decoder contains three hidden layers, each with 256 width. The coordinate-based MLP contains two hidden layers, the hidden layer width is set to 16. To evaluate DEM SR method, we calculate the root mean squared error (RMSE) for both elevation and slope.

$$\mathrm{RMSE} = \sqrt{\frac{\sum_{i=1}^{N}\left(O_i - \widehat{O}_i\right)^2}{N}} \tag{11}$$

where N is number of DEM cells, O_i and $\widehat{O}_i$ denotes the elevation or slope value in the generated SR DEM and the ground-truth HR DEM respectively. Note that lower RMSE means to better results.

4.2 Results

We first evaluate the SR performance of the proposed method in comparison with bicubic interpolation, SwinIR, TfaSR and EBCF. As shown in Table 1, EBCF achieves the best RMSE in both elevation and slope, while the proposed method clearly surpasses bicubic interpolation. The performance gap with dedicated SR methods is expected, as they are explicitly trained to learn mappings from low- to high-resolution DEM. Despite not achieving state-of-the-art accuracy, the proposed method offers distinct advantages in representation and applicability as further supported by the subsequent results.

The proposed method provides a continuous and differentiable elevation function via the coordinate-based MLP. Slope values can be computed using automatic differentiation rather than finite difference approximations. Figure 5 visualizes dx, dy and slope maps computed by automatic differentiation and finite difference, showing consistent results.

Table 1. Evaluation results of super-resolution performance.

	RMSE-Elevation (m)	RMSE-Slope (°)
Bicubic	4.7683	2.0021
SwinIR	1.6713	1.1853
TfaSR	1.5581	1.1318
EBCF	1.4735	1.1163
The proposed method	2.4091	1.6711

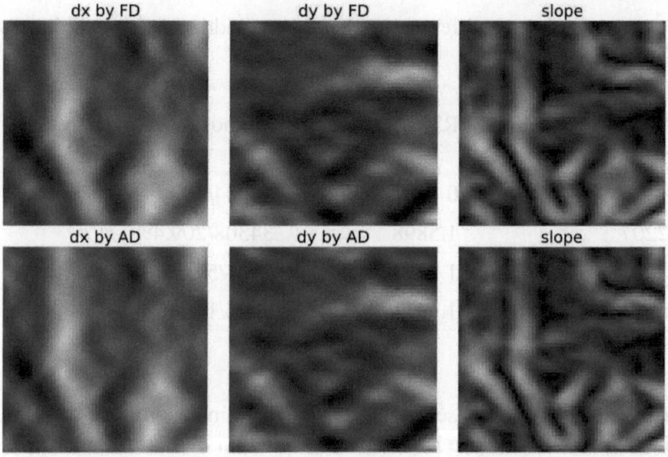

Fig. 5. The visualization of *dx dy* and slope. The first row shows the *dx*, *dy* and slope calculated by finite difference (FD). The second row shows the corresponding results of the SR DEM calculated by automatic differentiation (AD).

Another key advantage of the proposed method is memory efficiency. Since the DEM is represented by a coordinate-based MLP, the memory usage is determined by the network architecture. We compare the performance and memory footprint of three MLP configurations with different hidden layer widths (64, 32, and 16). As shown in Table 2, the model with a width of 16 requires only 14.9% of the memory compared to storing the full-resolution DEM, while maintaining comparable performance. Based on this trade-off, we adopt the MLP with a hidden layer width of 16 in the proposed method.

To further evaluate the advantages of our end-to-end method for generating coordinate-based MLPs, we compare it with two types of fitting-based baselines: (1) an MLP fitted to the ground-truth HR DEM, and (2) MLPs fitted to the SR DEMs generated by SwinIR, and TfaSR. Both MLPs are trained in a self-supervised manner using MSE loss for 1000 epochs with a learning rate of 0.0001. Their MLP settings are kept consistent with ours. As shown in Table 3, our proposed method achieves the lowest RMSE in both elevation and slope, outperforming the other fitted baselines. The SwinIR+MLP fitting exhibits the worst performance and also incurs significant computational overhead (6.112 ms for SR DEM generating and 1.22 s per-sample for MLP fitting), making it inefficient. In contrast, the proposed method directly generates the parameterized MLP from LR input in 8.134 ms, and completes full DEM generation (including MLP inference) in 8.463 ms. This highlights the advantages of the proposed method in both accuracy and efficiency.

Table 2. Evaluation results of different hidden layer widths. MLP-n indicates the feature dimensions of hidden layer is n.

	RMSE-Elevation (m)	RMSE-Slope (°)	Memory Size (Bytes)/Relative Memory (%)
HR DEM	0	0	16384/100%
MLP-64	2.2207	1.5898	34308/209.4%
MLP-32	2.3832	1.6373	8964/54.7%
MLP-16	2.4091	1.6711	2436/14.9%

Table 3. Comparison with fitting-based methods for generating coordinate-based MLPs. Metrics include accuracy (elevation and slope RMSE) and generation time.

	RMSE-Elevation (m)	RMSE-Slope (°)	SR DEM generate time	MLP parameter generate time per sample
HR DEM+MLP fitting	2.778	1.894	0 ms	1.22 s
Swinir+MLP fitting	3.243	2.096	6.112 ms	
TfaSR+MLP fitting	3.151	2.079	2.422 ms	
The proposed method	2.4091	1.6711	8.463 ms	8.134 ms

These results confirm that although the proposed method does not achieve the highest reconstruction accuracy, it offers a practical and efficient solution for vehicle motion simulation. By representing DEMs in a compact, continuous, and differentiable form, the proposed method enables accurate terrain interaction with low memory overhead, making it well-suited for integration into vehicle motion simulation systems.

5 Application in Vehicle Motion Simulation

5.1 Integration of DEM SR into Vehicle Motion Simulation

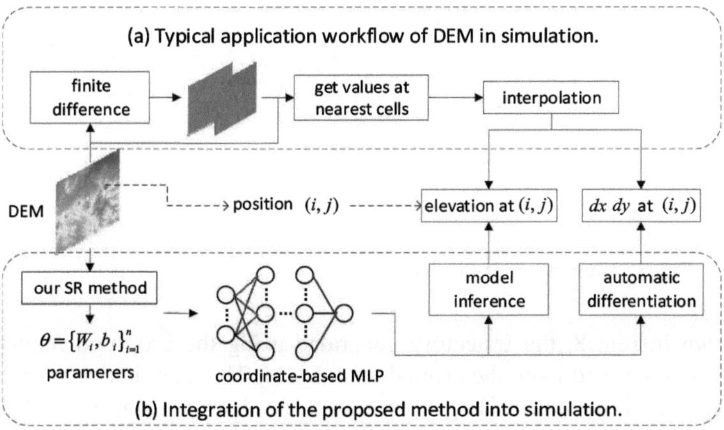

Fig. 6. Comparison of typical workflow and integration of the proposed method in vehicle motion simulation.

To demonstrate the practical applicability of the proposed method, we integrate it into the vehicle motion simulation system. The overall workflow is illustrated in Fig. 6. In the typical workflow, elevation and slope components (*dx* and *dy*) at arbitrary positions are obtained by computing finite difference and interpolating values from raster-based DEM. The workflow integrating the proposed method begins with a LR DEM and outputs the parameters of a coordinate-based MLP that represents the HR DEM as a continuous function. Unlike conventional raster-based DEM, the MLP allows for direct querying of elevation and slope components (*dx* and *dy*) at arbitrary positions via automatic differentiation, enabling accurate and efficient interaction during simulation.

5.2 Experiments and Results

We compare the proposed integrated method with the typical application workflow. We use the HR DEM as ground truth and take the LR DEM and the bicubic-interpolated DEM as baselines. The proposed method acts solely as a terrain service that returns elevation (and slope) at queried coordinates. The evaluation is conducted in a vehicle motion simulation system under a path planning scenario, where the simulated vehicle follows a sequence of predefined waypoints as shown in Fig. 7. At each simulation timestep, the simulator queries terrain at each timestep to update the vehicle state, and the resulting trajectory position (x, y, z) is recorded, and the root mean squared error (RMSE) with respect to the ground-truth trajectory is computed.

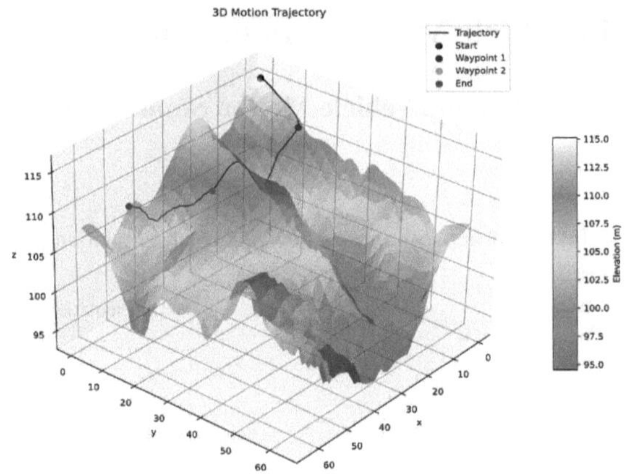

Fig. 7. Illustration of the 3D motion trajectory under path planning.

As shown in Fig. 8, the trajectory generated using the proposed method closely matches the one derived from the ground-truth DEM. The quantitative results, summarized in Table 4, show that the largest errors occurred when using the LR DEM. The proposed method outperformed bicubic interpolation, achieving more accurate simulation results. These findings demonstrate that the proposed SR method can effectively enhance simulation accuracy.

Table 4. RMSE of simulated vehicle position x and y under different inputs.

	RMSE-x (m)	RMSE-y (m)
LR DEM	0.8478	0.7608
Bicubic DEM	0.7791	0.4115
The proposed method	0.7338	0.3613

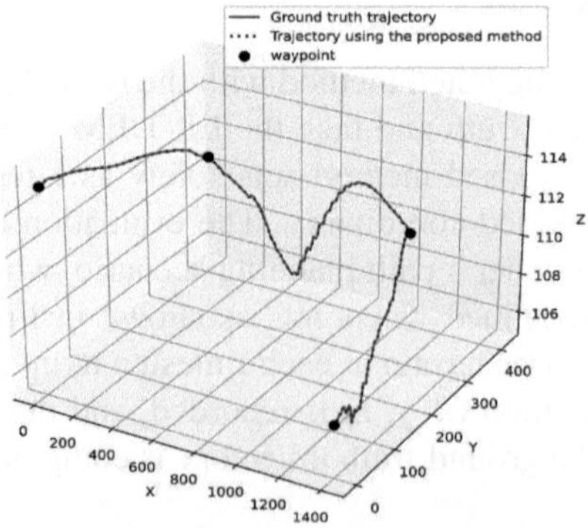

Fig. 8. Illustration of the trajectory generated by the proposed method and the ground-truth.

6 Conclusion

In this paper, we proposed a SR framework for DEM based on a coordinate-based MLP, which represents DEM as a continuous function over spatial coordinates. The MLP is constructed using periodic activation functions and supports direct querying of elevation and automatic computation of slope at arbitrary positions. A hypernetwork with an encoder–decoder architecture is employed to generate the MLP parameters from LR DEM in an end-to-end manner.

Experimental results demonstrate that the proposed method achieves higher accuracy than bicubic interpolation in both elevation and slope prediction, while requiring only 14.9% of the memory compared to storing full-resolution DEM. We further compared the proposed method with fitting-based baselines and showed that it offers better accuracy and significantly higher efficiency by eliminating the need for per-sample training. In addition, the proposed method can be seamlessly integrated into vehicle motion simulation systems, providing accurate, continuous, and differentiable terrain information for real-time trajectory planning. These advantages make the proposed method a practical and efficient solution for terrain-aware applications.

Nevertheless, the proposed method also has certain limitations. Its accuracy still falls behind state-of-the-art deep learning models that are explicitly designed for super-resolution. Future work will focus on validating the method across more diverse and complex terrains, as well as exploring advanced implicit representation architectures, thereby enhancing the robustness and broadening the applicability of the framework to more terrain-aware applications.

Disclosure of Interests. The authors have no competing interests to declare that are relevant to the content of this article.

References

1. Dong, C., Loy, C.C., He, K., Tang, X.: Learning a deep convolutional network for image super-resolution. In: Fleet, D., Pajdla, T., Schiele, B., Tuytelaars, T. (eds.) Computer Vision – ECCV 2014, pp. 184–199. Springer, Cham (2014)
2. Liang, J., Cao, J., Sun, G., Zhang, K., Van Gool, L., Timofte, R.: Swinir: image restoration using swin transformer. In: Proceedings of the IEEE/CVF International Conference on Computer Vision, pp. 1833–1844 (2021)
3. Lin, X., et al.: A DEM super-resolution reconstruction network combining internal and external learning. Remote Sens. **14**, 2181 (2022). https://doi.org/10.3390/rs14092181
4. Zhang, Y., Yu, W., Zhu, D.: Terrain feature-aware deep learning network for digital elevation model superresolution. ISPRS J. Photogramm. Remote Sens. **189**, 143–162 (2022). https://doi.org/10.1016/j.isprsjprs.2022.04.028
5. Yao, S., Cheng, Y., Yang, F., Mozerov, M.G.: A continuous digital elevation representation model for DEM super-resolution. ISPRS J. Photogramm. Remote Sens. **208**, 1–13 (2024). https://doi.org/10.1016/j.isprsjprs.2024.01.001
6. Wang, Y., et al.: TTSR: a transformer-based topography neural network for digital elevation model super-resolution. IEEE Trans. Geosci. Remote Sens. **62**, 1–19 (2024). https://doi.org/10.1109/TGRS.2024.3360489

7. Sitzmann, V., Martel, J., Bergman, A., Lindell, D., Wetzstein, G.: Implicit neural representations with periodic activation functions. In: Advances in Neural Information Processing Systems, pp. 7462–7473. Curran Associates, Inc. (2020)
8. Mildenhall, B., Srinivasan, P.P., Tancik, M., Barron, J.T., Ramamoorthi, R., Ng, R.: NeRF: representing scenes as neural radiance fields for view synthesis. Commun. ACM **65**, 99–106 (2021). https://doi.org/10.1145/3503250
9. Singh, R., Shukla, A., Turaga, P.: Polynomial implicit neural representations for large diverse datasets. In: Proceedings of the IEEE/CVF Conference on Computer Vision and Pattern Recognition, pp. 2041–2051. IEEE, Vancouver, BC, Canada (2023). https://doi.org/10.1109/CVPR52729.2023.00203
10. Xu, Q.-C., Mu, T.-J., Yang, Y.-L.: A survey of deep learning-based 3D shape generation. Comp. Vis. Media **9**, 407–442 (2023). https://doi.org/10.1007/s41095-022-0321-5
11. Chen, Y., Liu, S., Wang, X.: Learning continuous image representation with local implicit image function. In: Proceedings of the IEEE/CVF Conference on Computer Vision and Pattern Recognition, pp. 8628–8638. IEEE, Nashville, TN, USA (2021). https://doi.org/10.1109/CVPR46437.2021.00852
12. Lee, J., Choi, K.P., Jin, K.H.: Learning local implicit fourier representation for image warping. In: European Conference on Computer Vision, pp. 182–200. Springer, Cham (2022). https://doi.org/10.1007/978-3-031-19797-0_11
13. Xu, X., Wang, Z., Shi, H.: UltraSR: spatial encoding is a missing key for implicit image function-based arbitrary-scale super-resolution. arXiv (2022). https://doi.org/10.48550/arXiv.2103.12716
14. Jiang, Y., et al.: HIIF: hierarchical encoding based implicit image function for continuous super-resolution. arXiv (2024). https://doi.org/10.48550/arXiv.2412.03748
15. Ha, D., Dai, A., Le, Q.V.: HyperNetworks. arXiv (2016). https://doi.org/10.48550/arXiv.1609.09106
16. Klocek, S., Maziarka, Ł., Wołczyk, M., Tabor, J., Nowak, J., Śmieja, M.: Hypernetwork functional image representation. In: International Conference on Artificial Neural Networks, pp. 496–510. Springer, Cham (2019). https://doi.org/10.1007/978-3-030-30493-5_48
17. Demiray, B.Z., Sit, M., Demir, I.: D-SRGAN: DEM super-resolution with generative adversarial networks. SN COMPUT. SCI. **2**, 48 (2021). https://doi.org/10.1007/s42979-020-00442-2
18. Zhang, R., Bian, S., Li, H.: RSPCN: super-resolution of digital elevation model based on recursive sub-pixel convolutional neural networks. ISPRS Int. J. Geo-Inf. **10**, 501 (2021). https://doi.org/10.3390/ijgi10080501
19. Demiray, B.Z., Sit, M.A., Demir, I.: DEM super-resolution with efficientNetV2. In: Climate Change AI (2021). https://doi.org/10.48550/arXiv.2109.09661
20. Gao, R., Jaiman, R.K.: H-SIREN: improving implicit neural representations with hyperbolic periodic functions. arXiv (2024). https://doi.org/10.48550/arXiv.2410.04716

A Modeling Method for the Pressing Process of Explosive Molding Powder Based on Particle Size Distribution

Jin Luo, Yifan Li, Linjing Tang, Xuying Jiao, and Xianzhen Jia(✉)

National Key Laboratory of Energetic Materials, Xi'an Modern Chemistry Research Institute, Xi'an 710065, Shanxi, People's Republic of China
15793592612@163.com

Abstract. This research explores the deformation characteristics, pressure-density distribution patterns, and key influencing factors of explosive powder in the compression molding process. First, a theoretical analysis was carried out on the pressure distribution during molding, and a mathematical model for the compression process was further deduced. Subsequently, by utilizing ANSYS APDL software, a random packing model that integrates the particle size distribution of explosive powder was constructed. Relying on the principles of continuum mechanics and finite element analysis methods, the study examined the laws governing pressure and density distribution of explosive columns under dynamic compression conditions. The findings indicate that the established model can effectively simulate the actual pressing process of explosive powder. This effectiveness was verified through pressure-density curves as well as pressure distribution data obtained under compression scenarios. Specifically, pressure propagates from the upper and lower punches toward the center of the explosive column, showing a gradual decreasing trend during the propagation process. In terms of axial density distribution, the regions near the punch ends exhibit higher density values, while the density in the central area of the explosive column changes minimally. Overall, the proposed model offers a reliable analytical tool for optimizing process parameters in explosive powder compression molding and accurately predicting the forming density of the final product.

Keywords: Molding Powder · Pressing Formation · Particle Deformation · Pressure Distribution · Uniformity · Numerical Simulation

1 Introduction

Compression molding serves as a core process for shaping explosive powders, as its performance directly determines the quality and detonation efficiency of explosive components. In contrast to unidirectional pressing, this technique exerts pressure on both ends of the mold simultaneously, which helps reduce the density inconsistency induced by one-sided loading. At present, most research in this field adopts a combination of experimental characterization [1–4] and numerical simulation methods. For example, Hu et al.

W. Cai et al. (Eds.): AsiaSim 2025, CCIS 2727, pp. 115–123, 2026.
https://doi.org/10.1007/978-981-95-4472-1_10

[5] utilized in-situ scanning to reconstruct the 3D morphology of powders, and further developed a discrete element model (DEM) to analyze the evolutionary characteristics of particles during the compression process. Guo et al. [6] explored the compaction density, Brazilian strength, and crack propagation law of PBX explosives through experimental tests and DEM simulation analysis. Reaugh [7] employed 3D elastoplastic hydrodynamics to simulate the response of HMX-based PBX under pressure, while Khoei et al. [8, 9] put forward a finite element method (X-FEM) that considers frictional contact to assess the density distribution during powder compaction. Other research progress includes.

Nevertheless, the discontinuous medium models based on DEM often over-simplify the rigidity of particles, failing to take into account the subtle contact and deformation behaviors between particles [10–12]. Furthermore, there is a lack of research that integrates particle size distribution and interparticle interaction effects to conduct a systematic analysis of density uniformity during dynamic compression. To fill this research gap, this study proposes a new finite element model that incorporates the aforementioned factors. By using ANSYS APDL, a random packing structure is generated, and this model framework is designed to predict density distribution and optimize process parameters, thereby promoting the digital development of explosive powder molding technology.

To address the existing shortcomings, this study takes JH-15 molding powder as the research object and develops a new model for the dynamic pressing of explosive molding powder. For the first time, this model comprehensively considers the particle size distribution of the molding powder and the interparticle contact effects, and constructs a finite element model with random packing characteristics. Combining ANSYS APDL parametric design and LS-DYNA software, it realizes the simulation of dynamic pressing processes. This model can accurately calculate the forming density, pressure distribution and particle deformation, which helps to improve the digital level of the pressing process for explosive molding powder.

2 Establishment of the Finite Element Model

2.1 Physical Model

The explosive JH-15 provided by Xi'an Modern Chemistry Research Institute is selected as the material, prepared by suspension granulation method, and its physical form is white granular solid. The composition ratio of this explosive is 96% RDX, 4% binder and 1% wax, and its theoretical maximum density under standard conditions is 1.771 $g{\cdot}cm^{-3}$, and the measured bulk density is 0.81 $g{\cdot}cm^{-3}$. The particle size distribution of JH-15 is shown in Table 1.

Table 1. Particle size distribution of JH-15

Particle size distribution	0.92 mm	0.442 mm	0.272 mm
Weight(%)	49.7	43.4	2.8

In view of the magnitude difference between the average particle size ($\approx 200\ \mu m$) of the molding powder and the actual size of the explosive column (tens to hundreds of millimeters), to avoid excessive consumption of computational resources caused by a large number of meshes in the three-dimensional random packing model, this study simplifies it into a two-dimensional plane strain problem in combination with the structural characteristics of the mold-punch. Random packing in a 3D setup would require a more complex mesh manipulation. In this sense, the model cannot allow studying out-of-plane rearrangements or contact topologies unique to sphere packings: the results should be interpreted as a projection of the 3D process.

Based on the particle size distribution of the molding powder, three types of particles with characteristic particle sizes of 0.92 mm (49.7%), 0.442 mm (43.4%) and 0.272 mm (2.8%) are selected, and randomly packed within the plane domain of φ20 mm × φ40 mm using the APDL parametric design language.

A random packing model of particles with random distribution characteristics is obtained, as shown in Fig. 1.

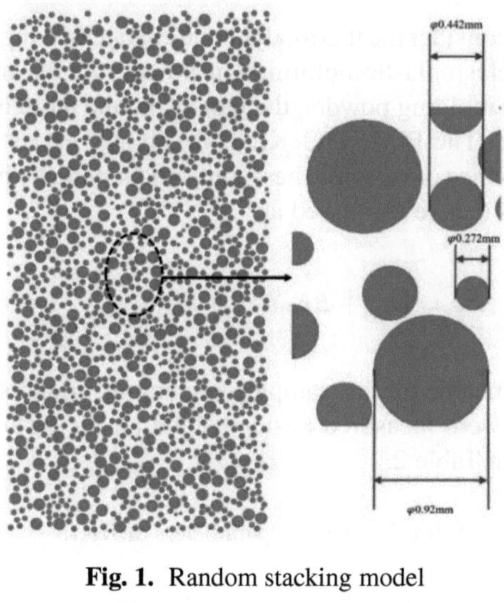

Fig. 1. Random stacking model

According to the random packing model, a unidirectional die pressing calculation model based on the finite element method is established, as shown in Fig. 2. The model is composed of the punch, the mold and the JH-15 explosive molding powder. Among them, the punch moves downward, and both the punch and the mold are made of steel materials. According to the bulk density of the JH-15 explosive, the initial height H_0 of the molding powder is calculated to be 40.0 mm.

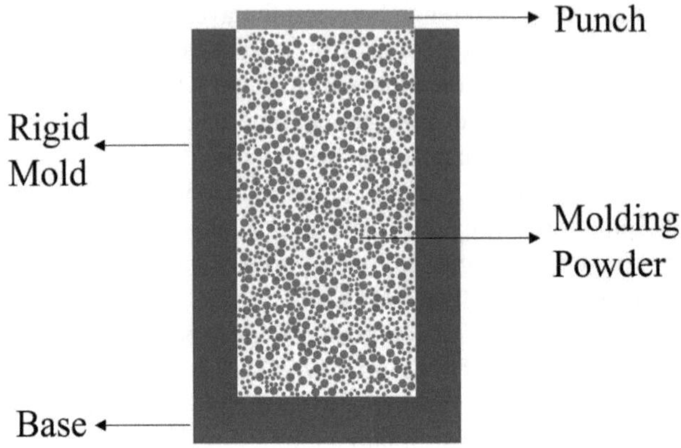

Fig. 2. Suppression model

2.2 Material Model

In this study, we do not consider the thermodynamic changes during the pressing process, and only explore the elastoplastic deformation process of the molding powder. The interaction between the molding powder, the punch and the mold is a dynamic response under a high strain rate. The PLASTIC_KINEMATIC [13] constitutive model, which combines the characteristics of isotropic hardening and kinematic hardening, is adopted. Its dynamic yield stress can be expressed as:

$$\sigma_y = \left(\sigma_0 + \beta E_P \varepsilon_p^{eff}\right)\left[1 + \left(\frac{\dot{\varepsilon}}{C}\right)^{\frac{1}{p}}\right] \quad (1)$$

The material parameters of the samples, including young's modulus, poisson's ratio, and yield stress, were measured through static tensile testing, the main material parameters are shown in Table 2.

Table 2. Material parameters of JH-15

Density/ $Kg \cdot m^{-3}$	Young's modulus/GPa	Poisson's ratio	Yield stress/ MPa
1771	10	0.3	5

2.3 Contact Algorithm and Boundary Conditions

In the simulation of dynamic pressing of the powder, the system includes three types of contact interfaces: the upper and lower punches-particles, between particles, and particles-mold. To suppress mesh distortion and reduce the hourglass effect, the penalty function contact algorithm [14] is adopted.

When the particles come into contact with the punch and thef mold, since the selection of the contact surface and the target surface is arbitrary in this system, the fully symmetric surface-to-surface contact in the LS-DYNA contact type is adopted. For the contact between the molding powders, considering the self-contact situation between particles, the single-surface contact in the LS-DYNA contact type is used. The contact pair types are defined as follows: punch/mold-particle: fully symmetric surface-to-surface contact; self-contact between particles: single-surface contact. The friction coefficient for the surface-to-surface contact is set to 0.5, and that for the single-surface contact is set to 0.4.

Constraints are set according to the motion characteristics of each component in the system. The mold and the base are both fixed constraint surfaces. The mold is constrained in both the X and Y directions. The punche is pressure-applying surfaces, constrained in the X direction while allowed to move in the Y direction.

3 Model Validation

3.1 Experimental Method

The density of the molding powder during compression molding increases with the increase of pressure. A higher density of the explosive column generally means better mechanical strength, enabling it to withstand greater external impacts and vibrations and reducing the risk of damage during transportation and use. A higher density usually leads to a higher detonation velocity and pressure, thereby enhancing the power of the warhead. An explosive column with a higher density can release chemical energy more effectively, increasing the destructive power and killing range of the explosion.

The mass remains conserved before and after pressing. According to the height, radius, and initial density of the explosive column before and after pressing:

The relationship of the density after pressing is obtained:

$$\rho_0 \frac{\pi D^2}{4} H_0 = \rho_1 \frac{\pi D^2}{4} H_1 \tag{2}$$

The relationship of the density after pressing is obtained:

$$\rho_1 = \frac{\rho_0 H_0}{H_1} \tag{3}$$

where $\rho_0 H_0$ is known, and H_1 is the height of the explosive column after pressing, which can be obtained from the displacement of the punch. Further, the change in the density of the explosive column during the pressing process can be calculated from the above formula. To obtain the change in the specific pressing pressure during the dynamic pressing process, points at equal intervals close to the punch can be selected as sampling points.

The compaction process was conducted at room temperature, with specific pressures set at 50 MPa, 100 MPa,..., 250 MPa, and 300 MPa. Under these pressure conditions, charge columns with a diameter of φ20 mm and a charge mass of 10 g were compacted. For each pressure condition, no fewer than three samples were prepared, ensuring three valid samples per batch. The density of the compacted samples was measured according to hydrostatic weighing method.

The average density of the three valid samples under each pressure condition was calculated and denoted as $\overline{\rho_i}$. The calculation is as follows:

$$\overline{\rho_i} = \frac{\overline{\rho_{i1}} + \overline{\rho_{i2}} + \overline{\rho_{i3}}}{3} \tag{4}$$

The measured charge densities under various pressure conditions are shown in Table 3.

Table 3. Charge density corresponding to each pressure

Pressure(MPa)	50	100	150	200	250	300
Density($g \cdot cm^{-3}$)	1.57	1.648	1.684	1.698	1.709	1.712

From the experimental data in Table 3, it can be observed that the higher the pressure, the slower the density changes, and the density changes become very slow after the pressure reaches 250 MPa. Since the model is a two-dimensional planar structure, while the actual molding powder is quasi-spherical, the contact between particles is more likely, resulting in greater elastoplastic changes compared to three-dimensional molding powder. Here, we validate the charge column density corresponding to pressures below 300 MPa. By processing the pressure-density curve obtained from the simulation results, the density values corresponding to each pressure for JH-15 explosive molding powder under both experimental and simulated conditions are shown in Fig. 3. The relative errors of the density values corresponding to each pressure are listed in Table 4.

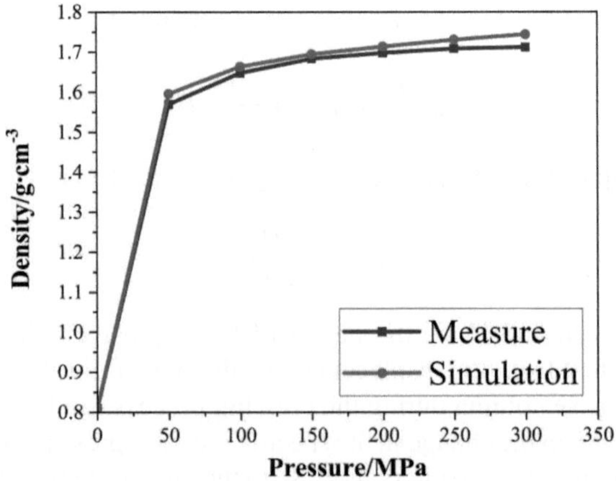

Fig. 3. Density values comparison

Table 4. Relative error of density corresponding to each pressure

Pressure(MPa)	50	100	150	200	250	300
Error(%)	1.656	0.971	0.653	0.942	1.287	2.044

Analysis shows that during molding powder dynamic compaction, particle rearrangement and elastoplastic deformation dominate at lower pressures; in 2D simulations, particle contact interactions are close to real conditions. As pressure rises, particle fragmentation, strain hardening [15, 16], and local shear become more obvious—these slow density growth. Thus, simulated density increases more sharply than experimental values at higher pressures, leading to larger errors. From Fig. 3 and Table 4, the model fits the compaction process well: maximum density error is only 2.044%, and the smallest error (0.534%) occurs at 150 MPa.

3.2 Single Directional Pressing

Select the parts close to the punch and the base to specifically analyze the pressure distribution of the entire explosive column. Three equally-spaced points are selected at the upper and lower parts as sampling points.

Taking the displacement of the punch as the x-axis, the pressure distribution of each sampling point, is shown in Fig. 4.

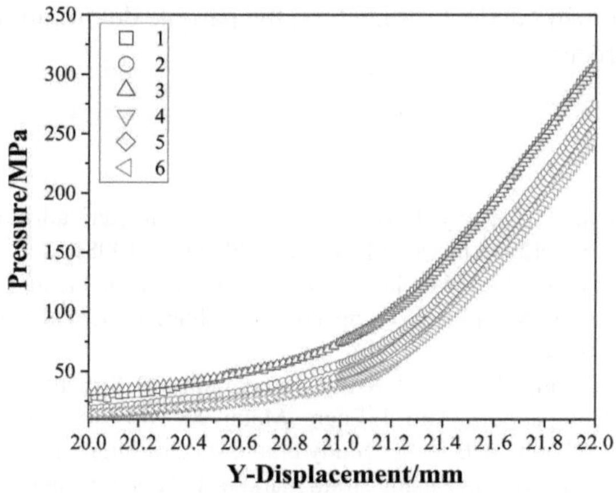

Fig.4. Pressure distribution near the punch and base

Further analysis of Fig. 4 reveals pressure-densities distribution differences between the punch and base ends:

1. **Punch end**: Pressure at both sides > center (symmetric on sides), so explosive column density at edges > center. Reason: Central particles face less downward resistance, while side particles bear greater friction from mold walls, increasing edge pressure and density.

2. **Base end**: Pressure at center > both sides (symmetric on sides), so explosive column density at center > edges. Reason: Central particles get counter-pressure from the base when moving down; edge force is consumed by friction and weakens with distance, increasing central pressure and density. This aligns with references [3, 16].

4 Conclusion

From the modeling process and pressing model verification, the numerical simulation method established in this study is highly effective and reliable for simulating molding powder dynamic pressing. Its accuracy stems from integrating four key elements:

- **Geometric modeling**: Multi-particle-size random packing algorithm constructs a particle model that truly reflects JH-15 explosive's particle size distribution.
- **Constitutive relationship**: Elastoplastic theory-based material model reasonably describes the mechanical response of the explosive's crystal-binder-wax composite system.
- **Contact algorithm**: Penalty function method solves complex multi-body contact (particle self-contact, mold/punch-particle surface contact) during pressing.
- **Boundary conditions**: Accurate motion constraints and load curves restore the dynamic pressing process.

Verification results confirm: Simulated pressure-density curves match experimental data well (error $< 3\%$), and pressure-density distribution follows the law of formed explosive columns.

In the future, we will conduct research on the particle deformation behavior during the grain forming process.

References

1. Burnside, N.J., Son, S. F., Asay, B.W. et al.: Particle characterization of pressed granular HMX, AIP Conf. Proc.**429**. American Institute of Physics, (1998)
2. Mamalis, A.G., Vottea, I.N., Manolakos, D.E.: Fabrication of metal/sheathed high superconducting composites by explosive compaction/cladding: numerical simulation. Mater. Sci. Eng. B **90**, 254–260 (2002)
3. Dai, B., Tian, Y., Zhang, W. et al.: X-ray Tomography of Structural Evolution of TATB Granules During Compaction. Chin. J. Energ. Mater. **23**, 982–988 (2015)
4. Dai, B., Lan, L.G., Zhang, W.B. et al.: Study on the state of internal stress and strain of tatb-based polymer bonded explosive using strain markers and cone-beam computed tomography. Central Eur. J. Energ. Mater. (14), 688–707 (2017)
5. Hu, G., Zhou, B., Fu, R. et al.: Discrete element modeling of the compression molding of polymer crystal composite particles. Powder Technol. **390**, 112–125 (2021)
6. Guo, Y., Liu, R., Chen, P. et al.: Mechanical behavior of PBX with different HMX crystal size during die pressing: Experimental study and DEM simulation. Compos. Sci. Technol. **222** (2022)
7. Reaugh, J. E.: Multi-scale computer simulation to study the reaction zone of soild explosives. Presented at 13th International Detonation Symposium. Norfolk, VA, United States, (2006)
8. Khoei, A.R., Shamloo, A., Azami, A.R.: Extended finite element method in plasticity forming of powder compaction with contact friction. Int. J. Solid Struct. **43**, 5421–5448 (2006)

9. Khoei, A.R., Biabanaki, S.O.R., Parvaneh, S.M.: Dynamic modeling of powder compaction processes via a simple contact algorithm. Int. J. Mech. Sci. **64**, 0020–7403 (2012)
10. Yeager, J.D., Manner, V.W., Stull, J.A. et al.: Importance of microstructural features in mechanical response of cast-cured HMX formulations. Am. Inst. Phys. **1979**, (2018)
11. Buechier, M.A., Luscher, D.J.: A semi-implicit integration scheme for a combined viscoelastic-damage model of plastic bonded explosives. Int. J. Numer. Meth. Eng. **99**, 54–78 (2014)
12. Manner, V.W., Yeager, J.D., Patterson, B.M. et al.: In situ imaging during compression of plastic bonded explosives for damage modeling. Mater. **10**, 638–651 (2017)
13. Hallquist, J.O.: LS-DYNA theory manual[Z]. Livemore Software Technology Corporation, Liver-more (2006)
14. Qingzhong, C., Derun, L., Junpei, X. et al.: Explosives and Charging Design. Beijing: Nation Defense Industry Press, pp. 222–226, (2019)
15. Wetler, R., Oliver, J., Sain, T., et al.: On the contact domain method: a comparison of penalty and Lagrange multiplier implementations[J]. Comput. Methods Appl. Mech. Eng. **205**, 68–72 (2012)
16. Seifried, R., Schiehlen, W., Eberhard, P.: The role of the coefficient of restitution on impact problems in multibody dynamics. Proc. Inst Mech. Eng. [K]: J. Multi-body Dyn. **224** (2010)

Simulation and Verification of Explosive Powder Compression Molding Based on Thermodynamic Elastoplastic Model

Jin Luo, Linjing Tang, Xuying Jiao, Yifan Li, and Xianzhen Jia(✉)

National Key Laboratory of Energetic Materials, Xi'an Modern Chemistry Research Institute, Xi'an 710065, Shanxi, People's Republic of China
15793592612@163.com

Abstract. To improve the compression molding quality of explosive powder, a modeling method that treats explosive powder as a continuum was adopted. Using an elastoplastic material model that considers thermodynamic changes, taking a specific size explosive column as an example, the DEFORM finite element software was employed to simulate the powder compression process, analyze the changes in relative density during the compression process, and study the density evolution law of the molded column. The results show that this simulation model can well simulate the powder compression molding process. For the pressure-density curve, the maximum relative error of density between the test and simulation under each specific pressure is only 0.996%. Regarding the density distribution of the column: the density distribution of the column near the punch end is such that the density at the edge is greater than that at the center; the density distribution of the column near the base end is such that the density at the center is greater than that at the edge, which is consistent with the results of relevant studies.

Keywords: DEFORM · Pressing Formation · Relative density · FEM · Numerical Simulation

1 Introduction

In the ammunition production process, the performance of charging equipment and the setting of process parameters directly determine the charging quality of ammunition. If the process parameters are improperly configured, the formed explosive is prone to problems such as cracks, bubbles, and uneven density distribution. Therefore, the quality of charging largely determines the overall quality of ammunition. With the popularization of finite element simulation and artificial intelligence technology in various industries, it has become a reality to use simulation methods to conduct numerical simulation of the explosive compression molding process. This method can not only significantly reduce research and development costs and shorten the research and development cycle, but also provide strong support for the rapid iteration of charging processes.

W. Cai et al. (Eds.): AsiaSim 2025, CCIS 2727, pp. 124–133, 2026.
https://doi.org/10.1007/978-981-95-4472-1_11

In terms of relevant research, in the early stage, researchers mainly carried out related studies by means of experiments and characterization methods [1–3]. These experimental studies provided basic data for a preliminary understanding of the laws of explosive powder compression molding by measuring and analyzing various parameters during the compression process, but only a series of observations could be made at the macro level. Reaugh from Lawrence Livermore National Laboratory [4] simulated the force, heat, and dynamic response of HMX-based PBX under pressure load based on the three-dimensional elastic-plastic hydrodynamics arbitrary Lagrangian-Eulerian finite difference method. Khoei A R et al. [5, 6] proposed a computational model based on the extended finite element method (X-FEM) to analyze the plastic behavior of powder compaction considering frictional contact, but the simplification of its contact algorithm may affect the prediction of molding density. Cao Xing [7] et al. regarded explosive powder as a continuous medium, established a powder compression model using MSC.Marc, and analyzed the evolution law of the relative density of explosive powder. However, this model failed to reflect the characteristics and interaction of particles.

In addition, in the research field of constitutive models and simulation methods related to powder compaction, Kuhn, Green, Shima et al. [8–10] constructed ellipsoidal yield models, and based on soil plasticity mechanics, the Drucker-Prager model [11], Cam-Clay model [12], etc. have also been developed. In subsequent studies, Myeong et al. [13] proposed a unified constitutive model applicable to both powder compaction and sintering processes based on plastic theory; Lee et al. [14] combined computed tomography technology with the finite element method to establish a finite element model that can reflect the actual pore size and morphology; Zhou et al. [15] used ABAQUS software and combined with the modified Drucker-Prager-cap model. It is worth noting that DEFORM software performs well in deformation analysis. In the field of powder forming, it uses the porous model to simulate the densification forming of porous materials during the compression process, which is still considered a relatively effective method.

Based on the practical background of the charging process, this study established a computational model for the continuum of explosive powder column compression molding using the advanced nonlinear finite element software DEFORM, and conducted numerical simulation of the compression molding process. Through the comparison between simulation and experiment, the pressure-density curve of powder compression molding and the variation law of the overall relative density of the formed powder column were obtained.

2 Finite Element Modeling

At present, most studies on mechanical models for the powder compaction process are based on the continuum hypothesis: that is, powder materials are regarded as compressible elastoplastic bodies. From an overall perspective, powder materials satisfy the condition of mass conservation, while from the perspective of local particles, they follow the principle of volume invariance. In this study, when simulating the compaction process of explosive powder, the continuum hypothesis is also adopted to model the explosive powder, and an elastoplastic mechanical model considering thermodynamic effects is introduced to analyze various variation laws during the compaction process.

2.1 Geometric Model

The schematic diagram of the compaction process for explosive molding powder (explosive powder) is shown in Fig. 2. The powder explosive is filled into the mold, with an initial bulk density of approximately 0.9 g/cm^3 and a height of about 140 mm. After leveling the surface, a punch (fixed on the press, which provides pressure; the press does not need to be modeled) is used to press down on the top of the explosive powder. The specific process parameters are shown in Fig. 1. The mold is cylindrical with a thickness of 20 mm and an inner diameter of 148 mm, and the punch diameter is 147.4 mm. After compaction, an explosive column of Φ148 mm × 70 mm is finally formed.

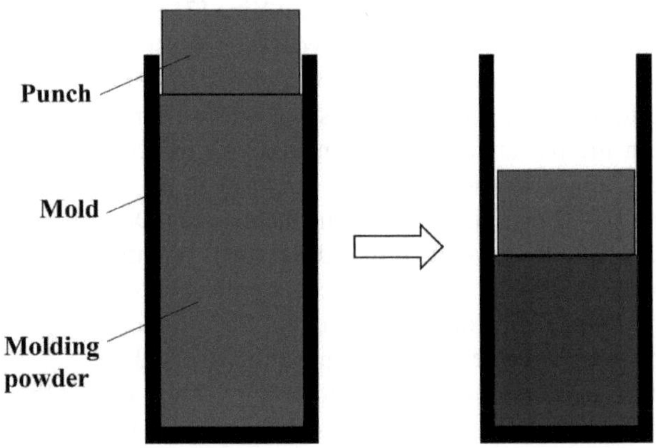

Fig. 1. Compaction model

2.2 Material Model

The actual compression molding process of powder materials is extremely complex, and some assumptions about powder materials need to be made here to enable the process to meet the requirements of mathematical simulation. The assumptions are as follows: the influence of the volume force of the powder material itself is ignored; the powder material is assumed to be homogeneous and its volume remains unchanged. Based on these assumptions, the powder explosive column can be regarded as a porous elastoplastic material considering thermodynamics, with a relative density of 0.4675 (the ratio of bulk density to formed density). The adopted constitutive model is as follows:

$$\bar{\sigma} = \bar{\sigma}\left(\overline{\epsilon}, \bar{\dot{\epsilon}}, T\right) \tag{1}$$

Where: $\bar{\sigma}$ is the equivalent stress; $\overline{\epsilon}$ is the equivalent strain; $\bar{\dot{\epsilon}}$ is the equivalent strain rate; is the temperature of the powder material. During the powder compaction process, as the temperature changes, the strain rate of the material also changes. Here, we set the changes in strain rate, strain, and flow stress under three temperature gradients, as shown in Fig. 2.

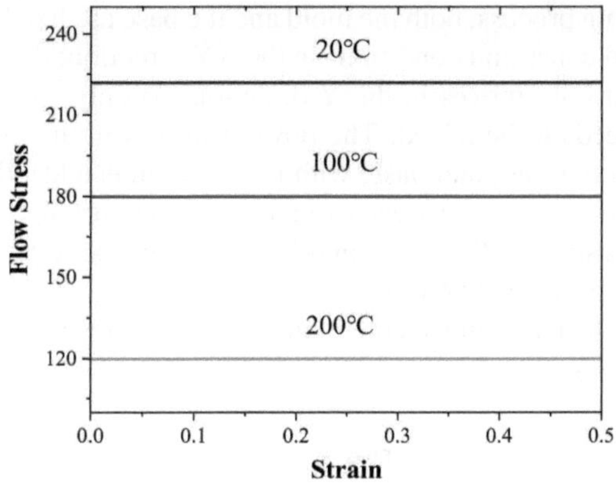

Fig. 2. Flow stress

The heat conduction equation describes the temperature change during the heat generation or heat dissipation process of powder materials, with the specific formula as follows:

$$\rho_1 c_p \frac{\vartheta T}{\vartheta t} = \nabla \cdot (k \nabla T) + Q \quad (2)$$

Where, ρ_1 is the material density, in kg·m^{-3}; c_p is the specific heat capacity of the material, in J·kg^{-1}·K^{-1}; k is the thermal conductivity, in W·m^{-1}·K^{-1}; t is time; Q is the spatial coordinate of heat generation rate.

Here, the contact among the mold, powder and punch follows Coulomb's friction law, and the frictional heat generation is:

$$q_f = \mu F_n V \quad (3)$$

Where, μ is the friction coefficient, F_n is the normal force, and V is the surface velocity of the part.

The relevant material parameters are shown in Table 1.

Table 1. Material parameters of powder

Density/ Kg · m^{-3}	Young's modulus/GPa	Poisson's ratio	Heat capacity/ J·kg^{-1}·K^{-1}	Thermal conductivity/ W·m^{-1}·K^{-1}
1925	10	0.3	1.2	0.5

2.3 Contact Algorithm and Boundary Conditions

In the entire powder pressing process, the magnitude of friction is related to the normal pressure between objects, and for dry friction between solid contacts, the Coulomb friction type is selected. Regarding the relative position accuracy of objects during contact, it can be adjusted by setting contact tolerances.

During the pressing process, both the mold and the base are fixed constraint surfaces, where we need to add constraint conditions in the XY direction; the punch is a pressure-applying surface that only moves in the Y direction, so only the constraint condition in the X direction needs to be added. The powder moves in the mold and comes into contact with the punch, mold, and base, with no constraints added here. Since this is a dynamic pressing process, it is necessary to apply a time-varying forced motion to the punch in this analysis stage as the load condition for the pressing process, and the punch moves at a constant speed (0.1666 mm/s).

The finally established finite element model for explosive powder compression molding is shown in Fig. 3.

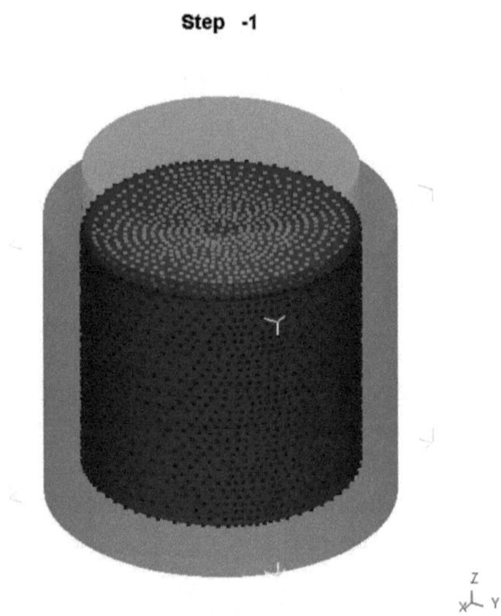

Fig. 3. FEM model

3 Model Validation

3.1 Experimental Method

The specific process flow of explosive powder compression molding is as follows:

The specific process of explosive powder compression molding is as follows:

1. Crush, sieve, and remove impurities from the explosive raw materials;
2. Select or process a special mold according to the designed shape of the powder column; clean and insulate the mold, etc.;
3. Quantitatively load the pretreated explosive raw materials into the mold to ensure uniform charging;
4. Place the loaded mold on the press, apply a predetermined pressure through the punch, and maintain the pressure for a certain period of time to reach the target density.

The pressing process is carried out at 80 °C and 100 °C. The specific pressure of the press is set to 98 MPa, 147 MPa, 196 MPa. For each specific pressure condition, no less than 3 samples are pressed to ensure that there are 3 valid samples in the same batch. The pressed samples are measured for density in accordance with GJB772A "Test Methods for Explosives" 401.2 (hydrostatic weighing method).

Table 2. Density of powder compaction under different pressures and temperature

Temperature		Pressure(MPa)	
	98	147	196
80 °C	1.747	1.807	1.822
100 °C	1.744	1.820	1.824

3.2 Stress-Density Curve Validation

In this simulation process, we have taken thermodynamic changes into account. Based on experience, the temperature rise during the pressing process is not drastic, so we only selected the density values corresponding to each pressure under the conditions of 80°C and 100°C as mentioned above.

The relationship of the density after pressing is obtained:

$$\rho_0 \frac{\pi D^2}{4} H_0 = \rho_1 \frac{\pi D^2}{4} H_1 \tag{4}$$

The relationship of the density after pressing is obtained:

$$\rho_1 = \frac{\rho_0 H_0}{H_1} \tag{5}$$

Where $\rho_0 H_0$ is known, and H_1 is the height of the explosive column after pressing, which can be obtained from the displacement of the punch. According to the relationship between punch displacement and loading force in the DEFORM post-processing software. The pressure-density curve of the entire powder pressing process is then derived by formulas (3) and (4), as shown in Fig. 4.

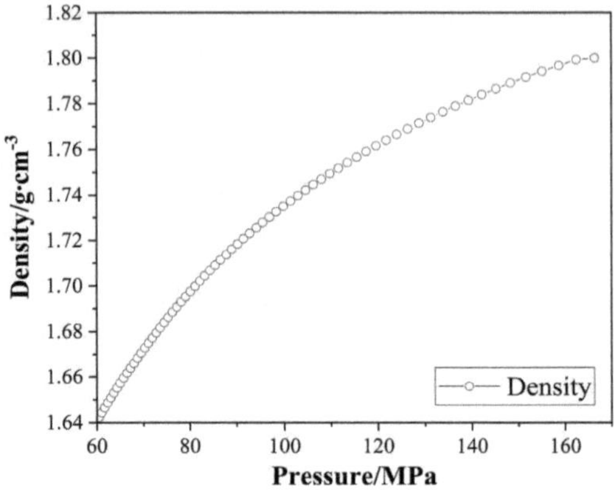

Fig. 4. Pressure-Density

Analysis of Fig. 4 shows that during the dynamic compaction of powder, when the pressure is relatively low, particle rearrangement and elastic-plastic deformation are the main occurrences. As the pressure increases, the particles will undergo strain hardening, and the short-term temperature rise will cause changes in the strain rate. The more obvious these phenomena are, the slower the density change will be.

The molding densities corresponding to the pressures under the simulation conditions in Fig. 5 were compared with those under the test conditions in Table 2, as shown in Table 3.

Table 3. Relative error of density corresponding to each pressure

Pressure (MPa)	98	147	166
Simulation-density ($g \cdot cm^{-3}$)	1.733	1.789	1.799
Error (%)	0.830	0.996	0.056

The results indicate that the model has a good effect in simulating the pressure-density curve during the powder pressing process. At a temperature of 80°C, the relative errors between the density values under the test and simulation conditions at various specific pressures are all within 1%, with the maximum being 0.996%; the error of the density value at 166 MPa in the experimental process of 3.1 is 0.056%.

3.3 Relative Density Distribution Validation

The parts close to the punch and the base are selected to specifically analyze the density distribution of the entire powder column. 10 equally spaced points are selected from the upper and lower parts as sampling points, as shown in Fig. 6.

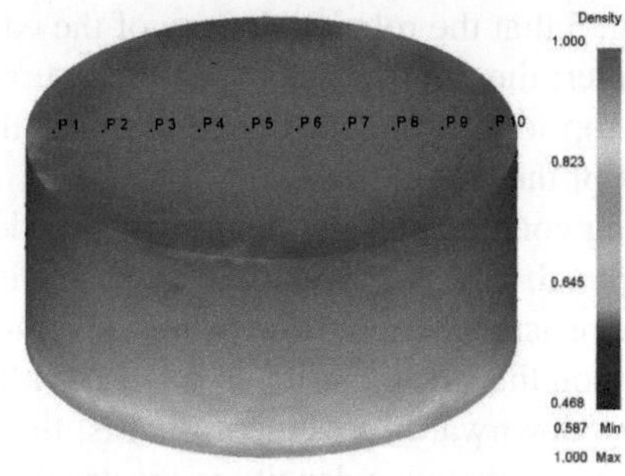

(a) Approaching the punch – cloud picture

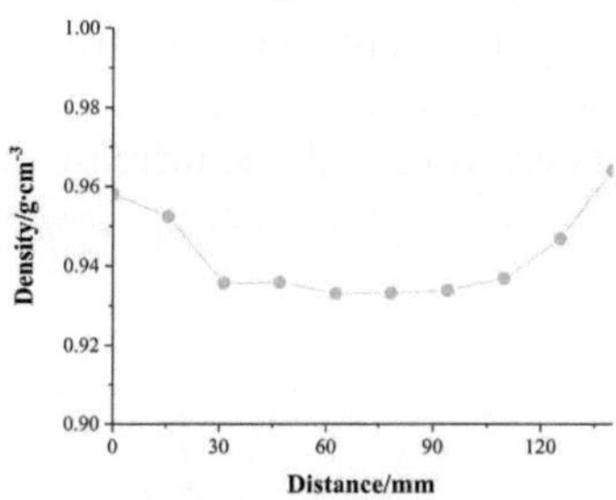

(b) Approaching the punch – curve picture

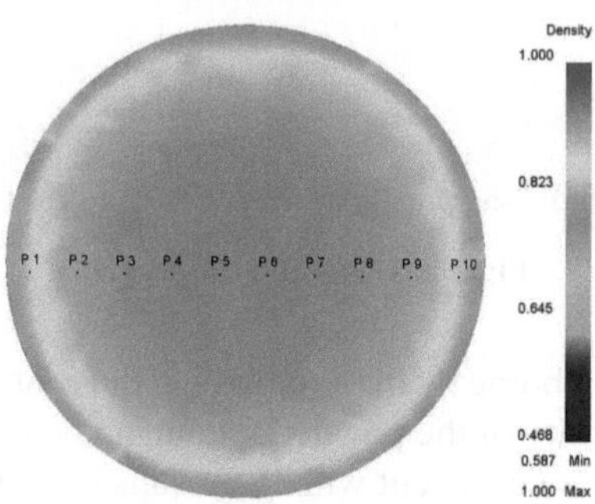

(c) Close the base – cloud picture

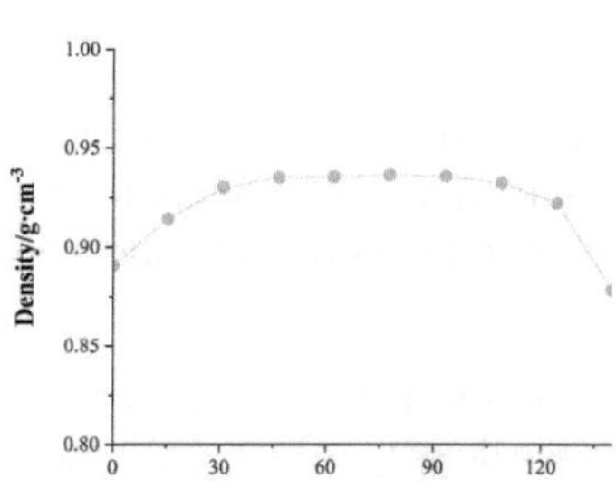

(d) Close the base – curve picture

Fig. 5. Relative density distribution

It can be seen from Fig. 5 that the relative density of the edge near the punch end is greater than that of the center; the relative density of the entire formed powder column gradually decreases from top to bottom; for the center near the base end, the relative density is greater than that of the edge.

From this, the following conclusions can be drawn: The density distribution of the powder column near the punch end is that the edge density is greater than the center density. This is because the resistance to the downward movement of particles at the axis is small; while the particles on the side experience friction with the mold wall, resulting in greater resistance during downward movement, that is, the particles at the edge are subjected to greater pressure, so the edge density is greater than the center density. The density distribution of the powder column near the base end is that the center density is greater than the edge density. The reason is that the downward movement of explosive particles in the center is resisted by the counter pressure from the base when reaching the base. However, during the transmission of the force at the edge, it is gradually consumed due to overcoming friction and decreases with the increase of distance.

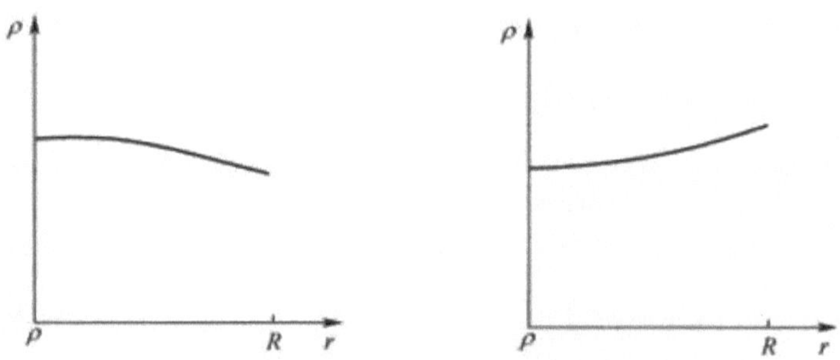

(a) Approaching the punch (b) Close the base

Fig. 6. Literature results [16]

As a result, the pressure borne by the explosive at the center is relatively greater than that at the edge, so the density of the powder column at the center of the base is greater than that at the edge. This is consistent with the results obtained in reference [16].

4 Conclusion

A powder compression molding model considering thermodynamic changes was established using the DEFORM finite element simulation software. The density evolution during the dynamic compression process of explosive powder was calculated, and the main conclusions are as follows:

1. The model exhibits a good performance in simulating the powder pressing process. The relative errors between the density values under the test and simulation conditions at various specific pressures are all within 1%.
2. The density distribution trends (edge > center near punch; center > edge near base) are consistent with prior literature.

References

1. Liangfei, B., Qiang, T., Xiaoqing, T. et al.: SANS Investigation on the effect of cold-pressed forming pressure on the microstructure of HMX-based PBX. Chin. J. Energ. Mater. **27**, 853–860 (2019)
2. Bin, D., Yong, T., Weibin, Z., et al.: X-ray Tomography of Structural Evolution of TATB Granules During Compaction. Chinese Journal of Energetic Materials **23**, 982–988 (2015)
3. Cheng, Z., Wang, J.: A particle-tracking method for experimental investigation of kinematics of sand particles under triaxial compression. Powder Technol. **328**, 436–451 (2018)
4. Reaugh, J.E.: Multi-scale computer simulation to study the reaction zone of soild explosives. Presented at 13th International Detonation Symposium, United States, 2006
5. Khoei, A.R., Shamloo, A., Azami, A.R.: Extended finite element method in plasticity forming of powder compaction with contact friction. Int. J. Solids Struct. **43**, 5421–5448 (2006)
6. Khoei, A.R., Biabanaki, S.O.R., Parvaneh, S.M.: Dynamic modeling of powder compaction processes via a simple contact algorithm. Int. J. Mech. Sci. **64**, 0020–7403 (2012)
7. Cao, X., Zhao, H.D., Cao, H.S. et al.: Influence of process parameters of explosive powder pressing on the quality of grain. Chin. J. Explos. Propellants (Huozhayao Xuebao) **44**, 72–77 (2021)
8. Kuhn, H.A., Downey, C.L.: Deformation characteristics and plasticity theory of sintered powder materials. Int. J. Powder Metall. **7**, 7–15 (1971)
9. Green, R.J.: Aplasticity theory for porous solids. Int. J. Mech. Sci. **14**, 215 (1972)
10. Shima, S., Oyane, M.: Plasticity theory for porous metals. Int. J. Mech. Sci. **18**, 285 (1976)
11. Drucker, D.C., Prager, W.: Soil mechanics and plastic analysis or limit design. Q. Appl. Math. **10**, 157 (1952)
12. Roscoe, K.H., Burland, J.B.: On the generalized stress-strain be havior of wet clay in engineering plasticity[M]. Cambridge University Press, Cambridge (1968)
13. Myeong, S.J., Jun, H.Y., Sung, H.R., et al.: A unified model for compaction and sintering behavior of powder processing. Finite Elem. Anal. Des. **53**, 56 (2012)
14. Lee, D.J., Jung, J.M., Latypov, M.I., et al.: Three Dimensional real structure-based finite element analysis of mechanical behavior for porous titanium manufactured by a space holder method. Comput. Mater. Sci. **100**, 2 (2015)
15. Rui, Z., Zhang, L.H., He B. et al.: Numerical simulation of residual stress field in green power metallurgy compacts by modified Drucker-Prager cap model. Trans. Nonferrous Met. Soc. China **23**, 2374 (2013)
16. Cui, Q., Liu, D., Xu, J. et al.: Explosives and charging design, pp. 222–223. Nation Defense Industry Press, Beijing (2019)

Research on Speed Control of Permanent Magnet Synchronous Motor Simulation Model Based on FOC

Yumu Luo[1], Zhenyu Zhang[1], Tan Li[1(✉)], Weining Song[2(✉)], Nanjiang Chen[1], Fangfang Gao[1], Wenjun Zhang[1], Congying Wu[1], Qi Wang[3], and Min Hu[4(✉)]

[1] Nanchang University, Nanchang, Jiangxi, China
someone8584@sina.com
[2] East China University of Technology, Nanchang, Jiangxi, China
[3] QuickTech Co., Ltd., Yizhuang, Beijing, China
[4] Jiangxi Science and Technology Normal University, Nanchang, Jiangxi, China

Abstract. With the improvement of industrial automation, energy saving and precision control demand, the speed control technology of permanent magnet synchronous motor (PMSM) has become a hot spot of industrial and academic research. This paper analyzes around the PMSM speed control, from theoretical modeling to simulation verification, adopts the magnetic field oriented control (FOC) strategy and combines with the SVPWM modulation technology to realize the decoupling of the motor multivariable and the precise control of the speed regulation; and puts forward the analysis of the motor speed control strategy based on the magnetic field oriented control method. The simulation model of PMSM speed control based on FOC is constructed by MATLAB/Simulink, and the speed control of PMSM is realized based on this model; and the stability of the control system under different working conditions, the rapidity of speed regulation and the effectiveness of the FOC control strategy are further verified through the comparative analysis of the motor running without and with load. The study provides a solid simulation basis for the ground application of motor speed control in industrial scenarios.

Keyword: Permanent Magnet Synchronous Motor (PMSM) · Speed Control · Theoretical Modeling · Field Oriented Control (FOC) · Simulation Model

1 Introduction

1.1 Research Background and Significance

With the increasing demand for motor performance in modern industries, motor drive systems are developing towards high efficiency, high precision and high stability. PMSMs are gradually being widely used in various industrial and consumer applications due to their high efficiency, high power density and reliability [1]. In this paper, we will analyze the need for PMSM speed control, discuss the technology behind it and the market demand, and explain its importance in the modern industrial environment.

W. Cai et al. (Eds.): AsiaSim 2025, CCIS 2727, pp. 134–147, 2026.
https://doi.org/10.1007/978-981-95-4472-1_12

As an advanced motor technology, PMSM has significant advantages in various types of applications; however, there are still difficulties and challenges to realize the high-precision speed control of PMSM; the traditional fixed-speed drive mode is difficult to meet the demands of complex working conditions [2]; in most applications, motors do not need to run at full load for a long time; and the constant speed control method is not conducive to achieving the energy-saving and environmentally friendly goals [3]; In addition, in application scenarios that require high dynamic response and precise position, the speed and torque of the motor need to be adjusted quickly according to the working conditions in order to realize the precise control requirements [4].

Based on the above problems, there are new and higher requirements for motor speed control; the need to adapt to the needs of variable working conditions, to be able to adjust the torque and speed of the motor in real time [5], to be able to cope with the realization of energy saving needs, motor speed control can be realized under different load conditions to achieve efficient operation [6]. Current speed control methods, such as field oriented control (FOC) and model predictive control (MPC), can not only realize precise control of PMSM speed and torque, but also greatly improve its dynamic response characteristics and efficiency [7, 8]. Through speed control, PMSM can be applied to a variety of complex working conditions and control requirements, and achieve the purpose of energy saving, high efficiency and precise control.

1.2 Analysis of the Current Status of PMSM Speed Control

Direct torque control (DTC), as one of the methods of motor speed control, is based on the direct control of motor torque and flux. At this stage, regarding the common problems of magnetic chain pulsation and torque pulsation in DTC research, methods such as SVM-DTC and model prediction DTC are proposed [9]; for problems such as the cost of sensors, DTC methods based on positionless sensors are proposed. And fuzzy control and variable structure control are combined on the basis of DTC, which are used to improve the robustness and real-time performance of the system [10].

Model predictive control (MPC), as a prospective control method, predicts future states by building a mathematical model of the motor [11]. At this stage, the research on MPC is mainly devoted to improving the response speed and dynamic performance of motors, and it is proposed to combine MPC with deep learning algorithms in order to optimize the prediction model and improve the adaptive capability [12, 13]; in the finite-control-set MPC-based method, some results have been achieved in reducing the computational burden by introducing advanced algorithms such as self-impedance control [14, 15].

The control method used in this paper is vector control, i.e., field oriented control (FOC); its basic principle is to realize the decoupling of the stator current components of the AC motor through coordinate transformation to form mutually perpendicular torque and excitation current components, so as to realize the control of the torque and speed [16]. The current research in magnetic field orientation control at home and abroad mainly focuses on improving the dynamic response and anti-interference capability of the system. For example, various advanced controllers have been introduced to enhance the robustness of the system [17]; model prediction-based vector control methods have been proposed to improve the control accuracy of the motor in high dynamic situations

[18]. In addition with the rapid development of artificial intelligence; in the future, neural networks, fuzzy control, etc. will be integrated into the control strategy to enhance the adaptive capability of the control system [19, 20].

1.3 Research Content and Objectives

This paper focuses on the FOC-based PMSM speed control strategy, establishes the mathematical model of PMSM, and designs the FOC-based speed control system, including spatial coordinate transformation, SVPWM technique and PI controller. MATLAB/Simulink is used to build the simulation model, and the performance of the system is simulated and analyzed to verify the effectiveness and feasibility of the control strategy. The research goal is to realize the high-precision speed control of PMSM and improve the dynamic response speed and stability of the system.

2 PMSM Mathematical Model

PMSM is a multivariable, strongly coupled nonlinear controlled object, with high power factor, efficiency and excellent control performance; where the strong coupling refers to the strong interdependence between the motor parameter variables, and in terms of PMSM control, it refers to the complex interrelationships between multiple state variables; that is, when regulating an input of the motor will affect multiple outputs of the motor. The existence of strong coupling relationships makes PMSM control complex, and simple control methods are difficult to effectively control such a system. In this paper, the decoupled d-axis and q-axis current information is used for vector control. The overall control schematic of motor speed control is shown in Fig. 1. Below:

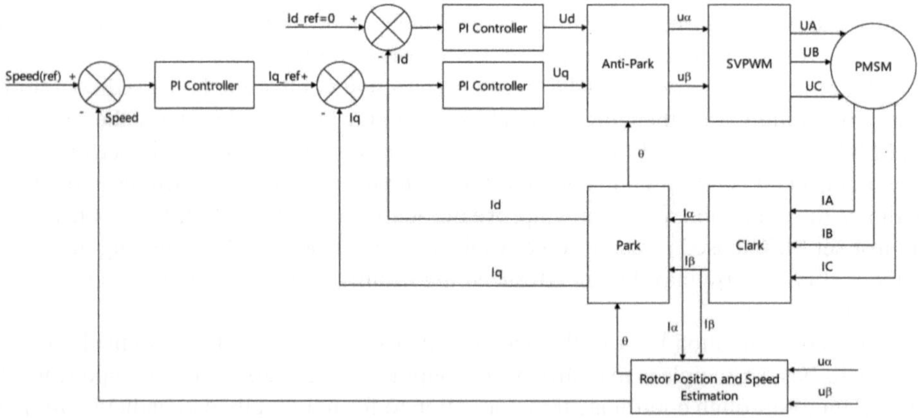

Fig. 1. Overall control principle diagram of PMSM

In the speed control of PMSM, to control the output speed of the motor is essentially by controlling the electromagnetic torque of the motor, and the generation of the electromagnetic torque of the motor relies on the interaction between the stator armature magnetic field and the rotor permanent magnets; the rotor magnetic field of the PMSM is generated by the built-in permanent magnets, and its magnitude is constant when ignoring the secondary factors such as temperature, magnetic saturation, and so on, while the magnitude of the stator armature magnetic field is determined by the current (or voltage) passed into the three-phase winding; therefore, the control of rotational speed can be realized by controlling the three-phase currents at the winding end; however, under the three-phase stationary coordinate system, there are nonlinearities and strong coupling among the three-phase currents ia, ib, and ic in the PMSM, which are difficult to be directly controlled; therefore, it is necessary to introduce the two-phase static and two-phase rotary coordinate system transformations to transform the three-phase currents ia, ib, and ic into the two-phase currents id, iq under the dq axis; and in the two-phase rotating coordinate system, the dq-axis currents of the PMSM are perpendicular to each other, i.e., the dq-axis currents are realized by decoupling control.

The mathematical model of PMSM under two-phase rotating dq coordinate system is as follows.

Voltage equation:

$$u_d = Ri_d + L\frac{di_d}{dt} - \omega_e \psi_q \tag{1}$$

$$u_q = Ri_q + L\frac{di_q}{dt} + \omega_e \psi_d \tag{2}$$

u_d, u_q, i_d, i_q, ψ_d, ψ_q: represents the stator voltage, current, and magnetic chain components in the dq-axis.

Magnetic chain equation:

$$\psi_d = Li_d + \psi_f \tag{3}$$

$$\psi_q = Li_q \tag{4}$$

Selecting id = 0 control mode, the torque equation is as follows:

$$T_e = \frac{3}{2}p_n(\psi_d i_q - \psi_q i_d) = \frac{3}{2}p_n((Li_d + \psi_f)i_q - \psi_q i_d) = \frac{3}{2}p_n \psi_f i_q \tag{5}$$

Know that the electromagnetic torque is directly controlled by the q-axis current iq (Achieved decoupling control).

Mechanical motion equation:

$$\frac{J}{p_n}\frac{d\omega_e}{dt} = T_e - \frac{B}{p_n}\omega_e - T_{\mathrm{L}} \tag{6}$$

ω_e: motor electrical angular velocity ($\omega_e = \omega_m p_n$), ω_m: motor mechanical angular velocity, B: viscous coefficient, J: rotational inertia, T_L: load torque.

3 PMSM Speed Control Design and Implementation

3.1 PMSM Speed Control Design

In the PMSM speed control, the FOC control strategy is selected, and the SVPWM signal modulation method; and in the system of the FOC control strategy, the control method of id = 0 is usually adopted, which is combined with the mathematical model of the motor under the dq-axis to know the torque equation as follows when id = 0:

$$T_e = \frac{3}{2}p_n(\psi_d i_q - \psi_q i_d) = \frac{3}{2}p_n((Li_d + \psi_f)i_q - \psi_q i_d) = \frac{3}{2}p_n\psi_f i_q \tag{7}$$

At this time, the electromagnetic torque of the motor is controlled only by the q-axis current iq, thus realizing the decoupling of the motor multivariable; from the general schematic diagram of the motor speed control, Fig. 1, it is known that the control system adopts a double closed-loop control structure, with the outer ring being the speed ring and the inner ring being the current ring. The output of the rotational speed loop is the given value of the current loop iq, and the input of the current loop is the deviation of the given and actual values of the d and q axis currents, which is used to regulate the output voltage through the PI controller, generate the driving signal through the SVPWM module, and control the switching state of the inverter, thus realizing the speed control of the motor.

3.2 Spatial Coordinate Transformation and Inverse Transformation

The three-phase current ia, ib, ic transformed from the three-phase stationary coordinate system to the two-phase stationary coordinate system is called Clark transform, and the expression of Clark transform is as follows.

$$\begin{bmatrix} f_\alpha \ f_\beta \end{bmatrix}^T = T_{3s/2s}\begin{bmatrix} f_A \ f_B \ f_C \end{bmatrix}^T \tag{8}$$

f: is not a specific physical quantity, it can be magnetic chain, voltage, current, etc.

$T_{3s/2s}$: is the coordinate transformation matrix.

$$T_{3s/2s} = k\begin{bmatrix} 1 & -1/2 & -1/2 \\ 0 & \sqrt{3}/2 & -\sqrt{3}/2 \end{bmatrix} \tag{9}$$

where the coefficient K = $\frac{2}{3}$ or $\sqrt{\frac{2}{3}}$, when k = $\frac{2}{3}$ represents constant amplitude, when k = $\sqrt{\frac{2}{3}}$ represents constant power, the exact value of k can be determined according to the constraints.

According to the above equation can be obtained:

$$I_\alpha = I_A - \frac{1}{2}(I_B + I_C) \tag{10}$$

According to the three-phase current at any moment relationship:

$$I_A + I_B + I_C = 0 \tag{11}$$

The following relationship can be obtained:

$$I_\alpha = \frac{3}{2} I_A \tag{12}$$

The Clark inverse transformation expression is as follows:

$$\left[f_A\, f_B\, f_C\right]^T = T_{2s/3s}\left[f_\alpha\ f_\beta\right]^T \tag{13}$$

where the coordinate transformation matrix $T_{2s/3s}$ is:

$$T_{2s/3s} = k\begin{bmatrix} 1\ 0 \\ -1/2\ \sqrt{3}/2 \\ -1/2\ -\sqrt{3}/2 \end{bmatrix} \tag{14}$$

The transformation of $i_\alpha i_\beta$ from two-phase $\alpha\beta$ stationary coordinate system to two-phase dq rotating coordinate system is called Park transformation, and the expression of Park transformation is as follows.

$$\left[f_d\ f_q\right]^T = T_{2s/2r}\left[f_\alpha\ f_\beta\right]^T \tag{15}$$

The coordinate transformation matrix $T_{2s/2r}$ is:

$$T_{2s/2r} = \begin{bmatrix} \cos\theta & \sin\theta \\ -\sin\theta & \cos\theta \end{bmatrix} \tag{16}$$

Combining the Clark and Park transformations, the transformation matrix $T_{3s/2r}$ is obtained for the transformation from the ABC coordinate system to the dq coordinate system:

$$T_{3s/2r} = k\begin{bmatrix} \cos\theta & \cos(\theta - \frac{2\pi}{3}) & \cos(\theta + \frac{2\pi}{3}) \\ -\sin\theta & -\sin(\theta - \frac{2\pi}{3}) & -\sin(\theta + \frac{2\pi}{3}) \end{bmatrix} \tag{17}$$

Combining Clark and Park inverse transformations, the transformation matrix of dq coordinate system to ABC coordinate system is $T_{2r/3s}$:

$$T_{2r/3s} = k\begin{bmatrix} \cos\theta - \sin\theta \\ \cos(\theta - \frac{2\pi}{3}) - \sin(\theta - \frac{2\pi}{3}) \\ \cos(\theta + \frac{2\pi}{3}) - \sin(\theta + \frac{2\pi}{3}) \end{bmatrix} \tag{18}$$

The three-phase voltage waveforms, the two-phase $\alpha\beta$ voltage waveforms obtained after Clark transformation, and the dq voltage waveforms obtained after Park transformation are shown in Fig. 2. Below; it can be seen from the figure that the three-phase coupled nonlinear sinusoidal voltage waveforms become two-phase perpendicularly linear voltage waveforms after the coordinate transformation; it is further verified that it is possible to decouple the difficult-to-control coupled variables through the coordinate transformation.

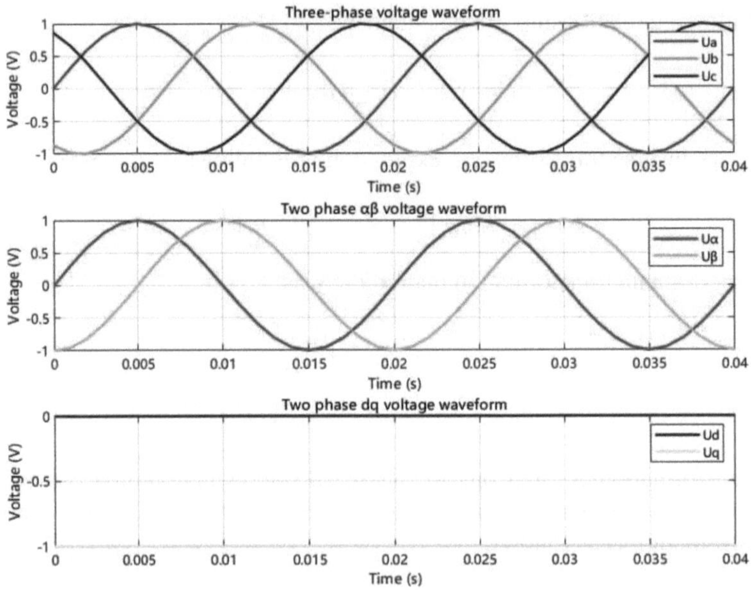

Fig. 2. Voltage waveforms in each coordinate system

3.3 SVPWM Modulation Technology

SVPWM (space vector pulse width modulation), compared with the traditional SPWM (sinusoidal pulse width modulation), SVPWM can make full use of the DC bus voltage, and can synthesize larger voltage vectors under the same bus voltage, which improves the speed control range and dynamic response capability of the motor.

The principle of SVPWM is the average equivalent principle, i.e., by adjusting the operating frequency and duty cycle of the PWM controller, the switching signal is converted into an average output in one cycle. In the motor speed control system, SVPWM is the core bridge connecting the motor control strategy and the power converter, and its core role is to convert the voltage vector command output from the control system into the switching signals of the power switching devices, so as to synthesize the required rotating magnetic field in the motor stator winding, and to realize the precise control of the motor speed and torque.

In the FOC control strategy, the SVPWM converts the ud and dq voltages obtained after coordinate transformation into the voltage vector magnitude and phase in the stationary coordinate system; and calculates the action time of each fundamental vector by selecting six non-zero fundamental voltage vectors (dividing the space plane into six sectors) and two zero vectors determined by the switching state, combined with the volt-second balance principle; thus, generating the inverter switching signals so that the inverter output pulse train is equivalent to the target voltage vector. The plane space sector division is shown in Fig. 3. Below.

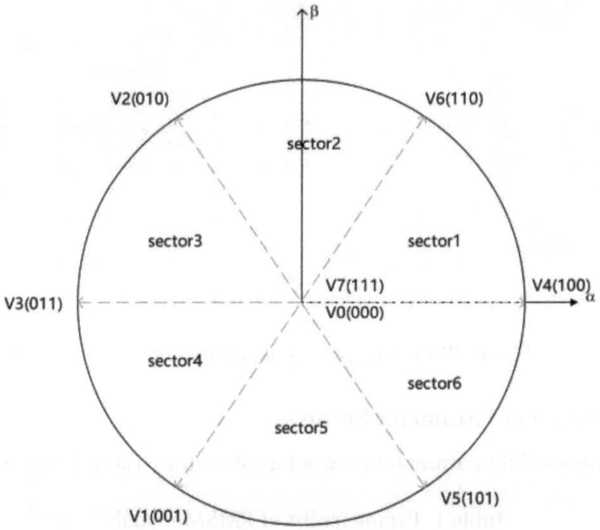

Fig. 3. Sector division of plane space

Analyzing the above figure, it can be seen that the six base vectors divide the plane space into six parts, and any synthesized vector in the plane space will fall in one of the six sectors, and the vector in any sector can be synthesized by the two base vectors in this sector, such as the vector in sector 1 can be synthesized by adjusting the time of action of V4, V6, and the zero vector (V0 or V7). That is to say, the dq plane is divided into 6 sectors, each sector is 60°; according to the sector where the reference voltage vector is located, the two adjacent basic voltage vectors and the zero vector are selected to be synthesized, and the synthesized voltage vectors are made close to the reference voltage vector by controlling the action time of each vector.

4 Simulation Model Construction and Analysis

4.1 Simulation Model Construction

MATLAB/Simulink is used to build a simulation model of FOC-based PMSM speed control system, as shown in Fig. 4. Below, including the PMSM module, coordinate transformation model, SVPWM module, PI controller module, inverter module and so on. Among them, the PMSM module is built according to the mathematical model above, the coordinate transformation module realizes 3s/2s transformation and 2s/2r transformation, the SVPWM module generates the switching signals of the inverter, and the PI controller module realizes the control of the speed ring and the current ring; and in the input side of the simulation model, this paper sets up the set speed wm = 50 rad/s and id = 0A.

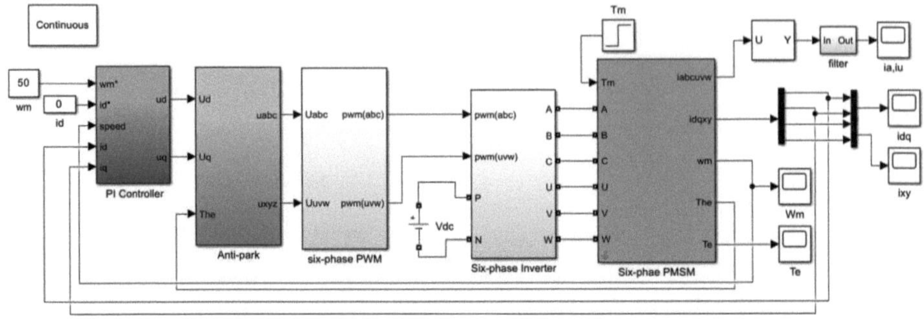

Fig. 4 PMSM speed control simulation model

4.2 PMSM Simulation Parameter Setting

PMSM simulation module parameters are set as shown in Table 1 below:

Table 1 Parameter list of PMSM module

Physical quantity symbol	Meaning	Unit	Setting value
R	Stator winding phase resistance	Ohm	1.4
Ld	d-axis inductance	H	0.008
Lq	q-axis inductance	H	0.008
Lz	Zero sequence inductance	H	0.0017
Flux	Magnetic Chain	Wb	0.68
J	Moment of inertia	$Kg.m^2$	0.015
F	Friction coefficient	N.m.s	0
P	Pole logarithm	—	3

Among them, the stator winding phase resistance R refers to the DC resistance of each phase winding; Ld, Lq is the equivalent inductance of d, q axis; zero-sequence inductance Lz is the path inductance of the zero-sequence current; the magnetic chain of permanent magnets Flux determines the amplitude of the reaction potential, which is the core source of torque; the rotational inertia J is the inertia of the motor rotor (including the load), which determines the dynamic response speed; the friction coefficient F is used to simulate the bearings, wind resistance, and other viscous friction. The friction coefficient F is used to simulate the viscous friction such as bearing and wind resistance, here in this paper, it is set to the ideal state, i.e., $F = 0$; the pole pair number P is the number of pole pairs of permanent magnets, which determines the relationship between the rotational speed and the frequency, and it is the core parameter of magnetic field orientation.

4.3 Analysis of Simulation Results

As shown in Fig. 4., at the input of the simulation model, this paper sets the set value of rotational speed as wm = 50 rad/s, id = 0A; the sampling time is 1s, and analyzes the system's speed regulation performance and stability by adding no load and adding load at time t = 0.2s.

In the case of no load, the rotational speed wm, the electrical angle the, the electromagnetic torque Te and the dq-axis current idq at the output of the simulation model speed control system are shown in the following diagrams.

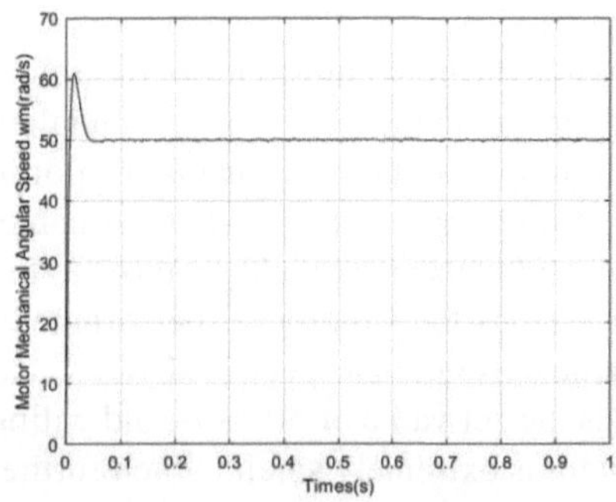

Fig. 5.1. Variation of motor speed

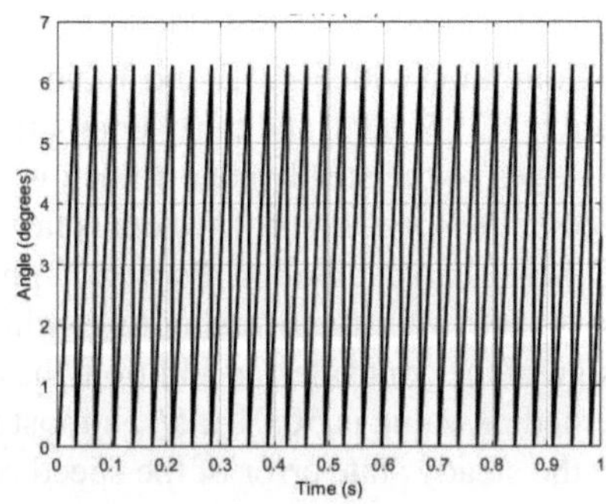

Fig. 5.2. Variation of electrical angle

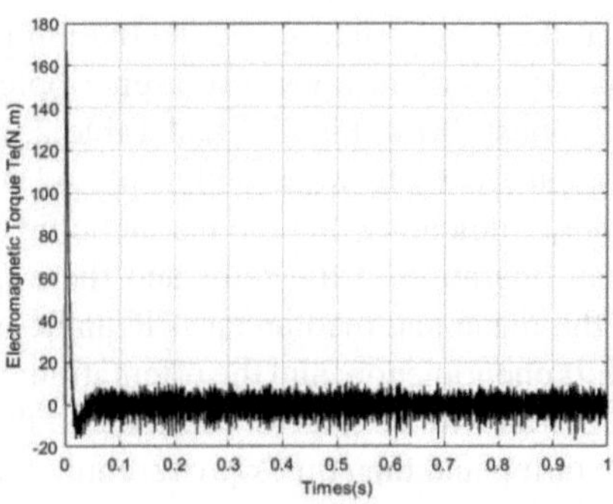

Fig. 5.3. Variation of electromagnetic torque Te

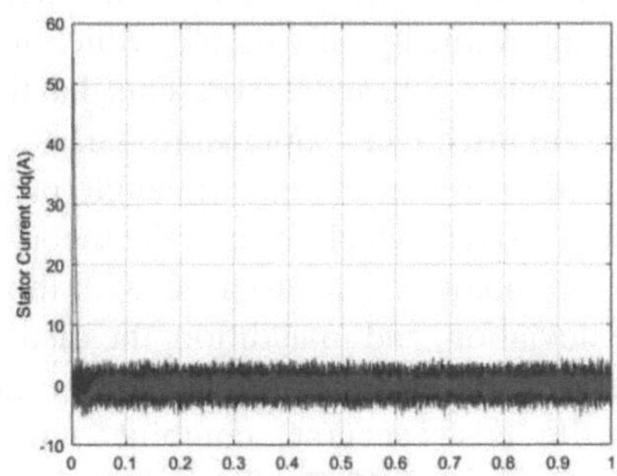

Fig. 5.4. Variation of dq axis current idq

Fig. 5 **(5.1)** Variation of motor speed **(5.2)** Variation of electrical angle **(5.3)** Variation of electromagnetic torque Te **(5.4)** Variation of dq axis current idq

The statistical information of the data of rotational speed wm, electrical angle the, electromagnetic torque Te, and dq axis current idq is shown in Table 2 below:

Table 2 Statistical information table of data variables under no load

	Rotational speed wm	Electrical angle the	Electromagnetic torque Te	Id current	Iq current
Maximum value	60.95	6283	166.7	4647	54.46
Mean value	50.00	3117	0.750	−1172	0.245
Median	50.01	3116	0.189	−1108	0.062

(continued)

Table 2 (*continued*)

	Rotational speed wm	Electrical angle the	Electromagnetic torque Te	Id current	Iq current
Root Mean Square RMS	50.08	3607	10.09	1626	3298

Combined with Fig. 5.1 and Table 2, it is known that the maximum value of rotational speed is 60.95 rad/s, and the overshooting amount appears in the starting stage, and then converges to the steady state value quickly, which indicates that the dynamic response speed of the speed control system is fast, and the damping characteristics are reasonable, and there is no oscillation dispersion phenomenon, and the speed quickly returns to the steady state after the overshooting, which further verifies the validity of the parameter design of the controller; in addition, the average value of rotational speed is 50 rad/s, and the median value is 50.01 rad/s, almost the same as the set value of 50 rad/s, indicating that the steady state error of the speed control system is extremely small, which further illustrates the high precision tracking ability of the vector control strategy on the speed; the root-mean-square value of the speed RMS is 50.08 rad/s, which deviates from the average value by only 0.16%, which indicates that the steady state speed fluctuation is extremely weak, and it represents that the PWM harmonics of the inverter, current ripple, etc. are effectively suppressed, i.e., the system is robust. From Fig. 5.2 and Table 2, it can be seen that the electric angle presents a regular sawtooth wave with a period of about 0.042s, which follows the theory of $\omega_e = p\omega_m$, indicating that the magnetic field of the motor is synchronized with the mechanical operation of the rotor and there is no deviation, and in addition, the distribution of the mean and median electric angle is symmetrical and uniform, i.e., there is no phase shift phenomenon, and the orientation of the d/q-axis is accurate; combined with Figs. 5.3, 5.4 and Table 2, it can be seen that the electromagnetic torque Te peaks to 166.7 N.m at startup and then quickly overcome the inertia to accelerate into a smooth state, iq current changes in the same way; combined with the above analysis, it can be concluded that in the absence of load through the use of magnetic field orientation control strategy to achieve efficient and accurate speed control of the motor.

In the case of adding load at t = 0.2s, the rotational speed wm, electrical angle the, electromagnetic torque Te and dq-axis current idq at the output of the simulation model speed control system are shown in the following figure (Fig. 6).

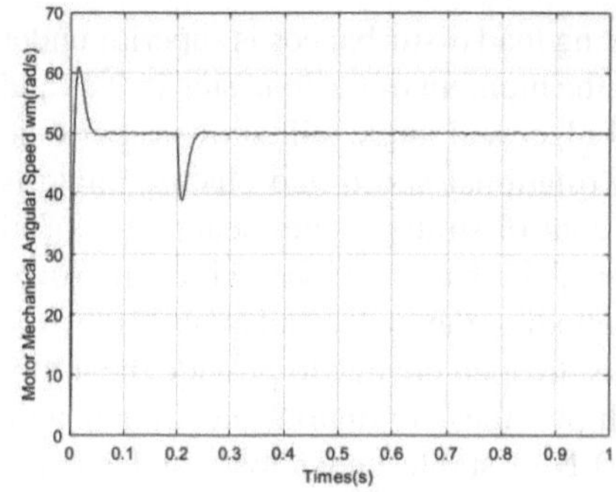

Fig. 6.1. Variation of motor speed

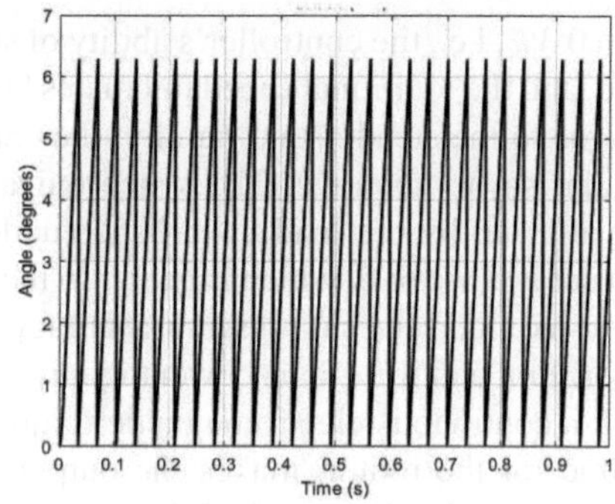

Fig. 6.2. Variation of electric angle

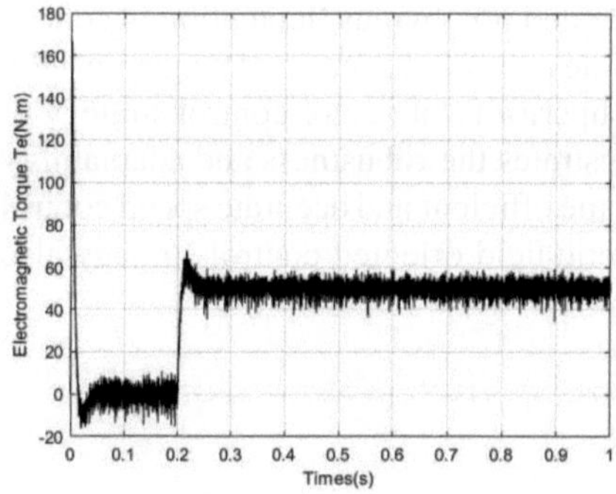

Fig. 6.3. Variation of electromagnetic torque Te

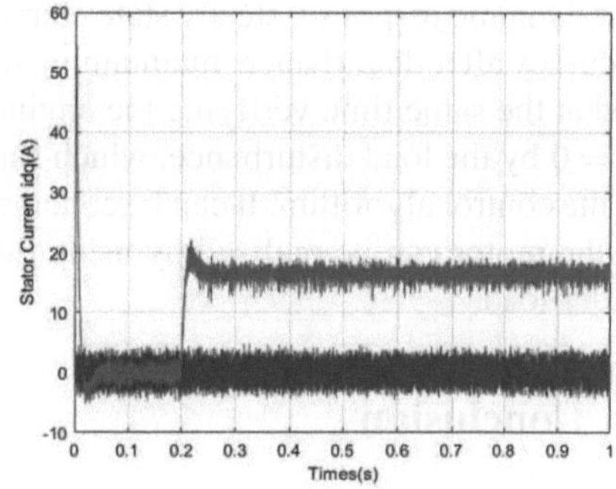

Fig. 6.4. Variation of dq axis current idq

Fig. 6 **(6.1)** Variation of motor speed **(6.2)** Variation of electric angle **(6.3)** Variation of electromagnetic torque Te **(6.4)** Variation of dq axis current idq

The statistical information of the data of rotational speed wm, electrical angle the, electromagnetic torque Te and dq axis current idq is shown in Table 3 below:

Table 3 Statistical information table for data variables under load

	Rotational speed wm	Electrical angle the	Electromagnetic torque Te	Id current	Iq current
Maximum value	60.95	6283	166.7	4816	54.46
Mean value	49.80	3109	40.75	0.00075	13.32
Median	50.01	3103	49.40	−0.021	16.15
Root Mean Square RMS	49.89	3601	45.89	1615	15.00

Combined with the above figures and Table 3, it can be seen that under load, the mean value of rotational speed is 49.80 rad/s, median 50.01 rad/s, which is only 0.4% deviation from the set value; the root-mean-square (RMS) is 49.89 rad/s, with a fluctuation of less than 0.3%, i.e., the controller's ability of suppressing load disturbances is superior under load, and the rotational speed fluctuates briefly in the moment of the load step in 0.2s and returns to the steady state rapidly; the change of electrical angle still shows a periodic regular sawtooth wave. The synchronization of rotational speed and electric angle is not affected by the load disturbance under this control strategy; the mean value of id current is close to 0, which is nearer to the set value than that of no load, which improves the d-axis current suppression accuracy and embodies the strong adaptability of the algorithm; and the q-axis current iq quickly tracks the load change to provide the motor with a continuous electromagnetic torque, which provides continuous electromagnetic torque for the motor, makes the output 40 ~ 50 N.m stable under load, and quickly adapts to make the speed of the motor track the set value stably under load addition; In conclusion, under load condition, the simulation model speed control system has fast dynamic response, steady state characteristics and no obvious fluctuation in control accuracy after disturbance, maintaining the accurate control of speed and magnetic field, and at the same time verifying the engineering superiority of vector control strategy of id = 0 by the load disturbance, which further illustrates the robustness and adaptability of the control algorithm. It can be concluded that the efficient and accurate speed control of the motor can be realized by using the magnetic field oriented control strategy also under load.

5 Conclusion

This paper focuses on the analysis of PMSM speed control, from theoretical modeling to simulation verification, through the analysis of the PMSM mathematical model and the construction of the simulation model, the decoupling of the multivariable coupling of the motor and the precise control of speed regulation are realized by using the magnetic field directional control strategy and combining with the SVPWM modulation technology; the adaptability and stability of the control algorithm in the case of the motor with and without load is also verified, providing a solid simulation basis for the application of motor speed control in industrial scenarios.

References

1. Zhao, C., Gui, B., Sun Y. Efficient control strategy of permanent magnet synchronous motor. Explosion-proof Motor **59**(05):25–28 (2024)
2. Ping, M., Jia, Z., Chen, Z. Design of DC servo motor drive based on hardware FOC. Power Electron. Technol. **58**(09):18–23 (2024)
3. Xu, J., Zhao, Q., Chen, Y., et al. Development of permanent magnet synchronous motor direct-drive speed control system for mining belt conveyor. Coal Technol. 1–8 [2025-07-03]. http://kns.cnki.net/kcms/detail/23.1393.td.20240701.1047.002.html
4. Lin, K., Gao, H. Y., Chen, Z. C. Research on compound control strategy of permanent magnet synchronous motorsspeed control system. Manufact. Technol. Mach. Tools **2024**(08):120–126+142 (2024).https://doi.org/10.19287/j.mtmt.1005-2402.2024.08.017
5. Hu, X., Xia, Y., Lendek, Z., et al. A novel dynamic prescribed performance fuzzy-neural backstepping control for PMSM under step load. Neural Networks, **2025**, 190107627–107627 (2025)

6. Zhang, H., Wang, H., Yang, J., et al.: Enhancing PMSM drive systems: an advanced three-vector model predictivecurrent control strategy. J. Phys. Conf. Ser. **3033**(1), 012023 (2025)
7. Chen, Y., Zhang, S.X.: Research on permanent magnet synchronous motor based on magnetic field oriented vector control. Silicon Valley **7**(20), 36–37 (2014)
8. Yifan, W., Yichime, S., Guoqiang, S., et al.: Research on vector control method of permanent magnet synchronous motor based on SVPWM. Microelectronics Machine **57**(09), 14–21 (2024). https://doi.org/10.15934/j.cnki.micromotors.2024.09.009
9. Luo, H., Wang, Z., Li, Y. Study on direct torque control strategy of PMSM without differential beat based on magnetic chain planning research. Electrical Drives, 1–9[2025–07–03].https://doi.org/10.19457/j.1001-2095.dqcd26481
10. Lu, C., Liang, H. Research on direct torque control of permanent magnet synchronous motor based on fuzzy tree model. Comput Meas Contr, 1–12[2025–07–03]. http://kns.cnki.net/kcms/detail/11. 4762.tp.20250421.1028.020.html
11. Huang, Y., Liu, S., Pang, R., et al.: Model predictive current control for six-phase PMSM with Steady-StatePerformance improvement. Energies **17**(21), 5273 (2024)
12. Zeng, X., Li, J., Yang, P., et al.: An echo state network approach for parameter variation robustness enhancement in FCS-MPC for PMSM drives. Appl. Sci. **15**(11), 6288 (2025)
13. Du, C., Gang, J. An optimal MPC control method for PMSM motor drive system based on Gray Wolf optimization process. J. Institut Eng (India): Series B, 2024, (prepublish): 1–8
14. Zhenbiao, Y., Jian, S.: Improved predictive speed control of permanent magnet synchronous motor with finite control set model. Motor and Control Applications **50**(12), 92–100 (2023)
15. Zhou, H., Li, L., Hu, Y., et al. Simplified finite control set modeling under five-phase PMSMsingle-phase open-circuit faults for pre measured torque and magnetic chain control. Chin. J. Electr. Eng., **45**(05):1958–1968 (2024).https://doi.org/10.13334/j.0258-8013.pcsee.232011
16. Hou, S., Gao, X.: Analysis of the principle and control mode of brushless DC motor balance car based on FOC control. Electron. Technol. **54**(01), 395–397 (2025)
17. Huang, G., Li, J., Yang, Y., et al.: An integral sliding-mode observer-based equivalent-input-disturbance methodfor fault-tolerant control of permanent magnet synchronous motor drive system. Vibration and Control **31**(13–14), 2920–2934 (2025)
18. Zhang, H., Wang, H., Yang, J., et al.: Enhancing PMSM drive systems: an advanced three-vector model predictive current control strategy. J. Phys. Conf. Ser. **3033**(1), 012023 (2025)
19. Yin, L., Tang, C., Wei, L. A PMSM speed control strategy of LADRC based on neural network load torque estimation. Int. J. Pattern Recogn. Artif. Intell., **39**(06) (2025)
20. Yu, Q., Pan, X., He, X., et al. Active disturbance rejection control strategy for PMSMs in electric tractors based on fuzzy cascaded extended observers. Comput. Electr. Eng. **2025**: 126110466–110466 (2025)

Modeling and Simulation of Underwater Active Electric Field Detection Based on Compact Electrode Structure

Yu Pei[1], Yong Cui[1](✉), Qinglei Hu[1], Huafu Cheng[2], Zirui Wang[1], Ke Bi[3], Jianchun Xu[3], and Huaining Wu[1]

[1] School of Automation Science and Electrical Engineering, Beihang University, Beijing, China
cuiyong@buaa.edu.cn
[2] Yichang Testing Technique R&D Institute, Yichang, China
[3] State Key Laboratory of Information Photonics and Optical Communications, School of Science, Beijing University of Posts and Telecommunications, Beijing, China

Abstract. Underwater active electric field detection is an important sensing technology applicable to turbid waters, low-light conditions, and other complex marine environments. Traditional low-frequency electric field sources usually adopt discrete paired electrode structures, and the large system size not only restricts the flexibility of deployment in narrow spaces but is also easily affected by environmental factors such as water disturbances, thereby reducing the stability and accuracy of detection. The emerging solution integrates the source electrodes in the single structure to achieve a compact design with miniaturization advantages, providing a solution to improve system integration and detection performance. In this paper, modeling and simulation studies are conducted on the underwater active electric field detection method. The theoretical model of the electric field generated by the compact electrode structure is established, the perturbation characteristics of typical underwater targets on the electric field distribution are analyzed, and the corresponding simulation model is constructed. The simulation results demonstrate that the compact electrode structure can effectively generate low-frequency electric fields and facilitate target detection. Furthermore, the influence of some structural parameters on detection performance is analyzed.

Keywords: Underwater Detection · Electric Field · Simulation

1 Introduction

Underwater active electric field detection mainly achieves target detection and identification by applying an electric field to the water and analyzing the target-induced perturbations in the electric field distribution. [1]. Compared with optical and acoustic detection, this method is characterized by low dependence on

W. Cai et al. (Eds.): AsiaSim 2025, CCIS 2727, pp. 148–158, 2026.
https://doi.org/10.1007/978-981-95-4472-1_13

water clarity, higher resolution at close range, and reduced susceptibility to multipath interference. [2–5]. Therefore, the underwater active electric field detection method has good adaptability in a variety of complex environments, especially in special conditions such as turbidity, low-light conditions, and rugged terrain.

The traditional implementation of electric field sources for underwater active electric field detection typically adopts discrete paired electrode structures [6, 7]. However, in order to generate a sufficiently strong electric field, it is often necessary to increase the distance between the electrodes. The larger size of the system structure will make it difficult to operate in narrow or complex underwater environments, and it is susceptible to disturbances brought by currents, water pressure and other complex underwater environments, which in turn affects the detection accuracy [8, 9].

To enable the miniaturization of low-frequency electric field sources, the integration of the source electrodes into a single structural unit offers a promising solution to achieve a compact design. Peng et al. designed a detection system with vertically arranged transmitting and receiving electrodes that allowed the location and tracking of underwater spherical targets [10]. Hu et al. designed a ring-distributed electrode arrangement, which can more fully utilize the spatial information of the electric field in the water [11]. Bai et al. integrated transmitter electrodes and receiver sensors in a capsule-like compact structure for underwater robotic electrical sensing [12].

In this paper, a theoretical analysis and simulation verification study is carried out around the application of underwater active electric field detection method. Firstly, the electric field model of compact electrode structure in the underwater environment and the equivalent model of the detected target are discussed respectively, and the perturbation law of the target to the spatial electric field is analyzed. Then the basic principle of active electric field detection of underwater targets is given. Next, the electric field characteristics and the underwater active electric field detection process are modeled and simulated, and the influence of some key parameters on the detection performance is discussed. Finally, the feasibility of the underwater active electric field detection method is verified by comparing the simulation results with the theoretical analysis, which provides a method reference for subsequent applications.

2 Underwater Active Electric Field Detection Method

2.1 Electric Field Model

In underwater active electric field detection, the higher conductivity of seawater will exacerbate the spatial attenuation of the electric field. In order to ensure detection coverage, extremely low frequency (ELF) or very low frequency (VLF) is often used as the operating frequency band. In complex media such as seawater or sedimentary layers, low-frequency signals compared to high-frequency signals have slower attenuation and can penetrate more effectively the conductive environment to achieve the detection of buried or obscured targets. VLF signals in the guarantee of a certain penetration ability at the same time can more effectively take into account the detection performance. The compact electrode structure illustrated in Fig. 1 is simplified as a cylinder, for which the electric field model is established based on equivalent dipole theory [13].

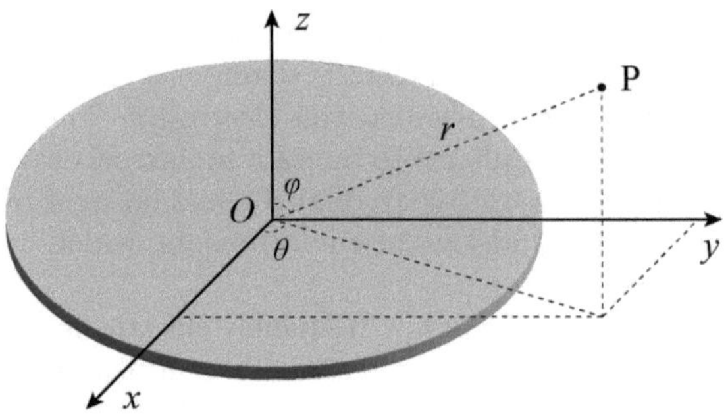

Fig. 1. Illustration of the electric field modeling for the compact electrode structure.

It is assumed that the compact electrode structure can be equated to an electric dipole placed along the z-axis with the electric dipole moment p_0. When the electric dipole moment varies sinusoidally, the vector potential $\boldsymbol{A}$ is obtained as follows.

$$\boldsymbol{A}(\boldsymbol{r}) = \frac{\mu}{4\pi}\frac{j\omega p_0}{r}e^{-jkr}\hat{\boldsymbol{\alpha}}_z \tag{1}$$

where $\boldsymbol{r}$ is the vector diameter to the observation point, μ is the magnetic permeability, ω is the angular frequency, k is the wave number, and $\hat{\boldsymbol{\alpha}}_z$ is the unit vector in the z-axis.

Expressed in spherical coordinates, the spatial electric field distribution is as follows.

$$\begin{cases} E_r = \frac{2p_0k^3}{4\pi\varepsilon}e^{-jkr}\left[\frac{1}{(kr)^2} - \frac{j}{(kr)^3}\right]\cos\theta \\ E_\theta = \frac{p_0k^3}{4\pi\varepsilon}e^{-jkr}\left[\frac{j}{kr} + \frac{1}{(kr)^2} - \frac{j}{(kr)^3}\right]\sin\theta \\ E_\varphi = 0 \end{cases} \tag{2}$$

where ε is the dielectric constant.

For underwater active electric field detection, the detection distance is usually less than the length of one wavelength. When the detection target is in the near-field region, the electric field strength amplitude is inversely proportional to the distance by a factor of three. This rapid decay characteristic makes the electric field energy concentrated near the compact electrode structure, reduces the influence of long-distance interference sources, and is conducive to high-precision detection of the target.

2.2 Underwater Active Electric Field Detection Model

In the research on underwater active electric field detection, targets are often simplified into idealized models with regular geometries to reduce the complexity of model construction and numerical calculations [14]. Equating a complex-structured target with a spherical conductor is a common and effective treatment method. This simplification strategy significantly reduces the need for modeling the geometric features of the target, thus simplifying the computational process of solving the boundary conditions and the electric field distribution. This not only helps to improve the overall simulation efficiency, but also makes the theoretical analysis more operable and universal, laying a foundation for the subsequent electric field distribution prediction.

The Rasnow model describes the perturbations produced by an ideal spherical conductor in a uniform background electric field [15]. In this model, the effect of the sphere on the distribution of the surrounding electric field can be described quantitatively based on the background electric field. Since the spherical conductor is a centrosymmetric structure, it can be simplified to a two-dimensional plane for analysis. A polar coordinate system is established with the center of the sphere of the spherical conductor as the origin. The background electric field E_0 is assumed to be uniform and oriented along the direction of the polar axis. Set the center of the sphere as the reference point for zero electric potential. Under steady-state electric field conditions, the potential $U(r,\theta)$ at any position (r,θ) in space can be obtained according to the following equation.

$$\frac{\partial}{\partial r}\left(r^2\frac{\partial U\left(r,\theta\right)}{\partial r}\right)+\frac{1}{\sin\theta}\frac{\partial}{\partial\theta}\left(\sin\theta\frac{\partial U\left(r,\theta\right)}{\partial\theta}\right)=0 \tag{3}$$

By applying the separation of variables method to Laplace's equation, based on the axial symmetry of the potential function, and combining the continuity boundary conditions of the potential and current density at the surface of the sphere, the expressions for the complete potential distributions induced by a spherical conductor in an applied electric field are obtained as follows.

$$U\left(r,\theta\right)=-E_0 r\cos\theta-E_0\frac{\rho_t-\rho_s}{2\rho_t+\rho_s}\frac{r_t^3}{r^2}\cos\theta \tag{4}$$

where r_t is the radius of the spherical conductor, ρ_t and ρ_s are the resistivity of the spherical conductor and the space medium, respectively.

For the potential distribution in the external region of the sphere, it can be considered as a superposition of two parts. One part is the potential distribution corresponding to the original background uniform electric field, and the other part is the perturbed potential due to the presence of the sphere. The latter can be equated to the additional potential generated by an electric dipole located at the center of the sphere and oriented in the same direction as the background electric field. This equivalent electric dipole model reflects the physical process of redistribution of free charges inside a conductor sphere under the action of an applied electric field, resulting in induced polarization. Since the background electric field is oriented horizontally, the polarized charges on the surface of the conductor sphere are also distributed along the horizontal direction, which makes the external perturbation potential exhibit obvious spatial variation characteristics in this direction.

2.3 Principle of Detection Method

The Rasnow model has a clear mathematical expression form and closed-solution structure, which provides a theoretical basis for simplifying the complex underwater target into an ideal conductor model. In the simulation process, the application of this model can simplify the setting of boundary conditions and reduce the geometrical complexity of the solution region, so as to improve the computational efficiency and stability of the solution. By combining the potential distribution perturbation generated by a spherical conductor in an applied electric field with the electric field model in a spatial environment, the detection of conductor targets can be realized.

In the absence of a target object, the voltage signal measured by the receiving electrode mainly originates from the electric field in the environment, which can be recorded as U_{env}. When the target object exists, its perturbation to the original electric field can be obtained according to Eq. (4), and its mathematical expression is shown below.

$$\Delta U = -E_0 r \frac{\rho_t - \rho_s}{2\rho_t + \rho_s} \left(\frac{r_t}{r}\right)^3 \cos\theta \tag{5}$$

The key step in underwater active electric field detection is to construct and optimize an objective function J that minimizes the difference between the voltage signal ΔU of the receiving electrodes obtained according to the theoretical model and the voltage signal U_{meas} received in the actual scenario.

$$J = \|\Delta U - (U_{meas} - U_{env})\|^2 \tag{6}$$

In practical scenarios, in order to obtain sufficient constraints and improve the uniqueness of the solution to the multivariate problem, an array of receiving electrodes is usually deployed to obtain measurement data from multiple locations in space. Another scheme is to obtain the received data at different moments through the movement of electrodes, thus realizing spatial-temporal data fusion. Among them, the moving electrode technique has better economy and stronger spatial adaptability in complex underwater environment, which can avoid the high demand for multichannel consistency for high accuracy, and the time series data acquired during the moving process can be supported for the analysis of dynamic changes in the target state. Therefore, the moving electrode technique is adopted as the primary approach for analysis.

3 Simulation Results and Discussion

3.1 Simulation Scenario and Modeling

The electric field in the environment is not homogeneous according to Eq. (2), which makes the theoretical analysis require the equivalent of a homogeneous electric field in a specific scale to realize the application of analytical models. Moreover, in complex underwater scenarios such as the detection of buried objects, it becomes difficult to accurately obtain the theoretical values due to the nonlinearity of the electric field, complex boundary conditions, and interference of ambient noise. The simulation method can realize the effective representation and efficient solution of the complex detection process by multi-physics modeling and combining with nonlinear boundary conditions [16]. At the same time, the simulation is also able to perform parameter analysis and law prediction without direct experimentation, which provides a basis for the design and optimization of the active electric field detection method.

The underwater active electric field detection method is simulated using COMSOL Multiphysics. The simulation scenario is shown in Fig. 2. The detection device consists of the compact electrode structure and a receiving electrode, which is located in the seawater region. The spherical conductor serves as the detection target and is located in the buried area. The horizontal movement of the detection device is simulated by changing the position of the spherical conductor, and the electric field signals obtained by the receiving electrode are simulated when the detection target is in different positions.

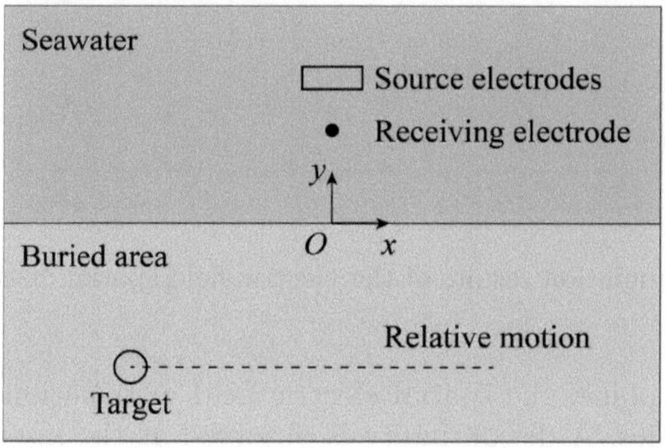

Fig. 2. Simulation scenario for underwater active electric field detection.

The size of the model is $2\,\text{m} \times 1\,\text{m}$, the height of the seawater area is $0.5\,\text{m}$ and the relative permittivity is 81. The height of the buried area is $0.5\,\text{m}$ and the relative permittivity is 40. A right-angle coordinate system is established with the center of the model as the origin. The compact electrode structure is modeled as a cylindrical structure with a radius of 25mm and a height of 3mm. It is centered at the coordinate point (0,0.2). The receiver electrode is positioned at the default location of (0, 0.1). The detection target is modeled as a solid sphere with a radius of 25mm, initially located at (0, −0.25). An infinite element domain is employed to simulate the open boundary conditions of the physical environment and to minimize artificial reflections.

3.2 Simulation Results of Electric Field Distribution

In the simulation process, the electric field perturbation caused by the detection target entering the underwater active electric field region is analyzed to study the effect of the target position change on the electric field distribution. As shown in Eq. (5), the key parameters affecting the detection results include the position of the receiving electrode, the resistivity of the target and its geometry. Systematically exploring the influence of these key parameters on the underwater active electric field detection method will provide theoretical support for system optimization and performance enhancement.

The simulation results show that when the frequency is 30kHz, the spatial distribution of the electric field is illustrated in Fig. 3.

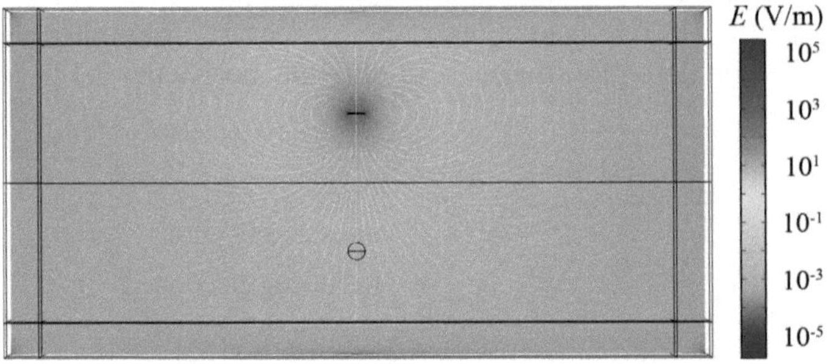

Fig. 3. Simulation results of the electric field spatial distribution.

In the vertical plane, the spatial electric field distribution exhibits axisymmetric characteristics. A discontinuity is observed at the interface between the seawater and the buried region. The simulation results are generally consistent with the theoretical analysis.

3.3 Simulation Results of Active Electric Field Detection

In order to simulate the moving process of the detection device, the detection target is set to move horizontally from coordinate $(-0.5, -0.2)$ to coordinate $(0.5, -0.2)$. At the same time, the positions of the receiving electrodes are changed to x-coordinate 0, -0.1, and -0.2, respectively. The underwater active electric field perturbation induced by the detection target, characterized by the voltage variation obtained by the receiving electrodes, is shown in Fig. 4.

In the simulation range, the extreme value of the voltage variation acquired by the receiving electrode occurs near the position where the detection target is closest to the receiving electrode. However, on both sides of this extreme value, the voltage variation does not exhibit the desired monotonicity. This is due to the electric field is non-uniform in space. The non-uniform electric field distribution couples with the perturbations induced by the detection target, which leads

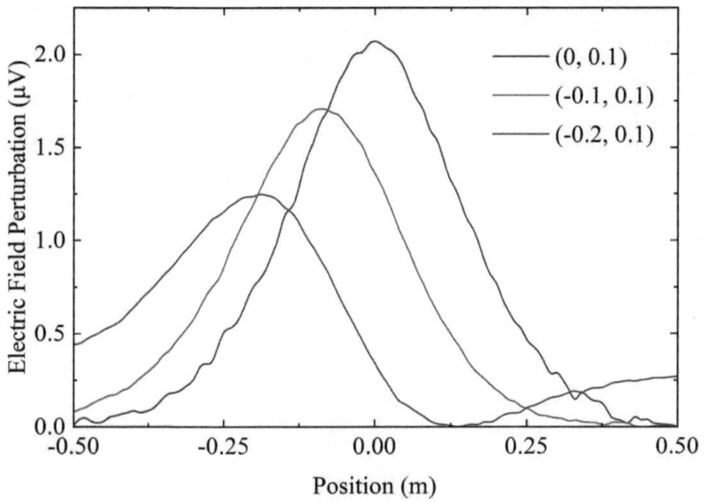

Fig. 4. Electric field perturbations obtained by receiving electrodes located at different coordinates during horizontal movement of the target

to the appearance of local minima. As the receiving electrodes gradually move away, the amplitude of the measured voltage changes tends to decrease overall. In order to obtain a stronger received signal to improve the detection accuracy, the position of the receiving electrode is fixed to (0, 0.1).

The influence of the detection target resistivity on the voltage variation measured by the receiving electrode is discussed, taking iron and polyethylene as examples. The simulation results are shown in Fig. 5, which shows the difference in the perturbation characteristics induced in the underwater active electric field for target objects with different conductivity.

When the detection targets are iron and polyethylene respectively, the variation patterns of the measured voltage amplitude at the receiving electrodes during the targets' horizontal movement are generally similar. However, there are numerical differences and an approximate multiplicative relationship between them. This is due to the contrast between the resistivity of the detection target and the surrounding medium. When the detection target resistivity is much smaller than that of the surrounding medium, it can be considered an ideal conductor. At this point, Eq. (5) can be simplified as follows.

$$|\Delta U| = E_0 r \left(\frac{r_t}{r}\right)^3 \tag{7}$$

When the resistivity of the detection target is much larger than that of the surrounding medium, it can be regarded as an ideal insulator. At this point, Eq. (5) can be simplified as follows.

$$|\Delta U| = \frac{E_0 r}{2} \left(\frac{r_t}{r}\right)^3 \tag{8}$$

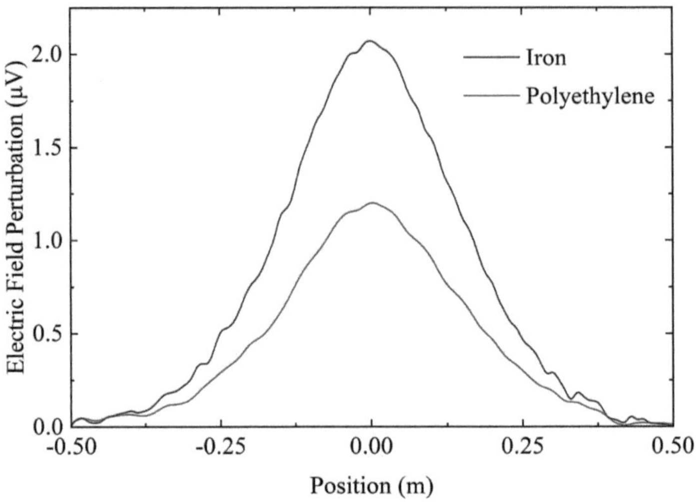

Fig. 5. Electric field perturbations at receiving electrodes during target movement for different target materials.

Therefore, for the two representative materials, iron and polyethylene, the coefficient differences derived from the theoretical analysis regarding resistivity effects show good agreement with the simulation results, validating the applicability of the theoretical model to targets with different electrical conductivity characteristics.

The effect of the target size on the voltage variation measured by the receiving electrode is explored by changing the radius of the spherical detection target with the target material fixed as polyethylene. The simulation results are shown in Fig. 6.

When the center of the spherical detection target is fixed, the amplitude of the voltage variation measured by the receiving electrode is approximately in a cubic relationship with the radius of the target, and this result is consistent with the theoretical analysis of Eq. (8). Therefore, for the received signals, target objects with higher electrical conductivity and larger geometric dimensions cause more significant electric field perturbations and are therefore easier to detect.

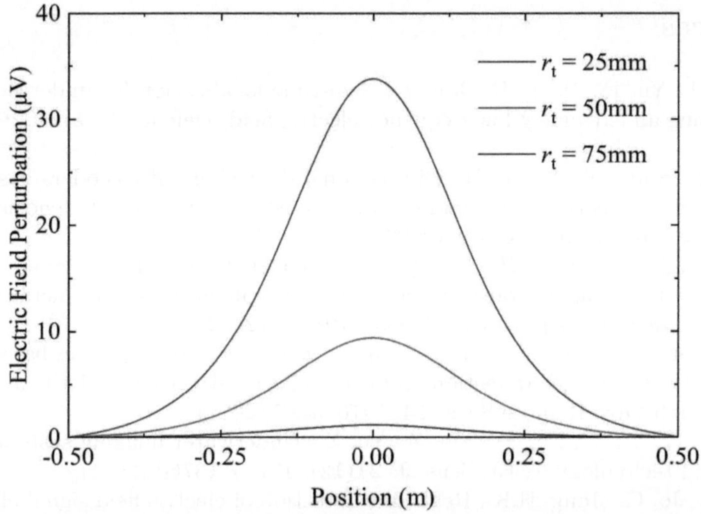

Fig. 6. Electric field perturbations at receiving electrodes during target movement with different spherical target radii.

4 Conclusion

In this paper, modeling and simulation studies are conducted to investigate underwater active electric field detection method. The study establishes a theoretical model of the electric field generated by the compact electrode structure and analyzes the perturbation characteristics of typical underwater targets on the electric field distribution, on the basis of which a simulation and analysis framework is constructed. The simulation results demonstrate that the compact electrode structure can effectively excite the low-frequency electric field and show the influence of some key parameters on the detection performance. The results provide a reference for the design of subsequent miniaturized and high-performance underwater electric field detection systems.

Acknowledgments. This work was supported by the National Natural Science Foundation of China under Grant 62271029.

Disclosure of Interests. The authors have no competing interests to declare that are relevant to the content of this article.

References

1. Zhang, J., Yu, P., Jiang, R., Xie, T.: Real-time localization for underwater equipment using an extremely low frequency electric field. Defence Technol. **26**, 203–212 (2023)
2. Dong, Y., Shen, X., Wang, H.: Bidirectional denoising autoencoders-based robust representation learning for underwater acoustic target signal denoising. IEEE Trans. Instrum. Meas. **71**, 1–8 (2022)
3. Shi, H., Li, J., Chang, H., Liu, L.: Research on passive localization method of shallow water acoustic source with single hydrophone based on hierarchical grid histogram filtering. Appl. Acoust. **194**, 108812 (2022)
4. Qi, J., Gong, Z., Xue, W., Liu, X., Yao, A., Zhong, P.: An unmixing-based network for underwater target detection from hyperspectral imagery. IEEE J. Sel. Top. Appl. Earth Obs. Remote Sens. **14**, 5470–5487 (2021)
5. Ouyang, F., Yu, J., Liu, H., Ma, Z., Yu, X.: Underwater imaging system based on light field technology. IEEE Sens. J. **21**(12), 13753–13760 (2021)
6. Kim, Y., Jo, G., Jung, H.K.: Real-time detection of electric field signal of a moving object using adjustable frequency bands and statistical discriminant for underwater defense. IEEE Trans. Geosci. Remote Sens. **60**, 1–8 (2022)
7. Cho, S.H., Jung, H.K., Lee, H., Rim, H., Lee, S.K.: Real-time underwater object detection based on DC resistivity method. IEEE Trans. Geosci. Remote Sens. **54**(11), 6833–6842 (2016)
8. Miller, L.M., Silverman, Y., MacIver, M.A., Murphey, T.D.: Ergodic exploration of distributed information. IEEE Trans. Rob. **32**(1), 36–52 (2015)
9. Lanneau, S., Boyer, F., Lebastard, V., Bazeille, S.: Model based estimation of ellipsoidal object using artificial electric sense. Int. J. Robot. Res. **36**(9), 1022–1041 (2017)
10. Peng, H., Jiang, G., Hu, Q., Fu, T., Xu, D.: Locating and tracking of underwater sphere target based on active electrosense. Sens. Actuators, A **363**, 114671 (2023)
11. Hu, S., et al.: A spatial field-aware underwater detection system based on active electrosense. IEEE Sens. J. **25**(5), 8828–8840 (2025)
12. Bai, Y., Snyder, J.B., Peshkin, M., MacIver, M.A.: Finding and identifying simple objects underwater with active electrosense. Int. J. Robot. Res. **34**(10), 1255–1277 (2015)
13. Schwinger, J., DeRaad, L.L., Jr., Milton, K., Tsai, W.: Classical Electrodynamics. CRC Press (2019)
14. Bazeille, S., Lebastard, V., Boyer, F.: A purely model-based approach to object pose and size estimation with electric sense. IEEE Trans. Rob. **36**(5), 1611–1618 (2020)
15. Rasnow, B.: The effects of simple objects on the electric field of apteronotus. J. Comp. Physiol. A **178**, 397–411 (1996)
16. Song, X., Xie, H., Sun, J., Han, D., Cui, Y., Chen, B.: Simulation of pedestrian rotation dynamics near crowded exits. IEEE Trans. Intell. Transp. Syst. **20**(8), 3142–3155 (2018)

Driving Closer to the Limit: Improved Virtual Racecar Drivers with Data-Driven Control

Ruslan Shaiakhmetov[1(✉)], Danilo Pianini[1], Valter Venusti[2], Gabriele D'Angelo[1], and Alessandro V. Papadopoulos[3]

[1] Alma Mater Studiorum—Università di Bologna, Cesena, Italy
{ruslan.shaiakhmetov,danilo.pianini,g.dangelo}@unibo.it
[2] Dallara Automobili S.p.A., Parma, Italy
V.Venusti@dallara.it
[3] Mälardalen University, Västerås, Sweden
alessandro.papadopoulos@mdu.se

Abstract. Accurate simulation of racing cars is crucial in motorsport to quickly identify effective setups before track testing. Typically, professional drivers provide feedback in simulation, but this process is costly and time-consuming. A capable virtual driver, combined with precise car simulations, could significantly speed up setup development. This paper proposes a data-driven predictive control approach, Data-enabled Predictive, for trajectory tracking in racing simulations. We compare our approach against an industry-standard Proportional-Integral-Derivative controller and a state-of-the-art Model Predictive Control controller, demonstrating that our method is feasible and yields substantial performance improvements, particularly when trajectories approach the car's physical limits.

Keywords: Machine Learning · Model Predictive Control · Autonomous Racing · DeePC · Trajectory Tracking · Racecar Simulation

1 Introduction

Professional racing teams heavily rely on simulators to refine car setups before events, significantly reducing track-time costs and environmental impacts. The relevance of simulation in motorsport has been growing steadily over the years, with teams investing millions of dollars to get ahead of their competitors[1]. A bet-

This work is supported by the project "Ottimizzazione computazione di un modello di simulazione dinamica del veicolo" funded by the European Union - NextGenerationEU and Dallara Automobili S.p.A. through the Italian "National Recovery and Resilience Plan" (PNRR) Mission 4, Component 2, Investment 3.3 (DM 352/2022) - CUP J33C22001400009 and the Swedish Research Council (VR) with the PSI project (No. #2020-05094).

[1] AMG Petronas Formula One Team—How Does F1 Simulation Work? https://archive.is/mrNjx, archived on 2024-04-02.

W. Cai et al. (Eds.): AsiaSim 2025, CCIS 2727, pp. 159–170, 2026.
https://doi.org/10.1007/978-981-95-4472-1_14

ter simulation infrastructure and high correlation between simulator and track can lead to significant gains: the base car setup can be found early, shrinking the search space and thus more effectively exploiting the free practice sessions to refine details. Increasing cost, environmental concerns, and regulatory constraints further amplify the role of simulation in motorsport [8].

Simulation at a professional level can be distinguished in two main categories:

1. *Driver-in-Loop (DiL)* simulators, where a human drives a model of the car;
2. *Virtual driver* simulators, where the car is driven by a computer program.

The requirement of a professional racing driver to be physically present in the simulator limits the extent to which DiL simulators can be used; on the other hand, accurate simulation of the driver's behavior (a task akin to programming virtually driven cars) is paramount to obtain valuable feedback.

In this work, we focus on the virtual driver simulator case, and, specifically, on the construction of a control system capable of tracking an ideal trajectory (e.g., coming from a real-world lap), for which we propose a data-driven predictive control approach. We compare our proposed approach with an industrial standard Proportional-Integral-Derivative (PID) controller and with academic state-of-the-art Model Predictive Control (MPC).

1.1 Problem Statement

Developing a virtual driver involves: (i) provided the track limits and car data, *generate an optimal reference trajectory*; and (ii) *compute the control inputs* to accurately follow it. Here we focus on the second task. In particular, we investigate the usage of data-driven control techniques for autonomous racing.

1.2 Contribution

This paper extends our previous work [17], where we introduced a data-driven predictive control approach for trajectory tracking in racing car simulation. In this extended version, we expand our analysis of the method including:

- the impact of key hyperparameters (prediction horizon and dataset size) on the controller's tracking performance;
- the controller's behavior on synthetic trajectories with progressively shorter lap times, evaluating its response when the reference becomes infeasible.

2 Related Work

The problem of tracking a reference trajectory is a common control challenge. Specifically, the control algorithm relies on feedback mechanisms to adjust the vehicle inputs in real-time.

A standard approach to trajectory tracking in virtual driver simulations and autonomous driving leverages PID controllers [5]. However, PID controllers lack anticipatory control capabilities.

MPC improves by predicting future states based on a model of the system dynamics [4], producing better driving performance [12], and as such becoming increasingly used in autonomous driving [2]. However, the improved performance comes at the cost of increased algorithmic complexity, as MPC requires a detailed and well-calibrated model of the system dynamics to make informed predictions, which can be time-consuming and resource-intensive [10].

Learning-Based Model Predictive Control (LBMPC) methods overcome model-building complexity by deriving dynamics directly from data. They are classified in three families [6], based on what is learned: (i) **system dynamics**: the algorithm improves its model of reality, either during operation or across multiple operational instances; or (ii) **controller design**: control parameters are adjusted to improve performance; or (iii) **constraints**: optimization and constraint satisfaction are decoupled, with MPC used to enforce constraints [9]. The approach closest to that proposed in this work belongs to the first category.

Some approaches treat the underlying system as a black box, using statistical methods to build a system model *implicitly* from data. Examples include methods based on deep neural networks [15] and statistical models (e.g., NARX [11]). DeePC [13] is part of this family. When real-world data is available, this approach can learn the input-output relationships. DeePC has shown promising in handling the nonlinear dynamics inherent in racing environments [3]. With sufficiently large datasets, DeePC can adapt to complex and dynamic scenarios, improving flexibility and robustness compared to traditional MPC approaches [7].

3 Proposed Approach

In this work, we investigate the use of DeePC to control a simulated racing vehicle, comparing it with a PID controller and a "classic" MPC controller.

3.1 DeePC

DeePC is a data-driven variation of MPC where the explicit model is substituted by a dataset. The intuition behind DeePC is that a linear combination of past realizations of the system could be used to match the current conditions and forecast future behavior. More formally, DeePC requires a dataset $\mathbf{H} \in \mathbb{R}^{\mathbf{N \times 2T}}$ of N past realizations of the system capturing T samples of the system state, namely T inputs $\mathbf{u}_t^s$ (input at time t of the s-th trajectory), and T outputs $\mathbf{y}_t^s$ (output at time t of the s-th trajectory).

Inputs and outputs are split into two subgroups each, representing the initial and the future state of the system, used respectively to match the current conditions and to forecast the future behavior. More formally: $\mathbf{u}_{\text{init}}$ (inputs selected to model the initial part of the trajectory across all N trajectories), $\mathbf{y}_{\text{init}}$ (outputs selected to model the initial part of the trajectory across all N trajectories), $\mathbf{u}_{\text{fut}}$ (inputs selected to model the future part of the trajectory across all N trajectories), and $\mathbf{y}_{\text{fut}}$.

Based on such dataset, the algorithm has to find a vector of coefficients $\mathbf{g}$, future predicted inputs $\mathbf{u}_{\text{fut}}$, and future predicted outputs $\mathbf{y}_{\text{fut}}$ such that: (i) there is no difference between the vector of previously known inputs $\mathbf{u}^*_{\text{init}}$ and outputs $\mathbf{y}^*_{\text{init}}$; (ii) the difference between the reference trajectory $\mathbf{r}$ and the predicted outputs $\mathbf{y}_{\text{fut}}$ is minimized, thus minimizing the amount of control exerted on the system (the norm of predicted inputs $\mathbf{u}_{\text{fut}}$). Formally, the optimization problem thus can be written as:

$$\begin{aligned} \underset{\mathbf{g},\mathbf{u}_{\text{fut}},\mathbf{y}_{\text{fut}}}{\text{minimize}} \quad & \sum \|\mathbf{y}_{\text{fut}} - \mathbf{r}\|_Q^2 + \|\mathbf{u}_{\text{fut}}\|_R^2 \\ \text{subject to} \quad & \mathbf{Hg} = \mathbf{L} \end{aligned} \tag{1}$$

where Q and R are weighting matrices that balance the trade-off between tracking performance and control effort. Optimization constraints can be expanded as:

$$\underbrace{\begin{pmatrix} \mathbf{u}^1_{\text{init}} & \mathbf{u}^2_{\text{init}} & \cdots & \mathbf{u}^N_{\text{init}} \\ \mathbf{y}^1_{\text{init}} & \mathbf{y}^2_{\text{init}} & \cdots & \mathbf{y}^N_{\text{init}} \\ \mathbf{u}^1_{\text{fut}} & \mathbf{u}^2_{\text{fut}} & \cdots & \mathbf{u}^N_{\text{fut}} \\ \mathbf{y}^1_{\text{fut}} & \mathbf{y}^2_{\text{fut}} & \cdots & \mathbf{y}^N_{\text{fut}} \end{pmatrix}}_{\mathbf{H}\in\mathbb{R}^{\mathbf{2T}\times\mathbf{N}}} \underbrace{\begin{pmatrix} g_1 \\ g_2 \\ \vdots \\ g_N \end{pmatrix}}_{\mathbf{g}\in\mathbb{R}^{\mathbf{N}}} = \underbrace{\begin{pmatrix} \mathbf{u}^*_{\text{init}} \\ \mathbf{y}^*_{\text{init}} \\ \mathbf{u}_{\text{fut}} \\ \mathbf{y}_{\text{fut}} \end{pmatrix}}_{\mathbf{L}\in\mathbb{R}^{\mathbf{2T}}} \tag{2}$$

Table 1 summarizes all symbols used in this section.

Linear Relaxation of Non-Linear Systems DeePC is working with the assumption that the controllable system is linear. If it's not the case, then non-linearities are accounted for by modelling them as noise through a so-called "discrepancy term" σ [3]. The problem can then be rewritten as:

$$\begin{aligned} \underset{\mathbf{g},\mathbf{u}_{\text{fut}},\mathbf{y}_{\text{fut}},\sigma}{\text{minimize}} \quad & \sum \|\mathbf{y}_{\text{fut}} - \mathbf{r}\|_Q^2 + \|\mathbf{u}_{\text{fut}}\|_R^2 + \|\sigma\|_{\lambda_y}^2 + \|\mathbf{g}\|_{\lambda_g}^2 \\ \text{subject to} \quad & \mathbf{Hg} = \mathbf{L} + \begin{pmatrix} 0 & \sigma & 0 & 0 \end{pmatrix}^\top \end{aligned} \tag{3}$$

Configuration of the Algorithm The algorithm can be configured with two key parameters representing the dataset size (N) and the prediction horizon (ph). We expect larger N to provide faster convergence and better overall performance at the expense of increased computational complexity. Instead, ph determines how far into the future the controller should look, and it is equivalent to the length of future input and output traces ($ph = |\mathbf{u}_{\text{fut}}| = |\mathbf{y}_{\text{fut}}|$). Selecting an appropriate prediction horizon impacts performance, as short horizons will may be insufficient to apply corrective actions, and performance will degrade for long horizons, as the learned behavior will slowly drift away from reality.

Table 1. Summary of the symbols used in Sect. 3

Parameter	Description
$\mathbf{g}$	Vector of coefficients for trajectories in dataset
$\mathbf{H}$	Matrix of dataset for DeePC
N	Number of trajectories in the dataset
T	Length of the trajectory in the dataset
$\mathbf{u}$	Input vector of the model
$\mathbf{y}$	Output vector of the model
Q	Cost weight matrix of output
R	Cost weight matrix of input
$\mathbf{r}$	Reference trajectory
λ_y	Cost weight matrix of discrepancy
λ_g	Cost weight of DeePC coefficients
σ	Discrepancy vector of non-linearities

3.2 DeePC for Simulated Racing Car Control

In this section, we apply DeePC to the problem of controlling a simulated racecar. We discuss the control parameters, the simplifications we introduced, and how to extend the model to account for greater complexity. We assume our controller acts on two inputs: acceleration control (throttle and brake) and steering.

Throttle and Brake. The acceleration control varies in a $[-1, 1]$ where negative values represent actions on braking, and positive values throttle. Thus, this model does not account for combined brake/throttle actions. Moreover, we assume that the car can always output its maximum torque, and thus we do not add gearshift control as an input. Both separated brake and throttle control and gear shifting can be included straightforwardly in the model, as the input and output spaces are not constrained by the algorithm.

Steering. steering is modeled as the angle between centerline of the vehicle and centerline of the front wheels, ranging in $[-15°, +15°]$; we thus model the input provided to wheels rather than the input to be provided to the steering wheel.

Outputs. The model's outputs are the following: (i) horizontal and (ii) vertical coordinates of vehicle's center of mass with respect to a global reference point (m) (iii) speed ($^m/_s$) (iv) heading angle with respect to a global coordinate directed towards east (rad). Thus, in total, the algorithm is subject to six channels: two inputs (every entry in $\mathbf{u}_{\text{fut}}$ and $\mathbf{u}_{\text{init}}$ will have two values) and four outputs (every entry in $\mathbf{y}_{\text{fut}}$ and $\mathbf{y}_{\text{init}}$ entry will have four values).

Dataset Size and Generation. DeePC requires a dataset of past realizations of the system to be able to predict future behavior. The quality of such dataset is paramount for the performance of DeePC. The dataset size N is tightly bound to the complexity of the model at hand. Constrained models generally require smaller datasets than less constrained and more complex models. For the problem at hand, even using our simplified racecar model (cf. Section 4.1), a dataset in the order of hundreds of trajectories is necessary. Thus, we run multiple instances of the racecar model, starting in the origin with a random speed, and record the car's paths in response to random control actions. We control the random generation by setting a different seed for each run to ensure reproducibility.

Dataset Roto-Translation. Trajectories must share the same reference frame, requiring roto-translation of either the dataset or the current trajectory. Here, we roto-translate the current trajectory into the dataset's frame.

4 Experimental Evaluation

In this section, we investigate: 1. how robust is DeePC to changes in the prediction horizon ph and dataset size N; 2. how DeePC compares to "classic" MPC and traditional PID controller in terms of tracking performance.

4.1 Experimental Setup

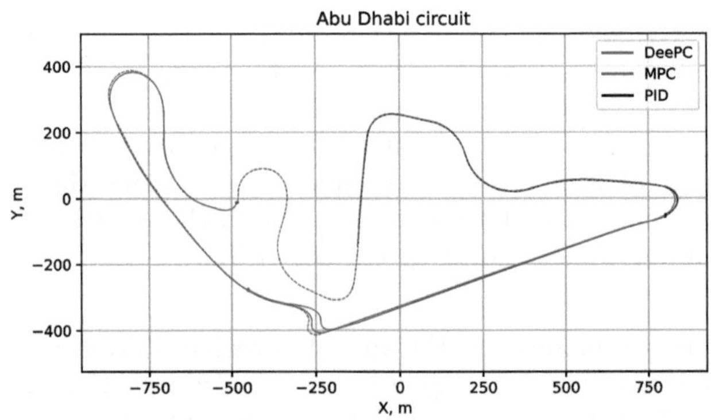

Fig. 1. Trajectory tracking in the Yas Marina circuit in Abu Dhabi. The dashed line defines the target trajectory, solid lines the trajectories as followed by the controllers. The controllers were initialized with time offsets to avoid overlap, which results in portions of the dashed line not being covered by any controller at a given time.

Metrics. In this evaluation, we employ the Residual Sum of Squares (RSS) method to gauge how accurately a vehicle follows the reference trajectory. Lower RSS values indicate better tracking performance.

Reference Trajectories. We test our algorithms on two different trajectory types: (i) a synthetic ∞-shaped Lissajous figure (Fig. 5); and (ii) a real-world trajectory of an open-wheel racecar in Yas Marina, Abu Dhabi (Fig. 1).

The Lissajous figure has been previously utilized in the literature [1] as a standard reference trajectory for evaluating the performance of trajectory tracking systems. It can be used to generate slower or faster trajectories for a given lap time τ:

$$\begin{cases} x(t) = 100 \sin\left(\frac{2\pi t}{\tau}\right) \\ y(t) = 100 \cos\left(\frac{4\pi t}{\tau}\right) \end{cases} \quad \text{for } t \in [0, \tau] \tag{4}$$

The Yas Marina circuit is a track where several major racing championships take place, including Formula 1. We use the real-world trajectory of the track to evaluate the performance of the algorithms in a more realistic scenario, with a variety of high and low-speed corners.

Table 2. Parameters of the racecar model

Param.	Description	Value
D_{RF}	Peak value of the friction coefficient (Pacejika D)	1.0
C_{RF}	Shape factor of the friction coefficient (Pacejika C)	1.1
B_{RF}	Stiffness factor of the friction coefficient (Pacejika B)	25.0
m	Racecar mass	896 kg
I_z	Moment of inertia	1500 kg·m^2
l_{RF}	Distance from Center of mass (CM) of Rear/Front wheel	1.125 m
ρ	Air density	1.225 kg/m^3
A	Cross sectional area	
C_D	Drag coefficient	$C_D A = 1.35$ m^2
C_L	Downforce lift coefficient	$C_L A = 4.31$ m^2
P	Motor power	620 hp

Racecar Model. For this initial study, we use a simplified model of a racecar based on the well-known "single-track model", in which the car is approximated as a two-wheeled vehicle with a fixed wheelbase, and the motion is described in terms of a few key parameters summarized in Table 2. In the model we consider nonlinear tire forces based on a simplified Pacejka model [14].

The state of the model is described by: (i) x, y: position of CM, (ii) ϕ: orientation of the model, (iii) V_x, V_y: velocity of CM, (iv) r: angular velocity of the model, (v) δ: steering angle of the front wheel, and (vi) Ξ: throttle; while its motion is governed by the differential equation:

$$\begin{bmatrix} \dot{x} \\ \dot{y} \\ \dot{\phi} \\ \dot{V}_x \\ \dot{V}_y \\ \dot{r} \end{bmatrix} = \begin{bmatrix} V_x \cos(\phi) - V_y \sin(\phi) \\ V_x \sin(\phi) + V_y \cos(\phi) \\ r \\ \frac{1}{m}(F_x - F_{Fy} \sin(\delta) - F_{Ax}) + V_y r \\ \frac{1}{m}(F_{Ry} + F_{Fy} \cos(\delta) - F_{Ay}) - V_x r \\ \frac{1}{I_z}(F_{Fy} l_F \cos(\delta) - F_{Ry} l_R) \end{bmatrix} \tag{5}$$

where the *tyres*' lateral forces are represented by F_{Fy} and rear F_{Ry}; the *aerodynamic* drag forces are represented by F_{Ax} and F_{Ay} (respectively, front and lateral[2]); and the *motor* force is represented by F_x. Tyre forces are computed as: $F_{RFy} = D_{RF} \sin\left(C_{RF} \operatorname{atan}\left(B_{RF}\alpha_{RF}\right)\right) W$ and $\alpha_{RF} = \operatorname{atan}\left(\frac{V_y - l_R r}{V_x}\right)$, where the weight ($W$) is computed as: $W = mg + \frac{1}{2}\rho A C_L \|V\|^2$. The aerodynamic drag forces are: $F_{Axy} = \frac{1}{2}\rho A C_D V_{xy}^2$.
Finally, the motor force is: $F_x = \min(\max(\Xi P V_x, -x_{WD_R}), x_{WD_R})$.

Car Parameters. For the experiments, we set the parameters of the car model to mimic a Formula 2 car[3] Their values are summarized in Table 2.

Optimization Criteria for DeePC. As optimization criterias we used $R = \text{diag}(0.1, 0.1)$, $Q = \text{diag}(1, 1, 1, 100)$, $\lambda_y = \text{diag}(200, 200, 200, 200)$, $\lambda_g = N/20$. Optimization criteria R and Q (for inputs and outputs, respectively) are chosen to balance the trade-off between tracking performance and control effort. Unlike MPC, DeePC has two additional parameters, λ_y and λ_g, that balance the trade-off between the uncertainty of initial conditions and the predicted trajectory based on the dataset. If $Q \ll R$, the controller deviates from the reference; while if $Q \gg R$, the system can become unstable. Similarly, if $\lambda_y \ll \lambda_g$ DeePC tends to ignore initial conditions in favor of making predictions, which can cause tracking deviations; opposedly, if $\lambda_y \gg \lambda_g$ the control becomes more random, decreasing control quality and possibly causing instability.

4.2 Baselines

We compare DeePC with two baselines: (i) a PID controller, and (ii) a "classic" MPC controller. In our paper, we employ the cascade scheme of four proportional controllers depicted in Fig. 2, which together compose a PID controller. The inner loops are responsible for controlling the steering and throttle based on the reference speed and heading. The outer loops integrate these inner loops and are

[2] Lateral aerodynamic forces are only relevant when the car slides.
[3] The parameters have been extrapolated with the help of domain experts from the data available at https://archive.fo/3erTM.

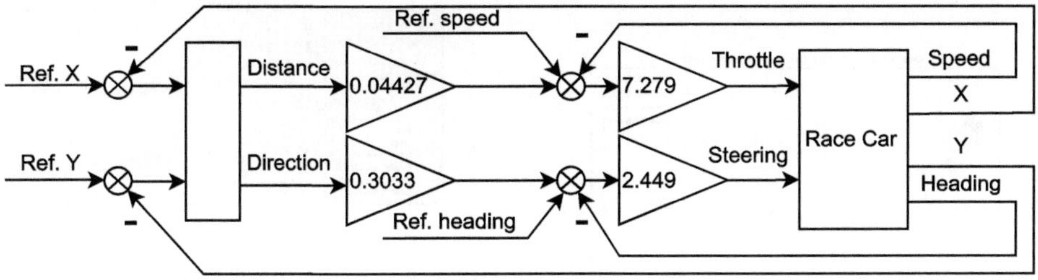

Fig. 2. PID controller scheme.

responsible for direction and distance control. The parameters have been found using random search optimization.

The MPC controller, instead, is based on a simpler *kinematic* model of the car, which does not consider friction. This way, we replicate the imperfect correlation between the real world and its simulated model.

Experiments and Reproducibility. We perform three experiments, meant respectively to: 1. evaluate the performance of DeePC with different choices of prediction horizon and dataset size; 2. compare the performance of DeePC with the state of the art on an artificial trajectory with varying lap times; and 3. compare the performance on a real-world trajectory of a race car to gather evidence of whether the approach can be applied to realistic scenarios.

The former two experiments have been opensourced[4] for reuse and reproducibility. An archival copy is also available at Zenodo [16]. The latter experiment could not be included, as the Yas Marina track trajectory is proprietary.

4.3 Impact of Dataset Size and Prediction Horizon on DeePC

As a first step, we investigated how the variation of prediction horizon and dataset size influenced the performance of DeePC. To do so, we generated a synthetic ∞-shaped trajectory largely within the capability of the car. We then let the prediction horizon range in $[20ms, 160ms]$ and we inspect the behavior of DeePC with dataset sizes $N \in \{50, 100, 200, 400\}$. For each combination of parameters, we run 30 repetitions differing by the seed used to generate the dataset.

Results are summarized in Fig. 3. The controller's ability to foresee into the future correlates positively with the overall quality of control. The best control quality is achieved at about $60ms$, however, this value may be different for different trajectories and car models.

4.4 Synthetic Trajectory Tracking

Next, we compare PID, MPC and DeePC on a synthetic ∞-shaped trajectory, with the goal of understanding how well they can cope with an increasingly

[4] https://github.com/Crylab/DeePC.

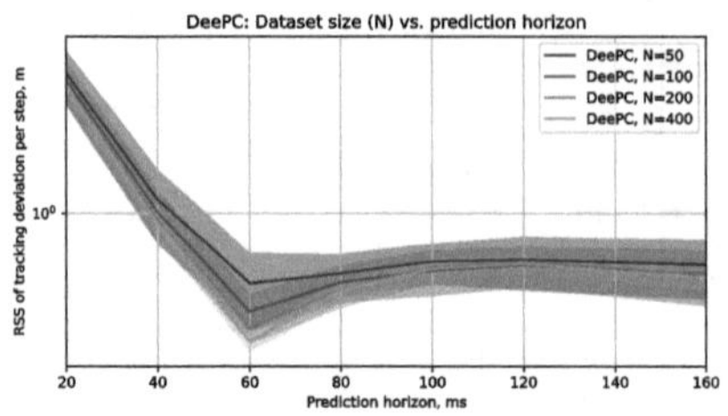

Fig. 3. DeepC performance with dataset size and prediction horizon. Solid lines represent the mean over 30 repetitions, while coloured shaded areas depict ± one standard deviation.

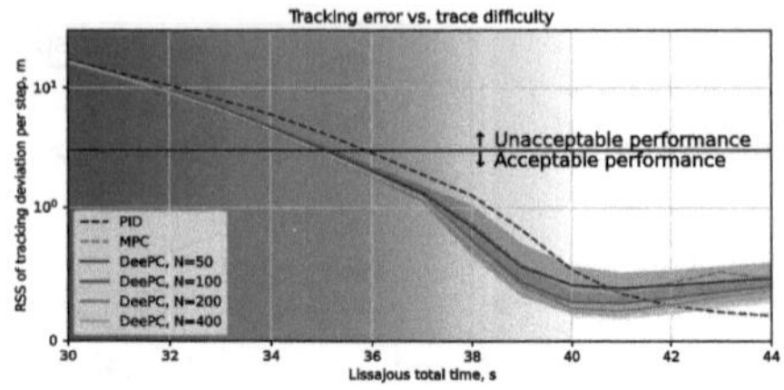

Fig. 4. Error with increasingly easy synthetic trajectories. When on the verge of the car capabilities, DeePC outperforms both baselines. Solid lines are averaged over 30 repetitions, coloured shaded areas depict ± one standard deviation. Acceptable performance is under 7 m.

difficult trajectory. In fact, we can apply Equation (4) to generate trajectories increasingly difficult to track, as the lap time τ decreases. In this case, we set the prediction horizon to $60ms$ for both MPC and DeePC.

The experiment results are depicted in Fig. 4, and show that the PID controller performs comparably to the predictive controllers for very easy trajectories; however, it quickly becomes the worst performer as the trajectory difficulty increases. MPC has better performance than the PID, and it is comparable to DeePC with $N = 50$. With a larger dataset, DeePC outperforms the baselines, especially for trajectories that sit close to the limit of the car performance.

Moreover, we found that the classic MPC approach is more sensitive to the precision of the numerical solver than DeePC: we encountered cases in which the resulting behavior is unstable for the same selection of optimization criteria for which DeePC is capable to follow the trajectory instead. An example is shown in Fig. 5, in which MPC accelerates too early and loses control of the car after a classic "pendulum" effect.

4.5 Real-World Trajectory Tracking

The last experiment is akin to the previous one, but the trajectory is a real-world lap of a racecar around the track of Yas Marina in Abu Dhabi. In this experiment we make the lap increasingly more difficult to follow by varying the peak friction coefficient of the tires, emulating the effect of an increasingly slippery track[5]. We analyze conditions that range from a slippery track in which the lap is plainly not achievable ($D_{RF} = 0.8$), to conditions of extremely high grip ($D_{RF} = 1.6$).

[5] Track conditions impact significantly the grip available to the car in real-world racing. Even if the track remains dry, the rubber laid down by the cars can make it more or less slippery, and the track temperature can also affect the grip. Moreover, the tire compound can be chosen to be more or less grippy, typically presenting a trade-off between peak performance and durability.

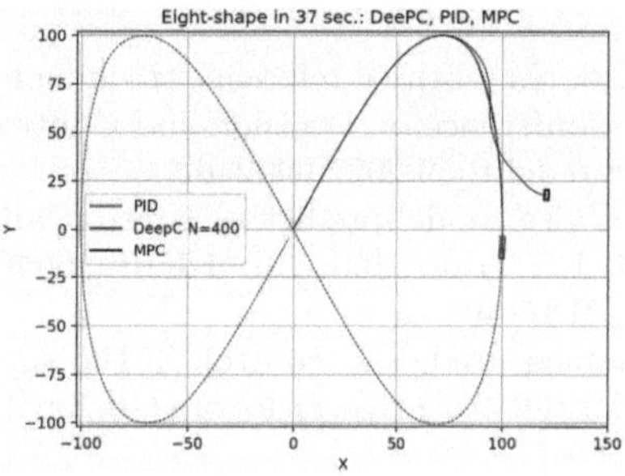

Fig. 5. ∞-shaped trajectory tracking with unstable MPC

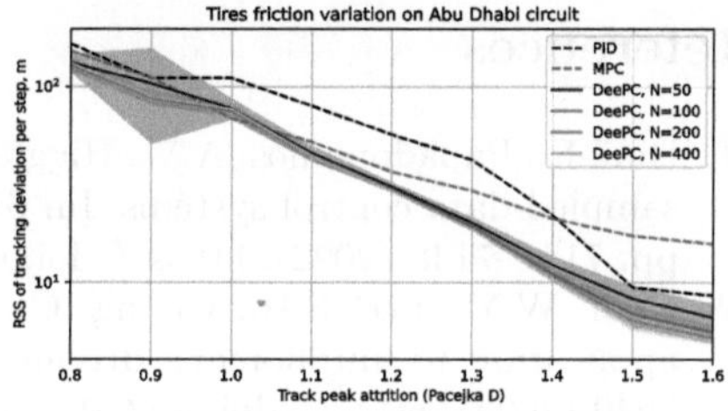

Fig. 6. Error with increasingly higher peak tyre friction in the Yas Marina circuit. DeePC outperforms both baselines. Solid lines are averaged over 30 repetitions, coloured shaded areas depict ± one standard deviation.

The resulting data is summarized in Fig. 6. In this test, with a much more complex trajectory featuring slow and fast turns, DeePC outperforms both baselines consistently. In this case, in fact, the simplified kinematic model of MPC is not capable to accurately predict the car's behavior in many conditions, while the data-based model internal to DeePC can produce more accurate predictions.

5 Conclusion and Future Work

In this paper, we extended our previous investigation of DeePC for trajectory tracking in race car simulation, investigating the impact of prediction horizon and dataset size on the controller's tracking performance and the controller's behavior on synthetic trajectories with progressively shorter lap times. We compared it against traditional PID and classical MPC controllers. Our results show DeePC is viable, outperforming traditional methods especially on complex tracks near the vehicle's limits. Its data-driven nature makes DeePC suitable even when building accurate real-world models is challenging, provided the dataset is sufficiently rich and the prediction horizon appropriately balanced.

Future work will extend the approach to advanced car models (including multibody dynamics, finite element tire models, and aerodynamics), improve dataset generation for greater efficiency, and tackle the separate problem of trajectory generation based on track and car characteristics, as discussed in Sect. 1.1. Moreover, we will more precisely characterize the efficiency profile of DeePC compared to MPC. In our experiments, execution times were comparable between the two methods; however, we expect DeePC to scale better than MPC with model complexity and prediction horizon. This expectation will be verified in future work.

References

1. Bini, E., Papadopoulos, A.V., Higgins, J., Bezzo, N.: Optimal reference tracking for sampled-data control systems. In: 61st IEEE Conference on Decision and Control, pp. 7141–7148 (2022). https://doi.org/10.1109/cdc51059.2022.9992462
2. Choi, W.Y., Lee, S.H., Chung, C.C.: Horizonwise model-predictive control with application to autonomous driving vehicle. IEEE Trans. Ind. Inf. **18**(10), 6940–6949 (2022). https://doi.org/10.1109/tii.2021.3137169
3. Coulson, J., Lygeros, J., Dorfler, F.: Data-enabled predictive control: in the shallows of the deepc. In: 18th ECC, pp. 307–312 (2019). https://doi.org/10.23919/ECC.2019.8795639
4. Darby, M.L., Nikolaou, M.: MPC: current practice and challenges. Control. Eng. Pract. **20**(4), 328–342 (2012). https://doi.org/10.1016/j.conengprac.2011.12.004
5. Farag, W.: Complex trajectory tracking using PID control for autonomous driving. Int. J. Intell. Transp. Syst. Res. **18**(2), 356–366 (2019). https://doi.org/10.1007/s13177-019-00204-2
6. Hewing, L., Wabersich, K.P., Menner, M., Zeilinger, M.N.: Learning-based model predictive control: toward safe learning in control. Ann. Rev. Control Rob. Auton. Syst. **3**(1), 269–296 (2020). https://doi.org/10.1146/ANNUREV-CONTROL-090419-075625
7. Huang, L., Lygeros, J., Dörfler, F.: Robust and kernelized data-enabled predictive control for nonlinear systems. IEEE Trans. Control Syst. Technol. **32**(2), 611–624 (2024). https://doi.org/10.1109/tcst.2023.3329334
8. Judde, C., Booth, R., Brooks, R.: Second place is first of the losers: an analysis of competitive balance in formula one. J. Sports Econ. **14**(4), 411–439 (2013). https://doi.org/10.1177/1527002513496009
9. Koller, T., Berkenkamp, F., Turchetta, M., Krause, A.: Learning-based model predictive control for safe exploration. In: IEEE CDC, pp. 6059–6066 (2018). https://doi.org/10.1109/cdc.2018.8619572
10. Kozak, S.: From PID to MPC: control engineering methods development and applications. In: K&I 2016 (2016). https://doi.org/10.1109/cyberi.2016.7438634
11. Limon, D., Calliess, J., Maciejowski, J.: Learning-based nonlinear model predictive control. IFAC-PapersOnLine **50**(1), 7769–7776 (2017). https://doi.org/10.1016/j.ifacol.2017.08.1050
12. Liniger, A., Domahidi, A., Morari, M.: Optimization-based autonomous racing of 1:43 scale RC cars. Optimal Control Appl. Methods **36**(5), 628–647 (2014). https://doi.org/10.1002/oca.2123
13. Markovsky, I., Huang, L., Dörfler, F.: Data-driven control based on the behavioral approach: from theory to applications in power systems. IEEE Control. Syst. **43**(5), 28–68 (2023). https://doi.org/10.1109/mcs.2023.3291638
14. Pacejka, H.B., Bakker, E.: The magic formula tyre model. Veh. Syst. Dyn. **21**(sup001), 1–18 (1992). https://doi.org/10.1080/00423119208969994
15. Rokonuzzaman, M., Mohajer, N., Nahavandi, S., Mohamed, S.: Model predictive control with learned vehicle dynamics for autonomous vehicle path tracking. IEEE Access **9** (2021). https://doi.org/10.1109/access.2021.3112560
16. Shaiakhmetov, R.: Crylab/deepc: Initial release (2024). https://doi.org/10.5281/zenodo.11515536
17. Shaiakhmetov, R., Pianini, D., Venusti, V., Papadopoulos, A.V.: A data-driven predictive control driver for racing car simulation. In: DS-RT, pp. 140–143. IEEE (2024). https://doi.org/10.1109/DS-RT62209.2024.00033

B-Spline Based Aerodynamic Table Look-up for Cyber in the Loop Simulation of Air Vehicle Cyber-Physical System

Bambang Sridadi[1](✉), Endra Joelianto[2], and Yul Yunazwin Nazaruddin[2]

[1] Doctoral Program in Engineering Physics, Faculty of Industrial Technology, Institut Teknologi Bandung (ITB), Bandung, Indonesia
33323006@mahasiswa.itb.ac.id

[2] Instrumentation, Control, and Automation Research Group, Faculty of Industrial Technology, Institut Teknologi Bandung (ITB), Bandung, Indonesia
{ejoel,yul}@itb.ac.id

Abstract. In complex continuous-time system models such as airborne cyber-physical systems (CPS), the equations of motion are expressed as a combination of mathematical functions and data tables obtained from laboratory measurements such as wind tunnels. For simulation purposes, a table look-up process is required as part of calculating the motion dynamics of an airborne vehicle to mimic the actual system. Currently, the table look-up process in flight simulations for pilot training purposes uses the piecewise linear interpolation (PLI) method. In this paper, the B-spline table look-up is formulated that can be used for engineering cyber in the loop simulation (CILS) of airborne cyber-physical systems. A flowchart and implementation of the B-spline table look-up in C/C++ have been developed. The results show that for table data with suddenly changes, the nonlinear B-spline table look-up method is superior to PLI. The nonlinear B-spline table look-up method includes and generalizes the conventional PLI. For m=1, B-spline interpolation is PLI. Furthermore, an adaptive interpolation is obtained by choosing the order m that corresponds to the characteristics (continuous differentiability) of the aerodynamic coefficient data under consideration.

Keywords: interpolation · simulation · nonlinear · air vehicle · B-spline

1 Introduction

In complex continuous-time system model such as air vehicle cyber-physical systems (CPS), the equations of motion are expressed as a combination of mathematical functions and data tables obtained from laboratory measurements such as wind tunnels. Depending on the form of the airborne model in question, i.e., whether it is a representation of total forces and moments or based on small perturbation equations, the aerodynamic data can be represented in various ways.

W. Cai et al. (Eds.): AsiaSim 2025, CCIS 2727, pp. 171–182, 2026.
https://doi.org/10.1007/978-981-95-4472-1_15

For a small perturbation model, the equations of motion coefficients are derivatives of the classical stability model, and a numerical table can describe the dynamics of the airborne model under a specific flight condition [1,2].

A pilot training simulation for flying an aircraft over a wide range of speeds, combined with various maneuvers involving varying angles of attack, will require a complex aerodynamic data and model. Forces and moments need to be expressed as functions of one or more of the following variables: angle of attack α, angle of sideslip β, control surface deflection, speed or Mach number, altitude [3,4]. Depending on the various flight tasks and missions, an appropriate level of complexity in the model and data representation are required. For example, during flight simulation scenarios involving extreme maneuvers such as dogfights flying, approaching to stall, flying follow the terrain, collision avoidance. This is where the form of the model and the accuracy of the data will have a significant impact on the natural dynamics.

For the design and implementation of an air vehicle CPS control system, a validation tool called simulator is required. Simulation as a validation tool requires precise models and data. Air vehicle CPS models can be a combination of mathematical formulations and data tables. In the early stages of designing a new CPS control system, a mathematical model and data should be developed, and rough variations in parameters can be made to identify sensitive areas and to indicate where to focus efforts to improve both the model form and the data. Simulation becomes essential here to evaluate the effectiveness of predicted performance and the operational procedures of proposed new designs. At the detailed design stage, a precise model and data can be essential for airframe and control system designers, providing a tool for evaluating alternative design strategies. This often demands detailed and precise modeling of the aircraft and its systems.

On the other hand, the B-spline, short for basis spline, is a type of spline function constructed to minimize overlap for a specified degree, level of smoothness, and arrangement of breakpoints (or knots that divide the domain). This efficient structure makes B-splines essential components for forming any spline function of the same degree. A B-spline is represented as a piecewise polynomial of order m, which corresponds to a polynomial of degree m. Any spline function with a given degree can be uniquely represented as a linear combination of B-splines of that degree, defined over the same set of knots [5–8].

Figure 1 shows the configuration of cyber in the loop simulation (CILS). The simulation system consists of physical subsystem and cyber subsystem. The cyber subsystem is containing inner-outer control law. Control input will influence the moments and forces of the air vehicle physical subsystem. The total force vector is $\mathbf{F} = f(F_x, F_y, F_z)$. The total moment vector is $\mathbf{M} = f(L, M, N)$. In the lateral dynamic, the moment on x-axis is $L = C_\ell \; qbar \; S \; B$. The force coefficients $C_\ell = f(\alpha, \beta, \delta_a)$ is function of angle of attack α, angle of sideslip β and aileron surface deflection δ_a. The same formulation for longitudinal directional dynamics, moments about the y-axis (M) and z-axis (N). The air vehicle parameters are dynamic air pressure $qbar$ in kg/cm^2, area of wing S in m^2, and span of wing B in m. The force and moment coefficient data is in the form of tabular data, so it requires interpolation calculations (table look-up) when compute simulations [2,4].

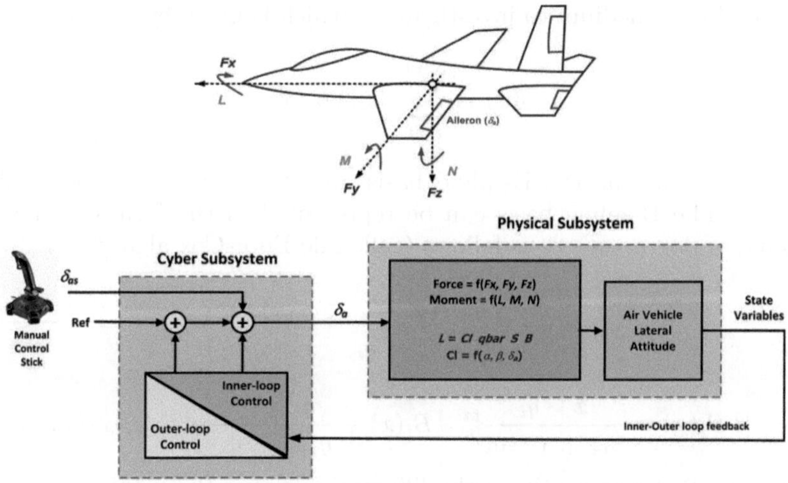

Fig. 1. Configuration of cyber in the loop simulation.

The characteristics of an air vehicle aerodynamic data are highly dependent on many variables and cannot be modeled in the form of mathematical function formulas but in the form of tabular data obtained from laboratory testing. To evaluate the tabular data in a simulation is known as a table look-up process, which is essentially a numerical interpolation process. In this paper, the author reports a study of a B-spline interpolation method that can be used for cyber in the loop simulation (CILS) of air vehicle cyber-physical systems.

2 B-Spline Function Spaces

This section sets up a function space built from B-splines. A B-spline of order m is a piecewise polynomial of degree m that is continuously differentiable $(m-2)$-times. When the order is 1 or 2, the B-spline corresponds to a step function or a piecewise linear (polygonal) function, respectively.

Consider a function space composed of spline function of order m (for m=1, 2, ...), as a subspace of $L_2(R)$ as follows [8,9]

$$ {}^{m}S := \left[{}^{m}_{[s]}B_k(x) \right]_{k=-\infty}^{\infty} \tag{1} $$

where we call ${}^{m}S$ the spline function space of order m. The basis $\{{}^{m}_{[s]}B_k(x)\}_{k=-\infty}^{\infty}$ is a spline sampling basis. The spline sampling basis satisfies

$$ s(x) = \sum_{k=-\infty}^{\infty} s_k \, {}^{m}_{[s]}B_k(x) \tag{2} $$

for any function $s(x) \in {}^{m}S$, where $s_k = s(x_k)(x_k = kh + (mh/2))$, is a sampling value. We call a function $s(x)$ the spline function, which is formed with the spline sampling basis ${}^{m}_{[s]}B_k(x)$ with the appropriate order m.

However, the spline sampling basis is not given explicitly. The B-spline basis shall be used as a medium to investigate it, which is given by

$$s(x) = \sum_{i=0}^{N-1} {}^{m}c_i {}^{m}_{[b]}B_i(x) \tag{3}$$

where ${}^{m}_{[b]}B_i(x)$ means the B-spline basis and ${}^{m}c_i$ is the B-spline coefficient of order m. The B-spline basis can be represented in the form of a piecewise polynomial of degree $m-1$ as follows (called de Boor-Cox algorithm) [10]

$${}^{1}_{[b]}B_i(x) = \begin{cases} 1, & (q_i \leq x < q_{i+1}) \\ 0, & (x < q_i, \quad x \geq q_{i+1}). \end{cases} \tag{4}$$

$${}^{m}_{[b]}B_i(x) = \frac{x - q_i}{q_{i+m-1} - q_i} {}^{m-1}_{[b]}B_i(x) + \frac{q_{i+m} - x}{q_{i+m} - q_{i+1}} {}^{m-1}_{[b]}B_{i+1}(x) \tag{5}$$

which is $(m-2)$-times continuously differentiable over the x-axis.

A B-spline function ${}^{m}_{[b]}B_\ell(x)$ possesses the following basic characteristics:

(a) it has finite (local) support in time

$${}^{m}_{[b]}B_i(x) = 0, \quad x \notin (ih, (i+m)h) \tag{6}$$

(b) it exhibits a shifting behavior

$${}^{m}_{[b]}B_i(x + kh) = {}^{m}_{[b]}B_{i-k}(x) \tag{7}$$

(c) it obeys certain symmetry properties

$${}^{m}_{[b]}B_i(-x) = {}^{m}_{[b]}B_{-m-i}(x) \quad \text{or} \tag{8}$$

$${}^{m}_{[b]}B_i(h - x) = {}^{m}_{[b]}B_{-m+1-i}(x) \tag{9}$$

The conditions that must be met for spline interpolation are as follows:

(a). The function values must be the same at the innermost nodes.
(b). The first and last functions must pass through the endpoints.
(c). The first derivatives at the innermost nodes must be the same.
(d). Assume that the second derivative is zero at the first point.

3 Table Look-up Interpolation

The rolling moment L of an air vehicle can be written as follows.

$$L = C_\ell \; qbar \; S \; B \tag{10}$$

where C_ℓ is the roll moment coefficient, $qbar$ is the dynamic pressure, S is the wing area, and B is the wing span. A plot of the coefficient C_ℓ versus the angle of attack α at various angle of sideslip β for an air vehicle can be seen in Table 1 and Fig. 2 [2,4].

It is possible to fit the data curve with a straight line passing through a specific range of α values. The coefficients of C_ℓ can be represented as the following linear function expression.

$$C_\ell = a_0 + a_1\alpha \tag{11}$$

This equation provides a fit to the data. If the change in the basic coefficients due to α is unacceptable for representation by such a simple expression, it is necessary to approximate to a nonlinear form such as a B-spline function. This approach has the advantage that once an α changes, a simple continuous expression is still available for computation. For angles α between defined values, a technique is required to interpolate appropriate values from the dependent coefficients such as a_0 and a_1. This is often referred to as table look-up. The following describes methods for looking up the table using piecewise linear interpolation (PLI) and nonlinear B-spline interpolation.

3.1 Piecewise Linear Interpolation

Given N data sets of values of a variable y as a function of a set of values x, where $y_i = f(x_i)$ [11]. The value of y for a given value of x can be obtained by interpolation between adjacent coordinate pairs. Thus, if

$$x_2 \leq x \leq x_3 \tag{12}$$

then

$$y = y_2 + \frac{(y_3 - y_2)}{(x_3 - x_2)}(x - x_2) \tag{13}$$

A comprehensive algorithm for this table look-up process must complete the following steps:

(1). Decide where the pair (x, y) is located in the table
(2). Calculate the local slope $(y_3 - y_2)/(x_3 - x_2)$
(3). Apply the interpolation formula (linear or nonlinear)

Special treatment must be taken if x is less than the lowest x value in the table, or greater than the highest x value in the table. Suppose the action is to assign y to the nearest end value, that is, to y_1 or y_n. An alternative would be to extend the slope of the last segment, that is:

$$x > x_n$$
$$y = y_n + \frac{(y_n - y_{n-1})}{(x_n - x_{n-1})}(x - x_n) \tag{14}$$

The procedure chosen will depend on the problem and the nature of the data. A more general formulation of a table look-up using PLI method can be formulated as follows. Considering one-dimensional linear interpolation data, the one-dimensional linear interpolation equation can be written as follows.

$$\begin{aligned} f(x) &= \frac{f(x_i) - f(x_{i-1})}{x_i - x_{i-1}}(x - x_{i-1}) + f(x_{i-1}) \\ &= \frac{f(x_i) - f(x_{i-1})}{\Delta_x}x - \frac{f(x_i) - f(x_{i-1})}{\Delta_x}x_{i-1} + f(x_{i-1}) \\ &= Ax + B \end{aligned} \tag{15}$$

where

$$\Delta_x = (x_i - x_{i-1}), A = \frac{f(x_i) - f(x_{i-1})}{\Delta_x}, B = -Ax_{i-1} + f(x_{i-1}) \tag{16}$$

Table 1 and Fig. 2 show examples of data on the aerodynamic coefficient of roll moment C_ℓ versus α at various values of β with piecewise linear interpolation. Table 1 shows a table of data on the roll moment coefficient of an air vehicle C_ℓ obtained from wind tunnel measurements [2]. The C_ℓ data is a function of the angle of attack α and the sideslip angle β. There are 12 data points of α ranging from –10.0° to 45.0°. There are 6 data points β ranging from –20.0 to 30.0°. So the number of C_ℓ data points is $12 \times 6 = 72$ data points. During the flight simulation, the equations of motion will be calculated continuously in real-time, one of which is calculating the magnitude of the roll moment L where it is necessary to first calculate the magnitude of the roll coefficient C_ℓ (see Fig. 1). The dynamics of the air vehicle's motion in the form of changes in α values (from –10.0° to 45.0°) and β (from –20.0 to 30.0°) will determine the values of C_ℓ which changes continuously at any time, so it requires a table look-up (interpolation) process.

Table 1. Air vehicle rolling moment coefficient data $C_\ell = f(\alpha, \beta)$.

Sideslip	Angle of attack α (deg)											
β (deg)	–10.0	–5.0	0.0	5.0	10.0	15.0	20.0	25.0	30.0	35.0	40.0	45.0
–20.0	–0.001	–0.004	–0.008	–0.012	–0.016	–0.019	–0.020	–0.020	–0.015	–0.008	–0.013	–0.015
–10.0	–0.003	–0.009	–0.017	–0.024	–0.030	–0.034	–0.040	–0.037	–0.016	–0.002	–0.010	–0.019
0.0	–0.001	–0.010	–0.020	–0.030	–0.039	–0.044	–0.050	–0.049	–0.023	–0.006	–0.014	–0.027
10.0	0.0	–0.010	–0.022	–0.034	–0.047	–0.046	–0.059	–0.061	–0.033	–0.036	–0.035	–0.035
20.0	0.007	–0.010	–0.023	–0.034	–0.049	–0.046	–0.068	–0.071	–0.060	–0.058	–0.062	–0.059
30.0	0.009	–0.011	–0.023	–0.037	–0.050	–0.047	–0.074	–0.079	–0.091	–0.076	–0.077	–0.076

Figure 2 shows a graphical representation of Table 1. The simplest interpolation from the table is by connecting two data points with a straight line, known as piecewise linear interpolation (PLI). The PLI method is widely used today in most flight simulators for pilot training purposes. However, flight simulators for engineering research require a more precise interpolation method, especially when the aircraft is moving with extreme maneuvers such as approaching to stall, flying follow the terrain, avoiding a collision.

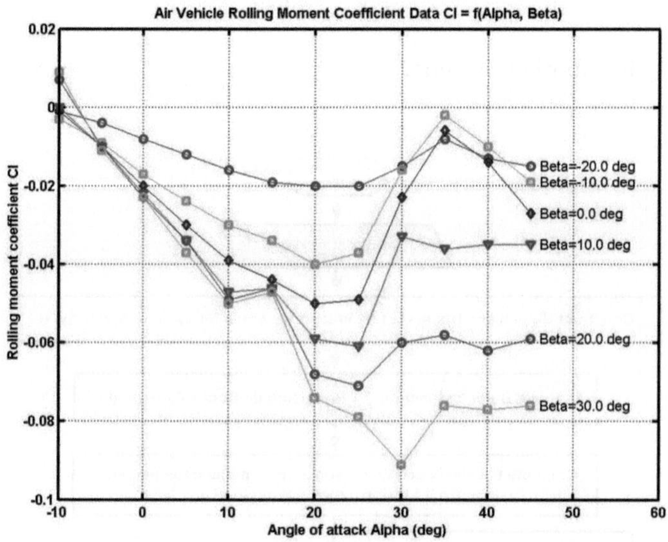

Fig. 2. Aerodynamic data C_ℓ versus α at various values of β.

3.2 Nonlinear B-Spline Function Interpolation

From Eq. (3), we can rewrite in the form of simultaneous equation system

$$\mathbf{A}(x)\ \mathbf{c} = \mathbf{y}(x) \tag{17}$$

where $\mathbf{A}(x)$ is the basis B-spline matrix and $\mathbf{c}$ is the B-spline coefficient vector.

$$\mathbf{A}(x) = \begin{bmatrix} {}^{m}_{[b]}B_0(x_0) & {}^{m}_{[b]}B_1(x_0) & \dots & {}^{m}_{[b]}B_{N-1}(x_0) \\ {}^{m}_{[b]}B_0(x_1) & {}^{m}_{[b]}B_1(x_1) & \dots & {}^{m}_{[b]}B_{N-1}(x_1) \\ \dots & \dots & \dots & \dots \\ {}^{m}_{[b]}B_0(x_{N-1}) & {}^{m}_{[b]}B_1(x_{N-1}) & \dots & {}^{m}_{[b]}B_{N-1}(x_{N-1}) \end{bmatrix}$$

$$\mathbf{c} = [\ c_0\ c_1\ \dots\ c_{N-1}\ ]^T$$

$$\mathbf{y}(x) = [\ y_0\ y_1\ \dots\ y_{N-1}\ ]^T$$

The nonlinear B-spline function table look-up (interpolation) process is as follows (see Fig. 3):

(1). Input the aerodynamic data x_i and y_i, where $y_i = f(x_i)$.
(2). Construct the system of simultaneous equations $\mathbf{A}(x)\ \mathbf{c} = \mathbf{y}(x)$.
(3). Solve the system of equations $\mathbf{c} = \mathbf{A}^{-1}\mathbf{y}$ using the LU decomposition method to obtain $\mathbf{c}$.
(4). Calculate the basis B-spline ${}^{m}_{[b]}B_i(x)$ using the de Boor-Cox algorithm.
(5). Calculate the nonlinear B-spline interpolation value $y(x)$ at point x.

$$y(x) = \sum_{i=0}^{N-1} {}^{m}c_i {}^{m}_{[b]}B_i(x) \tag{18}$$

(6). Go to (5) for another x value.

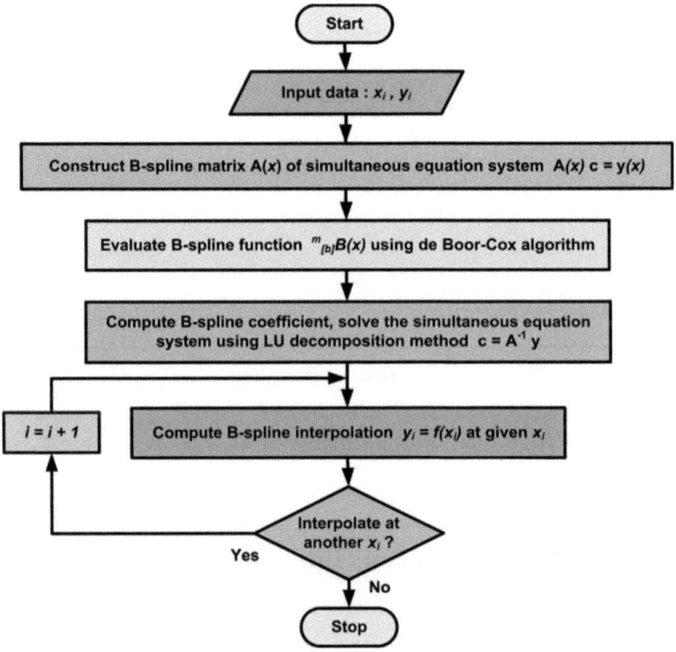

Fig. 3. Nonlinear B-spline table look-up (interpolation) process.

4 Experiment Results

An air vehicle model provides an example of data interpolation and can be applied in simulation practice. The aerodynamic coefficient of the roll moment can be expressed in the form of an equation as a function of the angle of attack α and the sideslip angle β given [2,4]:

$$C_{\ell tot} = C_\ell + (\Delta C_\ell)_{\delta_a} \tag{19}$$

Each term (item) in this expression is defined as follows. C_ℓ is basic roll moment coefficient for rigid air vehicles. $(\Delta C_\ell)_{\delta_a}$ is changes in the basic roll moment coefficient due to aileron control input δ_a where C_ℓ is a function of the angle of attack α and the angle of sideslip β. Note that each curve is for a different value of β, at different intervals, and that the origin for each curve has been displaced for clarity. The other terms in the C_ℓ equation are obtained from the figure and further data equations. It can be seen that the roll coefficients C_ℓ presented in relation to α and β described above constitute an extensive data package for a modern air vehicle that can be created there.

As an experiment, the C_ℓ data table (see Table 1) was used for a fighter aircraft with the following flight envelope: angle of attack α (deg) is [–10.0 –5.0 0.0 +5.0 +10.0 +15.0 +20.0 +25.0 +30.0 +35.0 +40.0 +45.0], sideslip angle β (deg) is [–20.0 -10.0 0.0 +10.0 +20.0 +30.0] and aileron control plane angle δ_a (deg) is [–21.5 0.0 +21.5].

The computation algorithm of nonlinear B-spline interpolation (table look-up) was then implemented as source code written in C/C++. The C/C++ source code was then compiled and linked using the Microsoft Visual Studio C/C++ compiler [12]. The bspline-init() function mpdule was called once, while the bspline-loop() function module was called repeatedly 60 times per second (or 60 Hz). The execution results of the C/C++ program can be seen in Table 2, Table 3 and Fig. 4.

Table 2 shows the results of the calculation of the B-spline coefficient ${}^m c_i$ using the LU decomposition method to solve the simultaneous equations (Eq. 18). At the sideslip angle position $\beta = 0.0°$, the change in the C_ℓ value with respect to the change in α will produce the coefficient ${}^m c_i$ values at orders m = 1,2, and 3. These ${}^m c_i$ values will be further used in the interpolation process in Fig. 3 (Eq. 18). Table 3 shows the results of the calculation of the B-spline coefficient ${}^m c_i$ at the sideslip angle position $\beta = 10.0°$.

Table 2. B-spline coefficient ${}^m c_i$ of order 1, 2 and 3 at $\beta = 0.0°$.

α (deg)	C_ℓ	${}^1c$	${}^2c$	${}^3c$
–10.000000	–0.001000	–0.001000	–0.001000	–0.001000
–5.000000	–0.010000	–0.010000	–0.007314	–0.006371
0.000000	–0.020000	–0.020000	–0.020017	–0.016758
5.000000	–0.030000	–0.030000	–0.030044	–0.029946
10.000000	–0.039000	–0.039000	–0.039721	–0.040160
15.000000	–0.044000	–0.044000	–0.043629	–0.043415
20.000000	–0.050000	–0.050000	–0.050504	–0.050182
25.000000	–0.049000	–0.049000	–0.053346	–0.055859
30.000000	–0.023000	–0.023000	–0.021422	–0.020382
35.000000	–0.006000	–0.006000	–0.002123	0.005977
40.000000	–0.014000	–0.014000	–0.016769	–0.022738
45.000000	–0.027000	–0.027000	–0.027000	–0.027000

Table 3. B-spline coefficient ${}^{m}c_i$ of order 1, 2 and 3 at $\beta = 10.0°$.

α (deg)	C_ℓ	${}^{1}c$	${}^{2}c$	${}^{3}c$
–10.00000	0.000000	0.000000	0.000000	0.000000
–5.000000	–0.010000	–0.010000	–0.006572	–0.004884
0.000000	–0.022000	–0.022000	–0.022166	–0.019232
5.000000	–0.034000	–0.034000	–0.033313	–0.032319
10.000000	–0.047000	–0.047000	–0.049957	–0.052220
15.000000	–0.046000	–0.046000	–0.042946	–0.040802
20.000000	–0.059000	–0.059000	–0.060368	–0.060574
25.000000	–0.061000	–0.061000	–0.066846	–0.070903
30.000000	–0.033000	–0.033000	–0.026558	–0.021815
35.000000	–0.036000	–0.036000	–0.037807	–0.045846
40.000000	–0.035000	–0.035000	–0.033797	–0.029327
45.000000	–0.035000	–0.035000	–0.035000	–0.035000

Figure 4 shows that first-order B-spline interpolation ($m = 1$) is essentially a piecewise linear interpolation (PLI). Thus, B-spline interpolation includes and generalizes the existing conventional PLI. By selecting an appropriate order m value, an adaptive interpolation is obtained, by selecting the appropriate order m according to the characteristic (continuous differentiability) of the aerodynamic table data we are dealing with. The nonlinear B-spline interpolation process calculates the roll moment coefficient C_ℓ as a function of the angle of attack α, sideslip angle β and aileron control angle δ_a. When the air vehicle is flying at an attitude of $\alpha = 26.39°$, $\beta = -19.12°$ and $\delta_a = 0.0°$, the B-spline interpolation process produces a roll moment coefficient value of $C_\ell = 0.052349$.

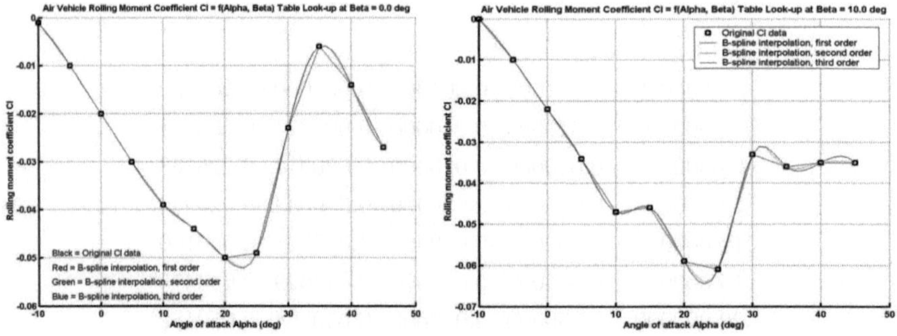

Fig. 4. B-spline interpolation of orders $m = 1, 2 and 3$.

Data interpolation computation as part of the simulation process requires precise and real-time computation, especially during extreme flight simulation scenarios such as dog fights, approaching to stall, flying follow the terrain, avoiding collisions. In these conditions, the PLI approach is not accurate enough, so it requires a nonlinear B-spline interpolation method. From Fig. 4 it can be seen that at alpha positions between 20.0–25.0° and 30.0–35.0°, B-spline interpolation is more precise naturally than PLI.

5 Conclusion

Nonlinear B-spline interpolation has been formulated for table look-up of aerodynamic coefficient data in airborne cyber-physical systems. A flowchart and implementation of B-spline table look-up interpolation in C/C++ have been developed for engineering cyber in the loop simulation (CILS) of airborne cyber-physical systems. The results show that for aerodynamic coefficient data with slowly changing curves, the piecewise linear interpolation is sufficient, but for data with sharply changing curves, nonlinear B-spline interpolation is required. It is shown that the table look-up interpolation process using the nonlinear B-spline method includes and generalizes the conventional piecewise linear interpolation (PLI). For m=1, B-spline interpolation is PLI. Furthermore, an adaptive interpolation is obtained by selecting an order m that matches the characteristics (continuous differentiability) of the aerodynamic (rolling moments) coefficient data under consideration. Future research will explore B-spline multi-variable table look-up methods that can be used in real-time cyber in the loop simulations.

Acknowledgments. This paper is the results of the research project funded by the Ministry of Education, Culture, and Technology of the Republic of Indonesia, the Doctoral Dissertation Research under grant contract No.: 036/E5/PG.02.00.PL/2024.

References

1. Alur, R.: Principles of Cyber-Physical Systems, 1st edn. The MIT Press, Cambridge (2015)
2. Stevens, B.L., Lewis, F.L., Johnson, E.N.: Aircraft Control and Simulation: Dynamics, Controls Design, and Autonomous Systems, 3rd edn. John Wiley and Sons Inc., Hoboken (2016)
3. Schreiter, K., Müller, S., Luckner, R., Manzey, D.: A flight simulator study of an energy control system for manual flight. IEEE Trans. Hum.-Mach. Syst. **49**(6), 672–683 (2019). https://doi.org/10.1109/THMS.2019.2938138
4. Zipfel, P.H.: Modeling and simulation of aerospace vehicle dynamics. In: AIAA Education Series, Reston, Virginia, 2nd edn (2007)
5. Cao, H., Zoldy, M.: Implementing B-spline path planning method based on roundabout geometry elements. IEEE Access **10**, 81434–81446 (2022). https://doi.org/10.1109/ACCESS.2022.3193667
6. Mitze, R., Dillkotter, D., Gros, S., Schild, A., Monnigmann, M.: Fast and smooth surface B-spline interpolation for regularly spaced data used in system modeling to make MPC real-time feasible. In: IEEE European Control Conference (ECC), Limassol, Cyprus, 12–15 June 2018 (2018)

7. Nguyen, N.T., Gangavarapu, P.T., Ernst, F.: B-spline-to-Bezier conversion and applications on path planning. In: 9th IEEE/IFAC International Conference on Control, Decision and Information Technologies (CoDIT 2023), Rome, Italy, 03–06 July 2023 (2023). 979-8-3503-1140-2
8. Schumaker, L.L.: Spline Functions: Basic Theory, 3rd edn. Cambridge University Press, Cambridge (2007)
9. Svoboda, M., Iovan, L.M., Andea, F.P.: B-spline interpolation technique for digital signal processing. In: IEEE International Conference on Information and Digital Technology (2015). 978-1-4673-7186-5
10. Boor, C.D.: A Practical Guide to Splines, rev Springer-Verlag, New York (2001)
11. Kreyszig, E.: Advanced Engineering Mathematics, Nine John Wiley and Sons Inc., New York (2006)
12. Press, W.H., Teukolsky, S.A., Vetterling, W.T., Flannery, B.P.: Numerical Recipes in C: The Art of Scientific Computing, 2nd edn. Cambridge University Press, New York (1992)

Spacecraft Evasive Maneuvering Based on Neural Network Pattern Recognition and an Improved SA-GA Algorithm

Yisong Wei[1,2], Ming Yang[1,2], Ping Ma[1,2], and Tao Chao[1,2(✉)]

[1] Harbin Institute of Technology, Harbin, China
chaotao2000@163.com
[2] National Key Laboratory of Modeling and Simulation for Complex Systems, Harbin, China

Abstract. For collision encounter scenarios between spacecraft and potentially threatening moving objects, this paper proposes the definition of a threat corridor and establishes its mathematical model. Based on neural network pattern recognition, the number of evasive maneuver impulses for spacecraft is determined. Based on this, an improved simulated annealing-genetic algorithm (SA-GA) is proposed to optimize spacecraft evasive maneuvers. Distinct from traditional evasive maneuver methods, this approach adopts the threat corridor as a novel evasion metric, extends evasive actions to multiple impulses, and fully integrates the global exploration capability of genetic algorithms with the local exploitation ability of simulated annealing in the improved SA-GA algorithm, achieving superior optimization results. Simulation results demonstrate that compared with conventional evasive maneuver methods, this approach ensures timeliness, effectiveness, and economy of evasive maneuvers while effectively overcoming the limitations of standalone genetic algorithms. It significantly improves the overall success probability of evasive maneuvers, providing new technical perspectives for spacecraft evasive maneuvers against potential threats.

Keywords: Spacecraft Evasive Maneuvering · Neural Network Pattern Recognition · Improved SA-GA Algorithm · Multi-impulse Maneuver · Threat Corridor

1 Introduction

In recent years, with the advancement of space technologies worldwide, the population of space debris has grown rapidly, and space-based active interception capabilities have significantly improved. These developments have led to escalating threats to spacecraft, making protective technologies a critical focus for nations globally. Among all spacecraft safety protection technologies, evasive maneuvering technology can effectively protect the spacecraft from interference and damage by external threats, ensure the continuous and stable operational capability of space systems, and possesses advantages such as simple technical implementation and wide application scenarios, gradually becoming a key focus of current research.

W. Cai et al. (Eds.): AsiaSim 2025, CCIS 2727, pp. 183–198, 2026.
https://doi.org/10.1007/978-981-95-4472-1_16

Currently, most research on spacecraft evasive maneuver methods treats the evasive maneuver problem as an optimization problem by setting optimization metrics such as terminal miss distance and collision probability.

For non-maneuverable threat objects such as space debris and defunct spacecraft, Reference [1] derived the optimal evasion direction for spacecraft by decomposing their relative motion with the target; Reference [2] developed a collision avoidance controller using the relative distance and its rate of change between the satellite and target; Reference [3] transformed the collision avoidance problem for satellite formation reconfiguration into a linear programming problem for solution; Reference [4] investigated collision avoidance within satellite formations using the potential function method; Reference [5] established a distance function between the maneuver point and predicted collision point, deriving the maneuver direction by maximizing miss distance; Reference [6] calculated optimal evasive maneuver direction and magnitude using collision probability.

For threatening objects with certain maneuvering capabilities such as autonomous rendezvous spacecraft, References [7] and [8] investigated high-precision guidance methods based on artificial potential functions for spacecraft dynamic obstacle avoidance; Reference [9] studied spacecraft pursuit-evasion games using differential game theory with miss distance as the payoff function; Reference [10] applied zero-sum differential game solutions to satellite interception and collision avoidance problems; References [11] and [12] considered the influence of relative motion on system observability and solved the optimal evasion problem using observability degree as the optimization objective; Reference [13] proposed a method for identifying non-cooperative spacecraft maneuvers using sparse orbital data; Reference [14] developed a deep reinforcement learning framework for autonomous game-theoretic evasion against proximity threats; Reference [15] presented a reachable-set-based approach in orbital elements for anti-encirclement evasion against multiple spacecraft.

However, current spacecraft evasion strategies are predominantly designed based on conventional metrics such as collision probability and miss distance, with focus primarily on the terminal encounter phase while lacking effective early warning for potential threat regions. Moreover, most evasion behaviors are limited to single short-duration maneuvers, which prove insufficient to completely eliminate threats when dealing with targets possessing rendezvous reconfiguration capabilities.

To address these limitations, this study first establishes a threat corridor model to delineate potentially hazardous regions along the threat object's trajectory, adopting it as the primary performance metric. Subsequently, neural network-based pattern recognition determines the required number of evasion impulses, extending evasion capability from single maneuvers to multiple impulses. Finally, an improved hybrid optimization strategy is developed using both threat corridor dimensions and impulse consumption as performance metrics to identify optimal evasion solutions.

Simulation results demonstrate that the proposed method effectively overcomes the limitations of conventional optimization algorithms, ensuring timeliness, effectiveness, and economy of evasion maneuvers while significantly improving overall mission success probability.

2 Threat Corridor Model

2.1 Scenario Description

A chaser spacecraft and a target spacecraft are in orbital motion. The chaser actively performs rendezvous with the target to execute a certain non-cooperative space mission. Under rendezvous time constraints and total delta-V budget, the chaser can only initiate rendezvous maneuvers from specific orbital regions. The target needs to determine optimal evasion strategies that minimize the aforementioned specific orbital regions. We define these specific orbital regions as the "threat corridor".

2.2 Chaser Rendezvous Maneuvering Strategy

The target operates in a near-circular orbit, and its trajectory can be approximated using the two-body motion model. Given the rendezvous time constraint Δt and the initial position/velocity state $X_{ti} = [R_{ti}\ V_{ti}]^T$ of the target at time t_i, the position/velocity state $X_{tf} = [R_{tf}\ V_{tf}]^T$ at time $t_i + \Delta t$ can be calculated according to the two-body motion model. This calculated position serves as the rendezvous point.

The Lambert two-impulse orbital transfer is selected as the chaser's rendezvous maneuvering strategy. Given the chaser's position/velocity state $X_{pi} = [R_{pi}\ V_{pi}]^T$ at time t_i as the initial maneuver condition, and the previously calculated rendezvous point's position/velocity state $X_{tf} = [R_{tf}\ V_{tf}]^T$ as the target condition, this Lambert strategy can uniquely determine the transfer trajectory and total required delta-V $\sum \Delta v_{pi}$ when the rendezvous time constraint Δt is specified.

2.3 Threat Corridor Modeling

Based on the aforementioned research scenario, we establish the mathematical modeling of the threat corridor as follows. Given the chaser's rendezvous time constraint Δt, any time instant after the initial epoch can serve as a potential maneuver initiation point. For each candidate initiation time, the corresponding total delta-V requirement can be computed following the previously described Lambert two-impulse orbital transfer strategy. Time t_i instant becomes infeasible when its $\sum \Delta v_{pi} > \Delta v_{\max}$, whereas any t_k satisfying $\sum \Delta v_{ki} \leq \Delta v_{\max}$ defines a threatening orbital position that enables successful interception, thereby creating vulnerability for the target. It follows that the threat corridor is constituted by the set of all time instants like t_k that satisfy the specified constraints. In this study, we characterize the size of the threat corridor by the arc length formed by these feasible points along the orbit.

The threat corridor is computed using a direct search method. Assuming the rendezvous is constrained within one orbital period, we initiate the computation from the chaser's initial state and systematically traverse all potential starting points along its orbit with a fixed step size h. For each candidate starting point, the total required delta-V for the chaser's orbital maneuver is calculated through the aforementioned chaser rendezvous maneuvering strategy. The resulting data is filtered by eliminating all starting points whose total required delta-V exceeds the allocated delta-V budget. The remaining

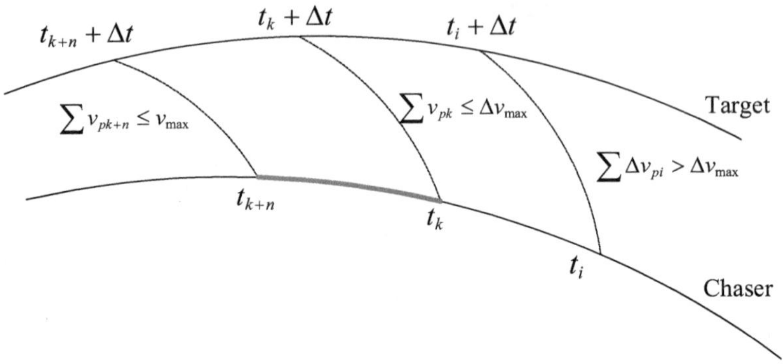

Fig. 1 Threat corridor schematic illustration

set of orbital points that satisfy all rendezvous constraints precisely defines the threat corridor. A schematic illustration of the threat corridor is presented in Fig. 1.

Let N_t denote the number of feasible points satisfying the rendezvous constraints. The temporal duration of the threat corridor is then calculated by Eq. (1).

$$T_t = (N_t - 1) \times h \tag{1}$$

Let T_c represent the chaser's orbital period. The arc length of the threat corridor is then computed by Eq. (2).

$$L_t = 2\pi \frac{T_t}{T_c} \tag{2}$$

3 Neural Network-Based Impulse Pattern Recognition

3.1 Analysis of Evasive Maneuver Impulse Patterns

When confronted with the chaser's threat, the target must execute evasive maneuvers through a series of impulsive maneuvers. In this process, the number of impulses determines the impulse pattern, and its determination must account for current conditions, particularly the initial position/velocity states of both the chaser and target. To address this, we employ neural networks to perform pattern recognition for identifying optimal impulse counts under varying scenarios.

3.2 Neural Network Model

This study adopts a multilayer neural network architecture based on backpropagation algorithm. The network comprises 1 input layer, 3 hidden layers, and 1 output layer, optimized using scaled conjugate gradient (SCG) method with cross-entropy as the loss function. All input features undergo min-max normalization preprocessing, while early stopping strategy is implemented to prevent overfitting.

The neural network's input layer consists of 12 neurons, corresponding to the 12 variables representing the initial positions and velocities of both the chaser and target. The output layer contains 5 neurons, representing the five impulse patterns ranging from 1 to 5 impulses. The hidden layers comprise 18, 24, and 36 neurons respectively.

The architecture of the neural network is illustrated in Fig. 2, while its architecture parameters and key hyperparameters are provided in Tables 1 and 2, respectively.

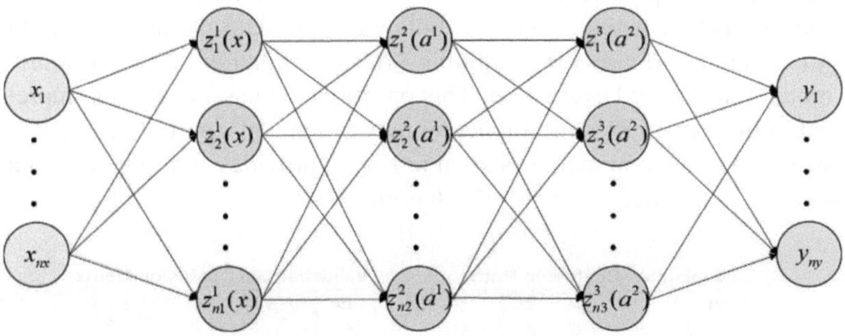

Fig. 2 Neural network architecture

Table 1 Neural network architecture parameters

Name	Parameter
Input layer	12
Hidden layers	18, 24, 36
Output layer	5
Hidden layer activation function	Sigmoid
Output layer activation function	Softmax

Table 2 Key hyperparameters of the neural network model

Hyperparameter	Value
Training epochs	3000
Learning rate	0.001
Target error	10^{-6}
Max validation failures	200

Excessively complex neural network architectures yield only marginal improvements in accuracy at the cost of significantly reduced efficiency. Based on a comprehensive trade-off between these two factors, the selected architecture is well-suited to requirements.

3.3 Neural Network Training and Evaluation

Through preliminary optimization simulations, we generated 10,000 training samples to construct the neural network dataset. Following the data partitioning strategy, the dataset was randomly divided into training (70%), validation (15%), and test (15%) sets for model training and evaluation. This partitioned dataset enables comprehensive assessment of the pattern recognition neural network model's performance.

The resulting confusion matrix, shown in Fig. 3, provides an intuitive visualization of classification performance across all categories.

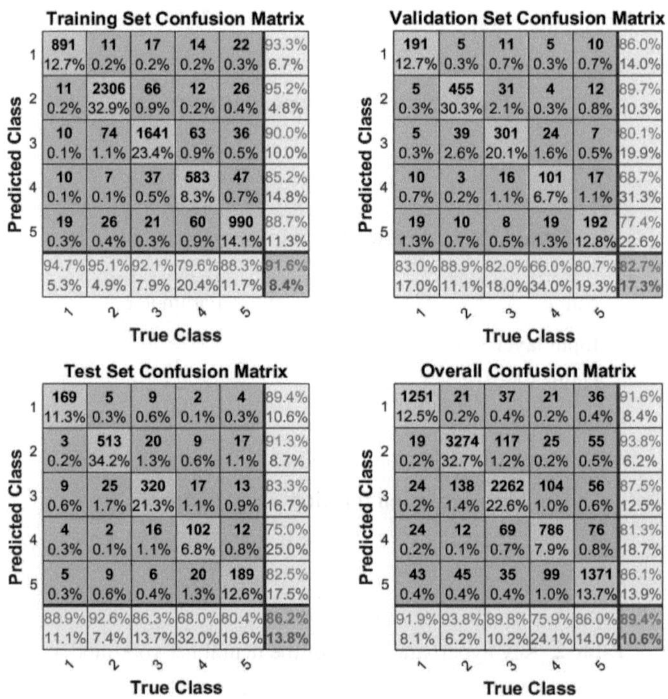

Fig. 3 Confusion matrix

As evidenced by the confusion matrix, the neural network model achieves approximately 90% classification accuracy across all five impulse patterns. This pattern recognition step provides a preliminary estimate of the optimal impulse count for the subsequent evasive maneuver optimization. The overall evasion effectiveness, however, is primarily determined by the subsequent optimization process, which exhibits a certain degree of robustness. Consequently, the achieved classification accuracy is sufficient to meet the preliminary requirements for determining the optimal impulse count in evasive maneuvers.

4 Design of Evasive Maneuver Optimization Method

4.1 Formulation of the Optimization Problem

The selection of optimization variables is determined by evasive maneuver performance metrics. Given a predetermined number of impulses, the maneuver effectiveness depends on three key parameters for each impulse: timing, direction, and magnitude. Consequently, these parameters are chosen as the optimization variables, as mathematically defined in Eq. (3).

$$D_{opt} = \left[t_1 \ \varphi_1 \ \psi_1 \ \Delta v_1 \ ... \ t_i \ \varphi_i \ \psi_i \ \Delta v_i \ ... \ t_n \ \varphi_n \ \psi_n \ \Delta v_n \right]^T \tag{3}$$

where t_i denotes the timing of the i-th impulsive maneuver, φ_i represents its pitch angle, ψ_i represents its yaw angle, Δv_i indicates the impulse magnitude, and n specifies the total number of maneuvers.

During multi-impulse evasive maneuvers, comprehensive constraints must be imposed on the timing, direction, and magnitude of each impulse.

The timing constraints require all impulses to be executed in chronological sequence and completed within a specified mission time window, as formally defined in Eq. (4).

$$0 \le t_1 \le ...t_i... \le t_n \le t_{\max} \tag{4}$$

The directional constraints bound the pitch and yaw angles of each impulse within predefined operational ranges, mathematically expressed in Eq. (5).

$$\begin{cases} \varphi_{\min} \le \varphi_i \le \varphi_{\max} \\ \psi_{\min} \le \psi_i \le \psi_{\max} \end{cases} \tag{5}$$

The magnitude constraints limit each individual impulse below the maximum allowable value while ensuring the cumulative total remains within the allocated delta-V budget, with both conditions specified in Eq. (6).

$$\begin{cases} \Delta v_i \le \dfrac{\Delta v_{\max}}{n} \\ \displaystyle\sum_{i=1}^{n} \Delta v_i \le \Delta v_{\max} \end{cases} \tag{6}$$

The objective of spacecraft evasive maneuvers is to minimize the threat corridor length within the shortest possible timeframe while simultaneously minimizing impulse expenditure during evasion. Therefore, the optimization objective comprehensively considers the threat corridor parameters (length and duration) along with maneuver impulse consumption, constructing the multi-objective weighted cost function as shown in Eq. (7).

$$J = w_1 \sum_{i=0}^{n} \sqrt{L_{ti} \frac{\Delta t_i}{\Delta t_{ref}}} + w_2 \sum_{i=1}^{n} \frac{\Delta v_i}{\Delta v_{ref}} \tag{7}$$

where L_{ti} denotes the threat corridor length after the i-th maneuver impulse (with $i = 0$ representing the initial corridor length); Δt_i indicates the current corridor duration, defined as the time interval between adjacent impulses (with $i = 0$ corresponding to the time of the first impulse); Δv_i stands for the impulse expenditure of the i-th maneuver; w_1, w_2 represents the weighting factor, whose value is problem-dependent; and Δt_{ref}, Δv_{ref} signifies the reference value used for non-dimensionalization, also determined by specific mission requirements.

In this study's optimization framework, the primary objective of evasive maneuvers is to maximize threat corridor reduction within minimal time, with impulse expenditure minimization being the secondary consideration. Consequently, the weighting coefficients for threat corridor parameters (length and duration) are set larger than those for impulse consumption, with specific values as formulated in Eq. (8).

$$\begin{cases} w_1 = 0.6 \\ w_2 = 0.4 \end{cases} \tag{8}$$

During the computation of the objective function, all optimization variables undergo non-dimensionalization to ensure the resultant values remain within a reasonable range. The reference values for this normalization are determined based on specific problem requirements, with the current study's reference values specified in Eq. (9).

$$\begin{cases} \Delta t_{ref} = 100 \\ \Delta v_{ref} = 300 \end{cases} \tag{9}$$

4.2 Integrated Optimization Framework for Evasive Maneuvers

The integrated evasive maneuver optimization algorithm proceeds through the following steps:

Step 1: Generate the initial population with randomized candidate solutions.

Step 2: Compute the population entropy and determine the current entropy phase (high/medium/low), then adaptively adjust genetic algorithm parameters (selection pressure, crossover probability, mutation probability) accordingly.

Step 3: Perform standard genetic operations (selection, crossover, mutation) to produce a new generation.

Step 4: Execute simulated annealing on the current optimal individual by generating neighborhood solutions through perturbation and accepting them according to the Metropolis criterion, iteratively cooling the temperature until it falls below the minimum threshold before updating the population's best solution.

Step 5: If the algorithm termination conditions are not satisfied, return to Step 2; otherwise, output the optimal evasive maneuver strategy derived from the final population's best individual.

Step 2 and Step 4 represent improvements addressing the limitations of "premature convergence" in the early stages and "stagnation" in the later phases of the genetic algorithm. The improved optimization approach combines the global exploration capability of the genetic algorithm with the local exploitation ability of the simulated annealing algorithm, denoted as the improved simulated annealing-genetic algorithm (SA-GA) approach.

4.3 Global Exploration Control Strategy

The "premature convergence" phenomenon in genetic algorithms fundamentally stems from the lack of effective control over the algorithm's global exploration, causing premature aggregation of most individuals around local optima and consequent loss of population diversity. To address this, we introduce population entropy as a diversity metric to regulate global exploration throughout the optimization process.

First, normalize each variable in the population, then discretize the normalized values by partitioning them into a predetermined number of equal-width bins. For these discretized variables, compute the probability distribution across bins and derive the entropy for individual variables as formulated in Eq. (10).

$$H(X_j) = -\sum_{i=1}^{B} p_{i,j} \log_2 p_{i,j} \tag{10}$$

For the entire population, the multivariate population entropy is calculated as specified in Eq. (11).

$$H = \frac{1}{M}\sum_{j=1}^{M} H(X_j) \tag{11}$$

where X_j represents the j-th variable in the population, $p_{i,j}$ denotes the probability of the j-th variable falling into the i-th bin, B indicates the total number of bins, and M specifies the total number of variables.

Population entropy serves as a crucial metric for quantifying population diversity, where higher entropy values indicate superior diversity with uniform individual distribution, while lower values signify poor diversity with converging individuals. We stratify the entropy into three distinct phases (high/medium/low) and adaptively adjust genetic algorithm parameters accordingly to regulate global exploration.

The selection pressure, crossover probability, and mutation probability adopted across different entropy phases are systematically summarized in Table 3.

Table 3. Genetic algorithm parameters at different entropy phases

Phase entropy	Selection pressure	Crossover probability	Mutation probability	Main strategy
High entropy	0.60	0.96	0.40	Exploration
Medium entropy	1.40	0.64	0.16	Convergence
Low entropy	1.80	0.48	0.10	Exploitation

4.4 Local Exploitation Control Strategy

The "stagnation" phenomenon in genetic algorithms fundamentally stems from the lack of effective control over the algorithm's local exploitation, which relies solely on late-stage population individuals lacking adequate perturbation mechanisms. To address this, we incorporate simulated annealing to enhance localized disturbances, thereby establishing effective control over the algorithm's local exploitation capability.

The simulated annealing algorithm exhibits strong local exploitation capabilities, with its core mechanisms being neighborhood solution generation and controlled cooling schedule management.

The simulated annealing algorithm perturbs the current best solution obtained by the genetic algorithm, generating new candidate solutions within its neighborhood and evaluating their fitness values. The perturbation magnitude is governed by the current annealing temperature, which dynamically controls the exploration range. The mathematical formulation for generating new solutions is provided in Eq. (12).

$$x_{new}^{(i)} = x_{cur}^{(i)} + \frac{T}{T_0}(UB^{(i)} - LB^{(i)})(\xi - 0.5) \tag{12}$$

where $x_{new}^{(i)}, x_{cur}^{(i)}$ represent the new solution and current solution for the i-th dimensional variable, respectively; T, T_0 denote the current temperature and initial temperature, respectively; $LB^{(i)}$, $UB^{(i)}$ indicate the lower and upper bounds of the i-th dimensional variable, respectively; and ξ is a uniformly distributed random number within the interval [0, 1].

The algorithm compares the new solution with the current best solution and determines its acceptance based on the Metropolis criterion: the improved new solutions are accepted unconditionally, while the degraded new solutions may be accepted with a probability influenced by the current annealing temperature. The acceptance probability calculation is formally specified in Eq. (13).

$$P = \begin{cases} 1, \Delta f \leq 0 \\ \exp(-\frac{\Delta f}{T}), \Delta f > 0 \end{cases} \tag{13}$$

where P represents the acceptance probability of new solutions, T denotes the current temperature, Δf indicates the fitness variation, $\Delta f = f(x_{new}) - f(x_{cur})$.

Following perturbation, the algorithm executes annealing by iteratively reducing the temperature until it falls below a predefined threshold or other termination criteria are met. The cooling process follows an exponential decay scheme as mathematically defined in Eq. (14).

$$T_{k+1} = \alpha_{co} T_k \tag{14}$$

where α_{co} represents the cooling rate and T_k denotes the temperature at the k-th iteration.

The key parameters of the simulated annealing algorithm are systematically configured as presented in Table 4.

Table 4 Parameters of the simulated annealing algorithm

Parameter	Value
Initial temperature	100
Cooling rate	0.95
Termination temperature	20

5 Simulation Results and Analysis

5.1 Simulation Scenario Configuration

To align with engineering practice, the deployed orbital altitude and rendezvous duration are configured with reference to typical LEO/MEO satellites, while impulse magnitudes are set according to standard orbital maneuver capabilities. The simulation assumes the chaser possesses superior maneuvering capability compared to the target, with detailed scenario parameters specified in Table 5.

Table 5 Simulation scenario parameter settings

Parameter	Value
Orbital altitude	1200 km
Rendezvous duration	2000 s
Total delta-V budget of chaser	1000 m/s
Total delta-V budget of target	300 m/s

The initial position and velocity state vectors of the target spacecraft are mathematically defined in Eq. (15).

$$\begin{cases} R_{tarM0} = \left[4597000\ 6135000\ 317000\right]^T m \\ V_{tarM0} = \left[5100\ -3100\ 200\right]^T m/s \end{cases} \tag{15}$$

The initial position and velocity state vectors of the chaser spacecraft are mathematically defined in Eq. (16).

$$\begin{cases} R_{purM0} = \left[4512000\ 6298000\ 331000\right]^T m \\ V_{purM0} = \left[4700\ -3200\ 230\right]^T m/s \end{cases} \tag{16}$$

5.2 Optimization Simulation Results

The initial state vectors of both target and chaser are input into the neural network model for evasive maneuver impulse pattern recognition, which identifies 3-pulse as the optimal impulse pattern.

Given the target's maximum total delta-V budget of 300 m/s, each individual impulse is capped at 100 m/s. Practical operational considerations limit the inter-pulse interval to 10–200 s, while impulse direction remains unconstrained. The complete boundary conditions for all variables are mathematically defined in Eq. (17).

$$\begin{cases} 10 \leq \Delta t_i \leq 200 \\ -\pi \leq \varphi_i \leq \pi \\ -\pi \leq \psi_i \leq \pi \\ \Delta v_i \leq 100 \end{cases} \tag{17}$$

The simulation results under the specified scenario conditions and constraints are presented in Table 6, which shows the optimal impulse sequence obtained through the optimization process.

Table 6 Multi-impulse maneuver optimization results

Impulse number	Impulse time (s)	Impulse pitch angle (deg)	Impulse yaw angle (deg)	Impulse magnitude (m/s)
1st	0	−160.39	−179.72	95.47
2nd	43.92	−116.31	180.00	50.61
3rd	222.61	−142.80	−62.44	8.05

The evasive maneuver executed according to the optimized impulse sequence results in threat corridor status quantitatively summarized in Table 7 and visually presented in Fig. 4 through Fig. 7.

Table 7 Threat corridor status during evasive maneuvers

Time	Threat count points	Orbital period points	Threat corridor length (rad)	Threat corridor ratio
Pre-maneuver	476	847	3.53	56.20%
After 1st impulse	367	847	2.72	43.33%
After 2nd impulse	75	847	0.56	8.85%
After 3rd impulse	39	847	0.29	4.60%

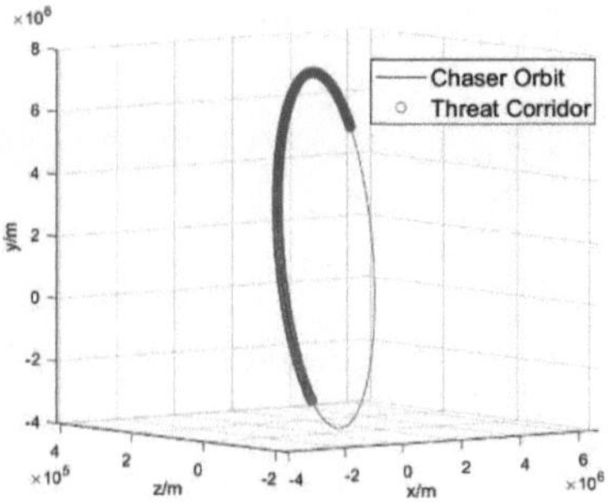

Fig. 4 Pre-impulse threat corridor

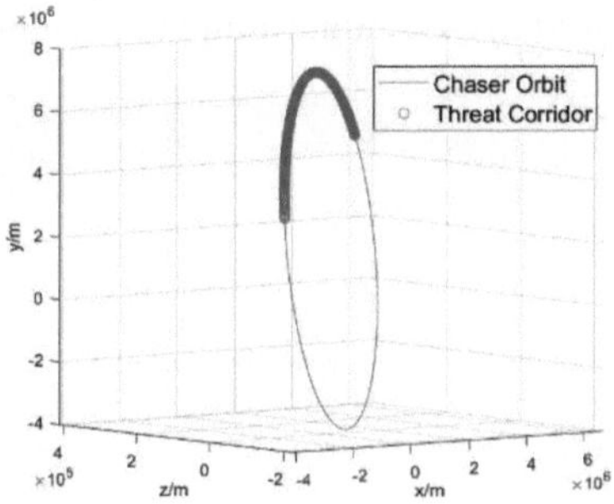

Fig. 5 Post-1st-impulse threat corridor

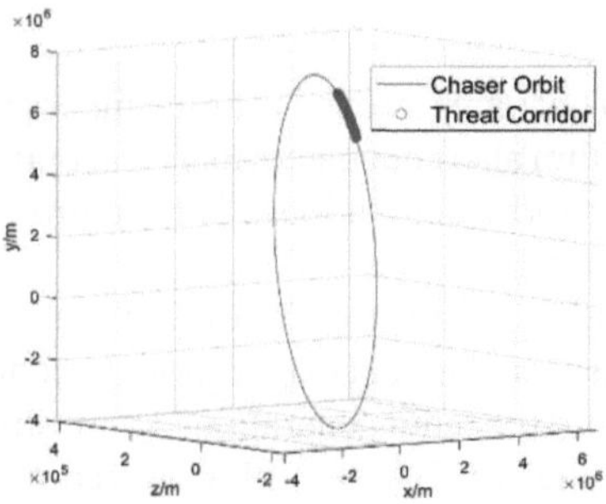

Fig. 6 Post-2nd-impulse threat corridor

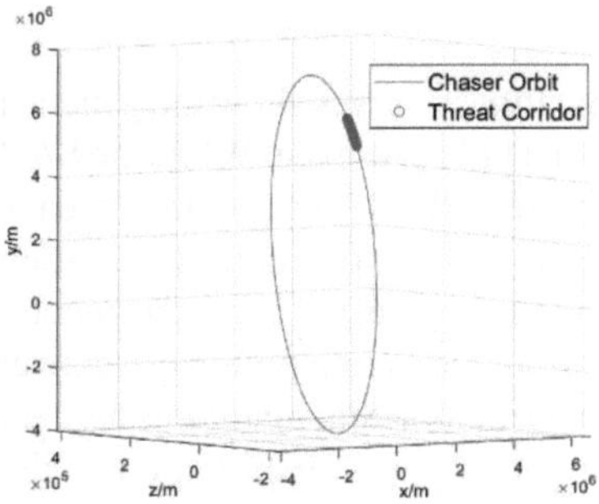

Fig. 7 Post-3rd-impulse threat corridor

Analysis of the simulation results reveals three key advantages of the proposed optimization algorithm:

Advantage 1: Timeliness Assurance.

The threat corridor ratio drops below 10% within merely 43.92 s after the second impulse, demonstrating the algorithm's capability to rapidly reduce threats during early-stage maneuvers.

Advantage 2: Effectiveness Assurance.

Final corridor ratio below 5% post-last impulse confirms near-complete evasion from the chaser's threat, ensuring mission-accomplishment reliability.

Advantage 3: Economy Assurance.

The total impulse consumption of 154.13 m/s (only 51.4% of the budget) with all three pulses complying with individual limits proves the algorithm's economic propellant utilization.

In summary, the optimization algorithm achieves exceptional evasive performance by simultaneously satisfying timeliness, effectiveness, and economy requirements.

5.3 Algorithm Comparative Analysis

The fitness and entropy iteration curve for both the standard genetic algorithm and the improved SA-GA algorithm are presented in Figs. 8 and 9, respectively.

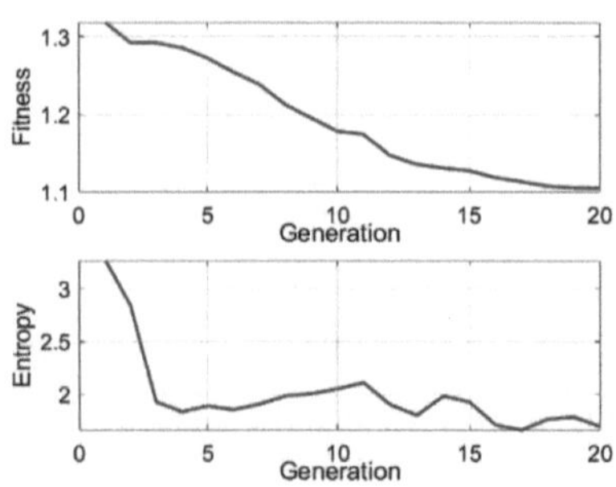

Fig. 8 Genetic algorithm iteration curve

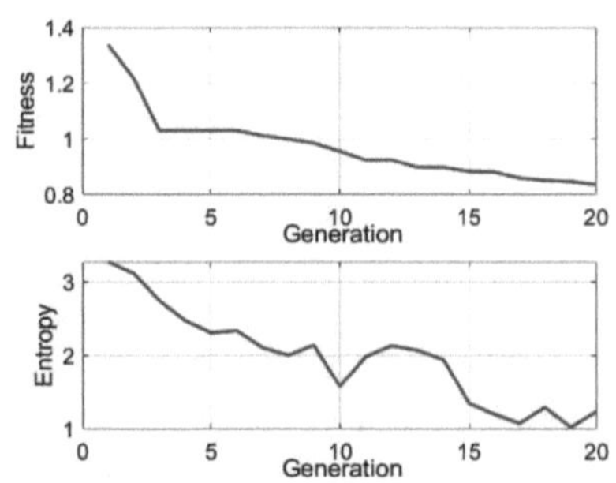

Fig. 9 SA-GA algorithm iteration curve

The fitness curves show the genetic algorithm becomes trapped near the fitness value of 1.1 and fails to escape. While the SA-GA algorithm also encounters this local optimum plateau near 1.1, it successfully breaks free after three generations. This confirms the SA-GA algorithm overcomes the "stagnation" limitation.

The entropy curves show the genetic algorithm's entropy drops below 2.0 by the third generation, indicating premature convergence that limits global exploration. In contrast, the SA-GA algorithm maintains higher entropy until the tenth generation, demonstrating effective early-stage exploration. This confirms the SA-GA algorithm overcomes the "premature convergence" limitation.

The overall algorithmic performance of both the standard genetic algorithm and the improved SA-GA algorithm is presented in Table 8.

Table 8 Performance comparison of optimization algorithms

Optimization algorithm	Time to reduce threat corridor ratio to 10%	Final threat corridor ratio	Total impulse consumption
Genetic algorithm	Failed to reach 10%	15.58%	205.07m/s
SA-GA algorithm	43.92s	4.60%	154.13m/s

The three parameters listed in the table respectively characterize the algorithm's timeliness, effectiveness, and economy, demonstrating that the improved SA-GA algorithm outperforms the standard genetic algorithm across all metrics.

6 Conclusions

This paper focuses on the spacecraft evasive maneuver problem and proposes an evasive maneuver method based on neural network pattern recognition and an improved SA-GA algorithm. After determining the number of evasive maneuver impulses through neural network analysis, the improved SA-GA algorithm is applied to optimize the impulse timing, direction, and magnitude for multiple maneuvers. This method overcomes the limitations of using standard genetic algorithm alone, minimizes the threat corridor length in the shortest possible time, and ensures the timeliness, effectiveness, and economy of evasive maneuvers, thus achieving near-total elimination of threats from chaser spacecraft, improving the overall success probability of evasive maneuvers, and providing certain safety guarantees for spacecraft when facing threats.

References

1. Yao, D., Wang, Z.: Autonomous collision avoidance strategy for on-orbit spacecraft. J. Natl. Univ. Defense Technol. **34**(6), 100–103, 110 (2012)
2. Wang, S., Schaub, H.: Spacecraft collision avoidance using coulomb forces with separation distance and rate feedback. J. Guid. Control. Dyn. **31**(3), 740–750 (2012)
3. Huang, H., Ma, G., Zhuang, Y.: Optimal trajectory planning for collision-free formation reconfiguration of satellite formation. Acta Aeronautica et Astronautica Sinica **31**(9), 1818–1823 (2010)
4. Zheng, Z., Song, S.: Adaptive cooperative control for formation flying satellites with collision avoidance. Acta Aeronautica et Astronautica Sinica **34**(8), 1934–1943 (2013)
5. Bombardelli, C.: Analytical formulation of impulsive collision avoidance dynamics. Celest. Mech. Dyn. Astron. **118**(2), 99–114 (2014)
6. Wang, H., Li, H., Tang, G.: Optimal collision avoidance maneuver for rendezvous and docking based on collision probability. J. Astronaut. **29**(1), 220–223 (2008)
7. Gao, P., Luo, J.: Adaptive artificial potential function guidance for spacecraft avoiding dynamic obstacles. Chin. Space Sci. Technol. **32**(5), 1–8 (2012)
8. Song, S., Zhang, D., Pei, R.: Non-cooperative autonomous rendezvous and docking guidance with dynamic obstacle avoidance. Chin. Space Sci. Technol. **30**(6), 39–48 (2010)
9. Zhang, Q., Sun, S., Chen, Y., et al.: Pursuit-evasion strategies for two spacecraft with fixed time and numerical solutions. J. Astronaut. **35**(5), 537–544 (2014)

10. Shen, D., Pham, K., Blasch, E., et al.: Pursuit-evasion orbital game for satellite interception and collision avoidance. Proceedings of SPIE **8044**, 284–287 (2011)
11. Yu, D., Luo, Y., Jiang, Z., et al.: Multi-objective evolutionary optimization of evasive maneuvers including observability performance. In: 2015 IEEE Congress on Evolutionary Computation (CEC), Sendai, Japan, May 25–28. pp. 603–610 (2015)
12. Yu, D., Wang, H., Zhou, W.: Anti-rendezvous evasion maneuver method considering spatial geometric constraints. J. Natl. Univ. Defense Technol. **38**(6), 89–94 (2016)
13. Zhao, J.: Threat analysis and countermeasure research for spacecraft proximity operations. Ph.D. Thesis, National University of Defense Technology (2021)
14. Zhang, H., Luo, J., Ma, W.: Machine learning-based game decision-making for spacecraft evasion target threat. Acta Aeronautica et Astronautica Sinica **45**(8), 249–264 (2024)
15. Xiao, Q., Li, L., Zhang, J.: Anti-encirclement evasion method for spacecraft under multi-satellite maneuvering proximity threat. J. Astronaut. **45**(10), 1578–1587 (2024)

Dynamic Modeling and Motion Control of a Thruster-Assisted Bipedal Robot

Ze Wei[1], Jiaying Tan[2,3], and Yan Huang[1](✉)

[1] School of Mechatronical Engineering, Beijing Institute of Technology, Beijing, China
yanhuang@bit.edu.cn

[2] School of Mechanics and Engineering Science, Peking University, Beijing, China

[3] Beijing Medical Robotics Industry Innovation Center, Beijing, China

Abstract. With the advancement of robotics technology, bipedal robots have become a key research focus in the field of intelligent robotics. To enhance their locomotive performance and environmental adaptability, existing studies have integrated thrusters into bipedal robots,which are intended to provide assistance. In this paper, we constructed the walking dynamics model of bipedal robots under the influence of external force fields realized by thrusters. A posture adjustment control strategy is also proposed for bipedal robots, which is used to control the pitch angle and yaw angle of the robot. Additionally, we quantitatively analyzed how external force fields of different magnitude and directions affect key performance metrics of bipedal robots, including lower limb joint torques, overall power consumption, and energy efficiency. Simulation results indicate that the thruster-generated external force field can play positive effects for posture adjustment and overall power consumption optimization of bipedal robots.

Keywords: Bipedal robot · External force field · Dynamics modeling · Motion control

1 Introduction

In recent years, bipedal robots have attracted widespread attention in the field of intelligent robotics due to their human-like movements, which enables them to traverse uneven terrains and overcome obstacles [1]. To enhance the stability and effectiveness of bipedal robots for dynamic motions such as jumping, climbing, and obstacle negotiation, researchers have proposed methods that employed rotors or ducted fans to assist bipedal robots [2]. By leveraging the external force field generated by these thrusters, bipedal robots can flexibly switch between hybrid modes, enhancing their ability to perform tasks in complex environments.

In exsiting studies, many researchers have proposed various control methods to enable bipedal robots with thrusters to switch between different motion modes, especially between aerial and terrestrial modes. Liang K et al. combined an Explicit Reference Regulator (ERG) with Model Predictive Control (MPC) for the Harpy robot,

W. Cai et al. (Eds.): AsiaSim 2025, CCIS 2727, pp. 199–210, 2026.
https://doi.org/10.1007/978-981-95-4472-1_17

bipedal robot with a pair of coaxial duct fans fixed to the torso, achieving efficient coordination of walking and jumping [3]. Sihite E et al. proposed a Model Predictive Control-based propulsion-enhanced dynamic wall jumping posture control method, and applied the method to the above-mentioned robot Harpy. The robot can successfully complete multiple wall jumps and climbing tasks in a vertical shaft [4]. Kim K et al. designed the LEO robot, which has a quadcopter force field to enable synchronous switching between hybrid terrestrial and aerial modes. The robot exhibited excellent adaptability and maneuverability in rope walking and skateboarding movements [5]. Huang Z et al. designed the HR1 robot with a duct fan propulsion and proposed a gait posture optimization method, which enabled the robot to cross large obstacles [7]. Subsequently, they designed the HR2 robot, which employed thrust vector control scheme. The robot could achieve stable takeoff (height exceeding 1,000 mm) at a thrust-to-weight ratio of 1.17, while effectively suppressing rotational and diving behaviors during takeoff [6]. Additionally, Zhao M et al. designed a quadruped robot SPIDAR with innovatively distributed spherical steerable rotors on the leg link units. With the assistance of the rotors, the robot achieved aerial transformation flight, and seamless switching between hybrid terrestrial and aerial modes [8].

Fig. 1. Robot simulation model

Above mentioned studies have significantly improved capabilities of motion mode switching and complex task execution of bipedal robots. The above-mentioned studies have significantly improved capabilities of motion mode switching and complex task execution of bipedal robots. However, these studies focused mainly on taking-off and landing of the robots, while dynamic bipedal walking with thrusters were rarely studied. Moreover, in these studies, the thrusters were mainly used to assist in switching modes, and there was a lack of analysis about the impact of thruster-generated force field on energy efficiency. In the present study, we designed a bipedal robot with four rotors in simulation (shown in Fig. 1). The robot's legs are designed with a posteriorly oriented configuration, similar to that of an ostrich, to enhance locomotion efficiency. We established the dynamic model and a control frame-work combining MPC and PD control. A posture-based external force field adjustment method was proposed to assist and optimize walking gaits of the bipedal robot. We quantitatively analyzed the impact of thruster-generated force fields with varying amplitudes and directions on energy efficiency of the robot. In simulations, this framework adjusts force fields based on the robot's posture. Qualitative analysis is conducted for the effects of force fields on joint torques and energy efficiency of the bipedal robot. Simulation results indicate that the thruster force field can provide positive effects for gait adjustment and energy consumption optimization of the bipedal robot.

2 Dynamic Model and Control Framework

This section focuses on the construction of a walking dynamics model and a motion control framework for a bipedal robot with thrusters. We modeled the force field generated by thrusters as a generalized force and used Lagrangian equation construct the robot dynamics model. Dynamics of bipedal walking was modeled during both the Double Support Phase (DS) and Single Support Phase (SS) phase. We combined Model Predictive Control (MPC) with PD control to develop a control framework suitable for bipedal robots assisted by thrusters.

2.1 Dynamic Model with Thrusters

We used the Lagrange equations to derive the dynamics, obtaining the Lagrangian quantity $\mathcal{L}(q_s, \dot{q}_s) = \mathcal{K}(q_s, \dot{q}_s) - \mathcal{V}(q_s)$, where $\mathcal{K}(q_s, q_s)$ is the kinetic energy and $\mathcal{V}(q_s)$ is the potential energy of the system. The resulting dynamic equations are expressed as follows:

$$D_s(q_s)\ddot{q}_s + C_s(q_s, \dot{q}_s)\dot{q}_s + G_s(q_s) = B_s(q_s)u + J_e^T F_e \tag{1}$$

where $D_s(q_s)$ is the symmetric inertia matrix, $C_s(q_s, \dot{q}_s)$ is the Coriolis term, $G_s(q_s)$ is the gravity term, $B_s(q_s)$ is the control matrix, J_e is the Jacobian matrix represents the mapping from state variables q_s to velocities of the robot's two feet, and F_e represents the ground reaction forces. $u = [u_j^\top, \lambda_{net}^\top]^\top$ is the control vector, which consists of the robot joint control vector u_j and the control vector λ_{net} introduced by the thrusters in the robot coordinate system. λ_{net} is obtained from the accompanying changes of the control vectors λ_i generated by the four rotors:

$$\lambda_{net} = \sum_{i=1}^{4} \begin{bmatrix} R_i & 0 \\ R_i S(d_i) & R_i \end{bmatrix} \lambda_i \tag{2}$$

where R_i is the rotation matrix of the thrusters relative to the robot, $\mathcal{S}(d_i)$ is a skew-symmetric matrix representing the cross product $d_i * F_j$, with d_i as the vector from the robot's CoG to the rotors and F_j as the thrust force generated by rotors.

In the SS phase, F_e consists solely of the stance leg GRF $F_{e,1}$. State vector q_s is determined by the trunk angle $q_p = [q_r, q_p, q_y]^\top$, thigh angle $q_{i,thigh}$, knee joint angle $q_{i,knee}$, thruster angle $q_{j,Thrust}$, and stance leg-end positions $p_1 = [p_{tx}, p_{ty}, p_n]^\top$.

$$q_s = [q_p, q_{iThigh}, q_{i,Knee}, q_{j,Thrust}, p_1^\top]^\top \tag{3}$$

The end of the SS phase is marked by the impact between the swing leg and the ground. During the DS phase, the ends of both legs (p_1 and p_2) are fixed to the ground till the rear leg leaves ground. F_e consists of ground reation forces $F_{e,1}$ and $F_{e,2}$. Considering the widespread application assumption of instantaneous duration and non-elastic rigid ground models, the posture of the system does not change ($q_s^- = q_s^+$).

Therefore, for the transition of the bipedal robot from SS phase to DS phase, swing leg end coordinate p_2 is introduced into the state vector such as $q_d = [q_s^\top, p_2^\top]^\top$. We assume that both feet are fixed to the ground and the foot tip velocities are 0 at the moment of collision. Thus we can obtain that the inertia matrix $D_d(q_d)$ is a positive definite square matrix, and $J_e(q_d)D_d(q_d)^{-1}J_e(q_d)^\top$ is full rank. The inverse operation can be performed to solve for the state and the ground reaction force after impacts:

$$\begin{bmatrix} \dot{q}_d^+ \\ F_e \end{bmatrix} = \begin{bmatrix} D_d(q_d^-) & -J_e(q_d^-)^\top \\ J_e(q_d^-) & 0^{6\times 6} \end{bmatrix}^{-1} \begin{bmatrix} D_d(q_d^-)\dot{q}_d^- \\ 0^{6\times 1} \end{bmatrix} \tag{4}$$

When entering the next SS phase, the support leg and the swing leg exchange with each other. This exchange can be described by a switching matrix R_s^d:

$$[q_e, \dot{q}_e]^T = R_s^d [q_d^+, \dot{q}_d^+]^T \tag{5}$$

2.2 Robot Motion Control

We used Model Predictive Control (MPC) and PD control as the walking control strategy for the bipedal robot. In the DS phase, we select the MPC framework to optimize GRF and torques [9, 10]. In this control framework, we define the robot state as $x = \left[p_c; \theta; \dot{p}_c; \omega\right]$, p_c is the center of mass position of the robot, θ is the Euler angle(roll angle, pitch angle, yaw angle) representing the robot's posture, $\dot{p}_c$ is the center of mass velocity of the robot, and ω is the angular velocity of the robot in the world coordinate.

Based on the angular momentum theorem and the force equilibrium equation, we can obtain the differential representation of the robot's state space.

$$\frac{d}{dt}\begin{bmatrix} \theta \\ p_c \\ \omega \\ \dot{p}_c \end{bmatrix} = A_c \begin{bmatrix} \theta \\ p_c \\ \omega \\ \dot{p}_c \end{bmatrix} + B_c u \tag{6}$$

We rewrite the dynamic equations in discrete form to obtain real-time solution. The optimization objective function is defined with two terms: first, the state tracking term minimizes the quadratic deviation between the predicted state and the reference trajectory, enabling the robot to closely follow the expected trajectory in the prediction time domain; second, the control input regularization term penalizes the torque magnitude, limiting the actuator output to a physically feasible range:

$$\min_{\boldsymbol{x},\boldsymbol{u}} \sum_{i=0}^{k-1} (x_{i+1} - x_{i+1_{ref}})^T Q_i (x_{i+1} - x_{i+1_{ref}}) + \|u_i\| R_i \tag{7}$$

In the SS phase, since the swing leg is not constrained by ground reaction force, PD control is used to control the swing leg [11]. The placement strategy of the swing leg is determined based on the position and speed feedback of the swing leg.

$$p_{\text{foot,d}} = p_{\text{c}} + \frac{\dot{p}_c \Delta_t}{2} + k_c(\dot{p}_c - \dot{p}_c^{cmd}) \tag{8}$$

where p_c is the position of the robot's center of mass in the world coordinate system, and $\dot{p}_c^{cmd}$ is the desired speed. Δ_t is the time when the support leg strikes the ground.

The swingleg force could be computed by treating the foot attached to avirtual spring-damper system. For the control of the swinging leg, we use PD control, treating the foot as attached to a virtual spring-damper system.

$$F_{\text{swing},i} = K_P(p_{\text{foot},d} - p_{\text{foot},i}) + K_D(\dot{p}_{\text{foot},d} - \dot{p}_{\text{foot},i}) \tag{9}$$

The swinging leg force is mapped to the corresponding joint using a Jacobian matrix.

$$\tau_{\text{swing},i} = J_v^T F_{\text{swing},i} \tag{10}$$

3 Simulation Result

In this section, based on the dynamic model and control framework, we conducted simulations to analyze the impact of force fields with different direction and magnitudes on the motion performance of the bipedal robot. First, in the simulation environment, force fields with different directions and magnitudes are applied to adjust the posture of the bipedal robot. Subsequently, force fields with different thrust-to-weight ratios are applied to investigate the impact of force field magnitudes on key variables of the bipedal robot, such as joint torque, overall power consumption, and Specific Resistance (SR).

3.1 Posture Adjustment

In this experiment, force fields with varying magnitudes and directions were generated via the rotational speed differences of the four rotors in the simulation, so as to adjust the robot's postures during walking. The direction of the force field and the torque generated by rotors are regulated via PD control, and the equations are as follows:

$$\theta_{\text{c}} = K_{\text{p,dir}\theta}(\theta_d - \theta) + K_{d,dir\theta}\frac{d}{dt}(\theta_d - \theta) \tag{11}$$

$$\tau_\theta = K_{p,\theta}(\theta_{\text{c}} - \theta) + K_{d,\theta}\frac{d}{dt}(\theta_c - \theta) \tag{12}$$

where θ_d is the desired pitch angle,θ is the current pitch angle which indicates the direction of the force field, and θ_c is the command pitch angle generated by the outer-loop PD controller. $K_{p,\theta}$, $K_{d,\theta}$, $K_{p,dir\theta}$ and $K_{d,dir\theta}$ are PD control gains.

In this trial, the robot's initial forward tilt angle is 5.3°. Approximately 0.2 s after applying the backward torque, pitch angle converges to target attitude, and thruster

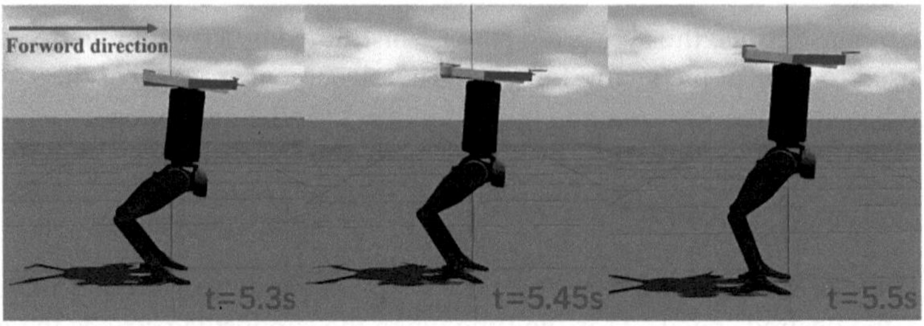

Fig. 2. Robot forward tilt posture adjustment. Robot legs adopt the posterior-oriented configuration. The robot moves towards right.

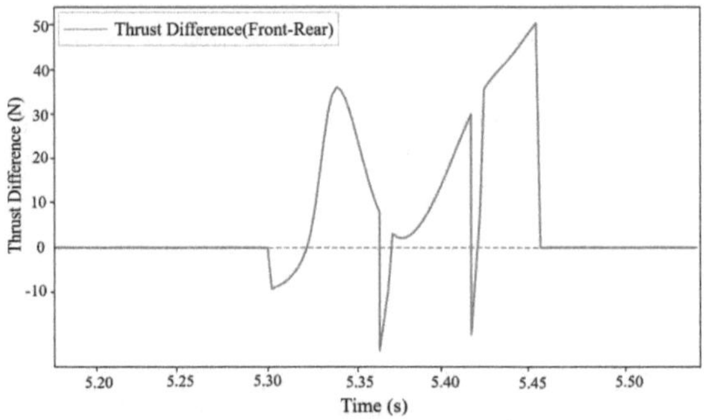

Fig. 3. Thrust magnitude difference in the forward tilt posture adjustment process

magnitude difference returns to zero. Figure 2 shows the adjustment process of the robot's forward tilt posture. The rotor speed is adjusted to generate a backward tilt torque, thereby adjusting the robot's posture. Figure 3 shows the thrust magnitude difference generated by the forward and rear rotors during this period.

Similarly, the direction of the force field and the roll moment magnitude equation used to adjust the robot's posture in the coronal plane are as follows:

$$\varphi_{\mathrm{c}} = K_{\mathrm{p,dir}\varphi}(\varphi_d - \varphi) + K_{d,dir\varphi}\frac{d}{dt}(\varphi_d - \varphi) \tag{13}$$

$$\tau_\varphi = K_{p,\varphi}(\varphi_c - \varphi) + K_{d,\varphi}\frac{d}{dt}(\varphi_c - \varphi) \tag{14}$$

where φ_d is the desired roll angle,φ is the current roll angle, and φ_c is the command roll angle generated by the outer-loop PD controller.$K_{p,\varphi}$, $K_{d,\varphi}$, $K_{p,dir\varphi}$ and $K_{d,dir\varphi}$ are PD control gains.

In this trail, the robot's initial right tilt angle is 7.3°. Force fields with different magnitudes and directions are used to adjust the robot's right tilt posture. Figure 4 shows the adjustment process and the thrust magnitude difference generated by the left and right rotors during this period.

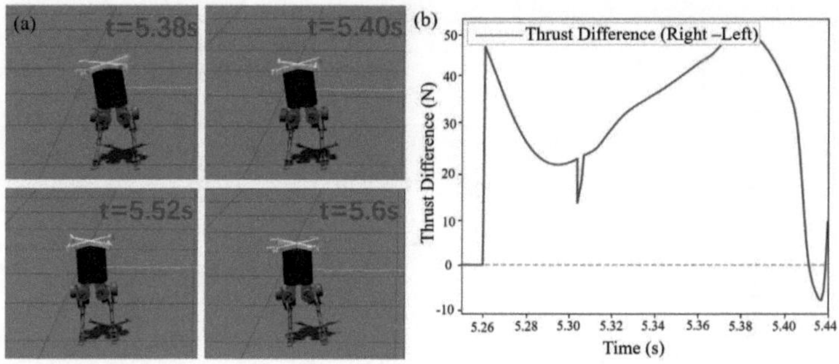

Fig. 4. Robot rightward posture adjustment and thrust magnitude change. (a) Robot right tilt posture adjustment. (b) Thrust magnitude difference in the process.

3.2 Effect on Joint Torque and Power

In this section, we analyzed the effects of thruster-generated force fields with different magnitudes on joint torque and energy consumption of the bipedal robot. A bipedal robot without an external force field was used as the control group. With an increase on thrust-to-weight ratio, the overall torque of the robot lower limb joints decreased. Figure 6 shows the Root Mean Square (RMS) torque values of the robot's lower limbs as a function of the thrust-to-weight ratio (Fig. 5).

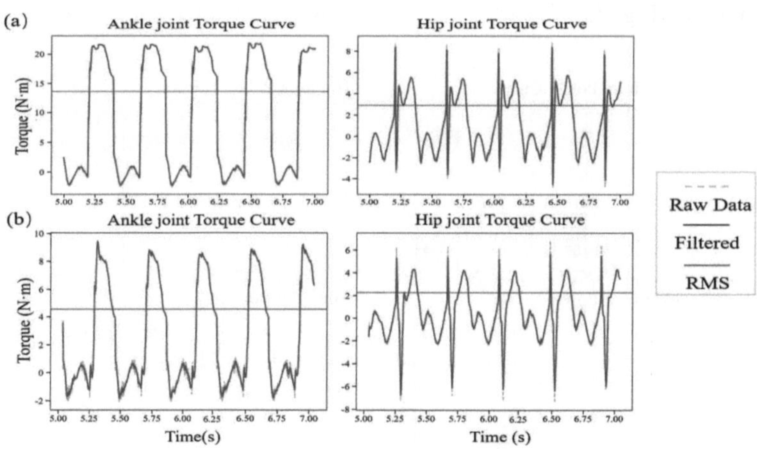

Fig. 5. Robot hip and ankle joints torques in simulation. (a) Joints torques with a thrust-to-weight ratio force field of 0.512. (b) Joints torques without external force field.

When walking without rotor assistance, the RMS of the ankle joint torque is 13.82 N·m, and the RMS of the hip joint torque is 2.85 N·m. When thruster-generated force field with a thrust-to-weight ratio of 0.512 is applied, the RMS of the torque at the ankle joint is 4.61 N·m, and the RMS of the torque at the hip joint is 2.13 N·m.

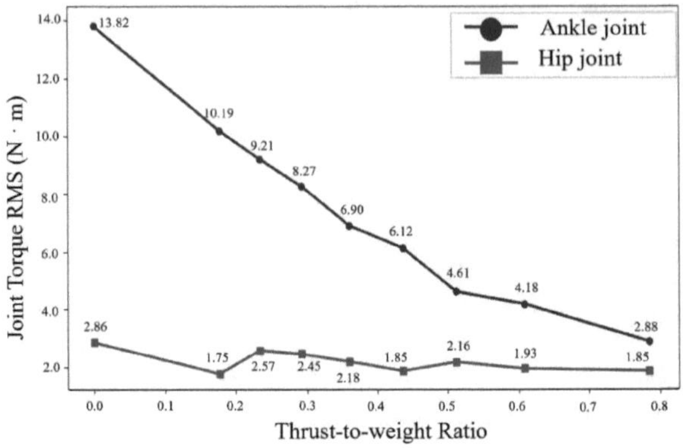

Fig. 6. RMS of joint torque of the bipedal robot with different thrust-to-weight ratios.

Analysis of lower limb joint power revealed that the average power of all joints decreased to cetain degrees after the application of an external force field. The average power of the ankle joint decreased from 4.36 W at a thrust-to-weight ratio of 0 to 2.97 W at a thrust-to-weight ratio of 0.436; the average power of the hip joint decreased from 1.37 W to 0.07 W. This trend indicates that the thruster-generated force field can effectively reduce the energy output requirements of the joints by providing low-gravity conditions. The instantaneous power of robot joints with thrust-to-weight ratio of 0 and 0.436 is shown in Fig. 7.

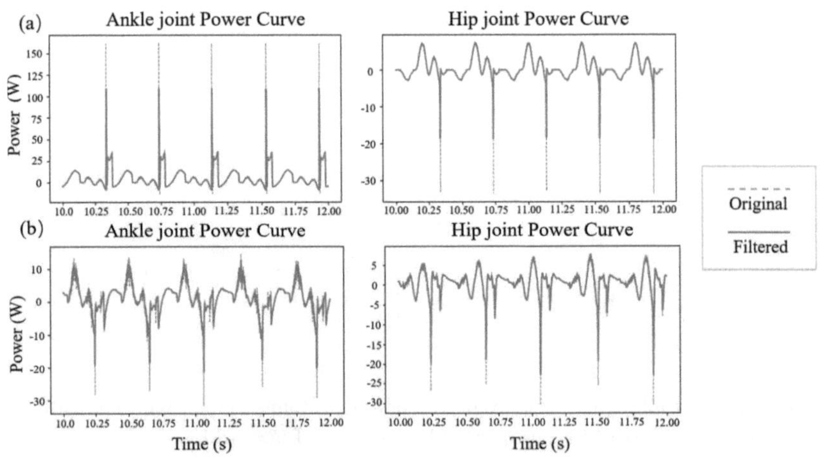

Fig. 7. Bipedal robot joint instantaneous power. (a) Robot without assistance. (b) Robot with 0.436 thrust-to-weight ratio force field.

It can be observed that with the assistance of an external force field, the fluctuation amplitude of the instantaneous power curve (the difference between the maximum and minimum power values) is significantly reduced. This indicates that the vertical force field not only reduces the average load on the joints, thereby lowering the instantaneous power peak during the transition between the stance phase to the swing phase, but also helps to reduce impact effects and lower the requirements on the drive system.

Based on the calculation of instantaneous power at each joint, the instantaneous power of all drive joints and rotor joints are summed to obtain the total instantaneous power during the robot's motion. The total instantaneous power during the robot's walking under different thrust-to-weight ratio conditions is shown in the table below. From the data in the table, it can be observed that when an external force field is introduced to assist the bipedal robot's movement, the joint power of the robot decreases as the thrust-to-weight ratio increases, but the system's total power does not continue to decrease. In fact, when the thrust-to-weight ratio exceeds 0.360, the system's total power increases due to the power consumption of the rotors. This indicates that total energy consumption of the robot is high when the thrust-to-weight ratio is relatively large, due to the significant energy consumption of the high-speed rotors (Table 1 and Fig. 8).

Table 1. Robot power under different thrust-to-weight ratios

Thrust-to-weight ratio	Total joint power (W)	Rotors power (W)	Total power (W)
0	32.5834	0	32.5834
0.176	29.8633	1.5942	31.5659
0.233	28.9037	3.8724	32.9377
0.292	26.9307	5.5132	32.6739
0.360	25.8233	7.5614	33.6995
0.436	24.5913	10.0646	35.0751
0.512	23.3034	13.0676	36.9156
0.609	21.079	16.6138	38.3852
0.784	21.9439	20.7508	42.5595

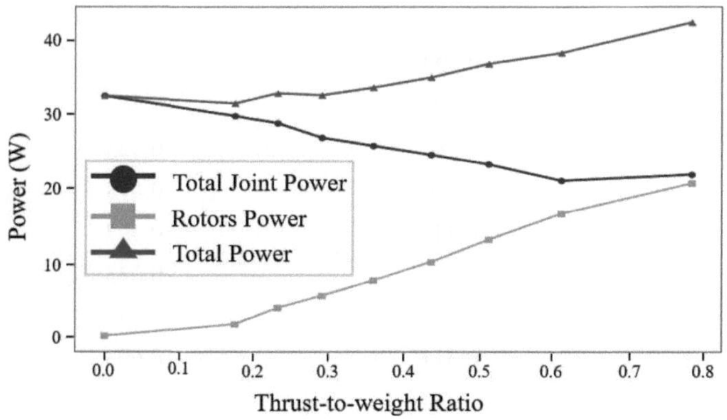

Fig. 8. Total power curve under different thrust-to-weight ratios force field

3.3 Effect on Specific Resistance

Previous studies have conducted quantitative analysis of the relationship between different force fields and joint torques and power of bipedal robots. However, the numerical values of torque and power parameters are constrained by specific robot dynamic parameters. In this study, we use specific resistance (SR) to evaluate the energy efficiency of the robot. SR is obtained by dividing total energy E consumed during movement by the product of the robot's gravitational force mg and traveling distance d [12].

According to previous researches, the energy efficiency of robot walking is lower than that of humans [13, 14]. The specific resistance value is approximately 0.2 during human walking. To illustrate the impact of force field with different magnitudes on walking efficiency of the bipedal robot, we analyzed the robot SR values and the total SR values in the simulated environment.The robot SR value is obtained without considering the rotor power consumption, while the total SR value is obtained with the rotor power consumption taken into account. Therefore, the robot SR value demonstrates the energy efficiency of the bipedal robot itself except for the rotors, and the total SR value denotes the energy efficiency of the overall system. The total mass of the robot was approximately 12 kg, and the walking speed was approximately 0.6 m/s.

External force fields have a significant reducing effect on the SR value. When the thrust-to-weight ratio increases to 0.292, the robot SR value decreases from 0.472 to 0.381. This indicates that the appropriate application of external force fields can optimize the robot's energy efficiency by providing low-gravity conditions. When the thrust-to-weight ratio is less than 0.360, the total SR value decreases with increasing thrust-to-weight ratio. When the thrust-to-weight ratio exceeds 0.360, as the thrust-to-weight ratio increases, the robot SR value decreases while the total SR value increases due to the rotor energy consumption. This trend reflects the existence of an optimal value of thrust-to-weight ratio for energy efficiency of the total system (Table 2).

Table 2. SR values of the robots under different thrust-to-weight ratios

Thrust-to-weight ratio	Robot SR value	Total SR value
0	0.472	0.472
0.176	0.423	0.447
0.233	0.409	0.466
0.292	0.381	0.463
0.360	0.366	0.478
0.436	0.349	0.497
0.512	0.330	0.523
0.609	0.299	0.544
0.784	0.311	0.603

4 Conclusion

In this study, we designed a bipedal robot with four rotors and constructed the dynamic model and control framework combined MPC and PD control. The proposed control framework were validated in simulation. The simulation results show that the force field generated by the rotors in simulation can effectively adjust the posture and gait characteristics of a bipedal robot during walking. The RMS value and power of the lower limb joint torque gradually decrease as the thrust-to-weight ratio increases. When the thrust-to-weight ratio is less than certain value, the system's total power remains at or below the level without assistance. These results indicate the existence of an optimal value of the thrust-to-weight ratio for energy efficiency. The quantitative analysis of experimental data provides a reliable basis for parameter optimization and engineering applications of thruster-assisted bipedal robots. In future work, we plan to conduct verification experiments on a physical robot prototype to further validate the effectiveness of the thruster-assisted strategy in real-world scenarios, and also further explore the role of thruster assistance in bipedal robot's movement across more motion modes including climbing stairs and traversing complex terrains, so as to provide more comprehensive support for its practical application.

Acknowledgement. This work was supported by the Beijing Institute of Technology Research Funds for High-Level Talents.

References

1. Li, H., Li, X., Millán, J.R.D.: Noninvasive EEG-based intelligent mobile robots: a systematic review. IEEE Trans. Autom. Sci. Eng. **22**, 6291–6315 (2025)
2. Earls, K.D.: Kinematics and mechanics of ground take-off in the starling Sturnis vulgaris and the quail Coturnix coturnix. J. Exp. Biol. **203**(4), 725–739 (2000)
3. Liang, K., Sihite, E., Dangol, P., Lessieur, A., Ramezani, A.: Rough-terrain locomotion and unilateral contact force regulations with a multi-modal legged robot. In: 2021 American Control Conference (ACC), New Orleans, LA, USA, pp. 1762–1769. IEEE (2021)
4. Sihite, E., Pitroda, S., Liu, T., Almanzor, D., Ramezani, A.: Posture manipulation of thruster-enhanced bipedal robot performing dynamic wall-jumping using model predictive control. In: 2024 IEEE-RAS 23rd International Conference on Humanoid Robots (Humanoids), Nancy, France, pp. 491–496. IEEE (2024)
5. Kim, K., Spieler, P., Lupu, E.S., Ramezani, A., Chung, S.: A bipedal walking robot that can fly, slackline, and skateboard. Sci. Robot. **6**(59), eabf8136 (2021)
6. Li, Y., Zhou, Y., Huang, J.: Jet-HR2: a flying bipedal robot based on thrust vector control. IEEE Robot. Autom. Lett. **7**(2), 4590–4597 (2022)
7. Huang, Z., Wu, K., Nie, L., Yang, L.: Planning and control of slide-steer gait for biped robot based on ducted fans. In: 2024 IEEE-RAS 23rd International Conference on Humanoid Robots (Humanoids), Nancy, France, pp. 98–105. IEEE (2024)
8. Zhao, M., Anzai, T., Nishio, T.: Design, modeling, and control of a quadruped robot SPIDAR: spherically vectorable and distributed rotors assisted air-ground quadruped robot. IEEE Robot. Autom. Lett. **8**(7), 3923–3930 (2023)

9. Li, J., Nguyen, Q.: Force-and-moment-based model predictive control for achieving highly dynamic locomotion on bipedal robots. In: 2021 60th IEEE Conference on Decision and Control (CDC), Austin, USA, pp. 1024–1030. IEEE (2021)
10. Liu, X., Rong, H., Neri, F., Liu, X., Zhao, M.: Human-simulated intelligent walking control for biped robots. IEEE Trans. Autom. Sci. Eng. **22**, 3237–3251 (2025)
11. Di Carlo, J., Wensing, P.M., Katz, B., Bledt, G., Kim, S.: Dynamic locomotion in the MIT cheetah 3 through convex model-predictive control. In: 2018 IEEE/RSJ International Conference on Intelligent Robots and Systems (IROS), Madrid, Spain, pp. 1–9. IEEE (2018)
12. Kashiri, N., Abate, A., Abram, S.J.: An overview on principles for energy effi-cient robot locomotion. Front. Robot. AI **5**, 129 (2018)
13. Tucker, V.A.: The energetic cost of moving about: walking and running are extremely inefficient forms of locomotion. Much greater efficiency is achieved by birds, fish and bicyclists. Am. Sci. **63**(4), 413–419 (1975)
14. McMahon, T.A.: The role of compliance in mammalian running gaits. J. Exp. Biol. **115**(1), 263–282 (1985)

Enhancing Nonlinear Dynamics and Processing Efficiency in Chaotic Stream Cipher via Branching Structures

Kentaro Yamada[1(✉)], Tatsuki Kamiya[1], Kouhei Kajima[1], and Hiroyuki Kamata[2]

[1] Graduate School of Science and Technology, Meiji University, Tokyo, Japan
{ce241021,ce241012,ce241014}@meiji.ac.jp

[2] School of Science and Technology, Meiji University, Tokyo, Japan
kamata@meiji.ac.jp

Abstract. The purpose of this research is to improve cryptographic security and processing efficiency by introducing a branching structure into chaotic stream cipher, thereby adding more nonlinearity to the overall system. The rapid advancement of IoT technology, has created a need for fast and secure cryptosystems suitable for environments with limited computational resources. Therefore, chaotic stream cipher based on deterministic chaos have been proposed, with security further enhanced through the introduction of Volterra filters and nonlinear functions to increase mathematical complexity. In contrast, this study proposes a new method that introduces a branching structure dynamically selected at runtime, rather than using a fixed equation to determine the internal state variables. This is expected to increase the system's structural complexity, even in low-computing-resource environments, while enhancing security and maintaining efficient key usage and processing speed.

Keywords: Deterministic chaos · Chaotic stream cipher · IoT

1 Introduction

Recently, the use of Internet of Things (IoT) devices has rapidly expanded in various areas of society, and the interconnection of these devices via the Internet has significantly increased user convenience. At the same time, as vast amounts of data are constantly communicated in the IoT environment, encryption technology to protect information is becoming increasingly important.

Considering the limited computing resources and power of IoT devices, there is a need to develop cryptographic schemes that offer high security with a low computational load [1, 2]. In this context, we have been conducting research on chaotic stream cipher based on chaos theory and deterministic chaos [3–5]. In our previous research, we have proposed methods to add chaos to ciphertexts by employing nonlinear functions and Volterra filters to increase the security of ciphertexts. In this study, we propose a new

W. Cai et al. (Eds.): AsiaSim 2025, CCIS 2727, pp. 211–221, 2026.
https://doi.org/10.1007/978-981-95-4472-1_18

chaotic stream cipher scheme that introduces a branching structure into the cryptosystem to enhance overall nonlinearities of the entire system and further improve the chaos and security of the ciphertext. The proposed method introduces nonlinearity by dynamically changing the system structure, representing a departure from the conventional approaches. By incorporating a branching structure at the system level, the overall behavior becomes more complex, while each construction formula can be simplified, leading to potential improvements in processing speed. In this study, we verify the effectiveness and practicality of the proposed method through comparative evaluation with conventional methods. We also compare the processing speed of the proposed method with that of the Advanced Encryption Standard (AES), which ensures high security through nonlinear processing (S-box), and clarify the superiority of the proposed method over conventional cryptographic methods in a low-computational-resource environment.

2 Methods

2.1 Deterministic Chaos

Deterministic chaos is a phenomenon in which the state transitions of a system are deterministic; however, the output signal exhibits disordered or irregular behavior owing to the nonlinear nature of the system [6]. Deterministic chaos has characteristics, such as orbital instability, long-term unpredictability, aperiodicity, and boundedness, making it suitable for cryptography.

2.2 Stream Cipher

Stream ciphers are a type of symmetric key cryptography in which the sender and receiver share the same encryption key. By encrypting data sequentially at the bit or byte level, they offer faster processing than block ciphers, which use the same symmetric key scheme, and is suitable for IoT devices requiring real-time performance [7].

In general stream ciphers, a keystream (pseudo-random bit string) is generated and combined with the plaintext using a bitwise exclusive OR (XOR) operation to produce the ciphertext. In this study, a scheme based on chaotic neurons is employed [8].

2.3 Fixed-Point Arithmetic

In this study, fixed-point arithmetic is employed to realize boundedness, a characteristic of chaos, by fixing the total bit number. An unsigned fixed-point format denoted as UxQy, represents values with x total bits and y fractional bits. This study adopts the U32Q20 format. Figure 1 shows the structure of the U32Q20 format [8].

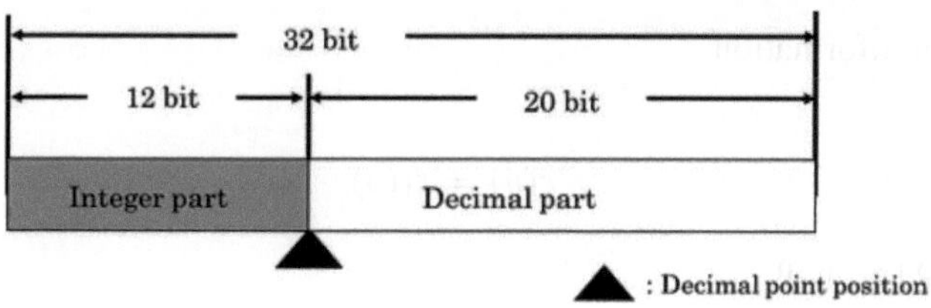

Fig. 1. U32Q20 format

3 Chaotic Stream Cipher

The flow of a chaotic stream cipher is as follows: the plaintext $s(n)$ is input into the cryptosystem, generating $r(n)$ as the transmitted data. The receiver obtains $r(n)$ and inputs it to the demodulation system to obtain the plaintext $s(n)$.

In contrast to ordinary stream ciphers, chaotic stream cipher do not generate and use an explicit keystream. Instead, the cryptosystem features a recursive and nonlinear structure, with the plaintext directly input into the system. This allows the ciphertext to be generated dynamically according to the internal state of the system.

The equations of the conventional and proposed schemes for chaotic stream cipher are shown below.

3.1 Conventional Methods

The conventional method used in this study is shown below [3]. Equation (1) incorporates the nonlinear function f shown in Eq. (8) in the chaotic neuron. To enhance resistance to cryptanalysis, Eq. (2), (3), (6) and (7) employ the Volterra filter in Eq. (9), which increases the key length [9]. In addition, Eq. (2), (3), (6) and (7) are synchronous equations, with the same equation structure for modulation and demodulation. This structure prevents accumulation of errors within the system, allowing self-synchronization even when errors occur during transmission [4]. Furthermore, the feedback function (Eq. (10)) prevents system simplification.

Here, $s(n)$ represents the plaintext, x is an internal state variable, and α, θ, and h are cryptographic keys, which must be shared before communication. In particular, θ_1, θ_2, and θ_3 are useful parameters to excite the system when no signal is present.

- Modulation system

$$x_1(n) = s(n) - f(x_1(n-1)) + \alpha x_3(n-1) + \theta_1 \tag{1}$$

$$x_2(n) = f_{volterra}(x_1(n-1), x_1(n-2), x_1(n-3), \theta_2) + f_c(x_2(n-1)) \tag{2}$$

$$x_3(n) = f_{volterra}(x_1(n-1), x_2(n-1), \theta_3) + f_c(x_3(n-1)) \tag{3}$$

- Transmission information

$$r(n) = x_1(n) \tag{4}$$

- Demodulation system

$$s(n) = r(n) + f(r(n-1)) - \alpha x_3(n-1) + \theta_1 \tag{5}$$

$$x_2(n) = f_{volterra}(r(n-1), r(n-2), r(n-3), \theta_2) + f_c(x_2(n-1)) \tag{6}$$

$$x_3(n) = f_{volterra}(r(n-1), x_2(n-1), \theta_3) + f_c(x_3(n-1)) \tag{7}$$

- Non-linear function

$$f(x) = \begin{cases} \kappa x + \sigma (x \leq -\epsilon) \\ 0(-\epsilon \leq x \leq \epsilon) \\ \kappa x - \sigma (\epsilon \leq x) \end{cases} \tag{8}$$

Where $\kappa = 10$, $\sigma = 5$, and $\epsilon = 9.78 \times 10^{-4}$.

- Volterra filter

$$f_{volterra}(x_1, x_2, \ldots, x_n, \theta) = \sum_{i=1}^{n} h_i x_i + \sum_{i=1}^{n} \sum_{j=1}^{n} h_{ij} x_i x_j + h_{12\ldots n} \prod_{i=1}^{n} x_i + \theta \tag{9}$$

- Feedback function

$$f_c(x) = 2^{26}(x) \tag{10}$$

3.2 Proposed Method

The equations for the proposed method are presented below. The encryption system is defined by Eq. (11, 12 and 13), with Eq. (14) representing the transmitted information. The demodulation system is described by Eq. (15, 16 and 17). The function f_c is defined as in the conventional method. The following section provides an overview of the proposed method.

The proposed method introduces two main modifications. First, it incorporates a branching structure. In conventional methods, the second and third equations are defined by a single fixed structure. In contrast, the proposed approach replaces them with a branching structure that selectively utilizes one of multiple equations. This branching mechanism adds nonlinearity and complexity to the system itself, which is expected to enhance security. In addition, the branching selection rule is determined based on the internal state variables and Nonce, as shown in Eq. (20). State Value is obtained by rounding off the sum of the internal state variable and Nonce with 30 bits and extracting the upper two bits. Consequently, State Value N assumes integers in the range 0 to 3, and the second and third equations are branching structures with four different states each.

The second modification involves simplifying the Volterra filter and eliminating the initial set of nonlinear functions. The Volterra filter reduces the number of input variables, shorting the equations and lowering the computational cost by replacing the multiplication with an XOR operation. This optimization is enabled by branching structure ensures sufficient randomness, which ensures sufficient randomness while enhancing processing efficiency.

The newly constructed Volterra filter is expressed in Eq. (18) and (19). As in the previous method, $s(n)$ denotes the plaintext and x denotes the internal state variable. Furthermore, α, θ, and h are cryptographic keys.

The number of encryption keys in this method is reduced to 20. As key lengths of 128 or 256 bits are commonly used in other cryptographic algorithms and the guidelines of the U.S. Department of Commerce's National Institute of Standards and Technology (NIST) recommend a cryptographic key length of 128 bits or longer after 2030, the key length of the proposed method is considered acceptable [10].

- Modulation system

$$x_1(n) = s(n) - \alpha x_1(n-1)x_3(n-1) + \theta_1 \tag{11}$$

$$x_2(n) = f_{v-col}(x_1(n-1), x_1(n-2), N_1) + \theta_2 \tag{12}$$

$$x_3(n) = f_{v-row}(x_1(n-1), x_2(n-1), N_2) + \theta_3 + f_c(x_3(n-1)) \tag{13}$$

- Transmission information

$$r(n) = x_1(n) \tag{14}$$

- Demodulation system

$$s(n) = r(n) + \alpha r(n-1)x_3(n-1) - \theta_1 \tag{15}$$

$$x_2(n) = f_{v-col}(r(n-1), r(n-2), N_1) + \theta_2 \tag{16}$$

$$x_3(n) = f_{v-row}(r(n-1), x_2(n-1), N_2) + \theta_3 + f_c(x_3(n-1)) \tag{17}$$

- Volterra filter

$$f_{v-col}(x_1, x_2, N) = \begin{cases} (h_{00} \bigoplus x_1 + h_{01} \bigoplus x_2)x_1 \bigoplus (h_{02} \bigoplus x_1 + h_{03} \bigoplus x_2)x_2 \ (N=0) \\ (h_{10} \bigoplus x_1 + h_{11} \bigoplus x_2)x_1 \bigoplus (h_{12} \bigoplus x_1 + h_{13} \bigoplus x_2)x_2 \ (N=1) \\ (h_{20} \bigoplus x_1 + h_{21} \bigoplus x_2)x_1 \bigoplus (h_{22} \bigoplus x_1 + h_{23} \bigoplus x_2)x_2 \ (N=2) \\ (h_{30} \bigoplus x_1 + h_{31} \bigoplus x_2)x_1 \bigoplus (h_{32} \bigoplus x_1 + h_{33} \bigoplus x_2)x_2 \ (N=3) \end{cases} \tag{18}$$

$$f_{v-row}(x_1, x_2, N) = \begin{cases} (h_{30} \bigoplus x_1 + h_{20} \bigoplus x_2)x_1 \bigoplus (h_{10} \bigoplus x_1 + h_{00} \bigoplus x_2)x_2 \ (N = 0) \\ (h_{31} \bigoplus x_1 + h_{21} \bigoplus x_2)x_1 \bigoplus (h_{11} \bigoplus x_1 + h_{01} \bigoplus x_2)x_2 \ (N = 1) \\ (h_{32} \bigoplus x_1 + h_{22} \bigoplus x_2)x_1 \bigoplus (h_{12} \bigoplus x_1 + h_{02} \bigoplus x_2)x_2 \ (N = 2) \\ (h_{33} \bigoplus x_1 + h_{23} \bigoplus x_2)x_1 \bigoplus (h_{13} \bigoplus x_1 + h_{03} \bigoplus x_2)x_2 \ (N = 3) \end{cases} \quad (19)$$

- State Value

$$N_m = (x_m(n-1) + Nonce) \gg 30(m = 1,2) \quad (20)$$

In the demodulation system, $x_1(n-1) = r(n-1)$.

4 Verifications

Simulations were performed using Visual Studio 2022, as detailed in Table 1. Additional Simulations in the low-computing environment were performed on the Raspberry Pi 4B, also listed in Table 1. The program was developed using Visual Studio 2022 on Windows 11 home, and subsequently deployed unchanged on the Raspberry Pi 4B for the experiments.

Table 1. Experimental environment

	Visual Studio 2022	Raspberry Pi 4B
OS	Windows11 home	Debian GNU/Linux 12 (bookworm)
CPU	12th Gen Intel Core I i5–12400 2.50 GHz	ARM Coertex-A72 @1.8 GHz × 4
Memory	16 GB	8 GB
Language	C++	C ++

4.1 Amount of Information Loss

In this verification, we evaluated the self-synchronization performance of the chaotic stream cipher by intentionally introducing errors and measuring the data loss until the errors converged. In this verification, error convergence and resynchronization were confirmed when the decrypted plaintext matched 10 consecutive samples following the transmission error. It was also assumed that the plaintext was consistently 0 and that the transmission error occurred in one bit of the transmission information. This measurement was performed 10,000 times using different encryption keys, and the mean value and standard deviation of the number of bits lost due to the error were calculated as a result of the verification.

4.2 Key Length

In this verification, the cryptographic keys of the system were evaluated. The verification method is as follows: First, the coefficient sensitivities of all cipher keys were measured using Eq. (21). Subsequently, a graph of the coefficient sensitivities was created, and from the graph, it was visually determined whether the encryption keys were valid or not. Based on this assessment, the number of valid keys, the system's key length, and the ratio of valid keys to the total number of keys the method has were calculated [5], where L is the number of samples, $s(t)$ is the plaintext, and $u(t)$ is the demodulation method.

$$D = \frac{1}{L}\sum_{t=0}^{L-1} |u(t) - s(t)| \tag{21}$$

When $D = 0$, the key is fully demodulated; when there is only one point with $D = 0$ and no clear regularity before or after that point, the key is considered to be a valid encryption key.

4.3 Processing Speed

The time required to encrypt and decrypt 10^6 samples was measured, and the processing speed, defined as the number of bits transmitted per second, was calculated. In this evaluation, in addition to the Visual Studio 2022 environment used in other experiments, tests were also conducted on a Raspberry Pi 4B to assess performance under low computational resources. In the Visual Studio environment, processing time was measured 100 times using different encryption keys, and the average was used to calculate the processing speed. In the Raspberry Pi 4B environment, the time to process 10^6 samples was measured once, and the processing speed was calculated similarly. Furthermore, a comparison was made with the conventional method and the widely used AES-CTR mode. The formula used to calculate the processing speed is shown below.

$$Processingspeed\left[Mbps\right] = \frac{10^6 \times 32[bit]}{10^6 \times ProcesingTime[ms] \times 10^{-3}} \tag{22}$$

4.4 Randomness

In this study, the NIST SP800-22 tool [11] published by NIST was employed to verify the randomness of the ciphertext. This tool consists of 16 statistical tests, and in each test, the result is regarded as a pass if the calculated $p - value$ is higher than the significance level α. For a 1 Mbit random sequence, each test was performed m times, and the pass rate was defined as r. If r falls within the range specified by Eq. (23) for all tests, the sequence is considered to be random.

In this study, 1 Mbit ciphertexts were generated and tested under the conditions of $\alpha = 0.01$ and $m = 1000$. As a result, if the pass rate r lies within the range of 98.0561% to 99.9439%, the generated ciphertexts were judged to exhibit randomness.

$$(1-\alpha) - 3\sqrt{\frac{(1-\alpha)\alpha}{m}} \le r \le (1-\alpha) + 3\sqrt{\frac{(1-\alpha)\alpha}{m}} \tag{23}$$

4.5 Orbital Instability

To verify the chaotic nature, orbital instability was evaluated using Lyapunov exponents calculated by the Sano Sawada method [12]. Orbital instability was considered when the largest of the three Lyapunov exponents was positive.

5 Results

5.1 Amount of Information Loss

The results of the verification of the amount of information lost are shown in Table 2. It can be observed that data loss decreases. The reduction in data loss is attributed to the modified argument of the Volterra filter, which decreases the number of residual errors.

Table 2. Results of information loss measurement

Verification details	Conventional method	Proposed method
Average [bit]	225.04	191.36
Standard deviation	0.18	0.13

5.2 Key Length

Table 3 presents the results of key length verification, and Fig. 2 shows a graph of key θ_2 as an example of a key judged to be valid. From the results in Table 3, it can be confirmed that the proposed method maintains a sufficient key length of 576 bits, although the key length has been reduced compared to the conventional method. In addition, the ratio of valid keys to total keys shows a slight improvement. These results suggest that the system's structural complexity has increased, allowing for more efficient utilization of encryption keys.

Table 3. Verification results of key length

Verification details	Conventional method	Proposed method
Total Number of Keys	23	20
Number of Valid Keys	20	18
Key length [bit]	640	576
Ratio of valid keys [%]	87.0	90.0

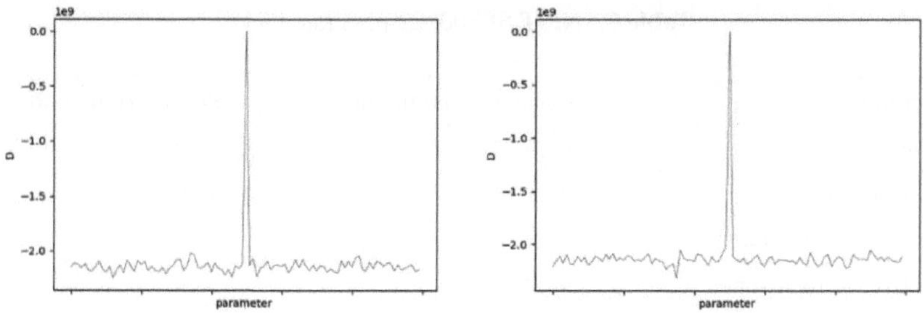

Conventional method　　　Proposed method

Fig. 2. Coefficient sensitivity D with respect to encryption key parameter θ_2 in each method (horizontal axis: value of parameter θ_2, vertical axis: coefficient sensitivity D).

5.3 Processing Speed

Table 4 presents the modulation and demodulation processing speeds for each method across two environments. The proposed method demonstrates faster processing compared to the conventional method and AES-CTR scheme. This improvement is attributed to the use of XOR operations in the Volterra filter and the reduction in input variables, which collectively reduce computational complexity.

Table 4. Verification of processing speed [Mbps]

Experimental environment	Verification details	Conventional method	Proposed method	AES-CTR
Visual Studio 2022	Modulation	2533	7232	
	Demodulation	2511	8852	
Raspberry Pi 4B	Modulation	846.850	1702.70	702.809
	Demodulation	839.529	1713.55	734.322

5.4 Randomness

The results of the randomness test are shown in Table 5. All values in Table 5 fall within the range specified by Eq. (23). Therefore, all tests were passed, indicating that both the conventional method and the proposed method produce ciphertexts with sufficient randomness.

Table 5. NIST SP800–22 pass rate [%]

Test method	Conventional method	Proposed method
Frequency	98.6	98.9
Block Frequency	98.8	98.9
Cumulative Sums forward	98.4	99.1
Cumulative Sums reverse	98.9	98.9
Runs	99	98.4
Longest Run	99.2	99.6
Rank	99	99.3
DFT	99	99
Non-Overlapping Template	98.9946	98.9642
Overlapping Template	98.6	98.3
Universal	98.3	98.5
Approximate Entropy	98.7	99.3
Random Excursions	98.6475	98.7083
Random Excursions Variant	99.071	99.0833
Serial	98.8	99.05
Linear Complexity	98.9	98.5

5.5 Orbital Instability

Figure 3 shows the evaluation results of α. For all encryption keys, both methods exhibited a positive maximum Lyapunov exponent, as illustrated in Fig. 3. This suggests that both methods possess orbital instability. In the proposed method, chaotic behavior was maintained despite the removal of nonlinear functions, which is likely due to the nonlinear dynamics introduced by the branching structure.

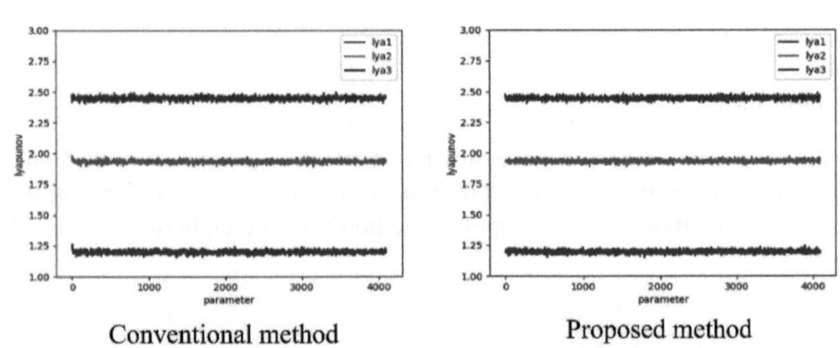

Fig. 3. Lyapunov exponent for each method when the encryption key α is varied. (horizontal axis: value of parameter α, vertical axis: Lyapunov spectra.)

6 Conclusion

In this study, we proposed a novel chaos stream cipher system incorporating a branching structure and evaluated its effectiveness. The results demonstrated that the equations used in the branching can be relatively simple, while maintaining randomness, sufficient key length, and chaotic behavior. This approach enhances improvements in processing speed and enables more efficient keys utilization. Furthermore, the introduction of the branching structure enhances the system's overall nonlinearity, aligning it more closely with the definition of deterministic chaos than conventional methods. Additionally, since the cipher generation process dynamically changes its structure, it becomes difficult for attackers to decipher, thereby improving resistance against structural analysis and brute-force attacks. Future research will focus on implementing encryption systems based on chaos theory and further verifying and improving the chaotic properties.

References

1. McKay, K.A., Bassham, L., Turan, M.S., Mouha, N.: Report on lightweight cryptography. NIST DRAFT NISTIR, pp. 1–29, (2016)
2. Singh, S., et al.: Advanced lightweight encryption algorithms for IoT devices: survey, challenges and solutions. J. Ambient Intell. Human Comput. **15**, 1625–1642 (2024)
3. Kono, S., Kamata, H.: Study on Evaluation of Resistance of Chaotic Stream Cipher to Transmission Errors. Proc. NOLTA, pp. 273–276 (2023)
4. Namba, R., Kamata, H.: Study on robustness evaluation of Chaotic stream cipher against transmission errors. Proc. NCSP'22, pp. 273–276 (2022)
5. Arai, T., Sato, T., Kamata, H.: Study on Chaotic Cipher with robustness and its characteristics. Proc. AsiaSim **2018**, 414–424 (2018)
6. Schuster, H.G., Just, W.: Deterministic Chaos: An Introduction, 4th edn. Wiley-VCH, Weinheim, Germany (2004)
7. Morii, M., Teramura, R.: The State of Stream Ciphers. IEICE Fundam. Rev. **2**(3) (2009)
8. Turuoka, Y., Nakasone, T., Kamiyama, K., Kamata, H.: The Development of the Chaotic Block Cipher. Proc. JSST, pp. 125–128 (2015)
9. Iwata, K., Nakamura, T., Ikeue, I., Irikura, H., Kamata, H.: Chaotic modulation with volterra filter for cipher. IEICE, Proc. NOLTA, pp. 216–219 (2007)
10. Baker, E.: Recommendation for Key Management: Part 1 – General. NIST Special Publication, pp. 800–57, (2020)
11. Rukhim, A., et al.: A Statistical Test Suite for Random and Pseudorandom Number Generators for Cryptographic Applications. NIST Special Publication 800–22, (2010)
12. Sano, M., Sawada, Y.: Measurement of the Lyapunov Spectrum from a Chaotic Time Series. Phys. Rev. Lett. **55**(10) (1985)

Mechanism Simulation of Lithium Polysulfide Conversion Catalyzed by Ti_3C_2 MXene with Different Terminals

Dezhi Yan[1], Fangchao Han[1], Qiang Lu[1], Ninghan Li[1], Qianfan Zhang[1], Yalan Xing[1(✉)], and Weining Song[2(✉)]

[1] Beihang University, Beijing 100191, China
xingyalan@buaa.edu.cn
[2] East China University of Technology, Nanchang 330013, China
201860174@ecut.edu.cn

Abstract. Lithium-sulfur batteries are regarded as ideal energy storage systems due to their high specific capacity and low cost. However, their large-scale application has been severely hindered by issues such as the shuttle effect and volume expansion, making the development of efficient catalysts imperative. This work utilized VASP simulation software to construct $Ti_3C_2T_2$ MXene models to deeply explore its catalytic mechanism for lithium polysulfide (LiPSs) conversion. The simulation results determined the site of MXene surface terminals, identified the most stable adsorption configurations of LiPSs, and quantify the corresponding adsorption energy. Furthermore, the intrinsic physical properties of $Ti_3C_2T_2$ MXene and the reaction energy barriers that catalyze the conversion of LiPSs were investigated. These findings provide a valuable insight into the catalytic mechanism of MXene for LiPSs conversion.

Keywords: Polysulfide · MXene · Model Validation · Catalytic Mechanism · VASP

1 Introduction

1.1 A Subsection Sample

Lithium-sulfur (Li-S) batteries are regarded as strong candidates for the next-generation energy storage system due to their extremely high theoretical energy density (2600 Wh kg^{-1}), low cost (< \$150 ton^{-1}) and environmental friendliness [1–3]. Conventional Li-S batteries utilize lightweight porous carbon as sulfur host, constructing a high-energy-density system through the complex 16-electron conversion process involving the sulfur reduction reaction and the reverse sulfur oxidation reaction [4]. However, their practical application faces significant challenges stemming from the polysulfide shuttle effect [5, 6], sluggish electrochemical conversion kinetics [7–9] and severe volume expansion [10, 11]. Hence, the development of effective catalysts is critically important for Li-S batteries. Furthermore, the large-scale application of wearable Li-S batteries requires the integration of flexibility, safety, and superior mechanical properties.

W. Cai et al. (Eds.): AsiaSim 2025, CCIS 2727, pp. 222–233, 2026.
https://doi.org/10.1007/978-981-95-4472-1_19

MXene is a class of transition metal carbon/nitride with a unique two-dimensional layered structure [12]. It demonstrates multiple advantages in Li-S batteries due to its high electrical conductivity, rich surface functional groups ($Ti_3C_2T_2$, where T stands for -O, -F, and -OH), and adjustable interlayer distance [13–15]. They serve not only as an efficient "sulfur host" to suppress the shuttle effect of LiPSs through physical confinement and chemical adsorption [16, 17], but also as a "catalytic center" to significantly reduce the conversion energy barrier of $S_8 \leftrightarrow Li_2S$ redox reactions, thereby enhancing the conversion kinetics of LiPSs [18, 19]. Meanwhile, its excellent mechanical flexibility provides the possibility of structural support and integrated design for wearable Li-S batteries [20, 21]. However, current research primarily focuses on macroscopic performance analysis, while systematic investigations into the microscopic catalytic mechanisms of different terminals and their sustainability implications remain insufficient, which hinders further optimization and application of MXene in Li-S batteries.

Simulation is indispensable in discovering efficient catalysts for Li-S batteries. Utilizing molecular dynamics (MD) and density functional theory (DFT), researchers can simulate the adsorption, conversion pathways and catalytic mechanisms of sulfur species at the atomic scale, rapidly screen potential catalyst materials (such as single-atom catalysts, metal compounds, etc.), predict their catalytic activity and stability, thereby minimizing experimental iterations [22, 23]. Simulation can also reveal the anchor-catalytic synergy mechanism of LiPSs, guiding the design of catalysts with high conductivity and abundant active sites, thereby optimizing the sulfur conversion kinetics of Li-S batteries, suppressing the shuttle effect, and promoting their practical application [24–27].

In this work, we used the Vienna Ab Initio Simulation Package (VASP) for DFT calculations [28, 29]. The Perdew-Burke-Ernzerhof (PBE) functional within the generalized gradient approximation (GGA) was utilized to describe the exchange-correlation potential [30, 31]. we systematically investigated the site of functional groups on MXene surface and their catalytic mechanisms for LiPSs conversion. The simulation results showed that the $Ti_3C_2O_2$ has a significant electron-donating capability, which not only demonstrated stronger adsorption for LiPSs but also significantly reduced the reaction energy barrier, efficiently catalyzing the reduction of S_8, thereby enhancing the electrochemical performance of Li-S batteries. These findings have pointed out the direction for the design and application of MXene in Li-S batteries.

2 Model Building

2.1 Theoretical Model

The first-principles method based on quantum mechanics, also known as ab initio calculation, employs non-empirical microscopic particle physics parameters to solve the Schrödinger equation. This approach yields the electronic structure information of materials, which can then be combined with principles from statistical physics to obtain a range of physical and chemical properties of materials in their ground or excited states, such as optical, magnetic, and mechanical properties.

The simulation process requires appropriate approximations to solve the Schrödinger equation while maintaining computational accuracy. First, an ideal crystal model with periodic translational structure is established. The multi-electron problem is then reduced to single-electron motion in a periodic potential field via the Born-Oppenheimer adiabatic approximation (2–1) and the Hartree-Fock single-electron approximation (2–2).

$$\hat{H} = -\frac{1}{2}\sum_{i}\nabla_i^2 + \sum_{i,I} V_I\left(\vec{r_i} - \vec{R_I}\right) + \frac{1}{2}\sum_{i \neq j}\frac{1}{|\vec{r_i} - \vec{r_j}|} \tag{2–1}$$

where Ĥ represents the Hamiltonian operator, $\vec{r}$ denotes the set of all electronic coordinates, and $\vec{R}$ is the set of coordinates of all nuclei. The three parts of the formula represent the kinetic energy of the electrons, the interaction energy between electrons and nuclei, and the Coulomb interaction energy among electrons, respectively.

$$\begin{gathered}\left(-\nabla^2 - V(r)\right)\psi_i(r) + \\ \sum_{i \neq j}\int \frac{|\varphi_j(r')|^2}{|r-r'|} dr' \varphi_i(r) - \sum_{i \neq j}\int \frac{\varphi_j^*(r')\varphi_i(r')}{|r-r'|} dr' \varphi_j(r) = E_i\varphi_i(r)\end{gathered} \tag{2–2}$$

where V(r) represents the potential field in which the particle is located, and φ_i (r) indicates that the state of the *i*-th electron located at r is φ_i

Subsequently, by incorporating DFT and separating the kinetic energy and electron exchange-correlation interaction energy of the multi-electron system, the Kohn-Sham equations are derived:

$$\rho(r) = \sum_{i=1}^{N}\left|\Phi_i(\vec{r})\right|^2 \tag{2–3}$$

$$\left[-\frac{1}{2}\nabla^2 + V_{KS}\left[\rho(\vec{r})\right]\right]\Phi_i(\vec{r}) = E_i\Phi_i(\vec{r}) \tag{2–4}$$

$$V_{KS}\left[\rho(\vec{r})\right] = v(\vec{r}) + \int dr\prime \frac{\rho(\vec{r}\prime)}{|\vec{r} - \vec{r}\prime|} + \frac{\delta E_{XC}\left[\rho(\vec{r})\right]}{\delta\rho(\vec{r})} \tag{2–5}$$

where ρ(r) represents the particle density, and E_i is the Lagrange multiplier.

Then, the complex interactions between electrons are simplified by employing the Local Density Approximation (LDA) or the Generalized Gradient Approximation (GGA).

$$E_{XC}^{LDA}[\rho] = \int \rho(\vec{r})\varepsilon_{XC}(\rho(\vec{r}))d\vec{r} \tag{2–6}$$

$$E_{XC}^{GCA} = \int f_{XC}(\rho_\alpha(\vec{r})), \rho_\beta(\vec{r}), \nabla\rho_\alpha(\vec{r}), \nabla\rho_\beta(\vec{r})d\vec{r} \tag{2–7}$$

where ε_{XC} represents the exchange-correlation energy per particle in a uniform electron gas with density ρ, $\rho(\vec{r})$ is the uniform electron density, and $\nabla\rho(\vec{r})$ is the electron density gradient

Finally, through the iterative calculation of the Self-Consistent Field (SCF), the convergence of the electron density distribution or the total energy of the system is taken as the criterion for the crystal structure to reach the equilibrium state, thereby yielding various physical properties of the materials.

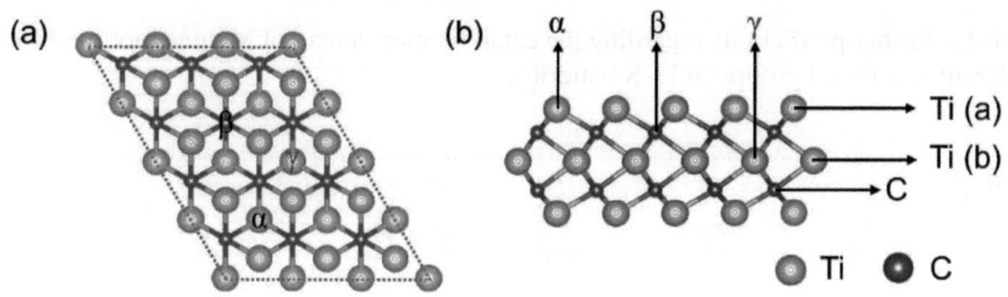

Fig. 1. Top (a) and side (b) views of the Ti_3C_2 MXene, The Greek letters in the figure are the possible adsorption sites.

2.2 Simulation Model

As one of the earliest synthesized and most common MXene materials, Ti_3C_2 exhibits a characteristic layered sandwich structure, consisting of alternating stacks of Ti and C atomic layers in a Ti-C-Ti-C-Ti sequence. In this structure, Ti_6C octahedral units are interconnected through edge-sharing configurations. The top and side views of the optimized Ti_3C_2 MXene structure are illustrated in Fig. 1.

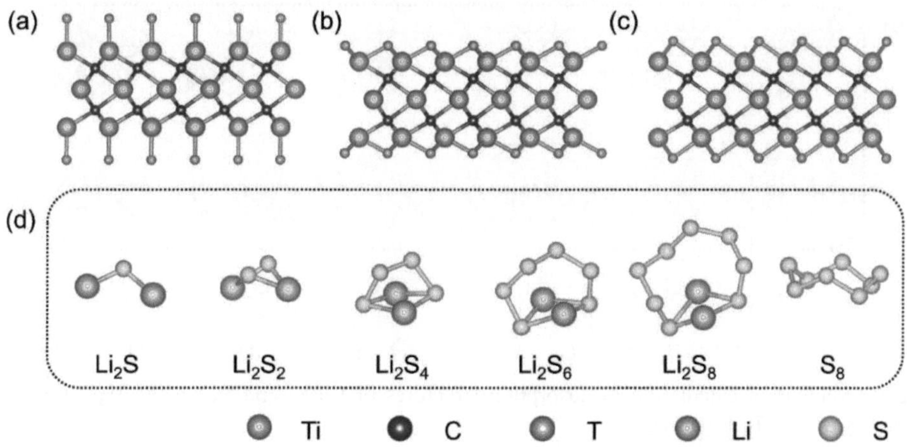

Fig. 2. The three possible simulation configurations for $Ti_3C_2T_2$: (a) Configuration I, (b) Configuration II, and (c) Configuration III. (d) Structural diagrams of LiPSs and S_8.

Based on the classical hydrofluoric acid (HF) etching process of Ti_3AlC_2 to synthesize MXene, this study systematically investigated three possible surface functional groups (–O, –F, and –OH) that can decorate the Ti_3C_2 structure, with the chemical formulas collectively represented as $Ti_3C_2T_2$. As shown in Fig. 2a-c, we identified three potential adsorption sites: the α site above the Ti(a) atom, the β site above the C atom, and the γ site above the Ti(b) atom. Through a comprehensive comparison of the total energy among the three configurations, we determined the most stable adsorption sites for each functional group on the MXene surface. These findings provide a structural basis for further predictions regarding the catalytic mechanism of MXene modified with different functional groups in Li-S batteries.

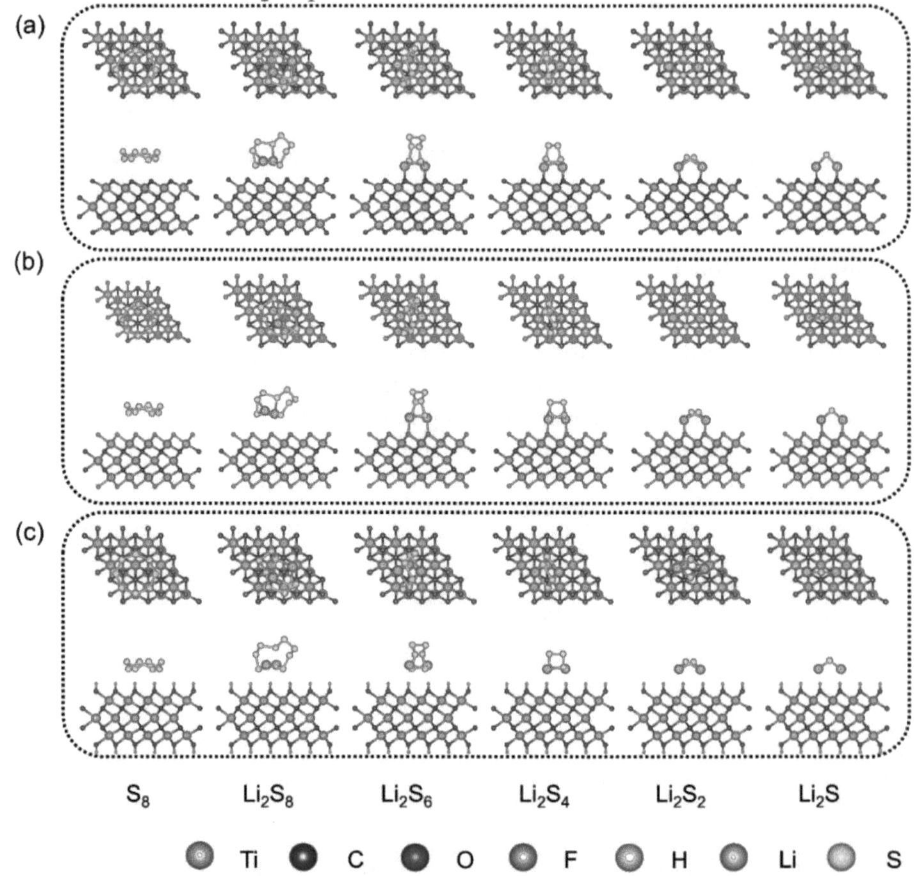

Fig. 3. Simulation calculation of adsorption structures of LiPSs and S_8 on (a) $Ti_3C_2O_2$, (b) $Ti_3C_2F_2$ and (c) $Ti_3C_2(OH)_2$.

To investigate the potential application of $Ti_3C_2T_2$ in Li-S batteries, we constructed the configurations of LiPSs and S_8 molecules (Fig. 2d), along with their adsorption models on $Ti_3C_2T_2$ surfaces (Fig. 3). The anchoring effect of $Ti_3C_2T_2$ on LiPSs was quantitatively evaluated by calculating the adsorption energy (E_{ad}), which is defined as follows:

$$E_{ad}=E_{slab}+E_{LiPSs}-E_{slab+LiPSs} \tag{2–8}$$

where E_{slab} and $E_{slab+LiPSs}$ represent the total energy of the system before and after LiPSs adsorption on the MXene, respectively, while E_{LiPSs} is the energy of LiPSs. A positive adsorption energy indicates that LiPSs can be stably adsorbed on the surface of

$Ti_3C_2T_2$. The same calculation method was applied to determine the adsorption energy of S_8.

3 Simulation Results and Discussion

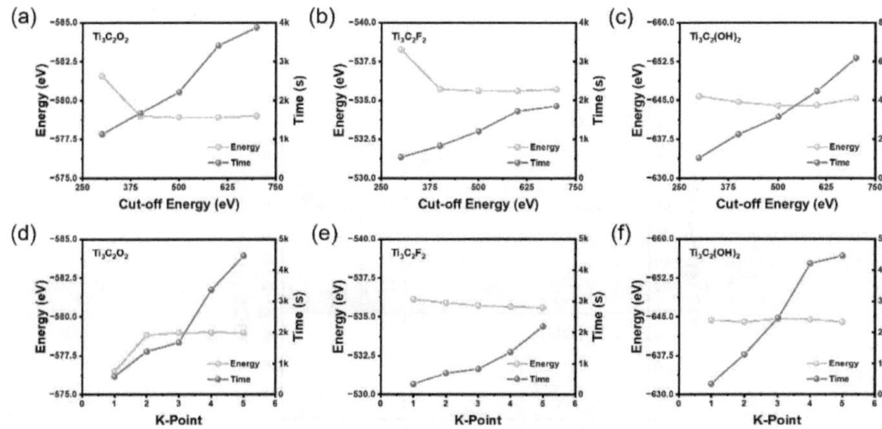

Fig. 4. Cut-off energy test and K-Point test for MXene calculations with different functional groups

Cut-off energy and K-point convergence tests are critical parameter optimization steps to ensure the reliability of simulation data. The cut-off energy test determines the energy cutoff value for the plane-wave basis set expansion, while the K-point test optimizes the sampling grid density in the Brillouin zone. Improper parameter selection may compromise result accuracy if too low or significantly increase computational costs if excessively high. As shown in Fig. 4, the test results for $Ti_3C_2T_x$ indicate that when the cut-off energy is increased to 400 eV, the total energy of the system tends to converge, while the computational cost increases exponentially with the increase of the cut-off energy. Based on this convergence criterion, 400 eV is selected as the cut-off energy in this simulation. Similarly, K-point testing achieved a balance between energy convergence and computational efficiency at a grid density of $3 \times 3 \times 1$, and this parameter was therefore adopted for subsequent simulations.

The most stable adsorption configurations were determined by comparing the total energy of functional groups at different adsorption sites on the Ti_3C_2 MXene surface. As shown in Table 1, the most stable configuration for $Ti_3C_2T_2$ is Configuration III with functional groups occupying the γ-site, In this configuration, the functional group is located above the hollow site of the second layer Ti atom in Ti_3C_2 MXene, forming coordination bonds with three adjacent C atoms and bonding with three surrounding Ti atoms. The corresponding total energy of this configuration are –578.98 eV for $Ti_3C_2O_2$, –535.73 eV for $Ti_3C_2F_2$, and –644.63 eV for $Ti_3C_2(OH)_2$. Based on these findings, Configuration III was adopted as the standard model for $Ti_3C_2T_2$ to further investigate its potential applications in Li-S batteries.

Table 1. The total energy of the three configurations $Ti_3C_2T_2$ with different functional groups (-O, -F, -OH).

	$Ti_3C_2O_2$	$Ti_3C_2F_2$	$Ti_3C_2(OH)_2$
Configuration I	–542.07 eV	–519.21 eV	–624.10 eV
Configuration II	–572.24 eV	–527.86 eV	–638.82 eV
Configuration III	–578.98 eV	–535.73 eV	–644.63 eV

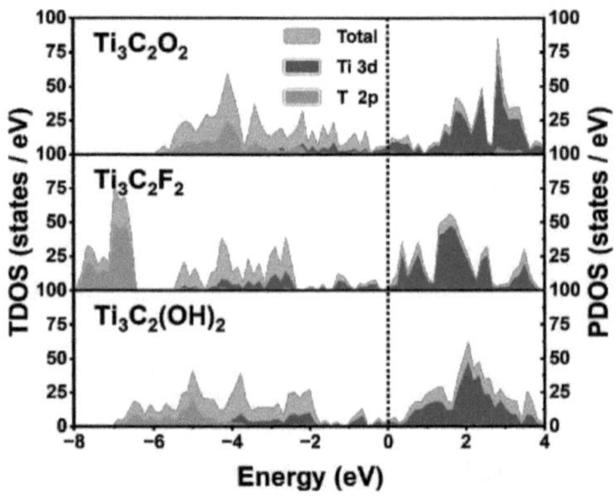

Fig. 5. Calculated DOS (left) and PDOS of Ti 3d (right) for $Ti_2C_2O_2$, $Ti_2C_2F_2$ and $Ti_2C_2(OH)_2$. The vertical dotted line at E = 0 eV represents the Fermi energy.

We systematically investigated the catalytic mechanism of $Ti_3C_2T_2$ in Li-S batteries through the analysis of the total density of states (DOS) and the partial density of states (PDOS) of the Ti 3d and T 2p orbitals. As a composite material for the S cathode, the electrical conductivity plays a decisive role in determining the battery performance. As shown in Fig. 5, $Ti_3C_2O_2$, $Ti_3C_2F_2$, and $Ti_3C_2(OH)_2$ all demonstrate excellent metallic conductivity, which can effectively compensate for the intrinsic low electronic conductivity of sulfur species, thereby effectively accelerating the rapid redox of LiPSs. The DOS and PDOS results indicate a significant hybridization of electronic states between the Ti 3d orbitals and the 2p orbitals of the functional groups, confirming the formation of polar covalent bonds. It is worth noting that the valence electron of $Ti_3C_2O_2$ near the Fermi level is significantly higher than that of $Ti_3C_2F_2$ and $Ti_3C_2(OH)_2$, indicating that it has a stronger electron donor capacity, which can provide more electrons to participate in the reduction reaction of sulfur species [32]. This characteristic makes it show a significant advantage in improving the performance of Li-S batteries.

The electronic localization function (ELF) and Bader charge analysis were conducted to further investigate the catalytic mechanism of $Ti_3C_2T_2$ in Li-S batteries. As shown in Fig. 6 and Table 2, compared with the $Ti_3C_2F_2$ and $Ti_3C_2(OH)_2$, a much more intense charge transfer was perceived in the $Ti_3C_2O_2$-Li_2S_6 interface, promoting the efficient anchoring and rapid conversion of LiPSs.

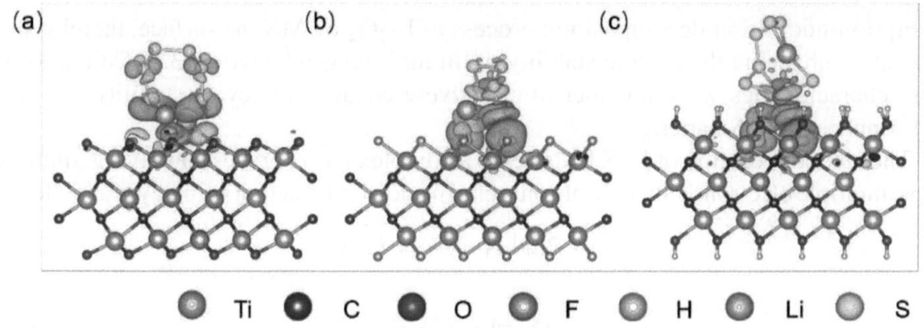

Fig. 6. Charge density difference for Li_2S_6 interacting with (a)$Ti_3C_2O_2$, (b)$Ti_3C_2F_2$, and (c) $Ti_3C_2(OH)_2$, respectively. The yellow and blue distribution corresponds to charge accumulation and depletion, respectively. The isosurface value was set to 0.003 e/Bohr^3.

Table 2. The Bader charge of the three configurations $Ti_3C_2T_2$ with different functional groups (-O, -F, -OH).

$Ti_3C_2T_2$	Bader
$Ti_3C_2O_2$	1.18 e^-
$Ti_3C_2F_2$	0.79 e^-
$Ti_3C_2(OH)_2$	0.68 e^-

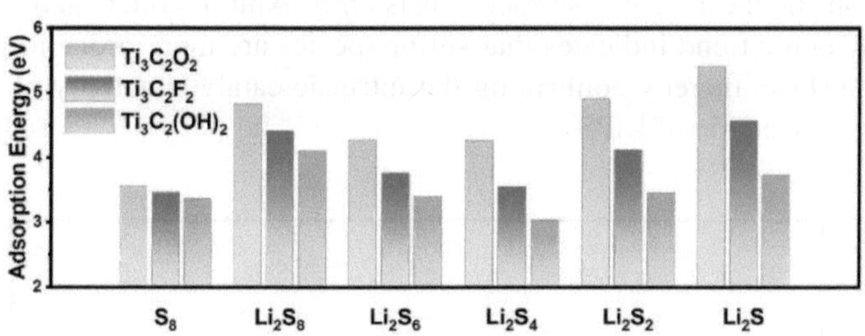

Fig. 7. Calculated adsorption energy for S_8, Li_2S_8, Li_2S_6, Li_2S_4, Li_2S_2, and Li_2S on $Ti_3C_2O_2$, $Ti_3C_2F_2$, and $Ti_3C_2(OH)_2$, respectively.

Furthermore, the adsorption energy of LiPSs and S_8 on the $Ti_3C_2T_2$ surface were calculated by DFT (Fig. 7). The calculation results are highly consistent with the Bader charge analysis, confirming that $Ti_3C_2O_2$ exhibits the strongest adsorption energy for LiPSs. This can be attributed to the polar characteristics of the Ti-O bond, which enhance the surface activity and form a stronger chemical bond between the -O and LiPSs. More importantly, this strong adsorption effect can significantly inhibit the shuttle effect of LiPSs, while providing more active sites for the redox reactions of sulfur species, Li et al. have also experimentally demonstrated that the catalytic capability of MXene is mainly derived from the decorated O group, which enables a stable and controllable adsorption-nucleation-decomposition process of Li_2O_2 on MXene surface, thereby significantly enhancing the cycling stability of lithium-oxygen batteries [33]. Collectively, these characteristics work together to effectively enhance the cycle stability and rate performance of Li-S batteries.

The cathode reaction of Li-S batteries is a complex redox process involving multiple steps, multiple electrons and multiple phases. The detailed reaction pathway is as follows:

$$S_8^* + 2Li^+ + 2e^- = Li_2S_8^* \quad (3\text{–}1)$$

$$\mathrm{Li_2S_8^*{=}Li_2S_6^*{+}\frac{1}{4}S_8} \quad (3\text{–}2)$$

$$\mathrm{Li_2S_6^*{=}Li_2S_4^*{+}\frac{1}{4}S_8} \quad (3\text{–}3)$$

$$\mathrm{Li_2S_4^*{=}Li_2S_2^*{+}\frac{1}{4}S_8} \quad (3\text{–}4)$$

$$\mathrm{Li_2S_2^*{=}Li_2S^*{+}\frac{1}{8}S_8} \quad (3\text{–}5)$$

To further investigate the catalytic mechanism of $Ti_3C_2T_2$, we compared the Gibbs free energy changes (ΔG) of LiPSs conversions on $Ti_3C_2O_2$, $Ti_3C_2F_2$, and $Ti_3C_2(OH)_2$ surface. As shown in Fig. 8, the ΔG values between adjacent sulfur species are labeled along the reaction pathway, providing a thermodynamic parameter to evaluate the spontaneity of each conversion step. Relative to $Ti_3C_2F_2$ and $Ti_3C_2(OH)_2$, the LiPSs conversion reactions on the $Ti_3C_2O_2$ surface consistently exhibit more negative ΔG values. This thermodynamic trend indicates that sulfur species are more prone to lithiation on the $Ti_3C_2O_2$ surface, thereby confirming the intrinsic catalytic activity of $Ti_3C_2O_2$ in promoting the conversion of LiPSs.

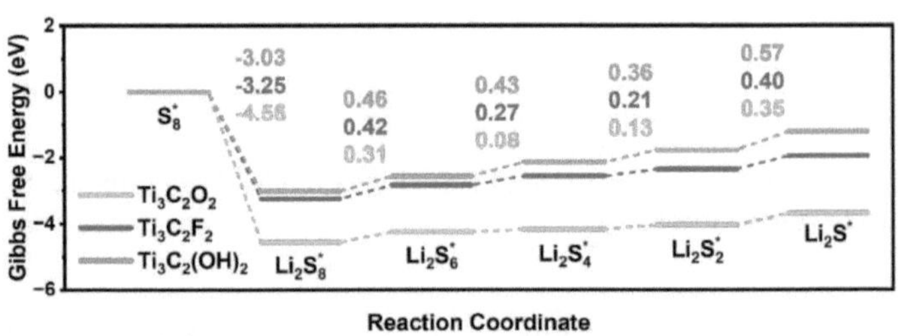

Fig. 8. Gibbs free energy for the reduction of LiPSs on $Ti_3C_2O_2$, $Ti_3C_2F_2$, and $Ti_3C_2(OH)_2$ substrates.

This intrinsic catalytic activity can accelerate the sequential conversion of LiPSs, thereby enhancing sulfur utilization, while concurrently suppressing the dissolution and accumulation of LiPSs in the electrolyte to effectively inhibit the shuttle effect, thereby enhancing the overall electrochemical performance of Li-S batteries. This finding provides a theoretical foundation for elucidating the catalytic mechanisms of MXene.

4 Conclusion

This work employs VASP simulation software to investigate the catalytic mechanism of Ti_3C_2 MXene with different terminal modifications toward LiPSs conversion. The simulation results reveal that configuration III possesses the lowest total energy and thus represents the most stable adsorption configuration. Further analyses demonstrate that $Ti_3C_2O_2$ exhibits superior electrical conductivity and stronger electron-donating capability, which can effectively facilitate the reduction of S_8. Moreover, $Ti_3C_2O_2$ exhibits a higher adsorption energy for LiPSs and a lower reaction energy barrier compared with other terminations, which is consistent with reported experimental results. This intrinsic catalytic activity can not only effectively suppress the shuttle effect, but also promote the rapid redox of LiPSs, thereby enhancing the electrochemical performance of Li-S batteries. This study helps to elucidate the mechanism of MXene-catalyzed LiPSs conversion, thereby providing new insights for the design of the cathode of Li-S batteries.

Acknowledgments. We are grateful to the Analysis & Testing Center of Beihang University for the facilities, and the scientific and technical assistance.

Disclosure of Interests. The authors have no competing interests to declare that are relevant to the content of this article.

References

1. Xu, J., Xu, L., Zhang, Z., Sun, B., Jin, Y., Jin, Q., et al.: Heterostructure ZnSe-$CoSe_2$ embedded with yolk-shell conductive dodecahedral as two-in-one hosts for cathode and anode protection of lithium-sulfur full batteries. Energy Storage Mater. **47**, 223–234 (2022)
2. Zhou, S., Shi, J., Liu, S., Li, G., Pei, F., Chen, Y., et al.: Visualizing interfacial collective reaction behaviour of Li-S batteries. Nature **621**, 75–81 (2023)
3. Liu, R., Wei, Z., Peng, L., Zhang, L., Zohar, A., Schoeppner, R., et al.: Establishing reaction networks in the 16-electron sulfur reduction reaction. Nature **626**, 98–104 (2024)
4. Hu, S., Huang, X., Zhang, L., Li, G., Chen, S., Zhang, J., et al.: Vacancy-defect topological insulators Bi_2Te_{3-x} embedded in N and B Co-doped 1D carbon nanorods using ionic liquid dopants for kinetics-enhanced Li-S batteries. Adv. Funct. Mater. **33**, 2214161 (2023)
5. Song, Y., Zhao, W., Kong, L., Zhang, L., Zhu, X., Shao, Y., et al.: Synchronous immobilization and conversion of polysulfides on a VO_2-VN binary host targeting high sulfur load Li-S batteries. Energy Environ. Sci. **11**, 2620–2630 (2018)
6. Feng, S., Singh, R.K., Fu, Y., Li, Z., Wang, Y., Bao, J., et al.: Low-tortuous and dense single-particle-layer electrode for high-energy lithium-sulfur batteries. Energy Environ. Sci. **15**, 3842–3853 (2022)
7. Han, F., Zhang, S., Xia, J., Yan, D., Xing, Y., Guan, X., et al.: Ultra-high rate and long cycle life sodium-based dual-ion batteries enabled by Li_2TiO_3-modified cathode-electrolyte-interphase. Energy Storage Mater. **74**, 103912 (2025)
8. Han, Z., Zhao, S., Xiao, J., Zhong, X., Sheng, J., Lv, W., et al.: Engineering d-p orbital hybridization in single-atom metal-embedded three-dimensional electrodes for Li-S batteries. Adv. Mater. **33**, 2105947 (2021)
9. Zhang, J., Chou, J., Luo, X.-X., Yang, Y.-M., Yan, M.-Y., Jia, D., et al.: A fully amorphous, dynamic cross-linked polymer electrolyte for lithium-sulfur batteries operating at subzero-temperatures. Angew. Chem. Int. Ed. **63**, e202316087 (2024)

10. Han, F., Zhang, S., Yan, D., Xing, Y., Xia, J., Guan, X., et al.: Constructing built-in electric fields in bimetallic selenide heterojunctions to bidirectional catalyze polysulfide conversion for flexible lithium-sulfur batteries. Chem. Eng. J. **516**, 164294 (2025)
11. Xia, J., Gao, R., Yang, Y., Tao, Z., Han, Z., Zhang, S., et al.: Ti_nO_{2n-1}/MXene hierarchical bifunctional catalyst anchored on graphene aerogel toward flexible and high-energy Li-S batteries. ACS Nano **16**, 19133–19144 (2022)
12. Liang, X., Rangom, Y., Kwok, C.Y., Pang, Q., Nazar, L.F.: Interwoven MXene nanosheet/carbon-nanotube composites as Li-S cathode hosts. Adv. Mater. **29**, 1603040 (2017)
13. Zhang, S., Zhong, N., Zhou, X., Zhang, M., Huang, X., Yang, X., et al.: Comprehensive design of the high-sulfur-loading Li-S battery based on MXene nanosheets. Nano-Micro Lett. **12**, 112 (2020)
14. Hussain, I., Kathiresan, M., Singh, K., Kalidasan, B., Mendhe, A.C., Islam, M.N., et al.: Interface and surface engineering of MXenes and COFs for energy storage and conversion. InfoMat **7**, e70011 (2025)
15. Luo, Z.-H., Zheng, M., Zhou, M.-X., Sheng, X.-T., Chen, X.-L., Shao, J.-J., et al.: 2D nanochannel interlayer realizing high-performance lithium-sulfur batteries. Adv. Mater. **37**, 2417321 (2025)
16. Wei, C., Wang, Z., Wang, P., Zhang, X., An, X., Feng, J., et al.: One-step growth of ultrathin $CoSe_2$ nanobelts on N-doped MXene nanosheets for dendrite-inhibited and kinetic-accelerated lithium-sulfur chemistry. Sci. Bull. **69**, 2059–2070 (2024)
17. Xiang, M., Shen, Z., Zheng, J., Song, M., He, Q., Yang, Y., et al.: Gas-phase synthesis of Ti2CCl2 enables an efficient catalyst for lithium-sulfur batteries. Innovation **5**, 100540 (2024)
18. Guo, M., Yuan, C., Xu, T., Zhong, S., Wang, W., Zou, T., et al.: In situ built nanoconfined TiO2 particles in robust-flexible MXene@rGO conductive framework enabling high-performance hybrid magnesium-sulfur batteries. Adv. Energy Mater. **13**, 2300417 (2023)
19. Raza, H., Bai, S., Cheng, J., Majumder, S., Zhu, H., Liu, Q., et al.: Li-S batteries: challenges, achievements and opportunities. Electrochem. Energy Rev. **6**, 29 (2023)
20. Gu, S., Jiang, H., Li, X., Dai, Y., Zheng, W., Jiang, X., et al.: Dispersing single-layered Ti3C2TX nanosheets in hierarchically-porous membrane for high-efficiency Li^+ transporting and polysulfide anchoring in Li-S batteries. Energy Storage Mater. **53**, 32–41 (2022)
21. He, Y., Zhao, Y., Zhang, Y., He, Z., Liu, G., Li, J., et al.: Building flexibly porous conductive skeleton inlaid with surface oxygen-dominated MXene as an amphiphilic nanoreactor for stable Li-S pouch batteries. Energy Storage Mater. **47**, 434–444 (2022)
22. Wang, Y., Guo, T., Alhajji, E., Tian, Z., Shi, Z., Zhang, Y.-Z., et al.: MXenes for sulfur-based batteries. Adv. Energy Mater. **13**, 2202860 (2023)
23. Liu, K., Fan, Y., Ali, A., Shen, P.K.: A flexible and conductive MXene-coated fabric integrated with in situ sulfur loaded MXene nanosheets for long-life rechargeable Li-S batteries. Nanoscale **13**, 2963–2971 (2021)
24. Gu, J., Shi, Z., Mu, Y., Wu, Y., Tian, M., Chen, Z., et al.: Sustaining vacancy catalysis via conformal graphene overlays boosts practical Li-S batteries. Energy Environ. Sci. **18**, 5940–5951 (2025)
25. Song, H., Münch, K., Liu, X., Shen, K., Zhang, R., Weintraut, T., et al.: All-solid-state Li-S batteries with fast solid-solid sulfur reaction. Nature **637**, 846–853 (2025)
26. Zhang, X., Zhang, X., Wang, X., Cui, G., Pan, H., Sun, W.: Engineering spin states of metal sites toward advanced lithium-sulfur batteries. Energy Environ. Sci. **18**, 3553–3567 (2025)
27. Du, Y., Chen, W., Wang, Y., Yu, Y., Guo, K., Qu, G., et al.: Quantum spin exchange interactions to accelerate the redox kinetics in Li-S batteries. Nano-Micro Lett. **16**, 100 (2024)
28. Kresse, G., Furthmüller, J.: Efficient iterative schemes for ab initio total-energy calculations using a plane-wave basis set. Phys. Rev. B **54**, 11169–11186 (1996)

29. Blöchl, P.E.: Projector augmented-wave method. Phys. Rev. B **50**, 17953–17979 (1994)
30. Perdew, J.P., Chevary, J.A., Vosko, S.H., Jackson, K.A., Pederson, M.R., Singh, D.J., et al.: Atoms, molecules, solids, and surfaces: applications of the generalized gradient approximation for exchange and correlation. Phys. Rev. B **46**, 6671–6687 (1992)
31. Perdew, J.P., Burke, K., Ernzerhof, M.: Generalized gradient approximation made simple. Phys. Rev. Lett. **77**, 3865–3868 (1996)
32. Yang, Y., Yao, M., Wang, X., Huang, H.: Theoretical prediction of catalytic activity of Ti_2C MXene as cathode for Li-O_2 batteries. J. Phys. Chem. C **123**, 17466–17471 (2019)
33. Li, J., Han, K., Huang, J., Li, G., Peng, S., Li, N., et al.: Polarized nucleation and efficient decomposition of Li_2O_2 for Ti_2C MXene cathode catalyst under a mixed surface condition in lithium-oxygen batteries. Energy Storage Mater. **35**, 669–678 (2021)

Short Papers

Analytical 3D Trajectory Solution and Simulation Analysis for Reentry Glide Vehicles Based on the Perturbation Method

Yujie Bai[1,2], Ju Huo[1,2], Zheng Mei[2,3], Songyan Wang[1,2], and Tao Chao[1,2](✉)

[1] Control and Simulation Center, Harbin Institute of Technology, Harbin, China
chaotao2000@163.com
[2] National Key Laboratory of Modeling and Simulation for Complex Systems, Harbin, China
[3] Beijing Simulation Center, Beijing, China

Abstract. Conventional analytical approaches for reentry glide trajectories often assume fixed flight profiles, limiting maneuverability. To overcome this, this paper presents an analytical method for three-dimensional glide-phase trajectory generation based on an altitude-velocity profile. The trajectory is decomposed into longitudinal and lateral components. The longitudinal motion is derived directly from the altitude-velocity relationship, while the lateral motion is modeled using a generalized latitude-longitude framework. A perturbation method breaks the lateral model into a sequence of lower-order sub-models, each solved recursively. Lagrange interpolation is used to approximate the integral terms, yielding an efficient analytical solution. Simulations confirm the method's accuracy, speed, and flexibility for diverse lateral maneuvers, highlighting its practical potential.

Keywords: Reentry Glide Vehicle · Analytical Trajectory · Perturbation Method

1 Introduction

Reentry Glide Vehicles (RGVs) are characterized by hypersonic speed, extended range, and maneuverability, making accurate and efficient trajectory prediction essential for guidance and mission planning [1]. Traditional Runge–Kutta (RK) integration provides accuracy but incurs high computational cost, unsuitable for onboard applications. Analytical methods can achieve comparable accuracy with two–three orders of magnitude faster computation [2].

Previous work focused on simplified longitudinal or lateral models. Bryant [3] developed drag–velocity relations; Xu [4] introduced quasi-equilibrium glide laws; Mititelu [5] derived 2D approximations; Dong [6] obtained semi-analytical solutions using H–V profiles. For lateral maneuvers, Zhang [7] proposed a generalized equatorial model, and Yang [8] extended it via Chebyshev-series solutions. However, most approaches rely on parameterized profiles, restricting adaptability.

This paper proposes an analytical 3D solution using non-parameterized H–V profiles. Contributions are:

W. Cai et al. (Eds.): AsiaSim 2025, CCIS 2727, pp. 237–243, 2026.
https://doi.org/10.1007/978-981-95-4472-1_20

1. For the longitudinal solution, analytical expressions of flight-path and bank angles are derived from the H–V profiles.
2. For the lateral solution, a generalized equatorial model is applied; perturbation decomposes the motion into sub-models, forming first-order ODEs solved progressively with Lagrange interpolation.
3. By combining longitudinal and lateral results, a complete 3D analytical trajectory is obtained, avoiding fixed profiles and enhancing vehicle maneuverability

The paper is organized as follows: Sec. 2 presents the model; Sec. 3 derives analytical solutions; Sec. 4 gives simulations for accuracy and efficiency; Sec. 5 concludes.

2 Mathematical Model

To facilitate analysis, the generalized equator is defined as the great circle through the initial position, tangent to the initial velocity. A reference coordinate system (RCS) is defined on the generalized equator, sharing the origin with ECEF,The $O_E X_A$ axis points toward the vehicle's position, the $O_E Z_A$ axis is normal to the generalized equatorial plane, and the $O_E Y_A$ axis follows the right-hand rule.

Analogous to ECEF, the generalized longitude $\tilde{\lambda}$, generalized latitude $\tilde{\varphi}$ and generalized heading angle $\tilde{\psi}$ are defined. Define H is the altitude, V is the velocity, γ is the flight-path angle, σ is the bank angle, R_e is the Earth's radius, L is the lift force, D is the drag force, m is the vehicle mass, and ω_e is the Earth's rotational angular velocity.

The model is given in Eq. (1).

$$\begin{cases} \frac{d\tilde{\lambda}}{dV} = -\frac{1}{D/m+g\sin\gamma} \cdot \frac{V\cos\gamma\sin\tilde{\psi}}{R^*\cos\tilde{\varphi}} \\ \frac{d\tilde{\varphi}}{dV} = -\frac{1}{D/m+g\sin\gamma} \cdot \frac{V\cos\gamma\cos\tilde{\psi}}{R^*} \\ \frac{dH}{dV} = -\frac{V\sin\gamma}{D/m+g\sin\gamma} \\ \frac{dt}{dV} = -\frac{1}{D/m+g\sin\gamma} \\ \frac{d\gamma}{dV} = -\frac{1}{D/m+g\sin\gamma} \cdot \frac{1}{V} \left[\begin{array}{l} \frac{L\cos\sigma}{m} - g\cos\gamma + \frac{V^2\cos\gamma}{R^*} + \omega_e^2 R^* \cos^2\varphi\cos\gamma \\ +\omega_e^2 R^* \sin\varphi\cos\varphi\sin\gamma\cos\psi + 2V\omega_e\cos\varphi\sin\psi \end{array} \right] \\ \frac{d\tilde{\psi}}{dV} = \frac{1}{D/m+g\sin\gamma} \cdot \frac{1}{V} \left[\begin{array}{c} \frac{L\sin\sigma}{m\cos\gamma} + \frac{V^2\cos\gamma\sin\tilde{\psi}\tan\tilde{\varphi}}{R^*} \\ +2V\omega_e \left(\begin{array}{l} \sin\varphi_0\cos\tilde{\varphi}\cos\tilde{\lambda} + \\ \cos\varphi_0\cos\psi_0\cos\tilde{\varphi}\sin\tilde{\lambda} + \cos\varphi_0\sin\psi_0\sin\tilde{\varphi} \end{array} \right) \end{array} \right] \end{cases} \tag{1}$$

3 Analytical Solutions

3.1 Longitudinal Trajectory

According to Eq. (1), the flight-path angel is given in closed form as follows:

$$\gamma = \arcsin\left(\frac{-D/m \cdot dH/dV}{V + g \cdot dH/dV} \right) \tag{2}$$

The vertical component of lift can be derived as:

$$u = \left[\frac{(D/m + g\sin y)\sin\gamma + \mathrm{d}^2H/\mathrm{d}t^2}{V\cos\gamma} + \left(\frac{g}{V} - \frac{V}{R}\right)\cos\gamma \right] mV \tag{3}$$

Subsequently, the bank angle can be computed as $\sigma = \arccos(u/L)\cdot sgnc$, and $sgnc$ denotes the sign of the bank angle, corresponds to the control reversal.

3.2 Lateral Trajectory

Decomposition of the Motion Model Based on the Perturbation Method. Considering $\tilde{\varphi} \approx 0°, \tilde{\psi} \approx 90°$, It is Assumed that $\tan\tilde{\varphi} \approx \tilde{\varphi}, \cos\tilde{\varphi} \approx 1, \sin\tilde{\psi} \approx 1, \cos\tilde{\psi} \approx \pi/2 - \tilde{\psi}$.

According to this, the model is linearized to reduce its nonlinearity and the high-order residual terms generated during the linearization are treated as perturbations.

Let $f_1(V) = 1/(D/m + g\sin y)$, $f_2(V) = V\cos\gamma/R^*$ and $f_3(V) = L\sin\sigma/(mV\cos\gamma)$,

by introducing a scaling parameter p, Eq. (1) Can be transformed as follows:

$$\frac{\mathrm{d}\tilde{\lambda}}{\mathrm{d}V} = -f_1(V)f_2(V)\frac{1 + p(\sin\tilde{\psi} - 1)}{1 + p(\cos\tilde{\varphi} - 1)} \tag{4}$$

$$\frac{\mathrm{d}\tilde{\varphi}}{\mathrm{d}V} = -f_1(V)f_2(V)\left[\frac{\pi}{2} - \tilde{\psi} + p\left(\cos\tilde{\psi} - \frac{\pi}{2} + \tilde{\psi}\right)\right] \tag{5}$$

$$\begin{aligned} \frac{\mathrm{d}\tilde{\psi}}{\mathrm{d}V} &= f_1(V)f_3(V) + f_1(V)f_2(V)[\tilde{\varphi} + p(\tan\tilde{\varphi} - \tilde{\varphi})][1 + p(\sin\tilde{\psi} - 1)] \\ &+ 2f_1(V)\omega_e\left[\begin{array}{l} a(1 + p(\cos\tilde{\varphi} - 1))(1 + p(\cos\tilde{\lambda} - 1)) + c(0 + p(\sin\tilde{\varphi} - 0)) \\ +b(1 + p(\cos\tilde{\varphi} - 1))(\tilde{\lambda} + p(\sin\tilde{\lambda} - \tilde{\lambda})) \end{array}\right] \end{aligned} \tag{6}$$

Let $\tilde{\lambda} = \tilde{\lambda}^{(0)} + p\tilde{\lambda}^{(1)} + p^2\tilde{\lambda}^{(2)}$, $\tilde{\varphi} = \tilde{\varphi}^{(0)} + p\tilde{\varphi}^{(1)} + p^2\tilde{\varphi}^{(2)}$, $\tilde{\psi} = \tilde{\psi}^{(0)} + p\tilde{\psi}^{(1)} + p^2\tilde{\psi}^{(2)}$, and expand the Eq. (4) to Eq. (6) into a power series of p. By matching the coefficients of each order in the power series expansion, the original nonlinear dynamic model can be decomposed into a sequence of simpler sub-models.

Zeroth-Order Approximate Analytical Solution.

Define $\sin\varphi_0 = a$, $\cos\varphi_0\cos\psi_0 = b$, $\cos\varphi_0\sin\psi_0 = c$,and define

$$S_0(V) = f_1(V)f_3(V) + 2f_1(V)\omega_e\left(a + b\tilde{\lambda}^{(0)}\right) \tag{7}$$

$$\begin{aligned} S_1(V) = 2f_1(V)\omega_e &\left[\begin{array}{l} a\left(-2 + \cos\tilde{\lambda}^{(0)} + \cos\tilde{\varphi}^{(0)}\right) \\ +b\left(-2\tilde{\lambda}^{(0)} + \tilde{\lambda}^{(1)} + \tilde{\lambda}^{(0)}\cos\tilde{\varphi}^{(0)} + \sin\tilde{\lambda}^{(0)}\right) + c\sin\tilde{\varphi}^{(0)} \end{array}\right] \\ &- f_1(V)f_2(V)\left(-2\tilde{\varphi}^{(0)} + \tilde{\varphi}^{(0)}\sin\tilde{\psi}^{(0)} + \tan\tilde{\varphi}^{(0)}\right) \end{aligned} \tag{8}$$

$$S_2(V) = 2f_1\omega_e\left[\begin{array}{l} c\tilde{\varphi}^{(0)}\cos\tilde{\varphi}^{(0)} + a\left(\begin{array}{l}(-1+\cos\tilde{\lambda}^{(0)})(-1+\cos\tilde{\varphi}^{(0)})\\ -\tilde{\lambda}^{(1)}\sin\tilde{\lambda}^{(0)} - \tilde{\varphi}^{(1)}\sin\tilde{\varphi}^{(0)}\end{array}\right)+\\ b\left(\begin{array}{l}\tilde{\lambda}^{(2)} - \tilde{\lambda}^{(1)} + \tilde{\lambda}^{(1)}\cos\tilde{\lambda}^{(0)} - \tilde{\lambda}^{(0)}\tilde{\varphi}^{(1)}\sin\tilde{\varphi}^{(0)}\\ +(\cos\tilde{\varphi}^{(0)} - 1)(\tilde{\lambda}^{(1)} - \tilde{\lambda}^{(0)} + \sin\tilde{\lambda}^{(0)})\end{array}\right)\end{array}\right] + f_1(V)f_2(V)\left[\begin{array}{l}-\tilde{\varphi}^{(0)}\tilde{\psi}^{(1)}\cos\tilde{\psi}^{(0)} - \tilde{\varphi}^{(1)}\tan^2\tilde{\varphi}^{(0)}\\ -\left(\sin\tilde{\psi}^{(0)} - 1\right)\left(-\tilde{\varphi}^{(0)} + \tilde{\varphi}^{(1)} + \tan\tilde{\varphi}^{(0)}\right)\end{array}\right] \tag{9}$$

The Zeroth-Order Differential Equations Are:

$$\frac{d\tilde{\lambda}^{(0)}}{dV} = -f_1(V)f_2(V) \tag{10}$$

$$\frac{d}{dV}\begin{bmatrix}\tilde{\varphi}^{(0)}\\ \tilde{\psi}^{(0)}\end{bmatrix} = -f_1(V)f_2(V)\begin{bmatrix}0 & -1\\ 1 & 0\end{bmatrix}\begin{bmatrix}\tilde{\varphi}^{(0)}\\ \tilde{\psi}^{(0)}\end{bmatrix} + \begin{bmatrix}-f_1(V)f_2(V)\pi/2\\ S_0(V)\end{bmatrix} \tag{11}$$

In Eq. (10), both $f_1(V)$ and $f_2(V)$ can be expressed in terms of V, so the integrand is approximated by a Lagrange interpolation polynomial. Zeros of the 10th-order Chebyshev polynomial are mapped to the interval as interpolation nodes. With the coefficients c_{1k} obtained, the integral is analytically expressed in Eq. (12).

$$\tilde{\lambda}^{(0)}(V) = \int_{V_0}^{V} -f_1(s)f_2(s)ds \approx \sum_{k=0}^{9} c_{1k}\frac{1}{k+1}\left(\frac{2}{V_0 - V_f}\right)^k\left[\left(V - \frac{V_0 - V_f}{2}\right)^{k+1} - \left(V_0 - \frac{V_0 - V_f}{2}\right)^{k+1}\right] \tag{12}$$

For the zeroth-order latitude and heading angle, as shown in Eq. (11), this equation is a linear nonhomogeneous ordinary differential equation (ODE) with constant coefficients. It can be solved by transition matrix and the integrand is approximated by a Lagrange interpolation.

Since $f_3(x)$ is influenced by the sign of the bank angel and is not a continuous function, it is replaced by $|f_3(x)|$.Integration is performed between two bank reversal points, from which the trajectory segments $P_2(V)$ and $P_3(V)$ are obtained.

Let $\widehat{V}_j, j = 1, 2...n$ denote the velocity at the bank reversal, then the solutions for the zeroth-order latitude and heading angle can be expressed as:

$$\begin{cases}\tilde{\varphi}^{(0)}(V) = \tilde{\varphi}^{(0)}(V_0)\cos\tilde{\lambda}^{(0)}(V) + \left(\frac{\pi}{2} - \tilde{\psi}^{(0)}(V_0)\right)\sin\tilde{\lambda}^{(0)}(V) + \\ \sin\tilde{\lambda}^{(0)}\sum_{j=1}^{n+1}(-1)^{j-1}\left[P_2(\widehat{V}_j) - P_2(\widehat{V}_{j-1})\right] + \cos\tilde{\lambda}^{(0)}\sum_{j=1}^{n+1}(-1)^{j-1}\left[P_3(\widehat{V}_j) - P_3(\widehat{V}_{j-1})\right]\\ \tilde{\psi}^{(0)}(V) = \frac{\pi}{2} + \tilde{\varphi}^{(0)}(V_0)\sin\tilde{\lambda}^{(0)}(V) + \left(\tilde{\psi}^{(0)}(V_0) - \frac{\pi}{2}\right)\cos\tilde{\lambda}^{(0)}(V) + \\ \cos\tilde{\lambda}^{(0)}\sum_{j=1}^{n+1}(-1)^{j-1}\left[P_2(\widehat{V}_j) - P_2(\widehat{V}_{j-1})\right] + \sin\tilde{\lambda}^{(0)}\sum_{j=1}^{n+1}(-1)^{j-1}\left[P_3(\widehat{V}_j) - P_3(\widehat{V}_{j-1})\right]\end{cases} \tag{13}$$

First-Order & Second-Order Approximate Analytical Solution. Higher-order corrections are expressed in terms of known lower-order states and polynomial approximations of the integral terms Eq. (14) ~ (17).

$$\begin{aligned}\tilde{\lambda}^{(1)}(V) = P_4(V) &= \int_{V_0}^{V} f_1(s) f_2(s)\left(\cos\tilde{\varphi}^{(0)} - \sin\tilde{\psi}^{(0)}\right)\mathrm{d}s \approx \int_{V_0}^{V} p_4(s)\mathrm{d}s \\ &= \sum_{k=0}^{9} c_{4k}\frac{1}{k+1}\left(\frac{2}{V_0 - V_f}\right)^k\left[\left(V - \frac{V_0 - V_f}{2}\right)^{k+1} - \left(V_0 - \frac{V_0 - V_f}{2}\right)^{k+1}\right]\end{aligned} \tag{14}$$

$$\begin{aligned}\tilde{\lambda}^{(2)}(V) = P_9(V) &= \int_{V_0}^{V} f_1(s) f_2(s)\begin{pmatrix} -\cos\tilde{\varphi}^{(0)} + \cos^2\tilde{\varphi}^{(0)} + \tilde{\psi}^{(1)}\cos\tilde{\psi}^{(0)} \\ +\tilde{\varphi}^{(1)}\sin\tilde{\varphi}^{(0)} + \sin\tilde{\psi}^{(0)} - \cos\tilde{\varphi}^{(0)}\sin\tilde{\psi}^{(0)}\end{pmatrix}\mathrm{d}s \\ &= \sum_{k=0}^{9} c_{9k}\frac{1}{k+1}\left(\frac{2}{V_0 - V_f}\right)^k\left[\left(V - \frac{V_0 - V_f}{2}\right)^{k+1} - \left(V_0 - \frac{V_0 - V_f}{2}\right)^{k+1}\right]\end{aligned} \tag{15}$$

Let $P_5(V), P_6(V), P_7(V), P_8(V), P_{10}(V), P_{11}(V), P_{12}(V)$ and $P_{13}(V)$ are polynomial approximations of the integrals of $f_1(V)f_2(V)\cos\tilde{\lambda}^{(0)}(\pi/2 - \tilde{\psi}^{(0)} - \cos\tilde{\psi}^{(0)})$, $f_1(V)f_2(V)\sin\tilde{\lambda}^{(0)}(\pi/2 - \tilde{\psi}^{(0)} - \cos\tilde{\psi}^{(0)})$,$\cos\tilde{\lambda}^{(0)}S_1(V)$, $\sin\tilde{\lambda}^{(0)}S_1(V)$, $f_1(V)f_2(V)\cos\tilde{\lambda}^{(0)}(-\tilde{\psi}^{(1)} + \tilde{\psi}^{(1)}\sin\tilde{\psi}^{(0)})$, $f_1(V)f_2(V)\sin\tilde{\lambda}^{(0)}(-\tilde{\psi}^{(1)} + \tilde{\psi}^{(1)}\sin\tilde{\psi}^{(0)})$, $\cos\tilde{\lambda}^{(0)}S_2(V)$ and $\sin\tilde{\lambda}^{(0)}S_2(s)$, the analytical solution can be obtained as follows:

$$\begin{cases} \tilde{\varphi}^{(1)}(V) = \cos\tilde{\lambda}^{(0)}(V)[P_5(V) + P_8(V)] + \sin\tilde{\lambda}^{(0)}(V)[P_6(V) - P_7(V)] \\ \tilde{\psi}^{(1)}(V) = \sin\tilde{\lambda}^{(0)}(V)[P_5(V) + P_8(V)] - \cos\tilde{\lambda}^{(0)}(V)[P_6(V) - P_7(V)] \end{cases} \tag{16}$$

$$\begin{cases} \tilde{\varphi}^{(2)}(V) = \cos\tilde{\lambda}^{(0)}(V)[P_{10}(V) + P_{13}(V)] + \sin\tilde{\lambda}^{(0)}(V)[P_{11}(V) - P_{12}(V)] \\ \tilde{\psi}^{(2)}(V) = \sin\tilde{\lambda}^{(0)}(V)[P_{10}(V) + P_{13}(V)] - \cos\tilde{\lambda}^{(0)}(V)[P_{11}(V) - P_{12}(V)] \end{cases} \tag{17}$$

By superimposing the state variables of all orders, an approximate analytical solution of the lateral trajectory can be obtained.

4 Simulation Analysis

The CAV-H is selected as the test case. Initial conditions are $H_0 = 60\,\mathrm{km}$, V_0=6800 m/s, γ_0=-0.2°,$\lambda_0 = 0°$,$\varphi_0 = 0°$,$\psi_0 = 90°$. The terminal conditions are $H_f = 25\,\mathrm{km}$, $V_f = 2000\,\mathrm{m/s}$. The $H(V)$ is shown in Fig. 1, in which the $H(V)$ are complex forms that are difficult to describe with simple mathematical expressions.

A comparative analysis showed in Table. 1 between the RK method and the analytical solution (ANA) method shows that the analytical solution yields longitude and latitude errors within 1°, as well as heading angle errors within 1°. Moreover, its efficiency is significantly higher than that of the numerical integration method (Fig. 2).

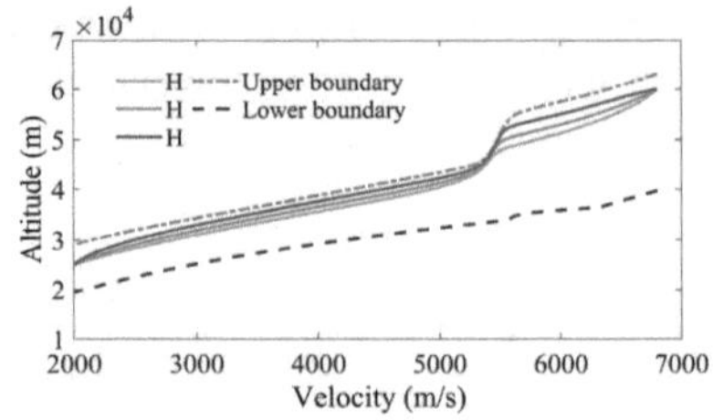

Fig. 1. Altitude-Velocity Profile

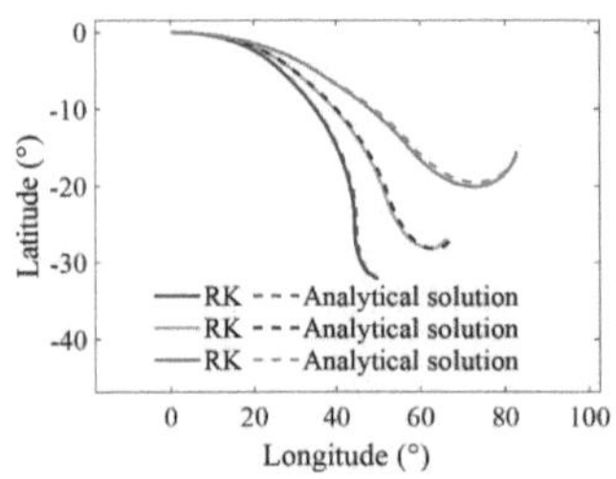

(a) 3-D track

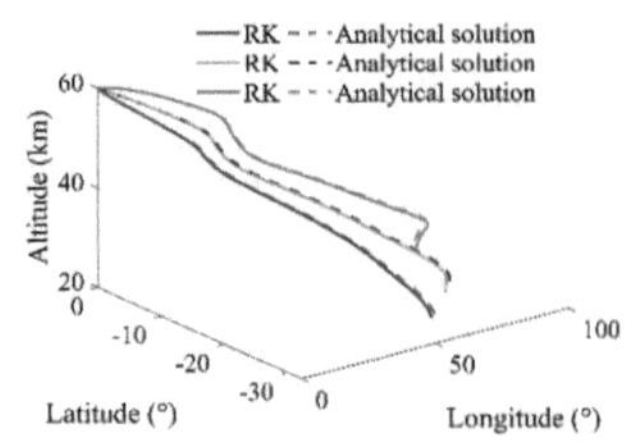

(b) Ground track

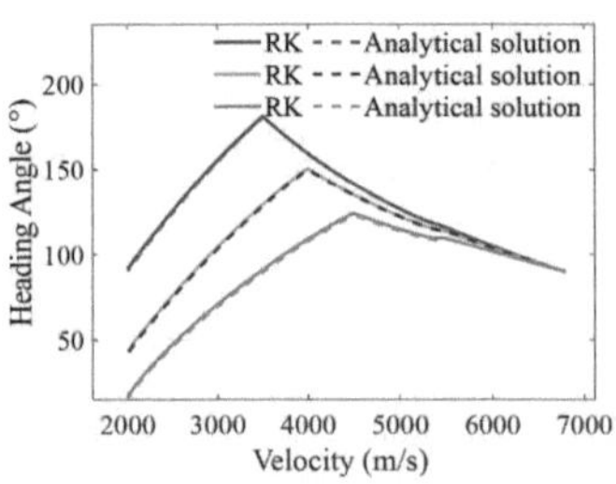

(c) Heading

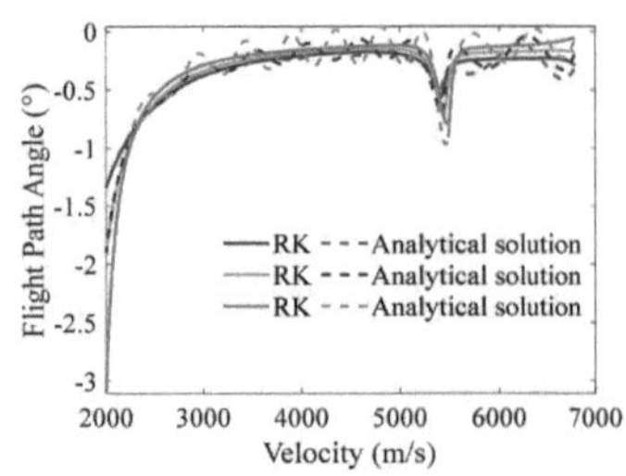

(d) FPA

Fig. 2. Comparison of results obtained by RK method and analytical solution.

Table 1. Comparative analysis between RK method and the ANA method

Case	Method	λ_f (°)	φ_f (°)	ψ_f (°)	Time(s)
Exp 1	RK	83.48	-14.77	91.67	0.495
	ANA	82.72	-15.30	91.39	0.027
Exp 2	RK	65.95	-26.97	42.30	0.349
	ANA	66.23	-27.00	42.49	0.020
Exp 3	RK	49.37	-31.79	17.31	0.715
	ANA	50.14	-32.09	16.12	0.016

5 Conclusion

In summary, the proposed analytical method demonstrates high accuracy and computational efficiency in reentry trajectory. Compared with the RK method, the analytical solution maintains longitude, latitude, and heading angle errors within 1°, while the small deviation in flight path angle has limited impact due to its inherently small magnitude. Furthermore, the method does not rely on parameterized altitude–velocity profiles, thereby offering greater flexibility and general applicability to various trajectory planning scenarios. Its significantly reduced computational load also makes it suitable for onboard or real-time applications.

Acknowledgments. This work is supported by the National Natural Science Foundation(NNSF) of China under Grant 62273119.

References

1. Richie, G.: The Common Aero Vehicle—Space delivery system of the future. In: *AIAA Space Technology Conference and Exposition*, Albuquerque (1999)
2. Pan, L., Peng, S., Xie, Y., Liu, Y., Wang, J.: 3D guidance for hypersonic reentry gliders based on analytical prediction. Acta Astronaut. **167**, 42–51 (2020)
3. Bryant, L.E., Tigges, M.A., Ives, D.G.: Analytic drag control for precision landing and aerocapture. In: *23rd Atmospheric Flight Mechanics Conference*, A98–37438 (1998)
4. Xu, M.L., Liu, L.H., Tang, G.J.: Quasi-equilibrium glide auto adaptive entry guidance based on ideology of predictor–corrector. In: *5th International Conference on Recent Advances in Space Technologies* (2011)
5. Mititelu, G.: Analytical solutions for the equations of motion of a space vehicle during the atmospheric re-entry phase on a 2-D trajectory. Celest. Mech. Dyn. Astron. **103**(4), 327–342 (2009)
6. Dong, C.: Adaptive finite-time guidance method for hypersonic glide vehicles. PhD thesis, Harbin Institute of Technology (2014)
7. Zhang, W., Chen, W., Yu, W.: Analytical solutions to three-dimensional hypersonic gliding trajectory over rotating Earth. Acta Astronaut. **190**, 702–716 (2021)
8. Yang, J., Yu, W., Chen, W.: Chebyshev-series solutions for nonlinear systems with hypersonic gliding trajectory example. *Aerosp. Sci. Technol.* (2023), 108024

Evaluating Hospital Disaster Resilience Using Simulation: Integrating Task Duration and Intra-Hospital Patient Transfer

Desak Ayu Clara Dewanti[1](✉), Taro Kanno[1](✉), Toshiki Nishimura[1], Kazumi Kajiyama[2], Michihiro Tsubaki[3], Sachika Sharikura[4], Misumi Yamazaki[5], Haruka Yoshida[6], Joniarto Parung[7], and Amelia Santoso[7]

[1] The University of Tokyo, Tokyo, Japan
{desakayuclara,tkanno}@g.ecc.u-tokyo.ac.jp
[2] Kitasato University Hospital, Sagamihara, Japan
[3] Kitasato University, Sagamihara, Japan
[4] Showa University Hospital, Tokyo, Japan
[5] Japanese Red Cross College of Nursing, Tokyo, Japan
[6] Nihon University, Tokyo, Japan
[7] University of Surabaya, Surabaya, Indonesia

Abstract. This study improves hospital disaster preparedness evaluation by developing a calibrated multi-layer discrete-event simulation (DES) model. The model integrates two types of data: Work-As-Done (WAD), collected from hospital disaster drills between 2022 and 2024, and Work-As-Imagined (WAI), derived from staff surveys and protocols. Extra Waiting Time (EWT), defined as the gap between WAD and WAI length of stay (LOS), was introduced as a resilience indicator. Results showed that the task-duration (Layer 1) was the dominant factor of EWT reductions, with values decreasing from 37.87 min in 2022 to 29.00 min in 2024. While the incorporation of transfer time (Layer 2) produced smaller additional decreases (−1.42 min in 2023 and − 0.18 min in 2024) but improved the attribution of delays by separating treatment from patient movement. Together, these findings demonstrate that while task execution is the primary influence on hospital resilience, explicit transfer modeling enhances accuracy and transparency. The framework offers a practical tool for quantifying operational inefficiencies, supporting hospital workflow evaluation under disaster conditions, and can be adapted to other mass-casualty scenarios.

Keywords: Disaster preparedness · Discrete-event simulation · Extra waiting time · Intra-hospital patient flow · Hospital resilience

1 Introduction

Japan is one of the most disaster-prone countries, especially with earthquake. Sudden patient surges during mass casualty incidents (MCIs) can overwhelm hospital capacity, even for disaster-base hospital [1]. With those conditions, disaster drills are essential

W. Cai et al. (Eds.): AsiaSim 2025, CCIS 2727, pp. 244–251, 2026.
https://doi.org/10.1007/978-981-95-4472-1_21

for testing preparedness. In addition, reflection, surveys, and checklists are widely used to evaluate the drills. However, current evaluation methods are often too subjective and lack detailed explanations of the systems [2, 3].

Unlike current evaluations, simulation modeling offers a more objective and reproducible method for analyzing hospital workflows during MCIs. Previous studies have demonstrated the effectiveness of simulation modeling for analyzing the efficiency of patient flow to resource allocation and throughput. Nevertheless, most models remain resource-focused [4, 5]. Without the incorporation of detailed task durations or intra-hospital transfer times, they are unable to capture intricacies of hospital drills [5]. Hence, detailed task durations and intra-hospital transfer times need to be integrated into the simulation model to comprehensively assessed the hospital drills.

To address this gap, this study develops a discrete-event simulation (DES) model that integrates both task duration and intra-hospital patient transfer time. By comparing Work-As-Imagined (WAI) with Work-As-Done (WAD), the model introduces Extra Waiting Time (EWT) as a new quantitative indicator to measure unexplained delays. Furthermore, the approach enables year-to-year comparison of disaster drill performance, offering hospitals actionable insights for strengthening preparedness and resilience for hospital during MCIs.

2 Methods

2.1 Performance Metrics

Hospital performance during disaster scenarios was evaluated using Length of Stay (LOS) as the primary outcome. Two models were compared: Work-As-Imagined (WAI), representing normative expectations based on protocols and staff surveys, and Work-As-Done (WAD), representing observed performance during real hospital disaster drills. The difference between the two models was expressed as Extra Waiting Time (EWT):

$$EWT_i = LOS_i^{WAD,clean} - LOS_i^{WAI,adjust} \quad (1)$$

where i indexes individual patients, $LOS_i^{WAD,clean}$ is the clinically cleaned observed duration from drills, and $LOS_i^{WAI,adjust}$ is the scope-adjusted normative estimate.

This inclusion allows for a more comprehensive estimation of LOS and provides deeper insight into operational delays that are often overlooked in simulations.

2.2 Data Sources

The WAD model captures the actual behavior and performance of the hospital observed during three years (2022–2024) of disaster training exercises. Data was collected from detailed hospital training logs and observational records [6]. Data included task durations and intra-hospital transfer times, incorporating natural variability from multitasking, prioritization, and staff availability.

In contrast, the WAI model represents an idealized view of hospital emergency operations. It reflects how processes are expected to operate under planned conditions, without disruptions. Data was derived from staff surveys and official protocols, reflecting expected task times under ideal conditions. Transfer times were estimated from department distances and average walking-speed distributions. Outliers were removed using interquartile range filtering.

Both models used consistent records data for staff numbers, equipment availability, and departmental capacity. With those data, the model enables the evaluation of delays and discrepancies between actual and expected performance, supporting the analysis of hospital preparedness and operational resilience.

2.3 Simulation Model

A discrete-event simulation (DES) was developed in AnyLogic to reproduce hospital workflows during MCIs. The model consisted of three integrated layers: (1) a task duration layer that models the time required for patients to progress through hospital stages such as triage, diagnostics, treatment, and discharge; (2) a transfer time layer that simulates intra-hospital patient movement delays between departments; and (3) a resource allocation layer that models the availability and usage of hospital staff, medical equipment, and beds.

The simulation operates at the individual patient level, where each agent interacts with the hospital environment (departments as nodes, hallways as transfer links). Each patient has properties including triage category, treatment needs, and routing path. This structure enables the model to capture how both treatment activities and patient movement contribute to overall LOS.

Figure 1 represents the simulation workflow. Hospital disaster drill data (WAD, 2022–2024) and survey-based estimates (WAI) were used as inputs for a multi-layer, discrete-event simulation that integrated task duration, transfer time, and resource allocation. Calibration factors (α and β for WAD and γ for WAI) were applied to remove non-clinical delays and align task scope, enabling fair comparison. The model was run separately using WAD and WAI data. The outputs, cleaned LOS for WAD and adjusted LOS for WAI, were then compared. The resulting extra waiting time (EWT) quantified hidden delays and served as the main resilience evaluation metric.

Table 1 summarizes the main parameters of the model. Task durations and transfer times were treated as stochastic, patient-specific variables, varying by triage color, examination area, and mobility method. Resource allocation data were derived from hospital records and applied consistently across WAD and WAI.

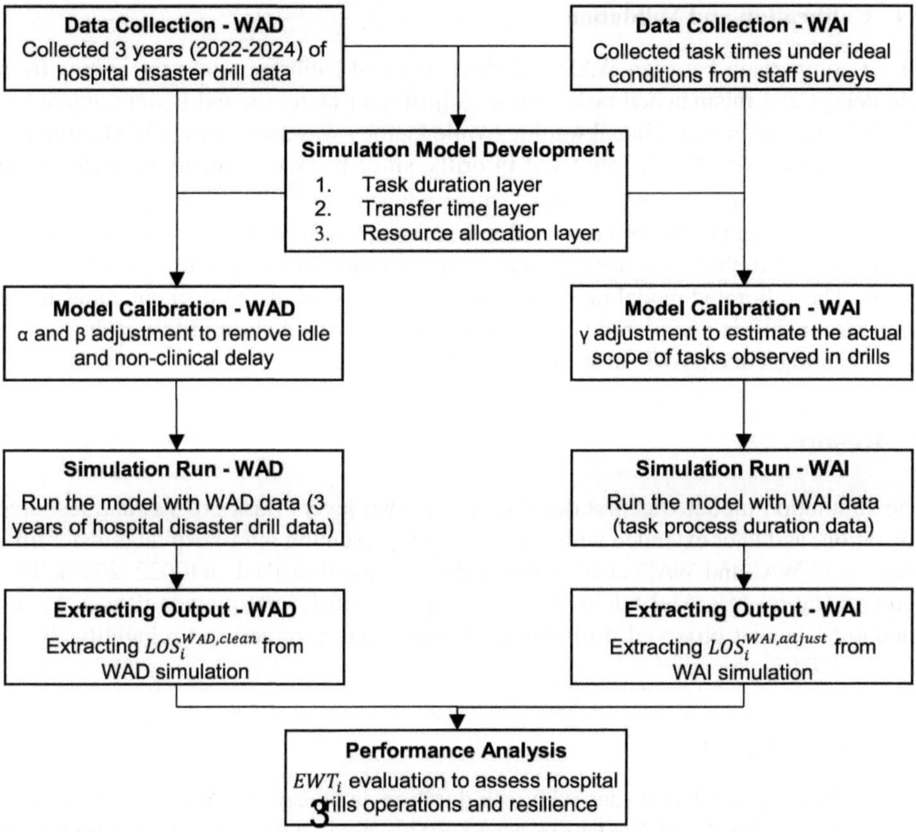

Fig. 1. Workflow for evaluating hospital disaster resilience using WAD–WAI comparison.

Table 1. Parameters and sources used in the simulation model.

Component	Description & Source	Notes on Variability
Task duration	From WAD drill logs (observed) and WAI staff surveys (expected)	Varies per patient ID and same task may differ across triage colors and examination areas
Transfer time	Derived from department distances and mobility method (walk, stretcher, wheelchair)	Patient and route-specific which distribution estimated from drills data
Resource allocation	Staff numbers, beds, and equipment from disaster drill records and hospital protocols	Applied consistently in WAD and WAI
Calibration factors (α, β, γ)	Adjust WAD for non-clinical waiting and align WAI to observed scope	Detailed formula reported separately

2.4 Calibration and Validation

Direct comparison between WAD and WAI required calibration to remove bias from idle delays and mismatched task scopes. Adjustment factors α and β were applied to WAD data to clean non-clinical waiting, while factor γ was used to align WAI estimates with the actual set of tasks observed in drills, since in practice many procedures are not fully performed during exercises. This produced $LOS_i^{WAD,clean}$ and $LOS_i^{WAI,adjust}$, enabling consistent LOS comparison. Detailed formulations of these factors are reported separately, but in this study, they are summarized as necessary steps to ensure fair evaluation. The calibrated model then was validated against observed drill outcomes using regression analysis and paired t-tests. Together, these steps ensured fair evaluation of Extra Waiting Time (EWT) as the key resilience metric.

3 Results

The simulation model was first developed with two layers (task process and resource allocation) and later extended with a third layer representing intra-hospital transfer time under both WAI and WAD conditions for three years of drills data (2022–2024). This addition improved model fidelity by capturing previously unexplained delays. Model validation against observed drill data confirmed high accuracy and reliability ($R^2 > 0.87$, $p < 0.05$).

3.1 Layer 1 Result

Figure 2 shows simulation runs with task duration as the sole layer showed consistent gaps between WAD and WAI LOS across 2022–2024. After applying calibration to remove idle and non-clinical delays, LOS was represented by stay time only, expressed as:

$$LOS_i^{WAD,clean} = T_i^{stay,WAD,clean} \tag{2}$$

EWT was highest in 2022, 37.87 min, then decreased to 34.65 min in 2023 and 29.00 min in 2024. The gradual decline suggests that, even without modeling transfers, hospital drills improved in operational efficiency over time.

3.2 Layer 2 Result

To better capture intra-hospital dynamics, a second layer was introduced by integrating transfer time into the simulation for 2023–2024 as shown in Fig. 3. After calibration, LOS was expressed as:

$$LOS_i^{WAD,clean} = T_i^{stay,WAD,clean} + T_i^{transfer,WAD,clean} \tag{3}$$

Incorporating transfer time slightly increased WAI LOS but reduced WAD LOS, leading to lower EWT values (from 33.23 min in 2023 to 28.82 min in 2024). This demonstrates that separating transfer from stay time normalizes hidden delays and improves the precision of resilience evaluation. Transfer data from 2022 were incomplete and therefore excluded from this analysis.

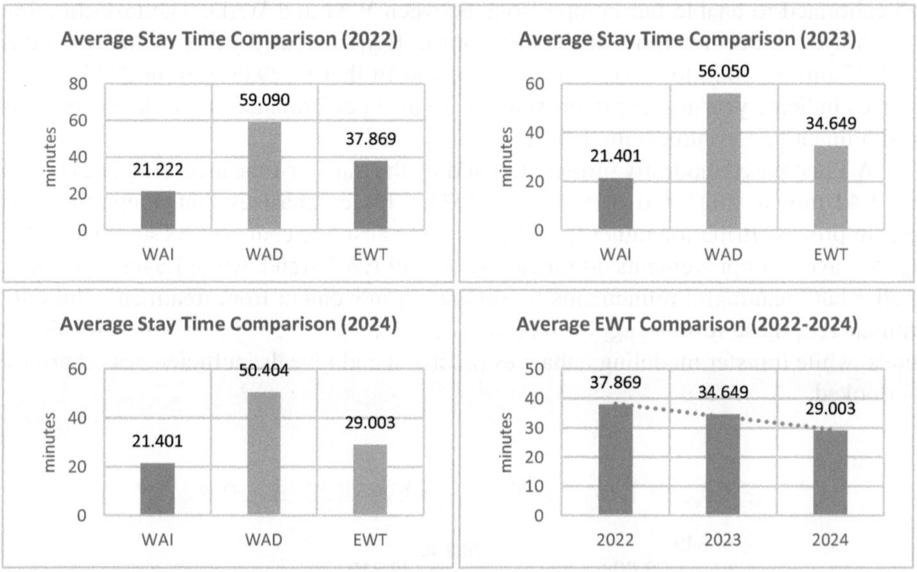

Fig. 2. Simulation results with Layer 1 (task duration only): WAI LOS, WAD LOS, and EWT comparison across 2022–2024.

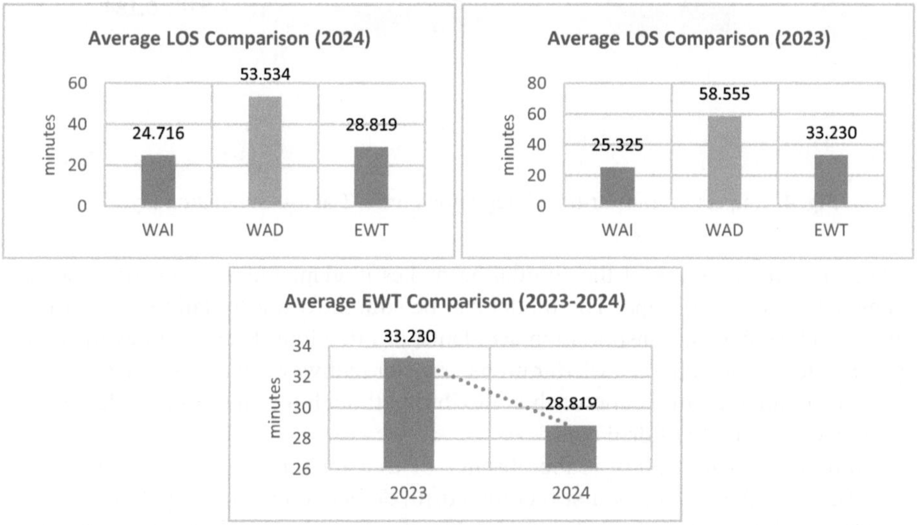

Fig. 3. Simulation results with Layer 2 (task duration + transfer time): WAI LOS, WAD LOS, and EWT comparison for 2023–2024.

4 Discussion

This study introduced a multi-layer simulation framework for hospital disaster drills and calibrated to enable fair comparisons between WAI and WAD. The task-duration layer (Layer 1) deemed most of the variation in EWT across 3 years, with reductions of 37.87 min in 2022 to 34.65 min in 2023, and further to 29.00 min in 2024. These changes indicate year-to-year improvements in drill performance and task execution is the dominant factor influencing EWT.

EWT decreased modestly further after adding the transfer-time layer (Layer 2) which was 1.42 min in 2023 and 0.18 min in 2024. This emphasizes that integrating this layer improves attribution rather than driving large absolute changes. As summarized in Fig. 4, Layer 1 improvements dominate the overall EWT trend, while Layer 2 provides smaller but meaningful refinements by separating movement from treatment. Unitedly summarized, these results suggest that task durations are the main driver of resilience trends, while transfer modeling enhances precision and reveals inefficiencies otherwise overlooked.

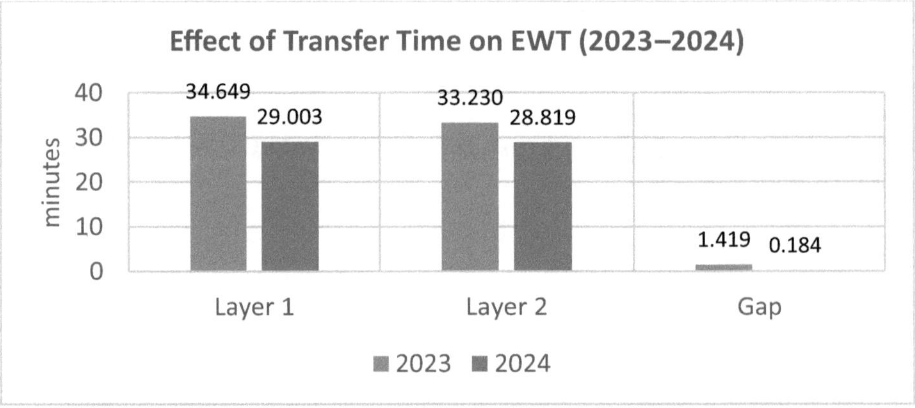

Fig. 4. Impact of transfer-time integration on EWT across simulation layers.

The modular structure of the simulation makes it adaptable to other MCIs scenarios beyond the current scope. The model can be straightforwardly tailored to different context, such as floods, transportation accidents, or infectious disease surges by adjusting parameters which are the task durations, transfer pathways, and resource allocation. The main advantage of this approach is flexibility, though it remains dependent on the availability and quality of drill data.

A limitation of this study is the absence of transfer-time data for the 2022 drill. Since 2022 was the hospital's first recorded drill, defective logging of patient transfers prevented the integration of this layer. Notably, the declining EWT trend is compatible with the hospital's own evaluation which identified 2024 as the best-performing year. However, staff were unable to fully explain why 2024 outcomes were superior, underscoring the added value of simulation in uncovering hidden dynamics behind observed performance.

5 Conclusion

This study developed a multi-layer simulation model to evaluate hospital disaster preparedness, introducing EWT as a metric to compare WAD and WAI. Results showed that task duration (Layer 1) was the dominant factor influencing EWT, with significant reductions observed from 2022 to 2024, while transfer-time (Layer 2) produced smaller decreases but improved attribution of delays by separating treatment from movement. Together, these layers provide a more realistic representation of hospital workflows and highlight trends consistent with the hospital's own evaluation, which identified 2024 as the best-performing year. Limitation of this study is the absence of transfer-time data in 2022, reflecting the challenges of early drill recording. Nevertheless, the framework demonstrates as a performance-monitoring tool for hospitals and can be adapted to other MCIs scenarios. Future work will extend the model to incorporate coordination and communication to enhance its ability to evaluate resilience in complex hospital environments.

Acknowledgments. This work was partly supported by KAKENHI (25H00777).

Disclosure of Interests. The authors have no competing interests to declare that are relevant to the content of this article.

References

1. Toida, C., Muguruma, T., Hashimoto, K.: Hospitals' preparedness to treat pediatric patients during mass casualty incidents. Disaster Med. Public Health Prep. **13**(3), 429–432 (2018). https://doi.org/10.1017/dmp.2018.98
2. Nekoie-Moghadam, M., Kurland, L., Moosazadeh, M., Ingrassia, P.L., Della Corte, F., Djalali, A.: Tools and checklists used for the evaluation of hospital disaster preparedness: A systematic review. Disaster Med. Public Health Prep. **10**(5), 781–788 (2016). https://doi.org/10.1017/dmp.2016.30
3. Ideguchi, T., Kanno, T., Umemoto, M., Kajiyama, K., Ikari, R., Yamazaki, M., Sharikura, S.: Extensive data collection in an in-hospital disaster response exercise for evaluating disaster resilience. AHFE Int. Conf. (2023). https://doi.org/10.54941/ahfe1003068
4. Trucco, P., Nocetti, C., Sannicandro, R., Carlucci, M., Weinstein, E.S., Faccincani, R.: Assessing hospital adaptive resource allocation strategies in responding to mass casualty incidents. Disaster Med. Public Health Prep. **16**(3), 1105–1115 (2021). https://doi.org/10.1017/dmp.2021.62
5. Umemoto, M., Kadono, S., Kanno, T., Kajiyama, K., Sharikura, S., Ikari, R., Yoneyama, M., Chuang, S.: Modeling and simulation of in-hospital disaster medicine in a mass casualty event for the resilience evaluation of BCPS. J. Disaster Res. **18**(2), 104–113 (2023). https://doi.org/10.20965/jdr.2023.p0104
6. Bito, Y., Kanno, T., Kajiyama, K., Yamazaki, M., Yoshida, H., Tsubaki, M., Sharikura, S.: Data collection and analysis of patient and document flow during a disaster exercise at a large hospital. AHFE Int. Conf. (2024). https://doi.org/10.54941/ahfe1004879

Personalized Federated Learning via Dual Alignment of Semantic Knowledge and Feature Prototypes

Bingli Sun[1], Yuchun Tu[1], Hongyan Quan[2], and Xiao Song[1](✉)

[1] School of Cyber Science and Technology, Beihang University, Beijing 100191, China
{youthbl,tuyuchun,songxiao}@buaa.edu.cn
[2] School of Computer Science and Technology, East China Normal University, Shanghai, China
hyquan@cs.ecnu.edu.cn

Abstract. Federated learning (FL) often suffers from client drift and inconsistent representations due to heterogeneous data distributions, limiting both generalization and personalization. Existing prototype-based methods partially address these issues but struggle to unify semantic representations across clients. In this paper, we propose **FedCoAlign**, a personalized federated learning (PFL) framework that jointly employs knowledge distillation and prototype alignment to enhance semantic consistency. Specifically, the global model output serves as soft labels to guide local training and mitigate client drift, while class prototypes are aligned with a global semantic space to improve representation consistency. Compared to existing personalized methods, FedCoAlign does not rely on complex task modeling but achieves performance improvements by introducing lightweight semantic consistency constraints. Experiments on multiple benchmarks show that FedCoAlign achieves superior performance and robustness, especially under highly heterogeneous scenarios, highlighting its effectiveness as a new paradigm for semantic-consistent personalization in federated learning.

Keywords: Personalized Federated Learning · Non-IID Data · Knowledge Distillation · Prototype Learning

1 Introduction

Federated learning provides a promising solution by keeping user data local and exchanging only model parameters [1]. However, in practice, FL often suffers from highly non-independent and identically distributed (Non-IID) client data. To address this, personalized federated learning has been proposed. Existing PFL strategies can be grouped into three categories: 1) data-level methods, which reduce heterogeneity through augmentation [2]; 2) model-level methods, which design parameter update strategies to adapt local models [3]; and 3) server-level methods, which perform personalized aggregation or client selection [4].

Prototype-based PFL has recently attracted attention [5], introducing class-centered prototypes as knowledge intermediaries to align representations across clients. While

W. Cai et al. (Eds.): AsiaSim 2025, CCIS 2727, pp. 252–258, 2026.
https://doi.org/10.1007/978-981-95-4472-1_22

effective, these methods still face two limitations: 1) prototypes are often obtained by simple feature averaging, which lacks semantic discriminability; and 2) prototype alignment does not fully exploit semantic relations between clients and the collaborative information from model outputs, limiting robustness under heterogeneous settings.

To overcome these challenges, we propose FedCoAlign, that achieves dual alignment of semantic knowledge and feature prototypes. Our contributions are threefold:

- This paper introduces semantic distillation by using global model outputs as soft labels to guide local training, mitigating client drift.
- We incorporate prototype alignment to ensure local representations remain consistent with global semantics, enhancing personalization.
- Extensive experiments across multiple datasets show that FedCoAlign achieves superior accuracy, robustness, and scalability.

2 Methodology

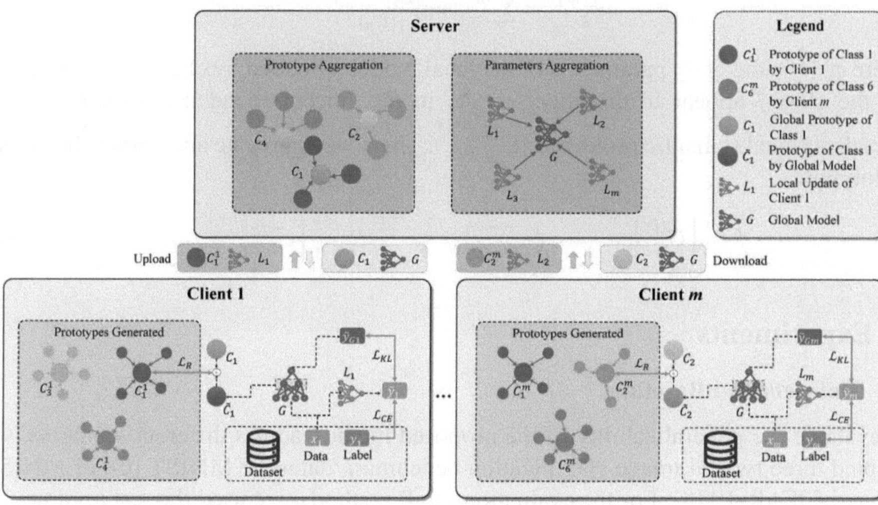

Fig. 1. Overview of FedCoAlign Framework

In this paper, we consider m clients $\{1,2,\ldots,m\}$, and each client i holds a local dataset $\mathcal{D}_i = \{(x_k^{(i)}, y_k^{(i)})\}_{k=1}^{|\mathcal{D}_i|}$. The objective function of FedCoAlign is:

$$\arg\min_{\omega_1,\omega_2,\ldots,\omega_m} \sum_{i=1}^{m} \lambda_i L(\mathcal{F}(\omega_i; x), y), \tag{1}$$

where $\lambda_i = {|D_i|}/{\sum_{n=1}^{m} |D_n|}$, $\mathcal{L}$ is the loss function, $|\mathcal{D}_i|$ denotes the number of samples.

The overall FedCoAlign framework proposed in this paper is depicted in Fig. 1. During local training, the objective function is formulated as follows:

$$\mathcal{L}_{local} = \mathcal{L}_{CE} + \beta\mathcal{L}_R + \gamma\mathcal{L}_{KL}, \tag{2}$$

where $\mathcal{L}_{CE}$ is the cross-entropy loss, and β and γ are hyperparameters. $\mathcal{L}_R$ is formulated as follows:

$$\mathcal{L}_R = \sum_j \|(C_G^{(j)} + \overline{C}_G^{(j)}) - C_i^{(j)}\|_2^2, \tag{3}$$

where $C_i^{(j)}$ denotes the prototype of client i on the j-th class, $C_G^{(j)}$ denotes the global prototype aggregated from all clients, and $\overline{C}_G^{(j)}$ denotes the prototype representation generated by the global model on local data. Additionally, this paper introduces a distillation loss based on the Kullback-Leibler divergence (KL divergence):

$$\mathcal{L}_{KL} = D_{KL}\left(q_\tau^S, q_\tau^T\right) = \sum_{c=1}^{\mathbb{C}} q_\tau^T(c)\log\frac{q_\tau^T(c)}{q_\tau^S(c)}, \tag{4}$$

where $q_\tau^S(c)$ is the prediction of local model for class c, $q_\tau^T(c)$ is the soft prediction of the global model for the same class c. $\mathbb{C}$ is the number of classes in the local dataset, and τ is the distillation temperature.

During global aggregation, the model parameter aggregation is shown as follows:

$$\phi_g^{t+1} = \sum_{i=1}^{m} \frac{|\mathcal{D}_i|}{\sum_{n=1}^{m}|\mathcal{D}_n|}\phi_i^{t+1}, \tag{5}$$

where ϕ_i^{t+1} is the body parameters of the local model uploaded by client i after training. Let the class j appear in the client set $\mathcal{N}_j$ in the current round. Each client $i \in \mathcal{N}_j$ uploads its local semantic prototype $\{C_i^{(j)}\}^{t+1}$. Then, we aggregate and update the global prototype:

$$\left\{C_G^{(j)}\right\}^{t+1} = \frac{1}{|\mathcal{N}_j|}\sum_{i\in\mathcal{N}_j} \frac{|\mathcal{D}_{i,j}|}{\sum_{n\in\mathcal{N}_j}|\mathcal{D}_{n,j}|}\left\{C_i^{(j)}\right\}^{t+1}. \tag{6}$$

3 Experiments

3.1 Datasets and Baselines

To evaluate the generalizability of the proposed method across different scenarios, we adopted three typical image classification benchmark datasets: MNIST [6], FEMNIST [7], and CIFAR-10 [8]. For the evaluation of all methods, we used the test accuracy of the best single global model as the metric for traditional FL methods, and the average test set accuracy of the best local models as the metric for PFL methods. We conducted a comprehensive comparison, including: Local, FedAvg [1], FedProx [9], FedPer [10], FeSEM [11], FedRep [12], FedProto [5].

3.2 Main Results

From the results in Table 1, FedCoAlign achieved the best performance in most heterogeneous settings. For example, on the MNIST dataset, FedCoAlign achieved an accuracy of 98.37% when n is 3, significantly outperforming FedProto (97.13%) and FeSEM (95.26%). This indicates that the dual semantic alignment mechanism and parameter decoupling strategy proposed in this paper are more advantageous in collaborative modeling of the semantic space.

Table 1. Comparison of FL methods on three benchmark datasets with non-IID settings

Dataset	Method	Stdev	Average Test Accuracy		
			$n = 3$	$n = 4$	$n = 5$
MNIST	Local	2	94.05 ± 2.93	93.35 ± 3.26	92.92 ± 3.17
	FedAvg	2	95.04 ± 6.48	94.32 ± 4.89	93.22 ± 4.39
	FedProx	2	96.26 ± 2.89	96.40 ± 3.33	95.65 ± 3.38
	FedPer	2	95.57 ± 2.96	96.44 ± 2.62	95.55 ± 3.13
	FeSEM	2	95.26 ± 3.48	97.06 ± 2.72	96.31 ± 2.41
	FedRep	2	94.96 ± 2.78	95.18 ± 3.80	94.94 ± 2.81
	FedProto	2	97.13 ± 0.30	96.80 ± 0.41	96.70 ± 0.29
	FedCoAlign	2	**98.64 ± 0.65**	**97.46 ± 0.38**	**96.75 ± 0.36**
FEMNIST	Local	1	92.50 ± 10.42	91.16 ± 5.64	87.91 ± 8.44
	FedAvg	1	94.50 ± 5.29	91.39 ± 5.23	90.95 ± 7.22
	FedProx	1	94.53 ± 5.33	90.71 ± 6.24	91.33 ± 7.32
	FedPer	1	93.47 ± 5.44	90.22 ± 7.63	87.73 ± 9.64
	FeSEM	1	93.39 ± 6.75	91.06 ± 6.43	89.61 ± 7.89
	FedRep	1	93.36 ± 5.34	91.41 ± 5.89	89.98 ± 6.88
	FedProto	1	96.82 ± 1.75	**94.93 ± 1.61**	93.67 ± 2.23
	FedCoAlign	1	**97.38 ± 1.66**	94.79 ± 2.04	**93.69 ± 2.36**
CIFAR-10	Local	1	79.72 ± 9.45	67.62 ± 7.15	58.64 ± 6.57
	FedAvg	1	81.72 ± 2.77	76.77 ± 2.37	75.74 ± 2.61
	FedProx	1	83.25 ± 2.44	79.20 ± 1.31	76.19 ± 2.23
	FedPer	1	84.38 ± 4.58	78.73 ± 4.59	76.21 ± 4.27
	FeSEM	1	80.19 ± 3.31	76.40 ± 3.23	74.17 ± 3.51
	FedRep	1	81.44 ± 10.48	76.93 ± 7.46	73.36 ± 7.04
	FedProto	1	84.49 ± 1.97	79.12 ± 2.03	77.08 ± 1.98
	FedCoAlign	1	**85.80 ± 1.88**	**80.88 ± 1.86**	**78.63 ± 1.75**

3.3 Effect of Hyperparameters

In this section, we discuss the impact of key hyperparameters on model performance in Table 2, including local batch size B, local epoch E, and the number of clients m.

a) Effect of B: Smaller B values enable the model to update gradients more frequently, enhancing generalization capabilities but potentially increasing variance. Moderately larger B values help stabilize training, thereby improving performance.

b) Effect of E: More local training stages enable each client to better adapt to its local data distribution, thereby improving the performance of personalized models. However, setting E too high may lead to issues such as overfitting or slowed convergence.

c) Effect of m: When $m = 20$, the model achieved optimal performance of 98.64% and 85.80% on MNIST and CIFAR-10, respectively. As m increases to 30 and 50, the model performance shows a slight decline. Furthermore, we visualized the accuracy and loss curves as the number of clients participating in training increased, as illustrated in Fig. 2. The above experiments thoroughly validate that our method can maintain the stability of the training process and the consistency of model performance even when the number of clients is expanded, demonstrating excellent generalization capabilities.

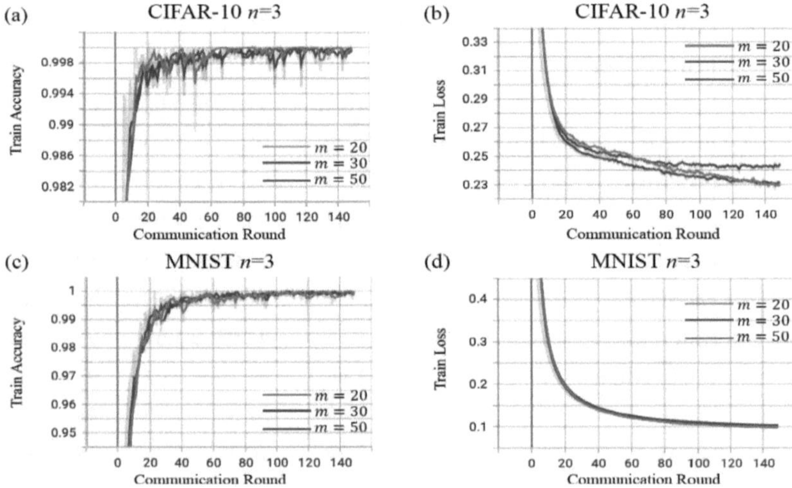

Fig. 2. Model training performance under different numbers of clients

Table 2. Discussion of hyperparameters on model performance

Hyperparameters	Settings	MNIST	CIFAR-10
Effect of B	$B = 4$	**98.64 ± 0.65**	59.29 ± 2.38
	$B = 8$	98.26 ± 0.52	79.14 ± 2.52
	$B = 16$	98.23 ± 0.39	**85.80 ± 1.88**
	$B = 32$	98.37 ± 0.43	84.77 ± 2.24
Effect of E	$E = 1$	96.25 ± 0.61	82.62 ± 2.53
	$E = 3$	96.87 ± 0.44	83.15 ± 2.37
	$E = 5$	97.36 ± 0.78	84.59 ± 2.51
	$E = 8$	**98.64 ± 0.65**	**85.80 ± 1.88**
Effect of m	$m = 20$	**98.64 ± 0.65**	**85.80 ± 1.88**

(continued)

Table 2. (*continued*)

Hyperparameters	Settings	MNIST	CIFAR-10
	$m = 30$	96.97 ± 0.38	82.32 ± 2.18
	$m = 50$	96.38 ± 0.46	82.73 ± 1.95

3.4 Visualization

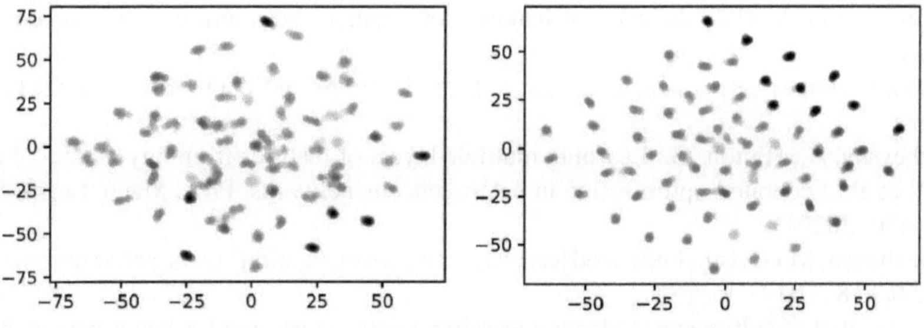

(a) FedPer (b) FedCoAlign

Fig. 3. Comparison of prototype representations for samples on MNIST

In Fig. 3, we used t-SNE to visualize the samples in MNIST test set and compared our method with FedPer to show the differences between the two methods in terms of prototype representation. It is evident that our proposed method achieves superior performance, as prototypes of different classes exhibit distinct boundaries.

4 Conclusion

We proposed FedCoAlign, a personalized federated learning framework that effectively mitigates client drift and enhances semantic consistency by aligning local prototypes with global semantics and incorporating soft-label guidance. Experiments across multiple datasets confirm its superiority over existing methods in accuracy, robustness, and scalability. In future work, we plan to integrate privacy-preserving techniques such as differential privacy to further enhance security and practical applicability.

Acknowledgments. This work was supported by the Beijing Natural Science Foundation (L233005) and the National Key Research and Development Program of China under Grant 2023YFB3308200.

Disclosure of Interests. No potential conflict of interest was reported by the author(s).

References

1. McMahan, B., et al.: Communication-efficient learning of deep networks from decentralized data. Artif. Intell. Stat. (PMLR) (2017)
2. Yoon, T. et al.: Fedmix: Approximation of mixup under mean augmented federated learning. arXiv preprint arXiv:2107.00233 (2021)
3. Chen, H.Y., Chao, W.L.: On bridging generic and personalized federated learning for image classification. arXiv preprint arXiv:2107.00778 (2021)
4. Morafah, M. et al.: Flis: Clustered federated learning via inference similarity for non-iid data distribution." IEEE Open J. Comput. Soc. **4**, 109–120 (2023)
5. Tan, Yue. et al.: Fedproto: Federated prototype learning across heterogeneous clients. Proceedings of the AAAI conference on artificial intelligence, vol. 36. No. 8 (2022)
6. LeCun, Y.:The MNIST database of handwritten digits (1998). http://yann.lecun.com/exdb/mnist/
7. Caldas, S. et al.: Leaf: A benchmark for federated settings. arXiv preprint arXiv:1812.01097 (2018)
8. Krizhevsky, A., Hinton, G.: Learning multiple layers of features from tiny images, 7 (2009)
9. Li, T. et al.: Federated optimization in heterogeneous networks. Proc. Mach. Learn. Syst. **2,** 429–450 (2020)
10. Arivazhagan, M.G. et al.: Federated learning with personalization layers. arXiv preprint arXiv: 1912.00818 (2019)
11. Long, G. et al.: Multi-center federated learning: clients clustering for better personalization. World Wide Web **26**(1), 481–500 (2023)
12. Collins, L. et al.: Exploiting shared representations for personalized federated learning. International conference on machine learning (PMLR) (2021)

A Chain-of-Thought-Based Model Auto-Configuration Method for Customized Production Simulation

Na Li[1], Yuanjun Laili[1,2,3(✉)], Lei Ren[1,2,3], and Lin Zhang[1,3]

[1] School of Automation Science and Electrical Engineering, Beihang University, 100191 Beijing, China
[2] Zhongguancun Laboratory, 100094 Beijing, China
[3] Hangzhou International Innovation Institute of Beihang University, 311115 Hangzhou, China
lailiyuanjun@buaa.edu.cn

Abstract. Simulation is a fundamental solution for investigating the capacity and efficiency of complex workshops in discrete manufacturing. With increasing custom production orders, it is more efficient to establish an extendable simulation model and make auto-configuration to analyze different kinds of reconfigurable production workspace, rather than construct a simulation model for each scenario. However, it is difficult to automatically configure a simulation model with long programming codes and complex coupled constraints among orders, materials, production machines, and production lines. To solve this problem, this paper establishes a key-value mapping rule to map key and repetitive information and decouple constraints among different parts of simulation model. Then, a chain-of-thought-based model auto-configuration method is proposed to configure a simulation model by using large-language model for programming code generation. To ensure correct and credible simulation model configuration, an automatic evaluation pipeline is also established. Experimental results on a typical extendable Anylogic simulation model for reconfigurable production workshop show that the proposed method can automatically generate appropriate simulation models for different scenarios with high precision greater than 90%.

Keywords: Simulation Model Auto-Configuration · Large Language Model · Key-Value Mapping Rule · Chain-of-Thought · Prompt Optimization

1 Introduction

Against the backdrop of digital transformation in the manufacturing industry, workshop production simulation has emerged as a critical tool for optimizing production processes and improving production efficiency and quality [1]. Industrial simulation software is commonly used to validate production plans, with

W. Cai et al. (Eds.): AsiaSim 2025, CCIS 2727, pp. 259–265, 2026.
https://doi.org/10.1007/978-981-95-4472-1_23

production parameters (equipment quantity, quality, production relationships) being key concerns; accurate configuration of these parameters ensures models operate as intended.

Large language models (LLMs) show potential in natural language processing and code generation but may underperform in automatically configuring workshop simulation models, struggling with configuration code structure or filtering interference. Machine learning, despite reducing reliance on professionals, is constrained by rigid templates, limiting non-professionals across scenarios. Although JSON is widely used in model configuration, JSON's lengthy, coupled nested outputs for configuration needs are ineffective for small-scale LLMs, necessitating intermediate rules to generate pre-configured data and optimize LLM output efficiency.

2 An Extendable Simulation Model for Customized Production

We adopted a workshop production simulation model with two core components: workshop operations (encompassing equipment and operational logic) and order allocation. Equipment parameters (location, quantity, efficiency) determine individual equipment performance, but their operation depends on other system components—mediated by operational logic. Equipment specifications are defined during initialization, remaining constant or changing only under specific conditions in a single run. However, the model's external interaction capability is equally critical [2]: order parameters enter dynamically/randomly during runtime to guide responses. Unlike preconfigured static or conditionally variable parameters, order parameters are not set beforehand.

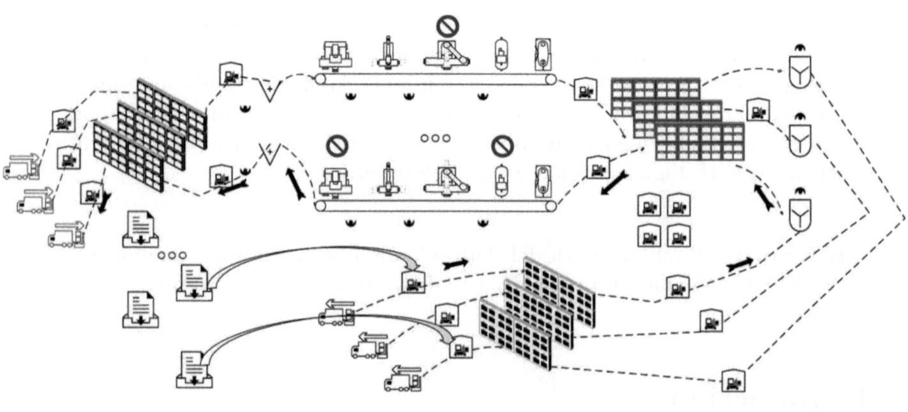

Fig. 1. Model Structure

The simulation model employed in this study can be roughly divided into four stages: raw material input, processing of raw materials into semi-finished products, assembly of semi-finished products into finished products, and finished product output (see Fig. 1).

3 A Chain-of-Thought-Based Model Auto-Configuration Method

3.1 The Key-Value Mapping Rule

When configuring workshop production simulation models, with x raw materials processed into y semi-finished products (xy references) and assembled into z finished products (yz references), describing these coupled parameters results in JSON keys with excessive characters but little useful information (Fig. 2).

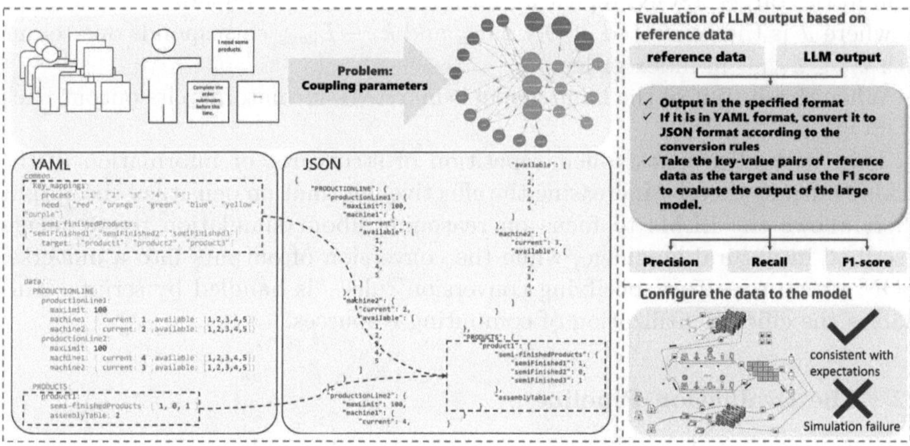

Fig. 2. Mapping rule, prompts and evaluation pipeline

We propose a YAML-based key-value mapping: generated YAML as pre-configuration to derive JSON avoids long LLM outputs, boosting information density. This reduces characters to 10%–50% of direct JSON (depending on independent/non-independent parameter ratio) while enabling full JSON restoration.

JSON stores parameters as key-value pairs (keys = parameter names, values = values). Duplicate keys form a list (L_{keys}) for reuse.

Let the YAML data be $Y = \{C, D\}$.The mapping rules specify YAML with two top-level keys:

- "common" section (C): Stores repeatable information (e.g., parameter name lists) identified by a common_key for later calls (L_{keys}).

$$C = \{K : L_{\text{keys}}\}, L_{\text{keys}} = [k_1, k_2, \ldots, k_n] \tag{1}$$

- "data" section (D): Uses common_key to pair originally repeated key structures with value lists (L_{vals}) for expansion ($L_{\text{vals},i}$).

$$D = \{d_i : \{K : L_{\text{vals},i}\}\}_{i=1}^{m}, L_{\text{vals},i} = [v_{i1}, v_{i2}, \ldots, v_{in}] \tag{2}$$

This unifies repeated information under one identifier and references it elsewhere, reducing characters and improving efficiency.

The mapping function $\Phi : Y \to J$ is defined as:

$$\Phi(Y) = \{d_i : \{K : \{k_j : v_{ij} \mid j = 1, 2, \ldots, n\}\} \mid i = 1, 2, \ldots, m\} \tag{3}$$

To convert YAML to JSON for model configuration: Using the "data" section as a template, recursively check for expandable keys (common_keys). For such keys, traverse L_{keys} and L_{vals}, form sub-key-value pairs in sequence, and store them in the target JSON, repeating until conversion is complete.

where J is the generated JSON data, and $k_j \in L_{\text{keys}}$ corresponds one-to-one with $v_{ij} \in L_{\text{vals},i}$ in index order.

When the output of the large model is in YAML format, map its output back to JSON.

This method avoids explicit repetition of structures or information in the LLMs's output, thereby increasing the effective information density of the output [3]. It allows the LLMs to focus on reasoning about simulation requirements described in natural language, while the conversion of outputs into a universal JSON structure—after specifying conversion rules—is handled by scripts. This enables the efficient utilization of computing resources.

3.2 The Evaluation Pipeline

The process is as follows: Since prompts mandate the model to output only configuration data (no irrelevant content), any output with extraneous information is invalid.

For valid outputs, format compliance is verified first. As configuration data here is based on JSON or YAML, subsequent evaluation proceeds only if the LLM outputs data in these standard formats.

The confusion matrix CM = {{TP, FN}, {FP, TN}} is used to evaluate text-based configuration data generation [4]:

$$\text{Precision} = \frac{TP}{TP + FP} \tag{4}$$

$$\text{Recall} = \frac{TP}{TP + FN} \tag{5}$$

$$F_1 = 2 \times \frac{\text{Precision} \times \text{Recall}}{\text{Precision} + \text{Recall}} = \frac{2TP}{2TP + FP + FN} \tag{6}$$

For standardized JSON output by the LLM, we conduct recursive, complete key-value matching against reference data: fully consistent key-value pairs are classified as TP; those in the reference(the original JSON in the dataset) but missing from the LLM output as FN; and those in the LLM output but not in the reference as FP. For standardized YAML output, we first convert it to JSON, then apply the above matching steps. After matching a sample, its evaluation metrics are calculated using Eq. (2), Eq. (3), and Eq. (4).

For this task—aimed at accurate configuration code generation via precise key-value matching—precision is the proportion of LLM-output key-value pairs present in the reference, and recall is the proportion of reference key-value pairs correctly output by the LLM.

4 Experiments

Without ambiguity, this article uses Qwen, Deepseek, and CodeLlama to refer to Qwen 2.5-coder-7b-instruct, Deepseek-coder-6.7b-instruct, and CodeLlama-7b-Instruct, respectively, which are the models we selected (Fig. 3).

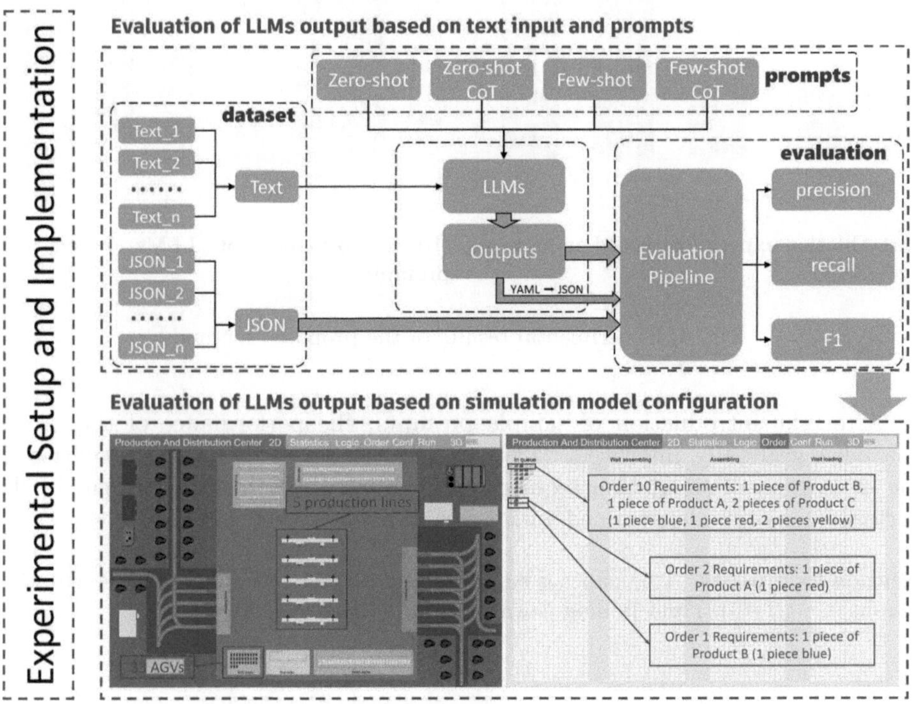

Fig. 3. Experimental Setup and Implementation

Ablation experiments are conducted using four types of prompts: Zero-shot, Zero-shot CoT [5], Few-shot [6], and Few-shot CoT [7] (Fig. 4).

Table 1. Ablation experiment and Performance of LLMs based on prompts

Experiment	prompt	LLM	Precision	Recall	F1-score
Ablation	Zero-shot		0.3412	0.3520	0.3444
	Zero-shot CoT		0.4097	0.4187	0.4125
	Few-shot	Qwen	0.8987	0.8700	0.8832
	Few-shot CoT		**0.9367**	**0.9051**	**0.9197**
Performance	Few-shot	Qwen	0.8987	0.8700	0.8832
		Deepseek	0.8577	0.8244	0.8399
		CodeLlama	0.1505	0.1479	0.1491
	Few-shot CoT	Qwen	**0.9367**	**0.9051**	**0.9197**
		Deepseek	0.8850	0.8518	0.8672
		CodeLlama	0.0950	0.0941	0.0945

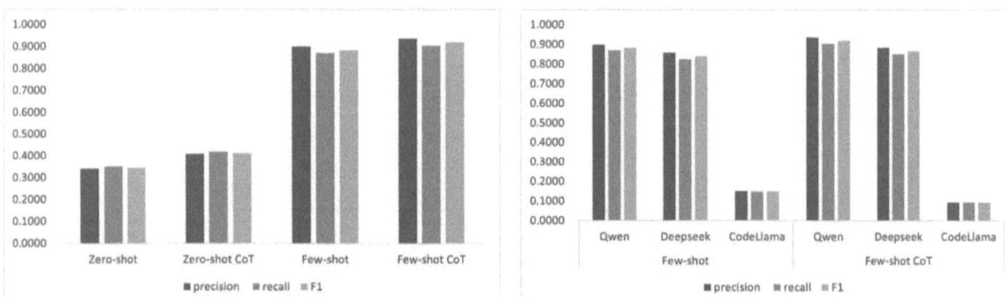

(a) Ablation experiment based on prompts (b) Performance of LLMs based on prompts

Fig. 4. Experimental results of the proposed method

After the introduction of sample prompts, the performance of the model has been gradually improved. Different models have different sensitivities to the expression of simulation requirements, which is particularly evident in the performance of models trained with less Chinese corpora.

Acknowledgments. This paper is supported by Beijing Natural Science Foundation (Grant No. L241018) and Beijing Nova Program (Grant No. 2024085).

References

1. Akhavan, A., Jalali, M.S.: Generative ai and simulation modeling: how should you (not) use large language models like chatgpt. Syst. Dyn. Rev. **40**(3), e1773 (2024)
2. Law, A.M., Kelton, W.D., Kelton, W.D.: Simulation Modeling and Analysis, vol. 3. Mcgraw-hill, New York (2007)
3. Min, S., et al.: Rethinking the role of demonstrations: what makes in-context learning work? arXiv preprint arXiv:2202.12837 (2022)

4. Powers, D.M.: Evaluation: from precision, recall and f-measure to roc, informedness, markedness and correlation. arXiv preprint arXiv:2010.16061 (2020)
5. Kojima, T., Gu, S.S., Reid, M., Matsuo, Y., Iwasawa, Y.: Large language models are zero-shot reasoners. Adv. Neural Inf. Process. Syst. **35**, 22199–22213 (2022)
6. Brown, T., et al.: Language models are few-shot learners. Adv. Neural Inf. Process. Syst. **33**, 1877–1901 (2020)
7. Wei, J., et al.: Chain-of-thought prompting elicits reasoning in large language models. Adv. Neural. Inf. Process. Syst. **35**, 24824–24837 (2022)

Entropy-Based Visualization of Missing Regions in 2.5D Cultural Heritage Point Clouds

Qingyu Mao[1], Liang Li[2(✉)], and Satoshi Tanaka[2(✉)]

[1] Graduate School of Information Science and Engineering, Ritsumeikan University, Osaka, Japan
is0597rs@ed.ritsumei.ac.jp

[2] College of Information Science and Engineering, Ritsumeikan University, Osaka, Japan
liliang@fc.ritsumei.ac.jp, stanaka@is.ritsumei.ac.jp

Abstract. 3D measurement point clouds have become a widely used medium for the digital archive of cultural heritage. However, for 2.5D data such as reliefs, scanning is typically performed from a frontal viewpoint, which often re-sults in missing regions, especially for areas with considerable thickness. In large-scale measurement tasks, detecting such incomplete areas is both chal-lenging and prone to low accuracy. In this paper, we propose a method based on the entropy of local linearity to effectively emphasize and visual-ize the boundaries of these missing regions within 3D point clouds. The approach demonstrates strong potential as an auxiliary tool for scanning quality assessment and for enhancing the geometric reliability of heritage point cloud datasets.

Keywords: Entropy · Point Clouds · Missing Regions

1 Introduction

With the advancement of 3D scanning technologies like laser scanning and photogrammetry [1], point clouds are increasingly used in fields such as cultural heritage preservation and virtual reality (VR) [2,3]. For outdoor cultural assets vulnerable to weathering, effective digital preservation is essential.

In computer vision, digital archiving has emerged as a key solution, enabling long-term storage and visualization without physical degradation. Advances in measurement and drone-based capture have further facilitated the acquisition of high-resolution 3D point clouds.

However, for large-scale outdoor heritage sites, missing regions due to incomplete scanning or sparse sampling are inevitable. These regions can hinder practical use. Manual annotation is labor-intensive and error-prone, and reconstruction methods often rely on speculation rather than true geometry.

This study proposes a method for effectively highlighting missing regions in 2.5D point clouds, namely, point clouds that capture relief-like shapes with

W. Cai et al. (Eds.): AsiaSim 2025, CCIS 2727, pp. 266–271, 2026.
https://doi.org/10.1007/978-981-95-4472-1_24

surface undulations, by statistically computing the local entropy of linearity. This helps during scanning by precisely identifying data loss. Future work includes extending the method to general point clouds with transparent visualization and exploring its use for detecting actual deterioration.

2 Brief Review of Point-Feature Extraction (PFE)

2.1 Overview

Point-Feature extraction (PFE) is the feature emphasis method we adopt in this work [4]. This method focuses on the local distribution of points and characterizes local geometric features by analyzing the eigenvalues of the covariance matrix obtained through Principal Component Analysis (PCA) of neighboring point coordinates.

Points with feature values exceeding a specified threshold are visually emphasized using highlight colors and point duplication [5], thereby enhancing their visibility in the final visualization.

2.2 Local Principal Component Analysis

For a given input point cloud, we compute a local 3D tensor, specifically, a covariance matrix, for each point based on the distribution of its neighboring points within a fixed radius. This radius is usually set to a few hundredths of the length of the bounding box diagonal.

From the covariance matrix, we obtain three non-negative eigenvalues, $(\lambda_1, \lambda_2, \lambda_3)$, sorted in descending order such that $\lambda_1 \geq \lambda_2 \geq \lambda_3$. The square roots of these eigenvalues reflect the rough extension of the neighboring points along the corresponding eigenvectors.

Points lying along strongly linear structures tend to have a significantly larger λ_1, while λ_2 and λ_3 are relatively small. To normalize the feature value, we define the local linearity score using the following equation:

$$\text{Linearity} := \frac{\lambda_1 - \lambda_2}{\lambda_1} \tag{1}$$

In this study, we normalize the linearity by dividing its value by the maximum value, allowing us to select an appropriate threshold within the range of zero and unity. This formulation will get a high value when λ_1 is dominant, indicating strong linearity structures. Points with linearity values exceeding a predefined threshold are classified as feature points and passed to the next stage for visualization.

2.3 Feature Enhancement and Visualization Results

As described in the previous section, feature points are typically visualized using a uniform highlight color and point duplication. Coloring helps make the feature re-gions visually prominent, while point duplication significantly increases the opacity of these regions in transparent visualization.

Fig. 1. where high-linearity regions are visualized in red, demonstrates the effectiveness of this approach in enhancing the visibility of structurally significant. (Color figure online)

3 Porposed Method

3.1 Overview

In this section, we present the specific method proposed in this paper. Our approach consists of two main stages:

In the first stage, we compute a local linearity measure for each point in the point cloud to evaluate its surrounding geometric structure. This linearity value is stored as an additional attribute for each point to support the subsequent processing.

In the second stage, we compute the information entropy of linearity values within a spherical neighborhood around each point. The resulting entropy characterizes the degree of structural disorder in the region. Points with entropy values exceeding a predefined threshold are emphasized as features and visualized together with the origi-nal point cloud.

3.2 Boundaries of Data Missing Regions

In 2.5D point clouds of planar carvings, data loss typically occurs in regions with physical thickness, particularly in raised structures that extend perpendicular to the base plane. Missing areas are almost always connected to well-measured regions, forming boundary zones where point cloud properties change abruptly. These transi-tional areas constitute the primary targets for our feature enhancement and visualiza-tion method.

Such boundaries often exhibit noticeable changes in point density. However, missing areas do not always imply a complete absence of data; in many cases, the point cloud may still contain scattered or patchy points within these regions(see Fig. 2).

Since our objective is to detect and emphasize these line-like transitional structures, we evaluate the local linearity of each point using the method described in Sect. 2. To capture the fine-grained local geometry around defect boundaries, we use a relative-ly small neighborhood radius for linearity estimation, typically set to 1/500 of the bounding-box diagonal length

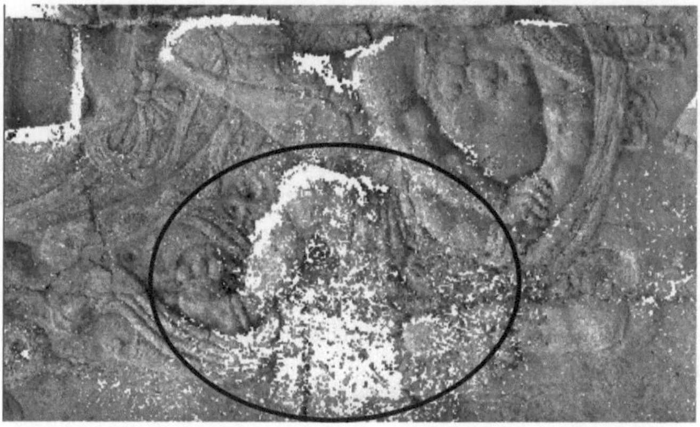

Fig. 2. Missing region in the point cloud (Juyong Pass, China)

3.3 Use of Entropy to Detect Boundaries of Data Missing Regions

As discussed in Sect. 3.2, the characteristics of missing regions in real-world 2.5D point clouds are often complex. Simple point density-based criteria are insufficient for reliably identifying the target regions. However, the transitional boundaries between well-scanned and missing regions are consistently accompanied by sharp variations in local linearity.

Even in missing regions where points are sparsely distributed in clusters, the inherent uncertainty of these areas leads to highly unstable and disordered linearity patterns. While other feature values may also exhibit inconsistency in such regions, our focus on line-like boundary transitions, combined with experimental observations, suggests that entropy computed from local linearity provides a more effective means of extracting the desired features.

In our method, information entropy is used to evaluate the degree of disorder in the local linearity distribution. Like the PFE approach, we focus on local geometric properties, but in contrast to the linearity computation stage, we typically use a larger neighborhood radius, e.g.$1/200$ of the bounding box diagonal length, for entropy estimation.

Since linearity values tend to be similar within small neighborhoods, a larger radius helps capture more diverse structures, thereby increasing the distinction between feature and non-feature regions.

To compute entropy, we divide the normalized linearity range $[0, 1]$ into N discrete bins and calculate the proportion of neighboring points falling into each bin. Intuitively, this corresponds to estimating the probability that a randomly selected point within the neighborhood has a linearity value falling into a specific subrange.

For each point, the disorder of linearity within its neighborhood is quantified using the following entropy-based formula.

$$E = -\sum_{i=1}^{N} p(i) \cdot \ln p(i) \tag{2}$$

where $p(i)$ denotes the proportion of points falling within each bin. As observed, the entropy value approaches zero when the proportion tends toward 0 or 1, indicating a relatively deterministic distribution. In contrast, higher values occur when the proportions are more balanced, reflecting a greater degree of disorder.

The boundary of the missing data region can be highlighted, as shown in Fig. 1, using feature-enhanced visualization that assigns distinctive colors to areas with high entropy.

4 Experimental Results

Fig. 3. A relief panel on the inner walls of the Cloud Platform at Juyong Pass, China

Fig. 4. Wall reliefs in the Borobudur Temple

Figure 3 and 4 show the feature-enhanced visualizations based on the entropy of definition (2). The upper image shows the result for a relief panel on the inner walls of the Cloud Platform at Juyong Pass, China, and the lower image for a wall relief of the Borobudur Temple, Indonesia. The boundaries of data missing regions are suc-cessfully extracted and visualized in red.

5 Conclusion

In this paper, we presented a method for highlighting missing regions in 2.5D cultur-al heritage point clouds based on the entropy of local linearity. By combining small-scale linearity analysis with large-scale entropy evaluation, our approach effectively emphasizes the structural inconsistency near data loss boundaries, which are often difficult to detect by traditional features such as point density or curvature.

The results show that the method can successfully visualize potential missing regions in relief-type point clouds, providing useful feedback for quality assessment.

In future work, we plan to extend the proposed method to more complex real-world 3D point clouds, and to incorporate transparent visualization techniques to facilitate rapid identification of missing regions, even in objects with intricate internal and external structures. Furthermore, we aim to explore the use of additional feature val-ues for evaluating not only geometric degradation but also surface color deterioration, with the goal of developing a more versatile and generalizable tool for point cloud analysis in cultural heritage contexts.

Acknowledgments. We would like to express our gratitude to Fadjar I. Thufail, Brahmantara, and Hiroshi Yamaguchi for their invaluable assistance in measuring the Borobudur Reliefs.

References

1. Baltsavias, E.P.: A comparison between photogrammetry and laser scanning. ISPRS J. Photogramm. Remote. Sens. **54**(2–3), 83–94 (1999)
2. Discher, S., Masopust, L., Schulz, S.: A point-based and image-based multi-pass rendering technique for visualizing massive 3D point clouds in VR environments (2018)
3. Thiel, F., et al.: Interaction and locomotion techniques for the exploration of massive 3D point clouds in VR environments. Int. Arch. Photogramm. Remote Sens. Spat. Inf. Sci. **42**, 623–630 (2018)
4. Dittrich, A., Weinmann, M., Hinz, S.: Analytical and numerical investigations on the accuracy and robustness of geometric features extracted from 3D point cloud data. ISPRS J. Photogramm. Remote Sens. **126**, 195–208 (2017)
5. Kawakami, K., et al.: Opacity-based edge highlighting for transparent visualization of 3D scanned point clouds. ISPRS Ann. Photogramm. Remote Sens. Spat. Inf. Sci. **2**, 373–380 (2020)

Modular Physics Simulation Approach for Amazon FC - Case Study

Sumant Joshi, Gandhi Chidambaram(✉), Tarciana Almeida, Anish Goyal, and Chin-Yuan Tseng

Worldwide Design Engineering, Amazon, Bellevue, WA, USA
gcchidam@amazon.com

Abstract. Physics simulation model have become essential tools in Amazon's fulfillment network for analyzing and optimizing material handling equipment (MHE) design. This paper presents a modular framework developed using Emulate3D to model MHE across multiple Amazon fulfillment facilities. The framework incorporates three main components: material to be handled module, material flow control module and package chute module. Through comprehensive validation against pilot results and statistical analysis, the model demonstrates high fidelity in replicating real-world operational dynamics. The framework's applications span from future automated conveyance flow control logic optimization to existing chute design retrofits. The physics model is used to identify chute jams before launch, location of sensors, optimal jam free merge logic, reducing time/cost for development. Key challenges including package softness, human operator behavior representation, and unexpected operational events are discussed. The study concludes by highlighting future directions in physics simulation to enhance simulation fidelity.

Keywords: Physics Simulation · Fulfillment center · Flow control · Package Merge simulation · Simulation driven decision · Logistics Simulation · Package Jam Detection · First Time Launch Quality

1 Background

Amazon's fulfillment facilities incorporate various automation technologies, multiple chute applications and miles of conveyance with sophisticated flow control logic. The design complexities necessitate sophisticated simulation tools for design validation against target system throughput and potential jam locations. Different vendors have different merge logic or chute designs. Modularization simplifies modeling of these similar components. Discrete event simulation modeling approach often struggles to capture the full complexity of these systems, particularly regarding package interactions. This study presents a modular simulation framework that addresses these challenges through flexible merge flow control configuration and chute testing module. The framework enables both

W. Cai et al. (Eds.): AsiaSim 2025, CCIS 2727, pp. 272–278, 2026.
https://doi.org/10.1007/978-981-95-4472-1_25

tactical optimization of current designs and strategic evaluation of future flow control concepts, while accounting for real-world constraints and operational variability.

2 Simulation Approach

A comprehensive physics simulation workflow traditionally encompasses three fundamental phases: CAD file import, custom feature setup, and results capture.

The initial phase begins with CAD geometry import through industry standard STEP/IGES formats, requiring careful attention to geometry preparation, automated mesh generation with quality checks, and appropriate material property assignments while preserving assembly relationships. The preparation process ensures geometric accuracy and mesh quality, forming the foundation for reliable simulation results.

The second phase, custom feature setup, represents the core of the simulation process. It involves defining the physics model through solver selection (volumetric, linear, and planar), specification of boundary and initial conditions, material handling configuration, and establishment of contact interfaces. A modular framework was developed using customized modules for material handling, flow control logic, and package chute simulation to accelerate model development. This framework includes a specialized material catalog and enables systematic testing of different merge control logic combinations. The system facilitates benchmarking of various merge control scenarios against target system throughput and potential package jams. For chute design validation, the framework incorporates a specialized testing module that analyzes package velocity, jams, and capacity.

The final phase focuses on results capture and analysis, encompassing real-time visualization, data extraction, and post-processing calculations. This includes generating comprehensive analytics such as package jam analysis, speed profile logging, and reporting package singulation percentages. The workflow concludes with systematic report generation, result validation, and data export in various formats (CSV, Images, Videos, HTML). The process operates iteratively, enabling continuous refinement based on initial results and optimization requirements, ultimately reducing the need for costly physical design iterations and prototyping (Fig. 1).

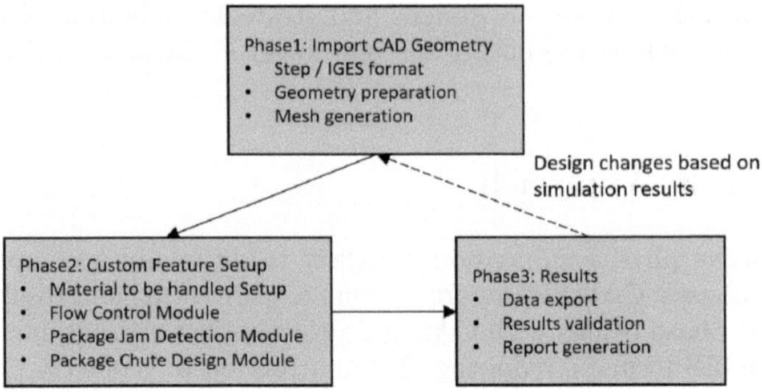

Fig. 1. Methodology

3 Literature Review

This literature review examines key developments in modular physics simulation approaches. Simulation modeling and analysis can be time consuming and expensive [1]. Simulations are primarily developed as decision support tools, where the objectives directly influence the selection of simulation models, input parameters, and desired output metrics, highlighting the need for standardized approaches in simulation development. McLean et al. [2] propose a framework for simulation standards development in manufacturing, emphasizing the importance of neutral model libraries and interface data standards to enhance the efficiency. Bernatovych et al. [3] proposes a novel software architecture for physics simulation that integrates three key concepts: a modular physics engine for flexibility, a structured physics pipeline for efficient resource management, collectively enabling more scalable and adaptable physics simulations. Negahban et al. [4] mentions physics-based simulation has become increasingly important in the logistics and warehousing domain. While traditional discrete-event simulation (DES) has been widely used, the integration of physics-based modeling enables more realistic analysis of conveyors. This review of existing literature reveals trend toward modular physics based simulation.

4 Case Study

4.1 Material to Be Handled

The properties of the material being handled are crucial for accurate physics simulations in flow control systems. Different package types were modeled using Blender software to incorporate different package textures, package material coefficient of friction, geometry and center of mass offset. These package types were further optimized to reduce the number of vertices for faster computation. The packages were imported as wavefront file format into Emulate3D software to create customized catalog items as shown in Fig. 2. Custom package generator also generates tote filled with different package types to incorporate accurate interactions between packages. The model's flexibility is further demonstrated with customized package generator using C# script to simulate instantaneous spikes in bulk package flow. Accurately modeling these properties in simulations ensures that the flow control logic and chute designs can be validated under realistic conditions, leading to more reliable and efficient system designs.

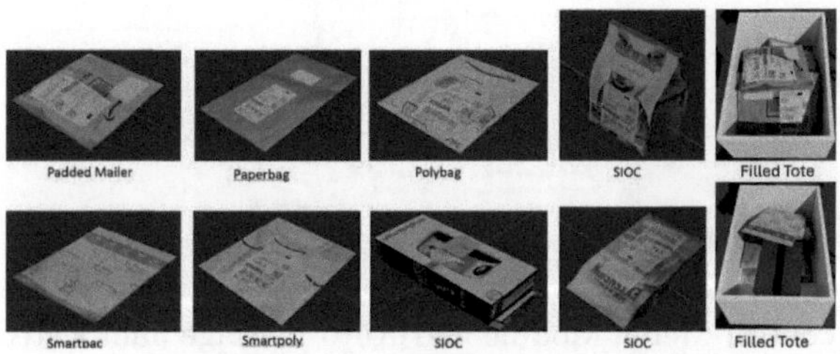

Fig. 2. Material to be handled

4.2 Flow Control Logic

Physics-based simulation proved instrumental in validating the flow control logic by accurately modeling package dynamics for Amazon fulfillment conveyance system. Customized package merge logic (i.e. opportunity merge, priority merge, timer based merge, slug merge and combinations of slug and opportunistic merge) were developed in Emulated3D using quicklogic scripting and saved as catalog items as shown in Fig. 3. This modular approach helped running different virtual scenarios that stakeholders could visualize without the costs and risks of physical testing. The simulation environment allowed for rapid iteration and refinement of merge logic, ultimately leading to a more robust and reliable system that could handle both steady-state operations and edge cases. Implementation of auto package jam detection module with an embedded C# script as shown in Fig. 3 automatically takes images of jammed packages and clears them while the simulation is running. This helps to expedite simulation runs. The physics simulation model guided the design and controls team choose optimized flow control logic with highest system throughput and no package jams.

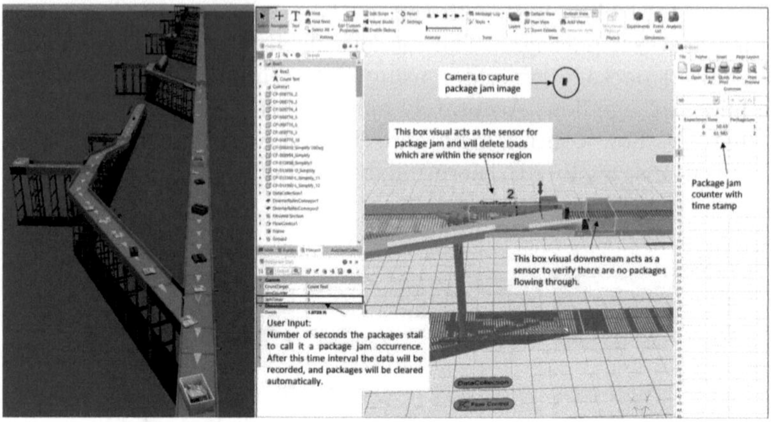

Fig. 3. Flow control Merge Module and Auto Package Jam Detection Module

4.3 Package Chute Design Optimization

Modular framework was further used to validate different chute design concepts, package exit velocity and cart fullness. The model incorporated packages diverting from cross-belt sorters into chutes and carts. The chutes are equipped with photo-eye sensors to monitor package fullness and prevent overflow. Package trajectory analysis was conducted using spaghetti diagrams to understand system dynamics to understand the impact of cart fullness and sensor location. The simulation model helps to identify optimised chute fullness sensor location which demonstrated a 10.72% improvement in cart utilization (from 64.04% to 74.72%) at the chute exit. The strong correlation between actual and simulated data is evidenced by an R-squared value of approximately 0.82, indicating high model accuracy. This significant finding was validated across 12 pilot locations, showing consistent improvement in cart utilization rates from 6% to 10%. The findings led to new network-wide standards for sensor positioning, resulting in enhanced cart and truck utilization while reducing both transportation costs and environmental impact. This implementation demonstrates how modular physics-based simulation modeling can effectively address complex operational challenges and establishes a framework for future optimization of material handling systems. Figure 4 shows package trajectories and cart fullness correlation data, supporting the conclusions about system optimization.

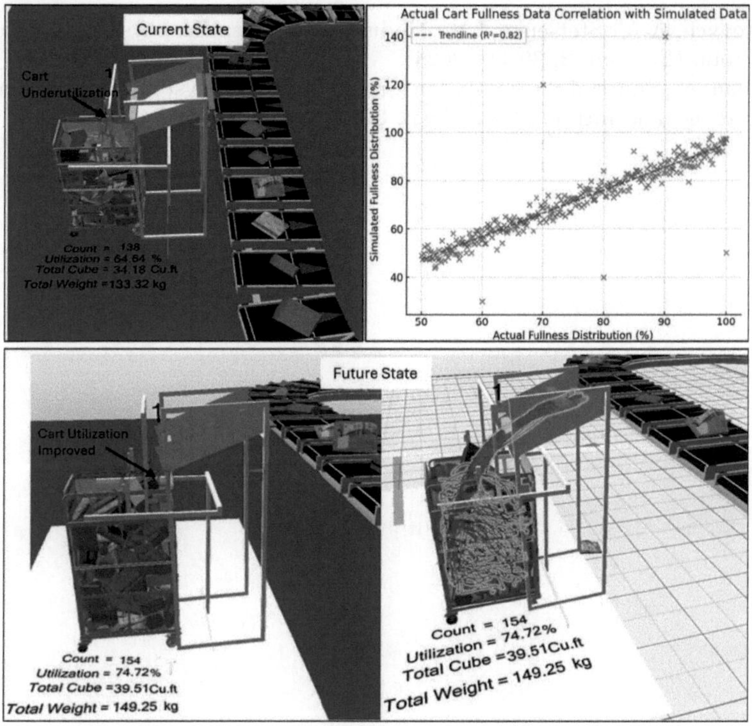

Fig. 4. Package Cart Fullness

5 Challenges and Future Direction

Current challenges center on the computational demands of modeling package softness and its effects on handling dynamics. Limited historical failure data and environmental factors like humidity and dust can impact system performance in ways that are difficult to predict and model effectively. These environmental and material factors create a complex web of inter-dependencies that further complicate the development of accurate simulation models. Looking forward, the physics simulation model connectivity with discrete event modeling tools could substantially reduce need for computational resources. The developed catalog modules will be used in cloud based collaborative platforms for faster model development. Controls emulation of recommended flow control logic will help to ensure First Time Launch Quality (FTLQ).

References

1. Banks, J.: Handbook of Simulation Principles, Methodology, Advances, Applications, and Practice, p. 12. Wiley, New York (1998)
2. McLean, C., Leong, S.: A framework for standard modular simulation. IEEE, San Diego (2003). https://doi.org/10.1109/WSC.2002.1166441

3. Bernatovych, A.A., Stetsenko, I.V.: Module-based scientific physics engine architecture. Probl. Program. **3**, 30–39 (2023)
4. Negahban, A., Smith, J.S.: Simulation for manufacturing system design and analysis: past, present, and future. Manuf. Syst. **33**, 161–176 (2014)

Knowledge Graph-Enhanced Large Language Model Approach for Device Fault Diagnosis Question Answering

Yuchun Tu, Bingli Sun, Zheng Wei, and Xiao Song(✉)

School of Cyber Science and Technology, Beihang University, Beijing, China
{tuyuchun,youthbl,SY2239209,songxiao}@buaa.edu.cn

Abstract. Large language models (LLMs) demonstrate exceptional performance in general natural language processing tasks but suffer from hallucination in domain-specific scenarios due to reliance on public internet data rather than expert knowledge. To overcome these challenges, we propose a hybrid question-answering (QA) architecture incorporating domain knowledge graphs. The system performs intent recognition, converts natural language queries to structured format, retrieves information from device fault knowledge graphs, and uses LLMs to generate accurate responses. Experimental results show substantial reduction in hallucination rates and improved accuracy compared to pure LLM approaches, providing a viable path for trustworthy domain-oriented QA systems.

Keywords: Knowledge graphs · Large language models (LLMs) · Intent recognition · Knowledge question answering · Prompt engineering

1 Introduction

Artificial intelligence technologies are transforming information access and knowledge services. Large language models (LLMs), such as GPT and BERT, have achieved groundbreaking progress in natural language understanding and generation [1,2]. These models are pretrained on vast textual data, acquiring linguistic knowledge and reasoning capabilities to perform complex language tasks in zero-shot or few-shot scenarios [7].

The remarkable success of large language models stems from their vast parameters and broad training data coverage. By training on trillions of internet tokens, these models develop comprehensive knowledge bases capturing human knowledge. They achieve near- or super-human performance in question answering, summarization, and dialogue generation, providing an unprecedented foundation for intelligent QA systems. However, widespread adoption has revealed inherent limitations. In expert-level knowledge-based QA scenarios, LLMs frequently fail to generate accurate responses due to constrained training data and deficiencies in knowledge acquisition mechanisms. While LLMs excel in

W. Cai et al. (Eds.): AsiaSim 2025, CCIS 2727, pp. 279–284, 2026.
https://doi.org/10.1007/978-981-95-4472-1_26

general-purpose language tasks, they face significant challenges in specialized domains: i) Limited knowledge coverage due to reliance on public internet sources while domain-specific knowledge remains confidential or inaccessible during pre-training; ii) Hallucination issues where models generate fluent but inaccurate responses instead of admitting knowledge gaps [4], potentially causing severe harm in critical domains like healthcare or legal consultations; iii) Knowledge lag as static post-training knowledge cannot accommodate frequently updated domain-specific information such as recent policies or evolving technical standards.

This study develops a question answering system preserving LLMs' strengths while ensuring domain expertise precision. The solution combines structured domain knowledge with large-scale model processing power. Knowledge graphs represent domain facts using entity-relation-entity triples, offering clear semantics and reasoning [3]. Domain knowledge graphs provide reliable factual basis, while LLMs convert natural language to structured queries and generate coherent answers. Specifically, the main contributions of this study are as follows:

- We propose a novel three-stage QA architecture consisting of intent recognition, knowledge graph querying, and LLM-based answer generation modules, preserving LLMs' language capabilities while ensuring reliability through structured domain knowledge.
- We develop an effective intent recognition method converting natural language questions into structured queries and design a knowledge integration strategy transforming retrieved information into high-quality answers. And we alleviate hallucination by grounding the system on trustworthy structured knowledge, significantly reducing hallucinated responses and improving factual accuracy in domain-specific QA.
- We conduct comprehensive experiments in a specific domain, demonstrating the superior performance of our proposed hybrid approach compared to conventional LLM-only baselines.

2 Methodology

2.1 Qwen2.5-7B-Instruct

Large Language Models (LLMs) adopt the decoder-only architecture based on Transformer's self-attention mechanism [11] and are trained through autoregressive next token prediction, learning linguistic knowledge from massive text [8]. LLMs demonstrate exceptional capabilities in question answering through in-context learning and instruction tuning [12]. However, purely parametric LLMs face incomplete knowledge coverage and hallucination in professional domains. Hybrid architectures like Retrieval-Augmented Generation (RAG) address this by incorporating external knowledge sources for reliable domain QA systems [5].

This study adopts the Qwen2.5-7B-Instruct model developed by Alibaba Cloud, an instruction-tuned version optimized for dialogue and instruction-following tasks. The 7-billion parameter model features advanced architecture with RMSNorm normalization [13], SwiGLU activation [9], and RoPE positioning [10]. It supports 128K token context length and is pre-trained on 18 trillion tokens of multilingual data covering 29 languages, followed by supervised fine-tuning and RLHF [6]. The model excels in mathematical reasoning, code generation, and multilingual understanding, with particular advantages in Chinese comprehension, making it suitable for Chinese professional domain QA systems (Fig. 1).

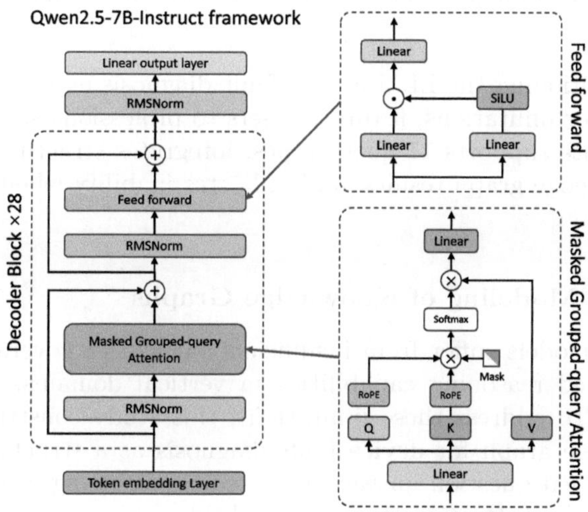

Fig. 1. The framework of Qwen2.5-7B-Instruct

2.2 Prompt Engineering

This study applies large language models to two core components of the device fault diagnosis intelligent Q&A system: user intent recognition and knowledge base-driven response generation. Corresponding prompt strategies are designed for different application scenarios to enhance model performance in specific domains. Through systematic prompt design methodology, as shown in Fig 2. This study achieves effective application of large language models in the device fault diagnosis domain, laying a methodological foundation for constructing high-quality intelligent Q&A systems.

Based on device fault diagnosis characteristics, a 12-category intent classification system is constructed. Eleven categories cover core scenarios including fault inquiry, solution consultation, component prediction, and maintenance inquiry. The 12th handles non-domain questions. Intent recognition uses Few-shot learning with designed examples, requiring only intent number outputs. Two response templates adapt to different scenarios. The general template uses

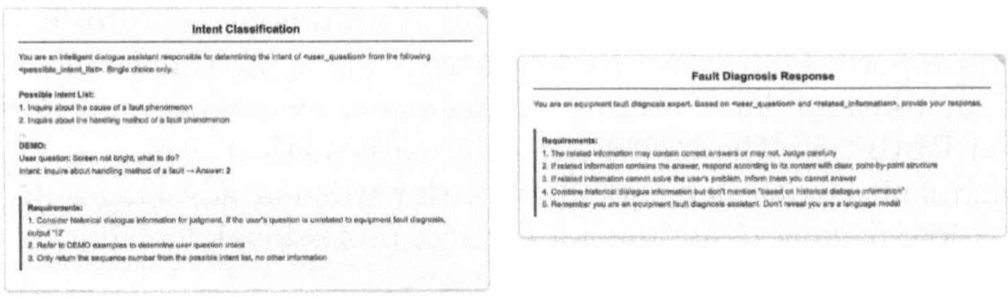

Fig. 2. Task-Specific Prompt Templates for Intent Recognition and Device Diagnosis

role-playing, positioning the LLM as a “”fault diagnosis expert” requiring concise responses. For limitations, it directs users to professionals. The knowledge-enhanced template supports 11 query types, integrates structured information, prioritizes knowledge graph results, and indicates inability when information is insufficient.

2.3 Ontology Modeling of Knowledge Graphs

Large language models suffer from insufficient knowledge coverage, poor timeliness, and limited reasoning capabilities in vertical domains, such as device fault diagnosis. To address these limitations, this study constructs a domain-specific knowledge graph for device fault diagnosis as a structured knowledge base for LLM-based question answering systems, enhancing accuracy and reliability in professional domains through a hybrid architecture combining graph retrieval and language model generation. By incorporating 732 entities and 1,781 relationships, we built a multi-dimensional knowledge graph for fault diagnosis, covering people, device, failures, and their resolutions. It serves as a structured knowledge base for intelligent diagnosis and maintenance.

3 System Implementation

In this section, we provide a detailed description of the system's runtime environment and its performance outcomes.

The system is deployed in a Windows 11 Professional environment and is powered by an Intel Core Ultra 9 285K CPU and an NVIDIA GeForce RTX 5090D GPU with 64 GB of dedicated memory. The software stack includes Python 3.9 and PyTorch 2.7.0, with CUDA 12.8. A Neo4j graph database is utilized for structured data management. The backend services are developed using Flask, while the frontend interface is built with Vue. Users interact with the fault diagnosis platform via a Vue.js web interface that processes inputs. Queries undergo semantic parsing to identify intent and extract entities, which are converted into Cypher queries for Neo4j graph database retrieval. Retrieved knowledge constructs prompts for LLM reasoning and diagnostic response generation. Flask backend returns results to frontend, while Redis caches dialogue states for multi-turn interactions.

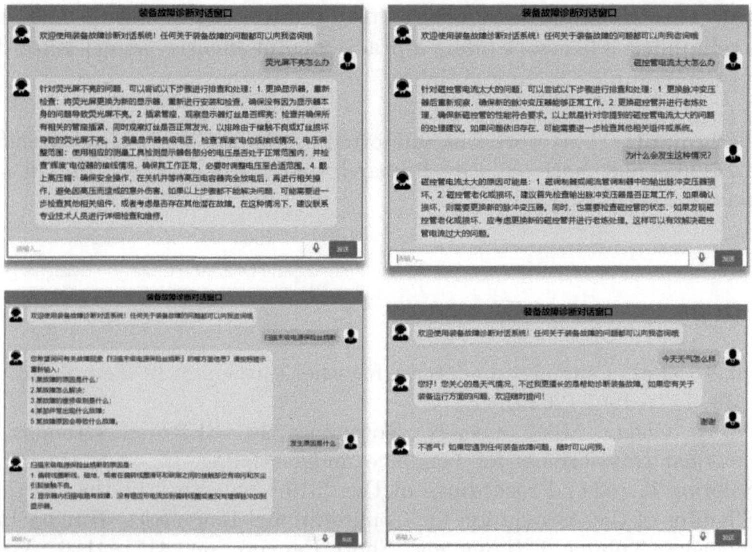

Fig. 3. Multi-turn Conversational Testing of Device Fault Diagnosis QA System

3.1 Result

To comprehensively validate the functional implementation of each module in the intelligent Q&A system for device fault diagnosis, we examined whether the system can stably produce expected outputs under various input conditions, ensuring functional completeness and logical correctness. We selected four distinct question-answering scenarios to present the test results: inquiries about device fault information, multi-turn dialogues, incomplete user input, and open-domain queries.

Figure3 shows system responses under four Q&A scenarios. Results indicate the system provides accurate single-turn answers and supports multi-turn interactions, effectively managing conversation states and maintaining coherence. When users ask open-domain questions unrelated to device faults, the system identifies them and guides users back to fault diagnosis. This delivers precise domain-specific answers while maintaining smooth user experience, demonstrating strong stability and effectiveness.

4 Conclusion

To improve the accuracy and efficiency of fault diagnosis in complex device, we propose a hybrid Q&A system that combines domain-specific knowledge graphs with large language models (LLMs). The system leverages intent recognition and semantic parsing to convert natural language queries into structured graph queries, enabling precise retrieval of domain knowledge. LLMs are then used to generate fluent answers based on the retrieved content. Experimental results show that this approach significantly reduces hallucination and enhances response reliability. This work offers a practical and effective solution for domain-specific QA in complex technical fields.

Acknowledgments. This work was supported by the Beijing Natural Science Foundation (L233005) and National Key Research and Development Program of China under Grant 2023YFB3308200.

References

1. Brown, T., et al.: Language models are few-shot learners. Adv. Neural. Inf. Process. Syst. **33**, 1877–1901 (2020)
2. Devlin, J., Chang, M.W., Lee, K., Toutanova, K.: BERT: pre-training of deep bidirectional transformers for language understanding. In: Burstein, J., Doran, C., Solorio, T. (eds.) Proceedings of the 2019 Conference of the North American Chapter of the Association for Computational Linguistics: Human Language Technologies, Volume 1 (Long and Short Papers), pp. 4171–4186. Association for Computational Linguistics, Minneapolis (2019). https://doi.org/10.18653/v1/N19-1423, https://aclanthology.org/N19-1423/
3. Hogan, A., Blomqvist, E., Cochez, M., d'Amato, C., Melo, G.D., Gutierrez, C., Kirrane, S., Gayo, J.E.L., Navigli, R., Neumaier, S., et al.: Knowledge graphs. ACM Comput. Surv. (Csur) **54**(4), 1–37 (2021)
4. Huang, L., et al.: A survey on hallucination in large language models: principles, taxonomy, challenges, and open questions. ACM Trans. Inf. Syst. **43**(2), 1–55 (2025)
5. Lewis, P., et al.: Retrieval-augmented generation for knowledge-intensive NLP tasks. Adv. Neural. Inf. Process. Syst. **33**, 9459–9474 (2020)
6. Ouyang, L., et al.: Training language models to follow instructions with human feedback. Adv. Neural. Inf. Process. Syst. **35**, 27730–27744 (2022)
7. Qiu, X.P., Sun, T.X., Xu, Y.G., Shao, Y.F., Dai, N., Huang, X.J.: Pre-trained models for natural language processing: a survey. SCI. CHINA Technol. Sci. **63**(10), 1872–1897 (2020). https://doi.org/10.1007/s11431-020-1647-3
8. Radford, A., et al.: Language models are unsupervised multitask learners. OpenAI blog **1**(8), 9 (2019)
9. Shazeer, N.: GLU variants improve transformer. arXiv preprint arXiv:2002.05202 (2020)
10. Su, J., Ahmed, M., Lu, Y., Pan, S., Bo, W., Liu, Y.: Roformer: enhanced transformer with rotary position embedding. Neurocomputing **568**, 127063 (2024)
11. Vaswani, A., et al.: Attention is all you need. Adv. Neural Inf. Process. Syst. **30** (2017)
12. Wei, J., et al.: Finetuned language models are zero-shot learners. In: International Conference on Learning Representations (2022)
13. Zhang, B., Sennrich, R.: Root mean square layer normalization. Adv. Neural Inf. Process. Syst. **32** (2019)

On Linking Learning and Game Goal in Serious Games Design

Mukarramah Yusuf[1(✉)], Elly Warni[1], M. Agung Sabillah[2], and Firmansyah Jaya Kusuma[1]

[1] Hasanuddin University, Perintis Kemerdekaan 10, Makassar 90245, Indonesia
mukarramah@unhas.ac.id

[2] MAS Studio, Poso Kota, Poso 94618, Indonesia

Abstract. Establishing a connection between educational and gaming objectives is a fundamental challenge in the development of serious games. In this paper, we delineate the design process of two serious games: one focused on history for high school students and the other centered on mathematics for middle school students. The design process adhered to established frameworks and methodologies recognized in the literature. Evaluated using GUESS, the math game achieved high scores in terms of visual and audio aesthetics, playability, and personal gratification. The History game was evaluated based on game flow elements and achieved the highest score for clear goals and feedback.

Keywords: serious game · design · learning objectives · game mechanics

1 Introduction

Translating learning objectives into game mechanics is a critical challenge in serious game design. This requires understanding both educational principles and game design elements to create effective learning experiences [1–3]. Designers must integrate learning goals into gameplay mechanics that are both engaging and educational. Game mechanics must motivate players while achieving learning objectives, often by breaking complex goals into manageable components within gameplay elements, such as progression systems and challenges.

Several existing frameworks and approaches have been developed to address this task, each offering unique methodologies and perspectives [1, 3–5]. These frameworks combine theory, research, and practical applications to offer complete solutions. They use ideas from psychology, sociology, and organizational behavior to build strong and flexible models. The variety of frameworks demonstrates this complexity. Some focus on specific parts, while others aim to be more widely applicable.

In this study, we present two serious games designed and developed following a structured approach that incorporates established frameworks and methodologies from the existing literature. The history-focused game for high school students and the mathematics-centered game for middle school students were developed with careful consideration of the educational objectives, target audience, and engagement factors.

W. Cai et al. (Eds.): AsiaSim 2025, CCIS 2727, pp. 285–290, 2026.
https://doi.org/10.1007/978-981-95-4472-1_27

These games aim to provide immersive learning experiences that complement traditional teaching methods, leveraging the power of interactive gameplay to enhance students' understanding and retention of key concepts in their respective subjects. We also present the results of the educational effectiveness and game flow evaluations.

2 Related Work and Design Process

Table 1 lists proposed models for translating learning objectives into game mechanics. Intrinsic integration [6] aligns game goals with learning goals through pedagogical approaches implemented within game mechanics. The 3i model [4] includes introduction, interpretation, and influence. The introduction integrates learning materials into gameplay where players learn through problem-solving. Interpretation converts learning tasks to game activities, where players complete tasks and receive feedback. Influence occurs when knowledge improves gameplay performance, with players gaining abilities as the game adapts to their level. The LM-GM model [7] combines game mechanics and educational components from game studies and learning theories, allowing designers to map key educational and entertainment aspects in order to guide the design process.

Table 1. Models for linking learning goals and game goals

Model	Guidelines
Intrinsic integration [6]	(1) Starting a learning goal and ending with the game goal, (2) Game goal is reach after the learning goal is reach, (3) Iterations for aligning the two goals
3i model [4]	Introduction, interpretation, and influence.
Learning Mechanic-Game Mechanic (LM-GM) [7]	Corresponding learning mechanics and game mechanics

For developing the two serious games, we applied the framework connecting software engineering, game design, and instructional design methodologies. The framework comprises four phases: analysis, design, development, and evaluation to meet educational objectives [8].

During design, game and educational objectives are aligned repeatedly [6]. The 3i model [4] divided alignment into smaller tasks like game setting and storyline. The game setting includes learning objectives comprising concepts, knowledge, and skills. The storyline, levels, and characters are derived from learning materials, with learning tasks embedded as game tasks. Completing game tasks accomplishes learning tasks in a spiral learning process [4]. Through the 3i model, game problems align with learning tasks while achieving the game goals. The game aims for players to achieve flow experience [9] through elements like usability, narratives, enjoyment, aesthetics, and social connectivity, or through control, skills, feedback, challenge, clear goals, and immersion [10, 11].

3 Results, Evaluation and Discussions

3.1 Story, Rules, Gameplay Elements

Following the design guidelines as above, we developed Geomecia, a serious game to learn Math, which is intended for year 7 students, and Homeland, a serious game to learn History, which is intended for high school students. Both games were developed using the Unity game engine and deployed as mobile Android applications.

Figure 1 (top) shows the menu features of Geomecia and Homeland. Both the History and Math games employ level-based dynamics, where players must complete a level to progress to the next. The levels in each game are designed to progress toward the learning topics in Geomecia, and time in Homeland. As time is crucial in history, the levels are designed to carry out the learning objectives concerning time and the chronological order of events in history. Geomecia is designed as an adventure game through medieval time in a foreign island.

Fig. 1. Menu features and a game task of the developed Math (top and bottom left) and History (top and bottom right) games.

In the History game, learning content is embedded through factual checkpoints that require players to correctly identify key events or figures before advancing. The Math game, in contrast, is structured around task-solving mechanics set within the foreign island adventure. These tasks present equations and problem sets of increasing difficulty, each designed to be solvable using knowledge acquired from earlier gameplay. Correct solutions allow progression and unlock subsequent levels, while incorrect attempts reduce the player's chance of winning.

Figure 1 (bottom) shows examples of the game tasks within one level of the game. The scene of Geomecia (bottom left) shows the climax of the story, where the hero needs to solve the game task (learning goal) in order to release his colleagues. The scene of Homeland (bottom right) shows the opening of the game task, where the learning materials (event name, date of occurrence, the people involved) are scattered around each scene and play task.

3.2 Evaluation Results

To measure educational effectiveness, we conducted pre- and post-learning assessments using test questions adapted from textbooks. There was a 13.6% increase in correct answers, rising from 80.7% in the pre-test to 94.3% in the post-test for the Homeland, and a 10.4% increase in correct answers, rising from 62.5% in the pre-test to 72.9% in the post-test for Geomecia.

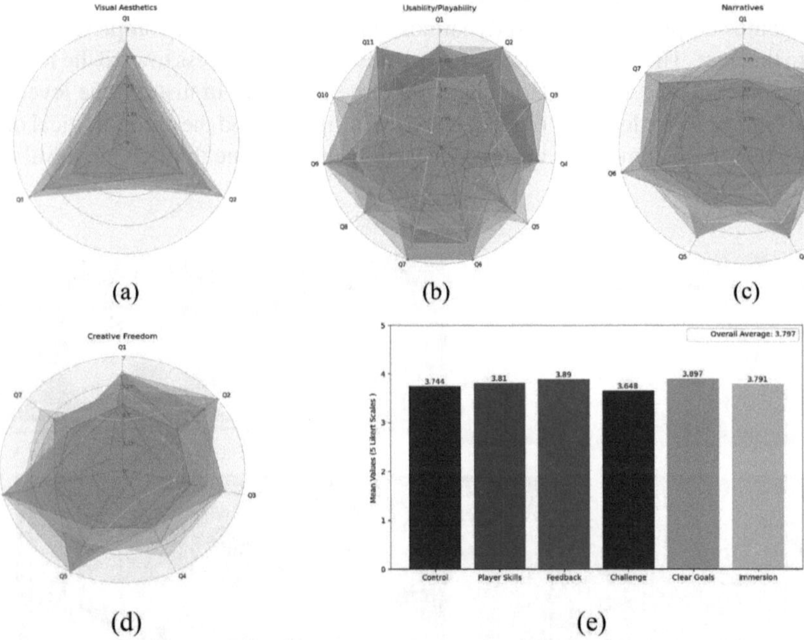

Fig. 2. Examples of evaluation results based on GUESS for the developed math game (a-d) and results based on GameFlow for the developed math game (e). At the top, left to the right are: usability/playability (a), personal gratification (b), and narratives (c). At the bottom are: creative freedom (d). Subscales of GameFlow are control, player skills, feedback, challenge, clear goals, and immersion

We used the Game User Experience Satisfaction Scale (GUESS) [10] to evaluate Geomecia, and Gameflow [11] to evaluate Homeland. Geomecia was tested by 21 students, and Homeland by 36 students. For Geomecia, all eight GUESS metrics received positive responses. The highest scores were for visual (Fig. 2a) and audio aesthetics, indicating that the game's visual and auditory elements were well received. Playability (Fig. 2b) and personal gratification also scored highly, indicating intuitive mechanics and interface. While narratives and creative freedom received lower scores (Fig. 2c-d), they maintained positive ratings. Figure 2e shows Homeland's evaluation results for control, player skills, feedback, challenge, clear goals, and immersion. All aspects received positive responses with an average of 3.8 from 5 Likert scales. Clear goals and feedback were rated highest, indicating well-defined objectives and good responsiveness.

Challenge and control scored the lowest, suggesting room for improvement in difficulty balance and player experience.

3.3 Discussions

The evaluation of game flow provides crucial information about engagement and educational value. The results offer insights into using frameworks for developing serious games in education, particularly for History and Mathematics. While literature on educational games for Math learning is abundant, this is not true for history learning. The history game for high school students presented challenges in translating the historical content into gameplay. The successful implementation shows historical concepts can be effectively gamified to increase student engagement. This approach could revolutionize history teaching by moving from textbooks to more interactive experiences.

Design challenges influenced the educational outcomes in both games. The History game balanced factual content with engagement by weaving learning goals into the game tasks. The Math game created scaffolded problem-solving tasks embedded in an adventurous journey to maintain engagement. The History game enhanced declarative knowledge through situated learning, while the Math game developed procedural fluency and reasoning skills. These differences show how subject matter affects design challenges and learning outcomes.

Both games incorporate mechanics for sustained knowledge retention. The History game uses retrieval practice through factual checkpoints to reinforce memory, while the Math game employs constructive learning for problem-solving skills.

4 Summary and Conclusion

The development of serious games presents a challenge in aligning educational goals with gaming objectives. This study explores this through case studies of history and mathematics games for high school and middle school students. The design process balances gameplay engagement with learning outcomes by integrating pedagogical principles with game design elements. This study evaluated game flow and educational effectiveness, examining player engagement through factors such as concentration, challenge-skill balance, goals, feedback, and control. The analysis provides insights into design effectiveness and the potential of serious games in education. Both games showed positive responses to game flow, although effectiveness may vary based on learning styles, gaming experience, and technological access. Future research should explore these variables and investigate the long-term educational impact of the games developed.

Acknowledgments. Hasanuddin University awarded a travel grant to attend the conference.

Disclosure of Interest. The authors declare no competing interests for this article.

References

1. Callaghan, M., Savin-Baden, M., McShane, N., Eguiluz, A.G.: Mapping learning and game mechanics for serious games analysis in engineering education. IEEE Trans. Emerg. Top. Comput. **5**, 77–83 (2015)
2. Cecotti, H., Callaghan, M.: Practical application of the learning mechanics-game mechanics framework for serious games design and analysis for the development of mental computation in virtual reality. In: 2021 IEEE International Conference on Engineering, Technology & Education (TALE). pp. 1067–1072. IEEE (2021)
3. Kalmpourtzis, G., Romero, M.: Constructive alignment of learning mechanics and game mechanics in Serious Game design in Higher Education. Int. J. Serious Games **7**, 75–88 (2020)
4. Shabalina, O., Mozelius, P., Malliarakis, C., Tomos, F., Balan, O.C., Blackey, H., Gerkushenko, G.: Combining game-flow and learning objectives in educational games. In: 8th European Conference on Games-based Learning (2014)
5. Hart, S., Halak, B., Sassone, V.: MOTENS: a pedagogical design model for serious cyber games. arXiv preprint arXiv:2110.11765. (2021)
6. van der Linden, A., van Joolingen, W.R., Meulenbroeks, R.F.G.: Designing an intrinsically integrated educational game on newtonian mechanics. In: Lecture Notes in Computer Science (including subseries Lecture Notes in Artificial Intelligence and Lecture Notes in Bioinformatics). pp. 123–133. Springer Verlag (2019). https://doi.org/10.1007/978-3-030-11548-7_12
7. Arnab, S., et al.: Mapping learning and game mechanics for serious games analysis. Br. J. Edu. Technol. **46**, 391–411 (2015)
8. Avila-Pesantez, D., Delgadillo, R., Rivera, L.A.: Proposal of a conceptual model for serious games design: A case study in children with learning disabilities. IEEE Access. **7**, 161017–161033 (2019)
9. Perttula, A., Kiili, K., Lindstedt, A., Tuomi, P.: Flow experience in game based learning–a systematic literature review. Int. J. Serious Games **4**, 57–72 (2017)
10. Phan, M.H., Keebler, J.R., Chaparro, B.S.: The development and validation of the game user experience satisfaction scale (GUESS). Hum. Factors **58**, 1217–1247 (2016)
11. Sweetser, P.: GameFlow 2020: 15 Years of a Model of Player Enjoyment. In: Proceedings of the 32nd Australian Conference on Human-Computer Interaction. pp. 705–711 (2020)

Author Index

A
Alagappan, Kalyani 55
Almeida, Tarciana 272
Andelfinger, Philipp 67

B
Bahsoon, Rami 90
Bai, Yujie 237
Bi, Jieyi 67
Bi, Ke 148

C
Cai, Wentong 67
Chan, Chew Wye 67
Chao, Tao 28, 183, 237
Chen, Nanjiang 134
Cheng, Hongbo 80
Cheng, Huafu 148
Chidambaram, Gandhi 272
Cui, Yong 148

D
D'Angelo, Gabriele 159
Dewanti, Desak Ayu Clara 244
Diamantopoulos, Georgios 90

G
Gan, Boon Ping 67
Gao, Fangfang 134
Gong, Guanghong 102
Gong, Jiabei 3
Goyal, Anish 272
Gu, Pengfei 40

H
Han, Fangchao 222
Hou, Guoqing 102
Hu, Jiangchuan 40
Hu, Min 134
Hu, Qinglei 148
Huang, Yan 199
Huo, Ju 237

J
Jia, Xianzhen 115, 124
Jiao, Xuying 115, 124
Joelianto, Endra 171
Joshi, Sumant 272

K
Kajima, Kouhei 211
Kajiyama, Kazumi 244
Kamata, Hiroyuki 16, 211
Kamiya, Tatsuki 211
Kanno, Taro 244
Kusuma, Firmansyah Jaya 285

L
Laili, Yuanjun 3, 259
Li, Liang 266
Li, Na 259
Li, Ni 102
Li, Ninghan 222
Li, Tan 134
Li, Yifan 115, 124
Lin, David Weidong 55
Low, Malcolm Yoke Hean 55
Lu, Han 80
Lu, Qiang 222
Luo, Jin 115, 124
Luo, Yumu 134

M
Ma, Ping 28, 183
Mao, Qingyu 266
Mei, Zheng 237

N
Nazaruddin, Yul Yunazwin 171
Nishimura, Toshiki 244

W. Cai et al. (Eds.): AsiaSim 2025, CCIS 2727, pp. 291–292, 2026.
https://doi.org/10.1007/978-981-95-4472-1

O
Omori, Haruki 16

P
Papadopoulos, Alessandro V. 159
Parung, Joniarto 244
Pei, Yu 148
Pianini, Danilo 159

Q
Qiao, Yiming 80
Qiao, Yu 28
Quan, Hongyan 252

R
Ren, Lei 3, 259

S
Sabillah, M. Agung 285
Santoso, Amelia 244
Shaiakhmetov, Ruslan 159
Sharikura, Sachika 244
Shimada, Mashiro 16
Song, Weining 134, 222
Song, Xiao 252, 279
Sridadi, Bambang 171
Sun, Bingli 252, 279

T
Tan, Jiaying 199
Tanaka, Satoshi 266
Tang, Linjing 115, 124
Theodoropoulos, Georgios 90
Tian, Bo 102
Tseng, Chin-Yuan 272
Tsubaki, Michihiro 244
Tu, Yuchun 252, 279
Tziritas, Nikos 90

V
Venusti, Valter 159

W
Wang, Kunyu 80
Wang, Qi 134
Wang, Shuaibo 102
Wang, Songyan 237
Wang, Zirui 148
Warni, Elly 285
Wei, Yisong 183
Wei, Ze 199
Wei, Zheng 279
Wu, Congying 134
Wu, Huaining 148

X
Xing, Yalan 222
Xu, Jianchun 148

Y
Yamada, Kentaro 211
Yamazaki, Misumi 244
Yan, Dezhi 222
Yang, Ming 28, 183
Yoshida, Haruka 244
Yusuf, Mukarramah 285

Z
Zhang, Bo 67
Zhang, Fei Fei 67
Zhang, Jiayi 3
Zhang, Jie 67
Zhang, Lei 80
Zhang, Lin 3, 40, 80, 259
Zhang, Qianfan 222
Zhang, Wenjun 134
Zhang, Yuteng 40
Zhang, Zhenyu 134
Zhou, Jianan 67
Zhu, Qiuyu 67

MIX
Papier aus verantwortungsvollen Quellen
Paper from responsible sources
FSC® C105338

If you have any concerns about our products,
you can contact us on
ProductSafety@springernature.com

In case Publisher is established outside the EU,
the EU authorized representative is:
Springer Nature Customer Service Center GmbH
Europaplatz 3, 69115 Heidelberg, Germany

Printed by Libri Plureos GmbH
in Hamburg, Germany